READINGS IN CULTURAL DIVERSITY AND CRIMINAL JUSTICE

READINGS IN CULTURAL DIVERSITY AND CRIMINAL JUSTICE

Edited by Lee E. Ross

University of Central Florida

SAN DIEGO

Bassim Hamadeh, CEO and Publisher
Jennifer McCarthy, Field Acquisitions Editor
Amy Smith, Project Editor
Celeste Paed, Associate Production Editor
Jackie Bignotti, Production Artist
Stephanie Kohl, Licensing Coordinator
Natalie Piccotti, Director of Marketing
Kassie Graves, Vice President of Editorial
Jamie Giganti, Director of Academic Publishing

cognella® | CUSTOM
3970 Sorrento Valley Blvd., Ste. 500, San Diego, CA 92121

CONTENTS

PREFACE

Having worked as a federal law enforcement officer many years ago, I have come to appreciate the importance of cultural diversity within American criminal justice systems—given the lack of diversity I experienced. In the mid-1980s, the demographic makeup of criminal justice personnel was noticeably different from what it is today. Moreover, there was far less diversity among key players and decision makers in terms of their race and ethnicity, color, religion, sexual orientation, handicap, family, or national origin. Like parents raising their first child, there was no manual (or book of instructions) to navigate through culturally related problems as they developed in a system sorely lacking in cultural diversity. Among practitioners and support staff, the lack of diversity was most apparent in three areas: race/ethnicity, gender, and sexual orientation. In many instances, I believe it was the lack of diversity that gave rise to past and recent practices of racial and gender discrimination, religious intolerance, racial profiling, malicious prosecutions, false convictions, disparate sentencing, and attitudes of indifference toward certain offenders, most of whom are people of color.

For nearly 30 years, I have taught courses along the lines of either race, crime, and justice or some variation of cultural diversity within the criminal justice system. Fortunately, there were some good scholarly resources available, clearly written and socially relevant. These resonated with students desiring to learn more about certain issues. However, most of the materials were either lacking in coverage or written in manner—perhaps too scholarly—that failed to capture the attention of the average student. Even today, many scholarly resources struggle to remain relevant and fall short of the gold standard of producing "cutting-edge research." As most textbooks are written as a standalone text and cover a tremendously wide range of materials, issues of diversity are usually 'lost in the sauce' and not explored in enough detail. Still other academic resources are written in very hegemonic and general terms—as though everyone, including criminal justice personnel, shares similar social histories. This book attempts to address some of these shortcomings by including readings that highlight elements of cultural diversity throughout the entire criminal justice system.

In doing so, it demonstrates the neglected role of cultural diversity and how this neglect affects the administration of justice.

Like many of you, I, too, believe that experience is the best teacher. It has been my learned experiences—both good and bad—that compelled me to edit this special collection of *Readings in Cultural Diversity and Criminal Justice*, a book that celebrates diverse voices and unique perspectives. Having grown up in a family of 15 children, some became "caught up" and processed through a predominantly White criminal justice system, unable to afford the kind of justice that would spare them the ordeal and preserve their sense of dignity and character. Unfortunately, I have also had a sibling literally murdered "in cold blood" where his perpetrator was not prosecuted because he was of the same race and social class as my brother. Sadly, another one of my siblings was a victim of police brutality, suffered from mental health–related issues as a result, and was diagnosed and treated by those who neither looked liked him nor were able to relate to him. While employed as a federal law enforcement officer, I witnessed racial profiling by coworkers on a daily basis and occasionally felt pressured to support practices I regarded as ostensibly racist—if not overtly biased. In these situations I have often wondered whether a more culturally diverse criminal justice system could have altered the context, narrative, and outcomes. For example, would it matter if the responding officer, defense attorney, prosecutor, and judge were not White—but rather people of color? Are there gender differences in how responding officers handle domestic violence incidents? Would a homicide be tried—rather than a dismissed—if the prosecutors were not White and did not appear indifferent to the plight and suffering of the victim's family? How might one's level of religiosity (or spirituality) matter in these instances? Moreover, would a customs officer—relying on a hunch—strip search a Catholic priest as readily as a traveling passenger appearing to be of Muslim or Arab descent? Clearly, each of these scenarios invites readers to consider the role and potential of culturally diverse perspectives in shaping certain outcomes.

This edited compilation covers a variety of topics that are critically important to the study of cultural diversity within the criminal justice system. Necessarily, these readings include overlapping terms and expressions common to issues of race, crime, and justice, terms such as "racial profiling," "intersectionality," and the "social construction of race." However, it differs from other readings in its focus on the origins of racism, the neglect of colorism, and the relevance of critical race theory. Gender dysphoria among practitioners, the prison industrial complex, and remedial efforts that espouse the importance of racial integration add currency to the importance of cultural diversity. Even more, the authors of these chapters are established academics and practitioners, representing a wide variety of disciplines, including medicine, sociology, criminology, criminal justice, political science, history, communications, and women's studies. Overall, *Readings in Cultural Diversity and Criminal Justice* meets the challenge of academic rigor and excellence, captures a wide range of issues, and targets a more culturally diverse audience.

INTRODUCTION

Readings in Cultural Diversity and Criminal Justice is designed primarily for under-graduate and graduate-level students desiring to learn more about the importance of cultural diversity in the criminal justice system and its relevance to issues of race, crime, and justice. Most contemporary criminal justice–related textbooks are written as a standalone text, covering a tremendously wide range of materials where issues of diversity are given less attention. This book attempts to address this shortcoming by focusing on readings that highlight elements of cultural diversity throughout the entire criminal justice system. These readings are cutting edge and reflect the contributions of scholars and practitioners across several disciplines, including medicine, sociology, criminology, criminal justice, political science, history, women's studies, and communications.

Designed as a supplemental text, Readings in Cultural Diversity and Criminal Justice invites readers to acknowledge and critically examine the importance of cultural diversity within the criminal justice system. While gender and ethnoracial differ-ences are often considered the foundational definitions of diversity, the operational meaning of diversity is defined by many different backgrounds and contexts. Diversity, as defined by Merriam-Webster dictionary (n.d,) is "the condition of having or being composed of differing elements: variety, especially the inclusion of different types of people (such as people of different races or cultures) in a group or organization."

Likewise, the term "culturally diverse" is often used interchangeably with the con-cept of "multiculturalism." Rosado (2010) defines multiculturalism as

> a system of beliefs and behaviors that recognizes and respects the presence of all diverse groups in an organization or society, acknowledges and values their socio-cultural differences, and encourages and enables their continued contribution within an inclusive cultural context which empowers all within the organization or society.

As such, this text promotes the idea that diversity of viewpoints is critically important and necessary to solve the problems we face individually and collectively. For the most part, this book encourages critical thinking, problem solving, and creativity regarding justice-related matters.

The benefits of promoting cultural diversity in the classroom are well documented (Clyne & Jupp, 2011). Research shows that diverse classrooms, in which students learn cooperatively alongside those whose perspectives and backgrounds are different from their own, are beneficial to all students—including middle-class White students—because these environments promote creativity, motivation, deeper learning, critical thinking, and problem-solving skills. Moreover, teaching diversity prepares students to be global citizens by exposing them to people from different cultures and social groups, enabling them to counter discriminatory stereotypes and practices (Page, 2008). It also increases cultural competence, which in turn allows students to be empathetic to the experiences and plights of others.

Readings in Cultural Diversity and Criminal Justice recognizes the importance of appreciating and understanding the role of diversity within our criminal justice system. Cultural diversity supports the idea that—despite our differences—each of us can make a unique and positive contribution to society at large and the justice system. However, we first we must have a level of understanding about each other in order to facilitate collaboration and cooperation to improve our systems of justice.

Organization of the Book

Divided into five parts, this book includes articles devoted to (a) an overview of racial and cultural diversity, (b) the historical and theoretical explanations of racism, (c) common diversity-related issues, (d) diversity matters within justice systems, and (e) the promise of cultural diversity within society and our justice systems. Taken collectively, the articles in each part include a wide range of issues and important concepts that promote a better understanding of the role of cultural diversity within the criminal justice system.

Part I consists of four introductory articles concerning colorism, the origins of racism, and how the media perpetuates racial stereotypes. The opening chapter, "Colorism in Mental Health: Looking the Other Way," is authored by Nadine Burnett (2015) and examines the importance of racial identity and the persistence of racism. In doing so, she identifies racial disparities based on skin color and sets the stage for understanding how skin color can ultimately affect our perceptions of guilt, innocence, and notions of deserved punishments. For example, research suggests that darker-skinned African American defendants were twice as likely to receive the death penalty for crimes involving White victims. Because colorism can negatively affect a child's self-esteem, it can conceivably fuel his or her involvement in harmful behaviors, including aggression, self-injury, and sexual promiscuity (Eberhardt, Davies, Purdie-Vaughns, & Johnson, 2006).

Chapter 2, "Racism: Origin and Theory," is authored by Benjamin P. Bowser (2017) and traces the theoretical development and promise of the concept of racism that evolved from the 1960s civil rights movement. Bowser reviews various forms of racism, including symbolic racism, color-blind racism, unconscious racism—as well as cultural, institutional, and individual-level racism. Fearing that the major concepts of racism did not fulfill its original promise, Bowser highlights the theoretical potential of *an activist concept* of racism to improve race relations. He prophesizes that once the notion of racial hierarchy is engrained in a culture, racism is permanent and the most we can ever hope for is to reduce racism as much as possible in each generation.

Chapter 3, authored by Mia Moody, Bruce Dorrie, and Harriet Blackwell (2009), attempts to demonstrate the effects of colorism and racism in society. Titled "How National Media Framed Coverage of Missing Black and White Women," the chapter argues that the media coverage of missing Black women, in comparison to coverage of missing White women, is biased and inadequate. Essentially, the media tends to rely on patriarchal representations of the world, which values (mostly White) women based on looks and body size. Since missing Black women do not receive as much media coverage, the implication is that they are deemed less valuable. Although the media acknowledges its role in framing the narrative of missing women, the disproportionate and unequal media coverage of missing Black females continues to the detriment of society.

Part I concludes with chapter 4, "Selling Savage Portrayals: Young Black and Latino Males in the Carceral State" by Natalie Byfield (2014). The author, a former columnist for the *New York Daily News*, revisits the story of the Central Park Five from her perspective as a Black female reporter. In doing so, she illuminates the race, class, and gender bias in the massive media coverage of the crime and the prosecution of the now-exonerated defendants. Her sociological analysis and first-person account persuasively argue that the racialized reportage of the case buttressed efforts to try juveniles as adults across the nation.

Part II consists of three articles specifically devoted to theory and designed to advance our understanding of the relations between cultural diversity, racism, and crime. Chapter 5, "Toward a Theory of Race, Crime, and Urban Inequality," is authored by Robert Sampson and William Julius Wilson (1995), who confront issues of race and violent crime head on. Most important is that the authors—alongside others—found that homicide was the leading cause of death among Black males. Their examination of firearm-related deaths provides clear evidence that African Americans continue to face dismal and worsening odds when it comes to crime in the streets and risk of incarceration.

In Chapter 6, "Rethinking Subculture and Subcultural Theory in the Study of Your Crime—A Theoretical Discourse," Chijoke Nwalozie (2015) offers a different perspective. The author argues that a reconsideration of subculture theory must ensure that youth subcultures are not benchmarked by those of Anglo/American cultural identities. Rather, they should refer to youths whose behaviors are oppositional to the mainstream culture, irrespective of the from which societies they come.

Chapter 7—written several years earlier—reflects the editor's contributions to this book and is titled "A Vision of Race, Crime, and Justice Through The Lens of Critical Race Theory." Here, Ross (2010) reasons that given ongoing practices and the condition of justice systems worldwide, an application of critical race theory (CRT) principles enables readers to examine social reality through a different (and more relevant) lens when addressing perceived injustices. Various principles of CRT are explained and applied to current practices, including interest convergence, White privilege, intersectionality, and storytelling, among other principles.

Part III comprises four readings in the areas of policing, prosecution, and punishment as chapter 8 begins with the article by Patrick Ibe, Charles Ochie, and Evaristus Obiyan (2012), titled "Racial Misuse of 'Criminal Profiling' by Law Enforcement: Intentions and Implications." This article examines critical issues regarding criminal profiling, its misuse by law enforcement, and the overreliance of this technique to solve serious crimes. The authors investigate the importance of racial profilig and its misuse in the United States and how it impacts African Americans and other minorities.

Chapter 9, authored by Lupe Salinas (2015), is titled "Abuses Resulting From Federal Immigration Enforcement Efforts." In this chapter, Salinas explores the degrading practices continually imposed on Latinx in the war against suspected illegal immigration. These include racial profiling, an approach used by both federal and state law enforcement agents, the abuse in immigration enforcement, and the use of deadly force against immigrants. As defendants navigating their way through the court system, the author discusses the communication barriers they encounter given their limited-English-proficiency and reliance on interpreters to understand the trial process. As a nation rich in ethnic and racial backgrounds, the United States, Salinas argues, should better strive to serve its principles of justice.

Chapter 10 is authored by Sparta Sah, Christopher Robertson, and Shima Baughman (2015) titled "Blinding Prosecutors to Defendant's Race: A Policy Proposal to Reduce Unconscious Bias in the Criminal Justice System." The authors provide readers an initial glance into issues of implicit biases. Behavioral science research has documented that prosecutors also harbor unconscious racial biases that affect their use of discretion when charging and prosecuting cases (Smith & Levinson, 2011). To reduce the risk of unconscious racial bias, the authors propose a policy change—through numerous techniques—that would blind prosecutors to the race of criminal defendant whenever feasible.

Chapter 11 concludes Part III with an article by Elizabeth Jones (2008), titled "Racism, Fines, and Fees and the U.S. Carceral State." This article suggests the need to move beyond traditional debates about mass incarceration in the United States to focus on the ubiquitous imposition of fines and fees for low-level offenses that carry wide-ranging poverty-enhancing and racially disparate consequences. The author argues that local government institutions, such as the police and courts, engage in daily practices that reflect the colorblind racism of neoliberalism, including revenue generation, which necessarily produces and reinforces race and class inequalities.

Part IV consist of five articles addressing issues of cultural diversity within corrections and correctional settings. It begins with the article in chapter 12 by A.E. Raza (2011) titled "Legacies of Racialization of Incarceration: From Convict-Lease to the Prison Industrial Complex." This article examines the current state of the U.S. prison system by historicizing it within the post-emancipation South. By concentrating on the history of the post-emancipation South and its prison system as it relates to African-Americans, this essay aims to show how anti-Black racism has been reinstituted in the current era of incarceration.

In chapter 13, Alessandro De Giorgi (2016) elaborates on the United States' love affair with imprisonment in the article "Five Theses on Mass Incarceration." Organized in the form of five short theses, the article assembles a critical map of some "discursive formations" that have emerged recently around the U.S. prison crisis. It concludes by offering some alternative ideas for a "radical reformist" agenda against mass incarceration.

Chapter 14 segues into the reality of sexual assault behind bars with the article "Women Behind Bars: An Illuminating Portrait," authored by Cathy McDaniels-Wilson and Judson L. Jefferies (2011). The authors provide readers with a sense of women's sexual abuse history across race by examining the staggering number of women inmates (in Ohio) who were sexually violated *before* entering prison. Concluding that the problem transcends race and age, the authors encourage readers to appreciate the consequences of one's history of sexual abuse, coupled with the complex needs of a steadily increasing prison population.

Chapter 15 is titled "Transgender Inmates: The Dilemma" and is authored by Hal Brotheim (2013). The author provides an in-depth examination of dysphoria and gender identity disorder, officially regarded as the presence of persistent and strong cross-gender identification. Although transgender arrestees experience much higher rates of sexual victimization, this chapter focuses on the potential for victimization, regardless of sexual orientation. Written with correctional personnel in mind, the chapter proposes the implementation of guidelines to ensure that contacts with transgender individuals are professional, respectful, and courteous and will not lead to complaints and lawsuits.

Chapter 16 is authored by Wesley Wagner and titled "Correctional Treatment: Developing a Successful Program." The author maintains that correctional treatment that offenders receive determines how productive they will be as members of society and whether they will contribute to recidivism. The article discusses correctional treatment programs that are being used in correctional facilities and whether they help inmates, regardless of race, become better individuals.

Part V concludes with three articles, starting with Chapter 17, "Dismantling the School-to-Prison Pipeline: A Survey From the Field." In this article, Matt Cregor and Damon Hewitt (2011) (both attorneys) document the meteoric rise of our nation's school discipline rates that have reached an all-time high. Moreover, racial disparities in suspensions, expulsions, and school-based arrests continue to widen. In their review of school discipline research, the article highlights promising efforts to eliminate racial disparities and to dismantle the school-to-prison pipeline.

Chapter 18, authored by Rachel D. Godsil (2015), is titled "Breaking the Cycle: Implicit Bias, Racial Anxiety, and Stereotype Threat." The author explores the dynamics of racial anxiety (often confused with racial threat) and cumulative racial advantages enjoyed by most Whites. He argues that these advantages have been embedded in society's structures and institutions and that structural racism cannot be successfully challenged without an understanding of how race operates psychologically. Godsil suggests that policy changes must address implicit biases that can affect political choices and can only be successful if the people implementing the policy changes are held in compliance.

The book concludes with chapter 19, authored by Elizabeth Anderson (2014), and goes the extra mile with the article titled "Why Racial Integration Remains an Imperative." The author notes that avoidance of integration is found across the political spectrum—often giving way to mythical remedial promises of racial justice, economic investments, and celebrations of multiculturalism. This article argues that all these purported remedies for racial injustice rest on the misguided illusion that racial justice can be achieved without racial integration.

Overall, these readings on cultural diversity within criminal justice systems provide a microcosm of the role of cultural diversity within the larger society. Each article is written by an equally diverse range of academics and practitioners spanning a variety of settings, including legal, medical, and social work. It is my hope that these 19 chapters demonstrate the importance of cultural diversity within our justice system and provide a framework for effective inclusive and interpersonal interactions. It also enables us to draw on our similarities and differences to break down stereotypes and prejudices. As educators, we must continually aspire to connect with all persons who are culturally, linguistically, racially, and ethnically diverse, particularly those who plan for careers in our justice systems.

References

Anderson, E. (2014). Why racial integration remains an imperative. *Poverty and Race, 20*(4), 1–19.

Brotheim, H. (2013). Transgender inmates: The dilemma. *American Jail Association, 27*(2) pp. 40–47.

Bowser, B. P. (2017). Racism: Origin and theory. *Journal of Black Studies, 48*(6), 572–590.

Burnett, N. (2015). Colorism in mental health: Looking the other way. *Journal of Colorism Studies, 1*(1), 1–5.

Byfield, N. (2014). Selling savage portrayals: Young Black and Latino males in the carceral state. In N. Byfield, (Ed.), *Savage portrayals: Race, media, and the Central Park jogger case* (pp. 168–181). Philadelphia, PA: Temple Univeristy Press.

Clyne, M., & Jupp, J. (2011). *Multiculturalism and integration: A harmonious relationship.* Canberra, Australia: Australian National University Press.

Cregor, M., & Hewitt, D. (2011). Dismantling the school-to-prison pipeline: A survey from the field. *Poverty & Race, 20*(1), 5–7.

De Giorgi. A. (2016). Five theses of mass incarceration. *Social Justice, 42*(2), 5–30.

Eberhardt, J. L., Davies, P. G., Purdie-Vaughns, V. J., & Johnson, S. L. (2006). Looking deathworthy: Perceived stereotypically of Black defendants predicts capital sentencing outcomes. *Psychological Science, 17*(5), 383–385.

Godsil, R. D. (2015). Breaking the cycle: Implicit bias, racial anxiety, and stereotype threat. *Poverty and Race, 24*(1), 1–10.

Ibe, P., Ochie, C., & Obiyan, E. (2012). Racial misuse of criminal profiling by law enforcement: Intentions and implications. *African Journal of Criminology & Justice Studies, 6*(1–2), 177–196.

Jones, E. (2018). Racism, fines, and fees and the U.S. carceral state. *Race & Class, 59*(3), 38–50.

McDaniels-Wilson, C., & Jeffries, J. L. (2011). Women behind bars: An illuminating portrait. *Journal of the Institute of Justice and International Studies, 11*, 129–144.

Merriam-Webster. (n.d.). *Diversity.* Retrieved from https://www.merriam-webster.com/dictionary/diversity

Moody, M., Dorries, B., & Blackwell, H. (2009). How national media framed coverage of missing Black and White women. *Media Report to Women, 37*(4), 12–18.

Nwalozie, C. J. (2015). Rethinking subculture and subcultural theory in the study of youth crime—A theoretical discourse. *Journal of Theoretical & Philosophical Criminology, 7*(1), 1–16.

Page, S. E. (2008). *The difference: How the power of diversity creates better groups, firms, schools, and societies.* Princeton, NJ: Princeton University Press.

Raza, A. E. (2011). Legacies of the racialization of incarceration: From convict-lease to the prison industrial complex. *Journal of the Institute of Justice and International Studies, 11*, 159.

Rosado, C. (n.d.). What makes a school multicultural? *Critical Multicultural Pavilion.* Retrieved from http://www.edchange.org/multicultural/papers/caleb/multicultural.html

Ross, L. E. (2010). A vision of race, crime, and justice through the lens of critical race theory. In E. McLaughlin & T. Newburn (Eds.), *SAGE Handbook of Criminological Theory* (pp. 391–409). Thousand Oaks, CA: SAGE.

Sah, S., Robertson, C. T., & Baughman, S. B. (2015). Blinding prosecutors to defendants' race: A policy proposal to reduce unconscious bias in the criminal justice system. *Behavioral Science & Policy, 1*(2), 69–76.

Salinas, L. (2015). Abuses resulting from federal immigration enforcement efforts. In *U.S. Latinos and Criminal Justice* (pp. 87–105). East Lansing, MI: Michigan State University Press.

Sampson, R. J., & Wilson, W. J. (1995). Toward a theory of race, crime, and urban inequality. In S. Gabbidon & H. T. Greene (Eds.), *Race, crime, and justice: A reader.* New York: N.Y., Routledge (pp. 37–56).

Smith, R. J., & Levinson, J. D. (2011). The impact of implicit racial bias on the exercise of prosecutorial discretion. *Seattle University Law Review, 35*(3), 795.

PART I

DIVERSE MATTERS OF PERCEPTION

"IF WE CANNOT NOW END OUR DIFFERENCES,
AT LEAST WE CAN HELP MAKE THE WORLD
SAFE FOR DIVERSITY."

– *John F. Kennedy*

Colorism in Mental Health

Looking the Other Way

Nadine Burnett

With major pharmacological advances there has been a shift in psychiatry to focus on biological factors versus environmental and social factors. However, as our minority population grows and disparities in health outcomes in these communities persist, it will become increasingly important to address underlying societal issues. In the 1970's, there was increased passion for and awareness of racial pride and identity (reflected in psychiatry with ample research which appeared in books exploring race and mental health) within the intellectual communities (of all races) and the minority community at large. When I first entered medical school, leaving out the racial identity of a patient was deemed as an unacceptable omission. Today, some 10 years after I left medical school, it has become commonplace for me to see "comprehensive" evaluations with no mention of race in my daily practice. This ambiguous identification of patients has become so normal that several of my colleagues argue that racial identification of patients only feeds into preconceived notions/biases, which cloud one's psychiatric assessment. This harmful misconception reflects a societal change, which is juxtaposed to the visible increase in people of color in powerful positions. This has all led to the fallacious belief that we now live in a "post racial" society. In the aggregate, these attitudes have led to the minimization of the importance of a patient's racial identity and ultimately the persistence of racism. Many are choosing to cling onto these exceptional examples and look away from the more painful reality. As we move towards this optimistic ideal of a colorblind society, it has become increasingly difficult to address colorism and its profound impact. There have been several studies to suggest higher social stressors related to colorism. Within minority populations, despite the amazing accomplishments, major disparities remain based on skin color.

For example:

- Lighter skinned African American males with less education and work experience were preferred to dark skinned African American males with more education and work experience (Harrison and Thomas, 2009).
- Darker skinned African Americans earned less than lighter skinned African Americans (72 cents to $1) (Hughes and Hertel, 1990).
- Light-skinned Latinos made $5,000 more on average than dark-skinned Latinos (Vedantam, 2010).
- Darker skinned African American defendants were twice as likely to receive the death penalty for crimes involving white victims (Eberhardt, Davies, Purdie-Vaughns, and Johnson, 2006).
- Lighter skinned African American women received shorter prison sentences than their darker skinned counterparts (Viglione, Hannon, and DeFina, 2011).

The above referenced information is shocking. Colorism has tainted darker minorities' American dreams, based solely on their pigmentation. As a child psychiatrist, I am particularly concerned about the impact of colorism on a developing child's mind.

Psychological abuse is defined as "a form of mistreatment in which there is intent to cause mental or emotional pain or injury including verbal aggression or statements intended to humiliate or insult" (Medical-Dictionary, 2014). It has been well documented that repeated negative messages delivered through the mechanism of emotional abuse may be internalized by a child and warps the way in which a child sees himself. Colorism as a form of emotional abuse can be expressed directly (through word and /or deed) from peers, family members and caregivers or it can be expressed indirectly via an unending chorus of negative stereotypes in the media. As such, this can have negative effects on the development of a child's self-esteem and self-worth. Poor self-esteem increases a child's likelihood of engaging in disruptive behaviors (e.g., criminal acts, substance abuse, promiscuity, or truancy) as well as increased vulnerability to psychiatric disorders (e. g., depression or anxiety disorders). These scars formed in early childhood will persist into adulthood, especially if left unaddressed.

In my practice, I have observed the effects colorism has on children daily. Comments from one child or a group of children (often within the same racial group) to another, such as "You are Black and Ugly!" can cause the preyed upon child to engage in desperate attempts to alter his or her appearance or increase his or her attractiveness in other, often drastic, ways. Unfortunately, no physical alteration of a child's appearance will eradicate the child's underlying feelings of inferiority. Colorism feeds into a child's feelings of low self-esteem, which ultimately spill over into and fuel their involvement in harmful behaviors (e.g., aggression, self-injury, substance abuse, sexual promiscuity, etc.). I have found that the hardest part of combating the cancerous effects of colorism on children is dealing with the perpetuation of colorism by the adults in their lives. On far too many occasions, I have heard adults (teachers/caregivers) support these distorted thoughts of victimized children rather than challenge them.

Preferential treatment of lighter skinned children by adults often causes children of lighter pigmentation to be ostracized and targeted by their peers. This sets up a maladaptive pattern, further feeding into the poisonous and maladaptive cycle. This "colorism cycle" reflects a common pattern of abuse, where those who are abused (particularly if the abuse is not professionally addressed or treated) will likely perpetuate this pattern and abuse others.

Colorism causes collateral damage beyond its effects on the child with darker pigmentation. Often lighter skinned children attempt to assert and prove their "blackness" by assuming negative stereotypes and trying to prove themselves by being overly aggressive (this is often a response to being the target of bullying by their peers). This bullying completes the cycle of abuse as darker children project their underlying feelings of anger towards these lighter skinned children in an effort to punish them for their perceived "birth rite" of an easier life.

The specific harms of colorism were driven home to me when I was completing a dermatology clerkship in medical school. An African American female in her mid-20's presented to the clinic requesting cream to correct the "dark spots" all over her skin. Upon my physical examination of the young woman, there were no signs of skin discoloration. I was confused by the patient's presentation, so I asked her to point to the "black spots" she was worried about. To my surprise and horror, the young woman pointed all over her body. The attending dermatologist (who was also a person of color) later evaluated the young woman and confirmed the absence of "black spots" or abnormalities. He knew what was going on and I knew what was going on and yet, he subsequently ignored this young woman's very real psychological issue and wrote her a prescription for a high dose bleaching cream. I am ashamed to confess that I did not even pursue a deeper conversation with the attending physician and I simply looked away to ease the discomfort and shame of the situation.

The exploration of colorism, its effects, and what we must do to eradicate this taboo topic is the call that I am trying to sound with this paper. I come from the perspective of one who has blood on my hands. I have been guilty of looking the other way, afraid of being perceived as radical, inflammatory or provocative. I have, at times pushed this topic back into the closet that it lives in for most of us people of color. Colorism is a painful and shameful reminder of our tortuous past. While it is far easier to minimize or ignore, this is not a solution. Given the pervasiveness of colorism and the colorism mindset throughout our society and its difficulty to prove with empirical data, a solution seems painfully illusive. Even as I sit here writing this article, any solution to this problem seems daunting and impossible. How can we address colorism when we cannot even engage in a non-threatening comfortable discussion? I believe that if each of us can challenge ourselves to speak up when faced with an issue that clearly is related to colorism we can begin to plant the seeds for change. We should speak up when negative comments are made which are attributed to darker skin tones. We must also speak out when we observe intimidating or bullying behaviors towards lighter pigmented individuals. We must all realize that colorism creates a dynamic, which perpetuates the harmful caste system of color created during slavery, which is the root to the problem. Let's shed the feelings of shame and embarrassment that have paralyzed us as individuals and ultimately as a country. We must not look away and avert our eyes; we must plant the seeds of change.

References

Eberhardt, J., Davies, P., Purdie-Vaughns, V. and Johnson, S. (2006). Looking deathworthy: perceived stereotypicality of black defendants predicts capital-sentencing outcomes. *Psychological Science,* 17 (5): 383–86.

Hamilton, D., Goldsmith, A. H. and Darity, W. (2008). Shedding "light" on marriage: The influence of skin shade on marriage for black females (Working Paper Series No. 16).

Harrison, M. S. and Thomas, K. M. (2009). The hidden prejudice in selection: A research investigation on skin color bias. *Journal of Applied Social Psychology,* 39, 134–168.

Hughes, M. and Hertel, B. R. (1990). The significance of color remains: A study of life chances, mate selection, and ethnic consciousness among black Americans. *Social Forces,* 68(2), 1105–1120.

Keith, V. M. and Herring, C. (1991). Skin tone and stratification in the black community. *The American Journal of Sociology,* 97(3), 760–778.

Psychological abuse. 2014. In *The Free Medical Dictionary*.com. Retrieved from http://medical-dictionary. thefreedictionary.com.

Viglione, J., Hannon, L. and DeFina, R. (2011). The impact of light skin on prison time for black female offenders. *The Social Science Journal,* 48:250–258.

Vedantam, S. (2010). *The hidden brain. How our unconscious minds elect presidents, control markets, wage wars, and save our lives.* New York: Spiegel & Grau.

Post-Reading Questions

1   In what ways is colorism harmful to the African American community? Are other persons of color equally affected by colorism? Why or why not?

2   Should we assume that all African Americans experience emotional abuse from the practice of colorism? Are the effects of colorism somewhat minimized by those oblivious to its reality? Please qualify your position.

3   In what ways is colorism manifested within interracial families and among biracial children and siblings?

4   To what extent should we be concerned about the impact of colorism on a developing child's mind? Is it plausible to assume that victims of colorism will internalize their abuse and perpetuate the abuse onto others? Please qualify your position.

5   How would you respond to the question, "How can we address colorism when we cannot even engage in a nonthreatening comfortable discussion?" Please qualify your position.

Racism

Origin and Theory

Benjamin P. Bowser

Racism's earliest usage has been traced to the 1902 edition of the *Oxford English Dictionary* as a description of U.S. policy toward Native Americans (Howard, 2016). For the first half of the 20th century, the term was used interchangeably with "racialism." The term's use is relatively new in the social sciences (Barot & Bird, 2001) and began with Ruth Benedict's *Race and Racism* (Benedict, 1945) and in Edmund Soper's *Racism: A World Issue* (Hankins, 1947). In both books, "racism" described incidences in the world community of animus between groups based on visible physical differences. With the possible exception of the term "prejudice," no other word gained such popular usage in the United States to describe social conflict as did racism in the second half of the 20th century.

Two developments popularized the term. The first was use as propaganda against anti-Semitism and the racial eugenics that targeted Jews in Germany in the 1930s and during the Second World War (Blaut, 1992). The second popularization came from U.S. civil rights activists during the 1960s. Activists saw the political independence of former colonies in Africa and Asia as hollow prizes that did not change the economic dependence of newly independent states on their former colonial masters (Nkrumah, 1965). Domestic U.S. civil rights victories did not lessen economic inequality between Black and White Americans in the South or elsewhere. In addition, a civil rights movement shortcoming was not having a specific strategy to effectively combat the covert and indirect ways that racial hierarchy was maintained in the North and Midwest; this shortcoming was the basis of the "black power" critique of the civil rights movement (Levy, 1998). Martin Luther King Jr. and the Southern Christian Leadership Conference highlighted this shortcoming in their unsuccessful attempt to address racial economic inequality in Chicago during the summer of 1966 (Ralph, 1993). A better understanding was needed of what they were up against and how to change it.

This [reading] has four objectives: The first is to revisit the concept of racism that evolved from 1960s civil rights activism, to note its theoretical promise. The second objective is to show that the major concepts of racism that took the place of the original notion in interpreting race relations since 1970 did not fulfill racism's early promise. The third objective is to outline what the activist concept of racism would be now if elaborated as theory and used in race relations. Finally, this article will suggest a way to advance the activist theory of racism and to make it a useful tool in contemporary research on race relations.

Racism: Emerging Concept

Members of the Student Nonviolent Coordinating Committee (SNCC) needed to make sense of what they were struggling against and how best to attack it (Forman, 1972). They needed a conceptual model. First, it was clear to them that the racial hierarchy they were up against dated back to slavery, was intergenerational, and part of the culture. Second, racial discrimination was institutionalized in different ways in the South and in the North. There was the overt and highly elaborate Jim Crow system in the South; then there was a covert and indirect system in the North. Third, they realized that individual acts of racial animus against African Americans were social in origin and did not originate solely from individuals actors. Individual Whites learned their animus as part of their socialization. What had to be worked out was how these three key realities were connected and operated and could be changed (Carmichael & Thelwell, 2003).

The first writing to connect two of the three realities, institutional racism and personal racial animus, was Stokely Carmichael (Kwame Ture) and Charles Hamilton's *Black Power* (1967). It was based on Kwame Ture's specific experience in Mississippi. The Jim Crow order of Southern small-town communities and expected social relations between races created a near perfect model of racial oppression. Carmichael and Hamilton first referred to this oppressive alignment as "personally and institutionally racist." The missing piece of history and culture was viewed as part of the institutional barrier. The first writing to describe all three pieces of the puzzle as distinct levels (cultural-historic, institutional, and individual) in a single concept of racism was James Jones' (1972) *Prejudice and Racism*. This early discussion was elaborated on in his later essay, "The Concept of Racism and Its Changing Reality" (Jones, 1981).

Theory Never Developed

Anyone familiar with 1960s liberation rhetoric heard racism described as "cultural, institutional and individual." The links between these levels were assumed. The three component concept of racism was primed for development as a theory. A ProQuest search of Sociological Abstracts of publications since 1990 using the terms "racism ... theory ... critiques" generated 637 references of discussions and research on racism. No publication elaborated on a theory of racism with cultural, institutional, and individual levels, phases or components. Based on monitoring the literature on racism, it is my contention that the literature on racism in its first three critical decades moved away from its early promise to develop a theory (Sage Race Relations Abstracts, 1981–2007). We now see each level (cultural, institutional, and individual) elaborated as distinct racisms. The original intent of linking the three levels in a single theory has been lost. Also lost is the promise that a theory of racism can come out of practice and be enhanced by further activism. What is now published are constructs that offer one-dimensional and reductionist explanations of race relations.

Racisms Without Theory

The government-compelled dismantling of Jim Crow segregation as legally sanctioned and overt practices in the South did not end institutional and individual racism. Covert expressions of racial animus replaced easily identifiable forms. The failure to create testable theories of racism left activists and academics alike without a conceptual tool to make sense of the post–civil rights racial divide. How well did sociological theory over the past 50 years accurately explain the relations between races? With the three levels of racism in mind as a basis for theory, a brief review of the four major propositions is in order.

Declining Significance of Race

Did race really decline in significance, heightening the importance of social class and culture (Wilson, 1978)? If you replace an overt system of racial hierarchy with a covert one, race's salience will appear to decline. However, a new system of controls where Whites are privileged and Blacks are disadvantaged still exists (Friedman, 1975). The only change is the institutional means to maintain inequality. Some theorists fell for this tactical shift in racism's institutional deployment. The outcome is the evolution of a new system of racial controls that is largely without description or commentary—referred to as a "new Jim Crow" (Alexander, 2011).

In retrospect, the idea of a declining significance of race should have been apparent as a missed reading of the 1970s. Covert racism in cities existed simultaneously with covert racism in the rural South. It is still very much with us. This includes steering by real estate agents and block busting (Kwate, Goodman, Jackson, & Harris, 2013); denying home loans and charging higher mortgage interests rates to Blacks (Woods, 2012); maintaining racially segregated schools by using unequal home values as the basis of school funding (Johnson, 2014); using seniority as a basis for employment (Byron, 2010), making Blacks the last hired and the first fired; and criminalizing Black men in the application of laws (Meares, 2014).

None of these practices is overtly racist. Schools, employers, police and courts, banks, and real estate function as they should. Racial motives are imminently deniable. Racism is evident only in outcomes. The declining significance of race is an insight about post-1960s institutional change that is simply incorrect. Race has not declined in significance. Only the institutional mechanics for maintaining racial hierarchy changed. More important is that there is no theory from this insight to explain current or future change.

Symbolic Racism

With the increasing sophistication of survey research and computer analyses, we can do more frequent and in-depth assessments of public opinions and beliefs. Important adjuncts to understanding modern race relations are explorations of White attitudes and beliefs toward Blacks and other people of color. Sears (1988) and Sears and McConahay (1973) first used the term "symbolic racism" to describe a new finding. White Americans supported the principles of equality for Black Americans, but at the same time do not support efforts to implement these principles. They decisively rejected the old Jim Crow racism and overtly racist sentiments, even in the South. In addition, Whites had much less personal animus against Black people than in the past and believed that White racism no longer existed. These researchers hypothesized that the origin of this conditional and relatively benign racism was in respondents' traditional conservative socialization, which held negative views of Blacks.

Oddly enough, there is no prior literature on traditional conservative socialization. With regard to racism's three levels, symbolic racism is a form of individual racism that is not influenced somehow by social structure or institutions. Perhaps, it is just a coincidence; symbolic racism appeared simultaneously with color-blind political conservatism. In which case, symbolic racism has institutional roots, just not the ones suggested by its authors. Here again is a post-1970s insight about race relations that is questionable as theory.

Color-Blind Racism

In the late 1980s, conservative talk radio discovered "color-blindness" as a solution to the race problem (Hilliard & Keith, 1999; Spence, 2006). Color-blindness is a direct application of indirection: If you do not know a person's race, you cannot discriminate against them. Conservatives saw color-blindness as a way to make unnecessary affirmative action, the Civil Rights Act, the Voting Rights Act, and all other measures they allege that discriminate against White people. Conservatives even advocated taking questions about race off the U.S. Census and any federally funded survey. Some White Americans even began to claim that they no longer saw a person's race or color. Therefore, they could not be racist nor act with racial bias.

Critiques of color-blindness both as public policy and as personal practice were to the point. While claiming color-blindness, advocates were hard at work trying to degrade institutions that maintain even an appearance of equity. Color-blindness was a central rationale for the conservative American Civil Rights Institute's promotion of California Proposition 209 outlawing the use of race, sex, or ethnicity in public life (Hicklin, 2007). Color-blindness was the rationale for Michigan's Proposal 2, which had the same objectives as Proposition 209. Both propositions are now law. There is no more direct translation of an idea into institutional life than making it a law. The bottom line is that people who claim color-blindness still manage to racially discriminate, and their color-blind public policies still have racially discriminatory outcomes (Bonilla-Silva, 2006). Racism has not gone away or disappeared under color-blindness. The result is only "color-blind racism." Here again, there is no theory.

Unconscious Racism

Unconscious racism focuses on the individual racism that affects institutional practice. The concept poses that racial bias exists subconsciously and is the source of discriminatory behavior against people of color in public accommodations, job applications, and court cases. Unlike other racisms, unconscious racism can be demonstrated in social psychological experiments (Eberhardt & Fiske, 1998). White subjects were shown people of different races in photos; their reactions were recorded showing unconsciously attributed racial stereotypes to these images. For example, dark-skinned Black men were closely associated with crime and danger; light-skinned men were more commonly associated with attractiveness and goodness. There are some questions as to how and to what extent conscious racism works beyond experimental settings; direct measures using surveys and interviews have not consistently supported this proposition (Blanton & Jaccard, 2008). However, the research on unconscious racism is the first attempt to isolate the subliminal connection between unconscious bias, discriminatory behavior, and racist institutional practices. What unconscious racism does not affirm is the source of unconscious bias in culture. What it does tell us is that culturally derived attitudes and beliefs regarding race are unconscious as well as conscious.

Other racisms. There are other descriptions of racism: laissez-faire racism, ideological racism, hi-tech racism, identity racism, environmental racism, and police racism. There are almost as many racisms as there are adjectives to describe racial encounters. What all of these racisms have in common is that the concept of racism has no theoretical content. What has been the outcome of decades of atheoretical racism?

A Consequence

The single most important organized effort since 1970 to push back civil rights gains and reaffirm racial hierarchy has been the rise of political conservatism. No theoretical construct in the social sciences regarding race saw this coming. President Johnson predicted that the Democratic Party would lose the South with passage of the 1964 Civil Rights Act. Opposition to two decades of civil rights reforms coalesced in 1981 with the election of Ronald Reagan as president of the United States. The key to Reagan's election and to reversing civil rights gains was the "Southern

Strategy" described by Lee Atwater, Reagan's campaign manager from South Carolina. Atwater's view was that there should be no more direct reference to Black people and to race. Indirection and "color-blindness" were the ways to do this.

> You start out in 1954 by saying, "Nigger, nigger, nigger." By 1968, you can't say "nigger"—that hurts you. Backfires. So you say stuff like forced busing, states' rights and all that stuff. You're getting so abstract now [that] you're talking about cutting taxes, and all these things you're talking about are totally economic things and a byproduct of them is [that] blacks get hurt worse than whites. And subconsciously maybe that is part of it. I'm not saying that. But I'm saying that if it is getting that abstract, and that coded, that we are doing away with the racial problem one way or the other. You follow me—because obviously sitting around saying, "We want to cut this," is much more abstract than even the busing thing, and a hell of a lot more abstract than "nigger, nigger." (Lamis, 1999, pp. 7–8)

With Atwater's quote, we see in stark relief the creation of a new expression of cultural racism (indirection). We also see the linking of cultural racism through indirection with the Republican Party's plans of action to shape American institutions for decades to come (Heatherly, 1981). The effective of using racial indirection soon became evident in surveys. White attitudes toward Blacks had steadily improved from 1963 to 1972, but began to reverse after the implementation of the Southern Strategy in the 1970s (Condran, 1979; Cummings, 1980). A plurality of Whites moved toward a broad based conservatism that analysts thought might be connected to racial attitudes (Chin, 1985; Sniderman, Piazza, & Tetlock, 1986). How did they explain such a reversal? A social psychological construct, working class authoritarianism, was posed as the explanation (Grabbs, 1980). Really? The intentionality and agency of Atwater and other shapers of public opinion were missed completely.

A hardening of White attitudes toward Blacks through indirection was necessary to put in place covert institutional efforts to roll back racial progress. For example, in urban centers with large Black populations, use of at-large elections was an indirect way to avoid "minority dominance" of Whites—Black majority rule. All through the 1980s, covert media appeals to race via the Southern Strategy called for "White" unity and resistance to Blacks (Hilliard & Keith, 1999; Spence, 2006). Attempts to elect Black mayors in Chicago and Los Angeles struggled against unspoken White voter opposition. Even the Ku Klux Klan leader, David Duke, retired his white Klan robe and hood, put on a suit and tie, and refused to directly refer to Black people. By doing so, he made a creditable run for governor of Louisiana (Ellison, 1991; Rose, 1992).

Media using the Southern Strategy convinced many Whites that racial discrimination no longer existed. Kluegel and Smith (1982) showed the extent to which these White beliefs about Black advancement were conditioned by the media. Another explanation for emerging White opposition to Black progress was White perceived self-interest and a sense that affirmative action violated their egalitarian principles (Kluegel & Smith, 1983; Smith, 1981). A decade later, a series of surveys reaffirmed that White opposition to redressing racial inequality was not due to racial prejudice per se, but was again a reflection of self-interest (Bobo & Kluegel, 1993; Kluegel, 1990; Schumann, Stech, & Bobo, 1985). Once more, social psychological phenomena explained away any intentional and institutional efforts to produce these outcomes. Meanwhile, Black gains had not only stopped, they were reversed in education, housing, income, and employment (Jaynes & Williams, 1989).

The Three Levels of Racism

If James Jones' three levels of racism evolved into a theory, what would it look like? Would this theory have anticipated the Southern Strategy? To see if should potential exists, we have to look specifically at each level and then outline how the levels link together.

Cultural Level

The cultural level is not a separate theory of racism (Blaut, 1992). It is one of three components of a theory. The cultural level of racism is an attempt to account for the following. Slavery in the U.S. ended in 1865 and was followed immediately by the Black Codes, which maintained Black subordination. By 1910, the Black Codes had evolved into a new system of Black oppression, Jim Crow (Ranney, 2006; Tischauser, 2012). Then, the 1964 Civil Rights Act ended Jim Crow, but the animus against Black people and efforts to subordinate them continued. Some point out that a third system of oppression is emerging—a New Jim Crow (Alexander, 2011; Massey, 2007). How do we account for the intergenerational continuity of racial animus despite efforts to eliminate it?

The dilemma is that racism defies legal solutions, social movements, and changes in economy, in people and in the times. There is only one explanation for the continuity of racism 50 years after activists posed the original concept of racism. Its transmission is cultural because it has distinct norms, attitudes, beliefs, and values and is a particular worldview. This transmission of racism is not a theory; it is an empirical fact. An ideology, philosophy, justification, or social theory based on this fact is not the same thing. In the original activist description of racism, its empirical reality was described as a cultural phenomenon.

Institutional Level

Civil rights activists who entered the Deep South in the 1960s were confronted by a total institution (Carmichael & Thelwell, 2003; Forman, 1972). In small Southern towns, every human institution was organized overtly around racial hierarchy—Jim Crow. Parks, schools, store entrances, courts, movie theaters, jobs, housing, churches, swimming pools, hospitals, and even cemeteries were racially segregated. Whites had the better facilities; Blacks had the worst. Blacks had to show deference to Whites. In contrast, Northern racism was indirect and faceless, the opposite of a total institution. Ironically, racial segregation of housing, jobs, and schools was more thorough than in the South (Massey, 2007). Public places were integrated. There were no formal racial codes of public etiquette. No one in prominence advocated racial segregation, admitted to it, controlled it, or took responsibility for it. Racism was covert with White-over-Black racial hierarchy as the outcome, just as it was in the South.

The difference between the North and South was in their institutional expressions of racism. They were two distinct ways to organizing racial hierarchy. Both ways had the same goal of Black subordination. It was at this institutional level of racism that activists focused their efforts (Better, 2008). Racial segregation laws could be reduced; schools integrated; curricula and pedagogy changed; housing, real estate, and bank mortgage practices scrutinized; and hiring goals could be established. Racial discrimination in voting rights could be eliminated. Racism nationwide could be addressed through institutional change, repeatedly and in each generation.

Individuals Level

Individual acts of racism constitute the third level of racism (Shah, 2008). To their credit, activists recognized that for most Whites the motivation of individual acts of racism was not innate. It was highly varied and conditional. Those who had lived and worked with Blacks as peers were less likely to be prejudice and might even oppose racism (Williams, 1975). Those who were better educated and well informed were also less likely to be prejudice; this characterized many fellow White civil rights activists. Where racial prejudice was not the norm and acts of racism were not tolerated, only a small minority of Whites were still compelled to act out racism (Pettigrew, 1981). It is hypothesized that this small group did so primarily out of some psychological and personality disorder. Most White Americans who were racist were malleable, were taught racism, and therefore, could be untaught.

Theory of Racism

Intrinsic to the 1960s activists' notion of racism was interaction between cultural, institutional, and individual levels. Think of racism as a stool; it stays upright and serves its purpose because it has three legs. Each leg is necessary and works in conjunction with the others. All three legs together are necessary and sufficient for the stool to stay upright; no one or two of the three legs can hold the stool up by themselves. The premises of this theory of racism follow:

1 Cultural racism (the presumption of White supremacy and Black inferiority) precedes and preconditions institutional expressions of racism. Without racist cultural scripts, institutional expressions of racism would not occur.

2   Cultural racism provides the blueprint and architecture for the organization of institutional racism, its objectives (White dominance), and criteria for success (White privilege). Cultural racism is passed on intergenerationally and is part of the content of White racial identity.

3   Institutional racism is essential for both the perpetuation of White privilege and of White dominance. Institutional racism keeps racism going within and across generations. It in turn reinforces cultural racism.

4   Institutional racism precedes and preconditions individual expressions of racism. Cultural racism is also a necessary precondition to individual racism, but its influence is mediated through institutional racism.

5   Cultural racism regulates the intensity and frequency of individual acts of racism by the extent to which institutional racism has been deployed. Hypothetically, if institutional racism is increasingly deployed, acts of individual racism will increase. If institutional racism is poorly deployed, individual acts will have little reinforcement.

The following illustration (Figure 2.1) shows the links and interdependencies between the levels of racism.

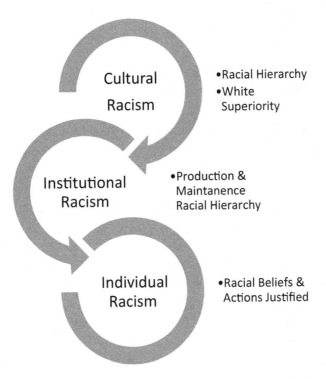

Figure 2.1   The activist theory of racism.

In the illustration, cultural racism is the blueprints for the operation of institutional racism in American life. It is the objective of institutions to fulfill cultural scripts. Through institutional racism, cultural racism gets operationalized within and across generations. Then, institutional racism in turn provides reinforcement for individual beliefs in racial hierarchy and provides justification for individual efforts to maintain racial hierarchy—individual racism.

The above premises that connect the three levels of racism have two corollaries for the functioning of the system as a whole.

> **System Maintenance:** Institutional racism requires institutions to rein-force one another to maintain White racial advantage.

For example, what if high school honors classes are used to privilege White students and the general education track disadvantages students of color? The solution is to make certain that White students who are not really honors material go into the general track and that students of color who are talented go into the honors track. Have you eliminated institutional racism? Not at all. One's struggle has only begun. Realignment back to White privilege becomes apparent when White parents, whose children were moved to the general track, sue and/or leave for private and alternative schools. White students still in the honors track will leave soon after as well. The school's principal will be criticized for driving White students out and eventually removed. The school budget will get cut. Eliminating one or two institutional practices will not end racism. The reaction of a series of other institutional players (district officials, teachers, courts, and parents) is to return to the cultural expectation of White racial privilege. Finally, if institutions do not fulfill their purpose, they can be abandoned.

> **Institutional Abandonment:** An institution will be progressively deval-ued and alternative ways will be sought to fulfill its role and functions if it no longer preserves White advantage.

When Whites are the predominant students in K–12 or in state universities, the quality of schools, teachers, faculty, and programs are maintained. Confidence in the systems and their graduates is high. The schools and universities are well funded even in hard times. If it is perceived that students of color are becoming the majority, efforts to maintain quality wane, confidence declines, and budgets get cut, repeatedly. If the non-White presence cannot be reversed by other institutional players (i.e., legislature, courts, criminal justice system), that institution will be allowed to decline until it collapses. Then, it will be reorganized, privatized, or have its function—educating students—distributed to other institutions.

In K–12, charter schools are a form of abandonment. Predominantly Black and Latino school systems are allowed to continue declining in exchange for a few charter schools that educate a small number of students. In public higher education, state governments will continue to defund public higher education until they reach a point where the only option will be to close or privatize them—to be taken over by for-profit educational corporations. In the same way, Black communities are redlined by banks and denied municipal services until they physically and socially collapse. Then, they are recycled for White use through gentrification. In both cases, White privilege and hierarchy are maintained.

Implications

When the three levels of racism get fully elaborated, it has implications. First, the theory of racism does not see racism as an outcome of some impersonal process "by which social, economic and political forces determine the content and importance of racial categories" as in racial formation theory (Omi & Winant, 1994, p. 61). A process does not necessarily have intentionality, the ability to refine, change, and redirect itself nor is a process motivated by status and material wealth, to name a few deficiencies (Feagin & Elias, 2013). If it is a process, racism is the unfolding of racial hierarchy as a culture script through institutional and individual levels of social organization. As long as the cultural content of White supremacy is unquestioned, institutional and individual racism are normal outcomes across time.

Second, there is a reason why the theory underlying racism was not developed. U.S. race relations literature has historically been about either finding a way to get Black people accepted by Whites or to resolving conflicts between the races (Pettigrew, 1991). Fundamentally, the "race problem" is thought to be a Black problem. This paradigm could not conceive of focusing the study of racism on Whites, specifically, asking what motivates some White people to act racist and others to be antiracist (Zuberi & Bonilla-Silva, 2008). Saenger (1965) commented two generations ago that "no objective research has been undertaken on the effects of social prejudice on those who harbor it" (p. 23) and Weston (1972) wrote "Whites have been neglected as a subject of study (in race relations)" (p. xiv). Little has changed. Application of the theory of racism could open this door. Without such a theory, the reaction to the civil rights movement and subsequent efforts to roll back its gains are missed for what they are by social scientists and activists alike. This theory could have anticipated the Southern Strategy and the rise of Trump because it focuses on White institutional responses to change. It focuses on the ways that racism adjusts to challenges.

Since 1981, no theory has developed as an alternative to the theory of racism that can anticipate and accurately identified changes in White racial attitudes and behaviors as the outcome of intentional human agency. To do this would minimally require monitoring new uses of cultural racism and the creation of new institutional practices. The theory of racism can do this only to the extent that changes in culture, institutional practices, and individual racial behaviors are viewed as integrated and preconditions to one another and mutually reinforcing.

Conclusion

There are fundamental questions about racism unexplained by the theory of racism. What would happen if the people who are considered racially inferior suddenly disappeared or were no longer identifiable? The answer from the current racial paradigm, where Black people are the sources of the race problem, is that racism would disappear. If Blacks disappeared, it might be that some other group may find themselves at the bottom of social hierarchy or it might be necessary to reinvent social hierarchy in the United States altogether. If the reality is the latter, the answer to this question might require replacing the theory of racism. The source of racial animus explained by the theory of racism may have some other and more fundamental motivation that we have yet to discover.

Another question is what if the central propositions in the theory of racism are simply wrong. We assume that if institutional racism ceases to exist for several generations, cultural racism would wane and eventually disappear. From an international and comparative perspective, there is evidence to the contrary. Cuba has been the best laboratory in the last half century in attempts to eliminate racism. Soon after the 1954 revolution, the new government passed laws against institutional barriers to racial equity and made very conscious efforts to eliminate racial hierarchy (Benson, 2016). After 60 years and almost three generations, Afro-Cubans enjoy the least racial inequality in education and health of any Afro-descendants in the West (Belizan, Cafferata, Belizan, & Althabe, 2007). Yet cultural racism still exists in Cuba (Bodenheimer, 2015) and new institutional barriers are already evident in tourism, where Black participation is clearly discriminated against (Roland, 2011). This suggests that once the notion of racial hierarchy is engrained in a culture, racism is permanent. The most we can ever hope for is to reduce racism as much as possible in each generation. The theory of racism may needs revision to reflect this reality.

The notion of cultural racism is also open to question. Cultural content virtually defies definition (Vandenberg, 2010). Culture is taken-for-granted shared attitudes, beliefs, and values. Anything cultural is difficult to measure. What is racism's specific content in the totality of American culture? Whatever it is, it too defies definition and measurement. How can we know whether this content exists and can be changed intentionally in any way? Likewise, can cultural racism be increased or decreased intentionally, and under what circumstances? Because we do not have answers to these questions, the theory behind the concept of racism is only as accurate as the concept of cultural racism. If we cannot get a better handle on what is cultural racism, then the idea of interaction between cultural, institutional, and individual racisms has limited utility. It took generations to create racist cultural content, but now can that content be upended and replaced in a few years or months (Mohammed, 2011)? The idea that deeply embedded cultural content such as racism or Whiteness can be upended by media turns on its head the idea that culture takes generations to produce (Llosa, 2015). Can one electoral or advertising campaign, that takes place over a few months, reinforce or undo cultural content that took generations to create? If this is the case, then electronic and social media are far more powerful and influential than we imagine.

A Contemporary Note

The need to advance the theory of racism and other notions that integrate culture, institutions, and individual influences could not be greater. Decades of continuous indirect appeals to affirm White racial superiority by the Republican Party have produced a monster. A segment of the conservative White electorate has rejected established Republican Party politics as unable to deliver on its ideological promises to reverse White working-class economic decline and to roll back big government, civil rights, globalism, and political correctness. The Tea Party in 2010 was the prelude, and now the Party has been taken over by its most extreme elements in a Donald Trump presidency. Race has not declined in importance. It was central to the 2016 election. The need to hide racism in symbolic indirection or color-blindness has been rejected. There is nothing unconscious about Trump and his electorate's racism. Lee Atwater moved conservatives away from direct racism. Donald Trump has brought them back.

If there was ever a bold and clear demonstration of the theoretic propositions of the theory underling racism, the Trump presidency is it. Cultural racism is evident in his appeals to return to the nostalgia of unquestioned White supremacy and paternity. Institutional racism is evident in the rejection of all institutional practices that constrain White supremacy in day-to-day life and in the lack of specifics as to what social and civil rights policies a Trump administration will pursue. Individual racism is already apparent in the violence and hostility of Trump supporters toward people of color. Their cultural views are linked to their institutional objectives to roll back civil rights gains. This real-life illustration of elements in the theory of racism strongly suggests that this theory is worth serious consideration and elaboration.

Acknowledgments

The author acknowledges James Forman, Walter Stafford, Robert Fullilove, and all of the other activists who risked their lives to end Jim Crow and to define racism.

Declaration of Conflicting Interests

The author declared no potential conflicts of interest with respect to the research, authorship, and/or publication of this article.

Funding

The author received no financial support for the research, authorship, and/or publication of this article.

References

Alexander, M. (2011). *The new Jim Crow: Mass incarceration in the age of color-blindness.* New York, NY: The New Press.

Barot, R., & Bird, J. (2001). Racialization: The genealogy and critique of a concept. *Ethnic and Racial Studies, 24,* 601–618.

Belizan, J. M., Cafferata, M. L., Belizan, M., & Althabe, F. (2007). Health inequality in Latin America. *Lancet, 370,* 1599–1600.

Benson, D. S. (2016). *Visions of power in Cuba: Revolution, redemption, and resistance, 1959–1971.* Chapel Hill: The University of North Carolina Press.

Benedict, R. (1945) *Race and Racism.* London, England: Routledge and Sons.

Better, S. J. (2008). *Institutional racism: A primer on theory and strategies for social change.* Lanham, MD: Rowman & Littlefield.

Blanton, H., & Jaccard, J. (2008). Unconscious racism: A concept in pursuit of a measure. *Annual Review of Sociology, 34,* 277–297.

Blaut, J. M. (1992). The theory of cultural racism. *Antipode, 24,* 289–299.

Bobo, L., & Kluegel, J. R. (1993). Opposition to race targeting: Self-interest, stratification ideology or racial attitudes. *American Sociological Review, 58,* 443–463.

Bodenheimer, R. (2015). *Geographies of Cubanidad: Place, race and musical performance in contemporary Cuba.* Jackson: University Press of Mississippi.

Bonilla-Silva, E. (2006). *Racism without racists: Color-blind racism and the persistence of racial inequality in America paperback.* Lanham, MD: Rowman & Littlefield.

Byron, R. A. (2010). Discrimination, complexity, and the public/private sector question. *Work and Occupations, 37,* 435–475.

Carmichael, S., & Hamilton, C. V. (1967). *Black power: The politics of liberation in America.* New York, NY: Random House.

Carmichael, S., & Thelwell, M. (2003). *Ready for revolution: The life and struggles of Stokely Carmichael* (Kwame Ture). New York, NY: Scribner.

Chin, J. (1985). Divergent trends in white racial attitudes towards Blacks. *International Journal of Sociology and Social Policy, 6,* 25–38.

Condran, J. (1979). Changes in White attitudes toward Blacks: 1963–1977. *The Public Opinion Quarterly, 43,* 463–476.

Cummings, S. (1980). White ethnics, racial prejudice and labor market segmentation. *American Journal of Sociology, 85,* 938–950.

Eberhardt, J. L., & Fiske, S. T. (1998). *Racism: The problem and the response.* Thousand Oaks, CA: Sage.

Ellison, M. (1991). David Duke and the race for the governor's mansion. *Race & Class, 33*(2), 71–79.

Feagin, J., & Elias, S. (2013). Rethinking racial formation theory: A systemic racism critique. *Ethnic and Racial Studies, 36,* 931–960.

Forman, J. (1972). *The making of a Black revolutionary.* New York, NY: Macmillan.

Friedman, R. (1975). Institutional racism: How to discriminate without really trying. In T. Petigrew (Ed.), *Racial discrimination in the United States.* New York, NY: Harper & Row.

Grabbs, E. G. (1980). Social class, authoritarianism, and racial contact: Recent trends. *Sociology and Social Research, 64*, 208–220.

Hankins, F. H. (1947). Soper, Edmund Davison. Racism, a World Issue. *The ANNALS of the American Academy of Political and Social Science, 252*(1), 162–163. New York: Abingdon-Cokesbury Press.

Heatherly, C. (Ed.). (1981). *Mandate for leadership: Policy management in a conservative administration.* Washington, DC: The Heritage Foundation.

Hicklin, A. (2007). The effect of race-based admissions in public universities: Debunking the myths about Hopwood and Proposition 209. *Public Administration Review, 67*, 331–340.

Hilliard, R. L., & Keith, M. C. (1999). *Waves of rancor: Tuning in the radical right.* Armonk, NY: M.E. Sharpe.

Howard, G. (2016, August 21). The easiest way to get rid of racism? Just redefine it. *The New York Times Magazine.* Retrieved from http://www.nytimes.com/2016/08/21/magazine/the-easiest-way-to-get-...package&version=highlights&contentPlacement=9&pgtype=sectionfront

Jaynes, G. D., & Williams, R. M. (Eds.). (1989). *A common destiny: Blacks and American society.* Washington, DC: The National Academy Press.

Johnson, O., Jr. (2014). Still separate, still unequal: The relation of segregation in neighborhoods and schools to education inequality. *Journal of Negro Education, 83*, 199–215.

Jones, J. (1972). *Prejudice and racism.* Reading, MA: Addison-Wesley.

Jones, J. (1981). The concept of racism and its changing reality. In B. P. Bowser & R. G. Hunt (Eds.), *Impacts of racism on White Americans* (pp. 27–50). Beverly Hills, CA: Sage.

Kluegel, J. R. (1990). Trends in whites' explanations of the black-white gap in socioeconomic status, 1977–1989. *American Sociological Review, 55*, 512–525.

Kluegel, J. R., & Smith, E. R. (1982). White beliefs about black opportunity. *American Journal of Sociology, 47*, 518–532.

Kluegel, J. R., & Smith, E. R. (1983). Affirmative action attitudes: Effects of self-interest, racial affect, and stratification beliefs on white views. *Social Force, 61*, 797–824.

Kwate, N. O. A., Goodman, M. S., Jackson, J., & Harris, J. (2013). Spatial and racial patterning of real estate broker listings in New York City. *The Review of Black Political Economy, 40*, 401–424.

Lamis, A. P. (1999). *Southern politics in the 1990s.* Baton Rouge: Louisiana State University Press.

Levy, P. B. (1998). *The civil rights movement.* Westport, CT: Greenwood Press.

Llosa, M. V. (2015). *Notes on the death of culture: Essays on spectacle and society.* New York, NY: Farrar, Straus and Giroux.

Massey, D. (2007). *Categorically unequal: The American stratification system.* New York, NY: Russell Sage.

Meares, T. L. (2014). The law and social science of stop and frisk. *Annual Review of Law and Social Science, 10*, 335–352.

Mohammed, S. N. (2011). *Communication and the globalization of culture: Beyond tradition and borders.* Lanham, MD: Lexington Books.

Nkrumah, K. (1965). *Neo-colonialism: The last stage of imperialism.* New York, NY: International Publishers.

Omi, M., & Winant, H. (1994). *Racial formation in the United States: From the 1960s to the 1990s* (2nd ed.). New York, NY: Routledge.

Pettigrew, T. F. (1981). The mental health impact. In B. Bowser & R. Hunt (Eds.), *Impacts of racism on White Americans* (pp. 97–118). Beverly Hills, CA: Sage.

Pettigrew, T. F. (1991). Normative theory in intergroup relations: Explaining both harmony and conflict. *Psychology and Developing Societies, 3*, 3–16.

Ralph, J. R. (1993). *Northern protest: Martin Luther King, Jr., Chicago, and the civil rights movement.* Cambridge, MA: Harvard University Press.

Ranney, J. A. (2006). *In the wake of slavery: Civil war, civil rights, and the reconstruction of southern law.* Westport, CT: Praeger Publishers.

Roland, L. K. (2011). *Cuban color in tourism and La Lucha: An ethnography of racial meanings.* New York, NY: Oxford University Press.

Rose, D. D. (Ed.). (1992). *The emergence of David Duke and the politics of race.* Chapel Hill: The University of North Carolina Press.

Saenger, G. (1965). *The social psychology of prejudice.* New York, NY: Harper & Row.

Schumann, H., Stech, C., & Bobo, L. (1985). *Racial attitudes in America: Trends and interpretations.* Cambridge, MA: Harvard University Press.

Sears, D. O. (1988). Symbolic racism. In P. A. Katz & D. A. Taylor (Eds.), *Eliminating racism: Profiles in controversy* (pp. 53–84). New York, NY: Plenum.

Sears, D. O., & McConahay, J. B. (Eds.). (1973). *The politics of violence: The new urban Blacks and the Watts Riot.* Boston, MA: Houghton Mifflin.

Shah, A. (2008). Are institutional and individual interpersonal racism the same? *The Psychiatric Bulletin, 32*(1), 32.

Smith, A. W. (1981). Racial tolerance as a function of group position. *American Sociological Review, 46,* 558–573.

Sniderman, P., Piazza, T., & Tetlock, P. (1986). Symbolic racism: Problems in motive attribution in political analysis. *Journal of Social Issues, 42*(2), 129–150.

Spence, G. (2006). *Bloodthirsty bitches and pious pimps of power: The rise and risks of the new conservative hate culture.* New York, NY: St. Martin's Press.

Tischauser, L. V. (2012). *Jim Crow laws.* Santa Barbara, CA: Greenwood Publisher.

Vandenberg, H. E. R. (2010). Culture theorizing past and present: Trends and challenges. *Nursing Philosophy, 11,* 238–249.

Weston, R. F. (1972). *Racism in U.S. imperialism: The influence of racial assumptions on U.S. foreign policy, 1893–1946.* Columbia: The University of South Carolina Press.

Williams, R. M. (1975). *The reduction of intergroup tensions: A survey of research on problems of ethnic, racial and religious groups* (3rd ed.). New York, NY: Social Science Research Council.

Wilson, W. J. (1978). *The declining significance of race: Blacks in changing American institutions.* Chicago, IL: The University of Chicago Press.

Woods, L. L. (2012). The federal home loan bank board, redlining, and the national proliferation of racial lending discrimination, 1921–1950. *Journal of Urban History, 38,* 1036–1059.

Zuberi, T., & Bonilla-Silva, E. (Eds.). (2008). *White logic, White methods.* Lanham, MD: Rowman & Littlefield.

Post-Reading Questions

1 What are the three levels of racism described by the author? What is the basic differ-ence between each level?

2 Why does the author claim that the original intent of linking the three level of racism has been lost?

3 What are some examples of covert racism? How would you distinguish between overt racism and covert racism?

4 To what degree can (or should) we hold someone accountable for racist attitudes when he or she may be unconscious of his or her racism?

5 In your estimate, what motivates some people to be racist and others to be anti-racists? How would you explain instances (of behaviors) of biracial individuals who harbor racist attitudes?

How National Media Framed Coverage of Missing Black and White Women

Mia Moody, Bruce Dorries and Harriet Blackwell

According to the Federal Bureau of Investigation, National Crime Information Center, there are 50,930 active missing adult cases in the United States as of January 31, 2007. Although the site does not make distinctions about missing persons by race, sex or demographics, clearly people vanish everyday in the United States, which lessens such stories' news value. However, each day a few stories about missing people slip through the news net and end up at the top lineup of newscasts.

In fact, in the early 2000s, stories about missing women became common fodder for front pages and lead television news items. The coverage of such stories became so popular during the mid-2000s that the media coined the term "Missing White Woman Syndrome," and "missing pretty girl syndrome," to refer to the form of media hype (Johnson, 2005). Conspicuously absent from headline news during the same time were similar articles about missing women of color, especially black women.

This textual analysis draws upon feminist and race paradigms to study black press and mainstream media representations of missing women to assess the ways, and to what effect, these signifiers of exclusion and domination play out in the media. Of interest were the following questions: 1) were stories about missing white women given more prominence than those about black women? 2) were missing women likely to be described from a patriarchal paradigm that values youth and beauty? 3) what frames emerged in the media's coverage of missing women?

Looking at this issue as it relates to race is fruitful as both interacting inequalities construct gender. Media send viewers, readers and listeners hidden messages that suggest a story's importance, and ultimately people's value within society. Early analyses (Ceulemans & Fauconnier, 1979; Gallagher, 1981) found the media to be deeply implicated in the patterns of discrimination operating against women in society-models, which, through their absence, trivialization or condemnation of women in media content amounted to their "symbolic annihilation" (Tuchman, 1978). Moreover, media attention can affect how local authorities handle a case. Victims who receive national attention, inevitably, receive more aid from local and national police and investigative teams.

Literature Review

Gans (1979) suggests that the basis of framing theory presumes the prevalent media will focus attention on newsworthy events and place them within a sphere of meaning, and that media professionals create frames in the context of complex organizations. The framing body of work shows that socioeconomic status, race and education can make a difference in how reporters frame certain issues. This is of significance, according to Gans (1979), because the majority of journalists come from an upper-middle to upper-class background, which he asserts is a distinctly white perspective. As a result, the framing of cultural groups has been negative and stereotypical (Martindale, 1990; Bagdikian, 1969; Entman, 1992; Dates & Barlow, 1993).

For feminist theorists, there is no dispute that media function ideologically, working with other social and cultural institutions to reflect, reinforce and mediate existing power relations and ideas about how gender is and should be lived (Enriques, 2001). Many feminist studies focus on the relationship between media portrayals of women and social reality. Studies give much attention to the gender-role messages in television programs, newspaper and magazine content. These studies found media often represent women as passive, submissive and dependent.

Sexism is compounded by racism for black women. The "ideal of female beauty in this country puts a premium on lightness and softness mythically associated with white women and downplays the rich stylistic manners associated with black women" (West, 2001, p. 130). Hooks (1992) and Moraga and Anzaldúa (1981) assert that black women's experience of various issues cannot be conceived as separable from their experience of racism. Therefore, they bear an altogether different burden from that of white women. For instance, Benedict's (1997) study found coverage to be not only racist, class-oriented and sexist, but inaccurate as well. Most rape stories contained the scenario of white female victims with African American male perpetrators. Similarly, Meyers (2004) used black feminist theory to determine how class, gender and race shape the way African American female victims and their perpetrators are portrayed. Meyers found that violence against African American female victims was seriously minimized and the victims blamed for their perpetrators' behaviors. Findings by Wilson, Gutiérrez & Chao (2003) support findings that coverage of victims reveals a hierarchy of white women above black women.

Findings and Discussion

Researchers found it impossible to include all women relevant to this study; therefore, they studied the reported cases of four missing women: Laci Peterson, 27; Lori Hacking, 27; Tamika Huston, 24; and LaToyia Figueroa, 24. Each of their cases reached beyond local coverage and occurred at different times from 2002 to 2005. Laci Peterson and Lori Hacking were perhaps two of the most discussed and analyzed women during this period. Tamika Huston and LaToyia Figueroa were perhaps the most publicized missing black women. Also of interest, three of the four women were pregnant, and the suspect accused in each of these cases was a husband or lover.

Investigators retrieved news transcripts using Lexis-Nexis for NBC and CBS networks and articles for *The Washington Post* and *USA Today*. Researchers looked at both newscasts and print media because news consumers tend to consult print news for the details, whereas and more people turn to television news than ever. Newscasts did not yield enough transcripts about black women for our sample. We referred to national newspapers in addition to *The Post* and *USA Today* to increase the number of texts. In the end, the sample included 40 texts that appeared during the first month of Peterson, Hacking and Figueroa's reported disappearances. Coverage of Huston did not appear until several months after her disappearance. The texts provided a comparative sample for all four women, as there were a small number of articles and transcripts about missing black victims.

The primary researcher read articles and transcripts multiple times and highlighted code words and themes. Cycling through data, the researcher was able to see similarities and differences in the articles and keep track of thematic elements (Squires, 2007). After compiling the sub-themes, an emergent pattern emerged, which provides the evidence for an argument about the nature of news media coverage of missing women.

Class and Coverage

There was a general template for how the press talked about missing women but it differed based on race. Mainstream press coverage of white women often included interviews of relatives and friends of the victim, a description of her neighborhood and lots of information about the person's personality. On the other hand, black-owned media and mainstream coverage of missing black women usually focused on the disparity in coverage, the person's dismal circumstances and the past of the victim's abusive mate.

Although the media did not overtly cover class in its analysis of missing victims, reporters used indicators such as occupations, homeownership and neighborhood descriptions help viewers and readers determine their social standing. For example, Lori and Mark Hacking were most likely middle-class: She was an assistant securities trader at a brokerage house, while he was a hospital orderly. Scott and Laci Peterson were middle class as ascertained from their occupations: Laci was *a former* substitute teacher and Scott was a fertilizer sales clerk. Many articles described their neighborhood as a nice, middle-class area. Other articles described Laci and Scott as attractive, middle-class people.

Conversely, LaToyia Figueroa and Tamika Huston were most likely lower- to middle-class. Figueroa was the single mother of a 7-year-old daughter and was five months pregnant at the time of her death. Articles often said Figueroa had "a solid work record" at a Center City restaurant. Signifiers of Huston's class were revealed in statements about joblessness and the fact that she was unmarried at the time she went missing from the Washington D.C. area. Because she was unemployed at the time of her death one might assume she was lower-class.

Sizing and Media's Coverage of Missing Women

The essence of framing according to Entman (1991) is sizing, or to what extent any depicted reality is magnified or miniaturized and thus, made more or less significant. Researchers found a combined 738 transcripts and articles about the subjects. Of that number, only 1.2% (n = 9) of them were about black subjects. Transcripts for Huston were found outside of the first month she was reported missing. On the other hand, Figueroa's transcripts were found during the first month of her disappearance, but they all were reported on the same day by CBS, which only had one transcript for Huston.

In contrast, researchers counted a substantial number of transcripts from each news organization for Peterson during the first month of her disappearance. The transcripts found for Hacking were 50% less than those found for Peterson. However, in comparison to coverage of Huston or Figueroa, the amount of transcripts about Hacking proved more than 80% higher. Clearly, there were significantly more transcripts about white women and very few transcripts about the black women.

Patriarchal Framing

Findings indicate that reporters often framed missing women in a patriarchal paradigm that related them to their roles as mothers, daughters and wives and discussed them in terms of youth and beauty. White women, in particular, were framed as sweet, valued loved ones placed on a pedestal by their family and community members. For example, a volunteer coordinator in a Jan. 2, 2003 NBC "Today Show" segment stated: "This community has wrapped their arms around the Peterson family ... Laci impacted this community because she was a substitute teacher so there were children across the Modesto community that have known her as well as people who have worked with her. The vigil the other night was the most emotional one I've ever been to."

Reporters also named or quoted Peterson's mother, husband, father, brother, sister-in-law, stepfather and stepmother throughout all of the 19 transcripts. Reporters encouraged them to talk about Peterson's normative behavior; specifically, NBC reporter Anne Curry on the Dec. 30, 2002 "Today Show" encouraged Laci's mother to talk about her missing daughter. Then she allowed her to describe Peterson with no interruptions. Peterson's mother lovingly described her daughter with four characteristics: happy, outgoing, friendly and greets everyone with a smile. Reporters vividly described the feelings of Peterson's relatives, e.g., "her family is distraught." In other cases, each time the reporter described Peterson, he or she used a different description, referring to a social role fulfilled, such as "the second-grade school teacher." These humanizing descriptions allow the audience to make connections with Peterson—who was a member of someone's family and made a meaningful contribution to society as a teacher.

Findings were similar for coverage of Hacking; however, the media placed a stronger emphasis on understanding her relationship with her husband whom police suspected in her disappearance. Lori Hacking was referred to as daughter, daughter-in-law, missing woman, Salt Lake City resident and jogger. As with Peterson, the details of her family life and her personal hobbies allowed readers to learn information outside of her name and location.

Although her case was similar to Laci Peterson's, reporters did not directly quote any of Figueroa's family members. She was five months pregnant, and the father of her child was the prime suspect in her disappearance. Instead, CBS reporters in many transcripts used the phrase "family members say" to suggest indirectly the source of information as exemplified in an Aug. 20, 2005 story on the "Saturday Early Show." In the same vague manner, journalists referred to Figueroa not by her name, but as "the Philadelphia woman." CBS's description of Figueroa is very detached and fits many female resident of that city.

Furthermore, reporters usually interviewed family members of missing black women in response to media attention garnered due to its lack of coverage. As a result, the interview usually focused on community activism and not the missing person's character or moral standing. For example, on Oct. 9, 2005, "Dateline NBC" journalists interviewed Huston's aunt and father for their efforts to get media attention for their loved one's case. Huston's aunt mentioned briefly Huston's disappearance as out of character. She stated: "She wouldn't just disappear. She knows without question that our whole family would be devastated." However, the reporter focused primarily on how the aunt had worked to gain national attention for the missing woman. There were no questions regarding the neighborhood where Huston resided or about her job or grieving family members.

In some cases, reporters highlighted the time that had passed during the investigations. This finding relates to Peterson, Hacking and Figueroa, all of whom were pregnant. In most cases, headlines about Peterson and Hacking emphasized that not only is a woman missing, but also a child is missing whose life depends on that woman being found. In this way, the reporters emphasized the tragedy of these cases, and the importance of a speedy recovery of the women to save two lives.

Reporters mentioned Peterson's pregnancy in all of the transcripts, and half of their headlines. The descriptions ranged from referring to her as "the pregnant woman" to including her gestation level, (eight months), due date (February 10), gender and desired name for her unborn child—Conner—as well as the relation of the fetus to Peterson. Teasers for stories about Peterson included: "Search for missing pregnant woman continues in Modesto, California," and "Family of a missing California pregnant woman continues to ask for help in locating her." Still prominent but less detailed, 15 of 19 transcripts about Hacking refer to her pregnancy, and her development (five weeks pregnant), which was unknown to most family members. Articles that included the information tended to mention the pregnancy prominently to add weight to the fact that her husband was a suspect in her murder case. For example, a July 23, 2004 "CBS Morning News" story included this blurb: "As we reported, there are bizarre, new developments in the case of a missing pregnant woman in Utah. Lori Hacking's husband is reportedly in a psychiatric ward and has been caught in a big lie."

Conversely, the media downplayed Figueroa's pregnancy. Journalists chose to identify Figueroa by her city and state. Headlines about her identified her as "the missing Philadelphia woman" or "Body of missing Philadelphia woman LaToyia Figueroa found in Chester City, Pennsylvania; suspect in custody."

Beauty and Youth in Coverage

In addition to being white, one's looks played a major role in whether she received media attention. Missing women who received a large quantity of media attention were usually young and attractive. Photos of the victims with their mates at social outings and smiling gaily for the camera were staples on nightly newscasts during the investigation into their cases. Laci Peterson is perhaps the best example of this trend. During her disappearance, particularly the early phases, newscasts frequently flashed pictures of the 27-year-old wearing her holiday best. Her glossy hair, big dimples and huge smile were often the lead topic in newscasts about the missing mother-to-be. For example, on a December 30, 2002 "CBS Early Show" edition, Peterson's sister-in-Law described her as always having a great smile, "you know, and those dimples, and—and she loved life, and loved the time of her life right now." Because of her attractiveness, journalists gave the Peterson tragedy the type of coverage usually reserved for more newsworthy stories such as catastrophic weather-related events and war.

Similarly, journalists placed value on all the victims' youthfulness. Most transcripts for white women, 60.5% (n = 23), mentioned their age, both 27 years old [...]. However, 39.5% (n = 15) did not, using instead the phrase 'young woman' as a substitute. The vast majority of the transcripts about black women, 88.9% (n = 8) drew attention to their age; both were 24 years old. Other examples include the description of Lori Hacking as "the pretty young Utah housewife." In another example, a source in the July 21, 2004 "CBS Early Show" said Hacking went for an early morning jog on Monday at a Salt Lake City park and had not been seen since. The transcript continues, "Now the desperate search is on for the young woman."

Media's Criticism of its Coverage

The discussion of a lack of articles about missing black women was a common thread in the sample, which may help explain why the media silence frame was the most prominent frame used for articles about missing black women. In articles using this frame, the media became part of the news. This type of article usually focused on one victim in the lead to illustrate the larger trend of missing women.

The disappearance of Tamika Huston was the first case that spawned controversy about media coverage of missing people and how cases get national attention. The "missing pretty girl syndrome," as coined by conservative pundit Michelle Malkin, drew attention to the neglect of missing non-white people. Journalist Gwen Ifill later described the phenomenon as the "Missing White Woman Syndrome."

Huston's aunt, Rebkah Howard, speculated that the choice to exclude missing black women is a conscious decision on the part of journalists who prefer to cover young, white, attractive, and middle- to upper-class women. Similarly, an August 15, 2005 *USA Today* article by Mark Memmott (2005) discusses the lack of interest in the Huston case briefly, and then focuses on the disappearance of Alabama high school student Natalee Holloway, 18, in Aruba. It included the question of whether networks push such stories about missing white women. In another example, *USA Today* began one story with a discussion of the "debate over whether national news organizations lack interest in missing people if they aren't young, pretty, white women." Similarly, NBC's hook or lead into a story stated its reporter was "taking a close look at TV's obsession with these missing women [Peterson, Hacking, and Seiler] when others [Huston] go unnoticed."

Obviously, there are many stories that go untold by both mainstream media outlets. Worth noting is the presence of newsworthiness in issues covered by the media. Perhaps it is not that these black women are not pretty or young enough, but that there are just too many that go missing to highlight them all. The media cannot cover every case equally. However, media outlets must devise fair ways to cover missing women.

Limitations and Conclusions

The study has implications for mass media scholars who have long argued that it is important to understand the ways in which the journalistic framing of issues occurs. However, as with any study, there were some limitations, particularly with the sample and period of study. A future study could include other racial or minority groups, such as Latina/Hispanic Americans and Asian Americans. However, based on our own news media exposure, researchers consider that an unlikely category for examination—for example, none of us have seen a case of a missing Asian American woman in national news media.

Similarly, it might be insightful to compare local news coverage of missing women to that of national news coverage. Evaluating the different practices and techniques these two distinct levels of news media use to generate interest in the stories of missing women could show more or less difference. Because local news stations tend to be community-oriented, their efforts to get public attention for missing black women might be more like that of national media coverage of white women.

Finally, a study that concentrates on the news coverage of missing men is overdue-although such research may exist, we found none in the literature review. More men than women go missing each year, but apparently, their disappearance is not as newsworthy, or examined in academic research about media coverage. Since society constructs gender-specific behavior for women and men (who are seen as strong, self-sufficient), then social norms and taboos might prohibit or at least discourage most news organizations from covering stories of missing men.

A sexist bias for covering stories of missing women may be based in our culture's existing power structures. Sexual violence is often an element of the crimes committed against abducted women, and an undercurrent in missing women stories. Media coverage about missing women may arouse a prurient interest in media audiences, and thus encourage modern-day yellow journalism in the race for higher ratings and readership.

Conclusion

The stories of the women in this study are strikingly similar and very emotional; the only significant difference among them is race. Our findings suggest a clear bias that favors young, attractive white women, almost to the exclusion of black women. Eugene Robinson, syndicated columnist and associate editor at *The Washington Post,* stated, "Something is at work here, at a conscious or at least subconscious level that leads them to choose victims of a certain type." The conscious level at which the decision to air or print specific stories of missing women fitting a certain category may never be known. At best, black women have unconsciously been overlooked in the media's coverage of missing women. At worst, the difference in coverage suggests a subtle form of racism.

Coverage of missing white women is more prominent, containing vivid details of ongoing investigations and personal connections; the same tactics are lacking in the coverage of missing black women. Additionally, findings indicate that media tended to depict white women within a patriarchal paradigm, emphasizing their physical appearance and feminine characteristics rather than providing details of ongoing investigations and personal connections.

Media's reliance on a patriarchal representation of the world, which values women based on looks and body size, forces the women's movement a step backward. Furthermore, the trend shows laziness on the part of journalists who frequently choose to play up stories about attractive, white women because such cases fit a convenient narrative pattern that storytellers have used for decades, a pattern that incorporates remnants of an outmoded view of women and black people and their roles in society. Furthermore, by vaguely covering the stories of missing black women, news outlets send a message of their insignificance to the larger society. Such tactics suggest white women are privileged members of society, deserving of more detailed, humanizing coverage and investigative effort from law enforcement officials.

Findings from this study have important implications for mass media scholars who have long argued that it is important to understand the ways in which the journalistic framing of issues occurs. To its credit, the media criticized itself for this type of coverage. However, the trend continues even today, to the detriment of society. Unfortunately, such framing influences public understanding and, consequently, policy formation. Because their disappearances seldom receive acknowledgment or get glitzy attention or prominence through coverage, black women—members of the non-dominant groups—are deemed less valuable.

Perhaps this study's evaluation of national television and print news coverage of missing black women might encourage policy changes and raise community awareness and sensitivity to the issue. Black Americans and people of minority groups, as well as whites, will benefit from more representative, fair coverage of these tragic social phenomena that cut across race and other dividing lines.

In a country with a Constitution that emphasizes equality and fairness for all citizens; black women and unattractive women go missing with little or no response from the Fourth Estate. Media might prove to be instrumental to the women's rescue. Unfortunately, if you are not white enough, pretty enough or young enough, then your family might not receive as much help from the media in your rescue efforts.

References

Bagdikian, B. H. (1969). *The press and its crisis of identity: Mass media in a free society.* Lawrence, KS: University of Kansas Press.

Benedict, H. (1997). Virgin or Vamp: How the press covers sex crimes. In L. Flanders (Ed.). *Real Majority, Media Minority* (pp. 115–118). Maine: Common Courage Press.

Ceulemans, M. & Fauconnier, G. (1979). *Mass Media: The image, role and social conditions of women.* Paris: UNESCO.

Chief Roy Wasden and volunteer coordinator Kim Petersen discuss the search and community support for missing pregnant woman Laci Peterson of Modesto, California. (Jan. 2, 2003). [Television broadcast transcript] NBC *Today Show.* Retrieved March 12, 2006 from Lexis-Nexis.

Dates, J. L. & Barlow, W. (1993). *Split Image: African-Americans in the Mass Media* (2nd ed.). Washington, DC: Howard University Press.

Enriques, E. (2001). An overview of various feminist strategies for reconstructing knowledge, 1998–2001: Isis International-Manila.

Entman, R. M. (1991). Framing U.S. coverage of international news: contrasts in narratives of the KAL and Iran air incidents. *Journal of Communication, 41*(4), 6–27.

Entman, R. M. (1992). African-Americans in the news: Television, modern racism and cultural change. *Journalism Quarterly, 69*(2), 341–361.

Gallagher, M. (1981). *Unequal opportunities: The case of women and the media.* Paris: UNESCO Press.

Gans, H. J. (1979). *Deciding What's News.* New York: Vintage Books. Hooks, B. (1992). *Black looks: race and representation.* Boston, MA: South End Press.

Johnson, A. (2005, June). A Missing Answer. *News-Record.com.* Retrieved March 6, 2007, http://bloe.newsre-cord.com/staff/outloud/archives/2005/06/a missing answe.html

Malkin, M. (2005, June 11). Missing pretty girl syndrome, blog posted to http://niichellemalkin.com/archives/002712.htm

Mankiewicz, J. (2005). *NBC Dateline: What Happened to Tamika?; Mystery of missing young woman solved.* [Television broadcast transcript]. NBC.

Martindale, C. (1990). Changes in newspaper images of African-Americans. *Newspaper Research Journal, 11*(1), 46–48.

Memmott, M. (2005, June 15). Spotlight skips cases of missing minorities. *USA Today,* p. 6A.

Memmot, M. (2005, August 22). Missing pregnant woman found dead. *USA Today,* p. 3A.

Missing Utah jogger's husband admitted to psychiatric ward amid revelations he lied about his college record. (July 22, 2004) *CBS Morning News.* [Television broadcast transcript] Retrieved March 13, 2005 from Lexis-Nexis.

Meyers, M. (2004). African American women and violence: Gender, race, and class in the news. *Critical Studies in Media Communication, 21,* 95–118.

Moraga, C. & Anzaldua, G. (1981). *This Bridge Called My Back: Writings by Radical Women of Color.* Watertown: Persephone.

NBC News, (2005, October 9). [Television broadcast transcript].

Philadelphia Police find body of missing pregnant women. (Aug. 20, 2005). *CBS Saturday Early Show.* [Television broadcast transcript] Retrieved March 12, 2006 from Lexis-Nexis.

Pregnant Laci Peterson Disappears Christmas Eve. Laci's Family And Police Chief Discuss Her Personality And Ongoing Search. (Dec. 30, 2002). *NBC Today Show.* [Television broadcast transcript] Retrieved March 12, 2006 from Lexis-Nexis.

Robinson, E. (2005, June 10). (White) women we love. *The Washington Post,* p. A23.

Search for Missing Philadelphia Woman May Be Over. (August 20, 2005). *The Saturday Early Show.* [Television broadcast transcript] Retrieved March 12, 2006 from Lexis-Nexis.

Still no sign of Salt Lake City jogger amid questions swirling around her husband. (July 23, 2004). *CBS Morning News.* [Television broadcast transcript] Retrieved March 12, 2006 from Lexis-Nexis.

Squires, C. (2007). *Dispatches from the color line: The press and multiracial America.* New York: State University of New York Press. Tuchman, G. (1978). *Making news: a study in the construction of reality.* New York: The Free Press.

Wasden, R., Modesto Co. Police Chief (2002, December 31). *CNN Live Today: Without a trace.* [Television broadcast transcript]. CNN.

West, C. (2001). *Race Matters.* Boston: Beacon Press. Originally published in 1993; reissued in 2001 in hardcover with new introduction.

What Happened to Tamika. Mystery of missing young woman solved. (Oct. 9, 2005) *Dateline NBC.* [Television broadcast transcript] Retrieved March 12, 2006 from Lexis-Nexis.

Post-Reading Questions

1   What evidence is there to suggests than missing White women are given prominence and more media coverage than missing Black and Latino women? In what ways is the choice to include coverage of missing women of color a conscious decision or an unconscious decision?

2   What are some of the "frames" that have emerged in the media's coverage of missing women? Have these frames changed over time—or have they remained somewhat constant?

3   What are some of the research limitations associated with the study of missing persons?

4   When reporting on missing women, why does the media appear to rely on patriarchal representations of the world?

5   Why does the media appear somewhat reluctant to give equal coverage to missing women who are viewed as physically unattractive or of a perceived lower social class?

Selling Savage Portrayals

Young Black and Latino Males in the Carceral State

Natalie Byfield

Fanning the Flames

As the Central Park jogger story unfolded, policy makers, academics, and other researchers from across the city and the nation weighed in on the significance of the attack and offered explanations and potential remedies for violence in the streets. Their solutions often leaned in the direction of more punitive law enforcement methods, as opposed to increasing social programs, banning weapons, or instituting other preventative measures. Nearly a month after the jogger was raped, on May 15, 1989, President George H. W. Bush announced a $1.2 billion anticrime spending package. In his statement announcing the plan, the president mentioned the rape of the jogger in Central Park, along with the murder of Michael Griffith in Howard Beach.[1] His plan called for the bulk of the allocation, $1 billion, to be spent on building new federal prisons (Weinraub 1989).

The focus on punitive as opposed to preventative measures could hardly have been a shock for New Yorkers. Their state was one of the first to rely on the adult criminal justice system to address the problem of juvenile crime. In 1978, New York state strengthened its juvenile offender law to incorporate violent juveniles into the adult court system. And across the nation a few states followed suit. But in the wake of the attack on the jogger, policy makers renewed their efforts to incorporate juveniles into the adult criminal justice system. Included in the public policy response to the rape was a sea change in the ways in which the majority of U.S. states addressed juveniles who committed violent crimes. Forty-four states across the nation began to embrace juveniles within the jurisdiction of the adult criminal courts. The new juvenile justice laws had their greatest impact on the lives of black and Latino youths. In the wake of the jogger incident the discourse from elected leadership, officials in the criminal justice system, and the media stoked fears around the issue of crime and the associations among race, crime, and youth. As a result of the ensuing moral panic, communities across the nation reshaped themselves.

Moral Panic, Wilding, and the War on Drugs

With the jogger case, the media introduced "wilding" into the public discourse as a new, depraved phenomenon in the ever-growing and increasingly heinous inventory of violent acts committed by young people. The New York City media appeared to be creating an association between acts of wilding and black and Latino youths. Moving forward after the rape of the Central Park jogger, the term "wilding" was reserved particularly for references to crimes committed by young blacks and Latinos (Welch, Price, and Yankey 2002, 2004).

The media construction of the wilding phenomenon as a part of the jogger incident allowed the case to have a greater significance for society than the traditional earlier associations of race and crime (Welch, Price, and Yankey 2002, 2004). "The term wilding made a greater impact on the culture by becoming another synonym for youth violence, contributing to fear of crime and moral panic" (Welch, Price, and Yankey 2002: 7). In this particular case, these researchers argue, the wilding incident caused a moral panic. But [...] juvenile crime and violence had been viewed in some sectors of the mainstream through a less hysterical lens up until the 1970s (Chang 2005). The circumstances surrounding the rape of the Central Park jogger were positioned far differently. While Welch and colleagues (2002) contend that the jogger incident facilitated a moral panic, I believe that the panic was already under way in U.S. society. While largely ignoring illegal drug use in white and affluent communities, law enforcement centered its attention instead on illegal drug use and the associated violence in minority urban communities; black and Latino youths became the focus of the panic. [...] The occurrence of the attack on the jogger during this period of heightened societal antagonism against young black and Latino males may have contributed to the level of sensationalism in the coverage of the case and the ease with which prosecutors drew the delusional conclusions they did. The jogger case is just another example of how a phenomenon exaggerated during a moral panic not only distorts the immediate reality but has the potential to transform future society in ways that suit the interests of the ruling groups that instigated the panic.

The notion of a moral panic is based on the work of Stanley Cohen (2002), who argues that individuals, groups, or events can sometimes be defined as a momentous threat to society and singled out for action. Through a commingling of interests, the media, clergy, elected officials, and criminal justice officials exaggerate the threat and use their resources to come up with self-serving solutions. Cohen's concept of moral panic (as expressed in his *Folk Devils and Moral Panics,* first published in 1972) was the basis of work by Stuart Hall et al. (1978) that examined the so-called problem of muggings in England in the 1970s. Hall et al. (1978) found that reports in the British press about the crisis related to this "new" phenomenon called "muggings" were really just exaggerated claims "factualized" in the media with the help of elected officials and the criminal justice system. Hall et al. (1978) concluded that these groups together set off the moral panic around the muggings. The moral panic represented a crisis in hegemony within the British state. They found that this crisis was, in part, created by changing attitudes among young immigrants, primarily black Caribbeans, who unlike their parents were not political accommodationists and were growing increasingly disenfranchised as an economic recession took hold and they became the targets of racist policies (Hall et al. 1978: 348–355).

In the United States in the 1980s, the moral panic around illegal drug use and the concomitant violence that goes along with the drug trade had already begun to single out young black and Latino males among the group targeted for extraordinary punishment by the state. This moral panic had the earmarks of a contemporary racial project for its potential to reorganize the society's relationship to blacks and Latinos. The type of marginalization experienced by young black and Latino males is tantamount to permanently kicking them out of or keeping them out of the "system," that is, denying them any type of access to mainstream life. Researchers have found a relationship among the nation's transition to a service economy from a manufacturing economy, high rates of unemployment for members of racially marginalized urban groups, and participation in the drug trade by members of these groups (Alexander 2010: 50; Bourgois 1995). While the economy was undergoing this structural transformation, federal, state, and local governments were also changing their criminal justice policies and policing practices to fight crime, specifically launching the so-called War on Drugs. Once they have been incarcerated, these young men have slim chance of finding regular gainful employment upon release.

Michelle Alexander (2010) argues that the War on Drugs was born out of a political response forged by conservative ruling elites threatened by African American demands for equality. This response began in the 1960s civil rights era as a backlash against the seeming social, economic, and political gains being made by African Americans (Alexander 2010). Crime became the rallying cry of right-wing and conservative politicians on their long march back from Barry Goldwater's 1964 Republican Party, as they sought to regain power and control over the social and political agendas of the United States (Pager 2007). The conjoining of the civil rights, black power, and middle-class (largely white) antiwar movements in the mid- to late 1960s so concerned those in power, primarily the political conservatives, that federal and state systems responded with a moral crusade implemented through stricter anticrime measures (Murch 2010; see also Pager 2007).[2] The Nixon administration, which came to power in 1969, gave birth to the Omnibus Crime Control Act in the early 1970s and initiated the War on Crime. Anticrime measures were so much a feature of the identity of the Republican Party that members of even the liberal wing of the party joined the anticrime crusade (Pager 2010). Governor Nelson Rockefeller of New York instituted the Rockefeller drug laws in the early 1970s, which imposed mandatory sentencing for even low-level drug dealers and drug addicts at the street level. These draconian measures disproportionately punished blacks and Latinos.

The conservative movement of the 1960s and 1970s blossomed into the Reagan adminis-tration, whose drug war policies instituted in the early 1980s became the most important piece of a "moral crusade" against the upheavals of the 1960s. The law-and-order, anticrime agenda at the federal level was supposed to return moral order to the nation (Alexander 2010; Pager 2007). This new conservative political movement interpreted the social and political agenda associated with liberal programs like the War on Poverty as "permissive" and sought to frame society's conflicts over the appropriate socioeconomic and political path forward as a "problem of moral order" (Pager 2007: 17). The War on Crime, which began in the Nixon administration, would continue through subsequent administrations, each with its own focus and each incorpo-rating more punitive means to address what was defined as the nation's crime problem. Reagan brought the crime-fighting focus to drugs, and in the mid-1980s, with the introduction of crack cocaine into the cornucopia of illegal drugs already used in the United States, the nation expe-rienced dramatic changes in patterns of incarceration. Crack cocaine's marketability—given its relatively low cost—to poor urban kids, and the participation of the unemployed urban poor in the sale of crack through low-level street hustling, allowed for an association among drug use, drug-related crimes, and race. This association was seen as particularly strong in a relatively insulated arena of illegal drug activities in the United States—the segregated, isolated black and Latino "margins" in urban areas. But, due to the ongoing moral panic over crime and drug abuse, an association among youth, drug crimes, and race became defined as a societywide problem, with black and Latino youths demonized as the new folk devils (Reinarman and Levine 2006). This allowed the mainstream media to more fully participate in a racial project that began with the political right's attempt to reimpose the moral order.

Symbols in Defense of the New Political Economy

After the introduction of crack cocaine into the illegal drug markets of the United States, the media became an important site for the government's advance campaigns in the War on Drugs (Alexander 2010: 50–51; Reinarman and Levine 2006). Alexander noted:

> The Reagan administration leaped at the opportunity to publicize crack cocaine in inner-city communities in order to build support for its new war.
>
> In October 1985, the DEA sent Robert Stutman[3] to serve as director of its New York City office and charged him with the responsibility of shoring up public support for the administration's new war. Stutman developed a strategy for improving relations with the news media and sought to draw journalists' attention to the spread of crack cocaine. (2010: 51)

The administration of George H. W. Bush launched the first campaign in its War on Drugs in the press. President Bush appointed William Bennett as his "drug czar," the media title for the head of the newly formed Office of National Drug Control Policy. Bennett had held a cabinet post from 1985 to 1988 as President Ronald Reagan's secretary of education, and he developed Bush's contribution to the drug war in a plan called "The National Drug Control Strategy." The plan, which would increase federal antidrug spending, cited crack as the cause of "the intensifying drug-related chaos" in U.S. society (Bennett 1989: 3). In selling this plan to the public, the Bush administration deliberately misrepresented the drug problem in the Washington, D.C., area. The first salvo came in a speech from the Oval Office:

> On September 5, 1989, President Bush, speaking from the presidential desk in the Oval Office, announced his plan for achieving "victory over drugs" in his first major prime-time address to the nation, broadcast on all three national television networks … . During the address, Bush held up to the cameras a clear plastic bag of crack labeled "EVIDENCE." (Reinarman and Levine (2006: 48)

Bush announced that the evidence had come from Lafayette Park, across the street from the White House, in an attempt to illustrate how overrun the whole society had become by drugs (Bush 1989). However, the drug bust had been set up by Bush officials. The press would later expose the lengths the Bush administration officials had gone through to construct the scenario. Citing the September 22, 1989, *Washington Post* story written by Michael Isikoff, Reinarman and Levine wrote:

> White House Communications Director David Demar[e]st asked Cabinet Affairs Secretary David Bates to instruct the Justice Department "to find some crack that fit the description in the speech." Bates called Richard Weatherbee, special assistant to Attorney General Dick Thornburgh, who then called James Mil[l]ford, executive assistant to the DEA chief. Finally, Mil[l]ford phoned William McMull[a]n, special agent in charge of the DEA's Washington office, and told him to arrange an undercover crack buy near the White House because "evidently, the President wants to show it could be bought anywhere" (Isikoff, 1989).
>
> Despite their best efforts, the top federal drug agents were not able to find anyone selling crack (or any other drug) in Lafayette Park, or anywhere else in the vicinity of the White House. Therefore, in order to carry out their assignment, DEA agents had to entice someone to come to the park to make the sale. Apparently, the only person the DEA could convince was Keith Jackson, an eighteen-year-old African-American high school senior …. (Isikoff, 1989). (Reinarman and Levine 2006: 49)

Revelations about these obvious attempts at public deception did not deter the Bush administration from its course in the drug war. Bennett planned to solve the nation's drug problems by pumping disproportionately larger amount of funds into law enforcement as opposed to treatment (Berke 1989). According to a 2007 report analyzing twenty-five years of the War on Drugs produced by the Sentencing Project, a nonprofit advocacy group focused on criminal justice policy issues, "Drug arrests have more than tripled in the last 25 years, totaling a record 1.8 million arrests in 2005" (Mauer and King 2007: 2). Law enforcement methods targeted street level dealers and the users of crack cocaine rather than users of powder cocaine (Alexander 2010; Reinarman and Levine 2006). "Drug offenders in prisons and jails have increased 1100% since 1980. Nearly a half-million (493,800) persons are in state or federal prison or local jail for a drug offense, compared to an estimated 41,100 in 1980" (Mauer and King 2007: 2).

This strategy incarcerated disproportionately large numbers of blacks and Latinos, who filled the ranks of street level dealers and who were predominantly users of crack cocaine, as compared to whites, who typically abused power cocaine (Reinarman and Levine 2006). While African Americans made up 14 percent of regular drug users, non-Hispanic whites 69.2 percent, and Hispanics 12.4 percent, "African Americans are 37% of those arrested for drug offenses and 56% of persons in state prison for drug offenses," according to the Sentencing Project report (Mauer and King 2007: 19–20). Media coverage of these law enforcement practices often ignored the racial disparities in the treatment of black and white offenders within the criminal justice system, reinforcing in the public discourse the association between black race and crime, particularly violent crime, and further advancing this association as some type of race-based biological imperative for crime and violence (Reinarman and Levine 2006).[4]

The news media were an important site for reconstructing the definition of black and Latino male youth as the War on Drugs got under way. The rape of the Central Park jogger in the midst of all this only amplified the existing state of moral panic. As it was represented in the media, the case heightened in the public's mind the type of threat that young black and Latino males represented in society. In my content analysis of the Central Park jogger press reports, I examined the features of an individual's social location that played a major role in the coverage—features of race, class, victimhood, gender, and age.[5] Here I highlight how the press reports of the jogger incident defined the suspects and the jogger in relation to each other.

While indicators for race were dominant in the press reports, indicators for class were the features of individual identities most often used to mark membership within categorical groupings. This made class the concept that appeared most frequently to readers.[6] Ninety-eight percent of the articles had at least one indicator for class [...]. In my study, three class indicators represented identity: runner, jogger, and avid runner. Nine class indicators represented institutions: jogger's universities, jogger's family and friends' universities, jogger's family and friends' jobs, jogger's non-Salomon job, Salomon Brothers, investment banker, schools suspects attended, suspects' family and friends' schools, and suspects' family and friends' jobs. Three class indicators represented social structure: jogger middle class, suspects' moderate income, and suspects' middle-class lifestyles. [...]

From a sociological point of view, most of the indicators of class used in the jogger coverage were based on institutions. Thus, the meaning that the concept of class took on in the coverage was largely as an important societal institution. Given this link in the press reports, it is possible that the coverage left audiences with the impression that the attack on the jogger represented an attack on important institutions. The jogger worked for the now-defunct investment bank Salomon Brothers, one of the powerhouses of the Wall Street community at the time [...]. This new economic system had shrugged off the manufacturing jobs that had at one time sustained the people in the margins. In their content analysis of the jogger coverage, which was organized differently from mine, Welch, Price, and Yankey came to a similar conclusion: "The rape of the 'young Manhattan investment banker' seems to represent a symbolic attack on the political economy by the so-called dangerous class" (2002: 21).

In the context of the press reports on the jogger's rape, the concept of gender was largely based on issues of identity. Seven of the ten indicators for gender were words related to gender identity: female, woman, pretty, attractive, bubbly, she/her, and breast. Three of the indicators for gender were based on violent social acts that subordinate: rape, sodomy, and gang-rape. The two most frequently used indicators for gender were "rape," which appeared in 84 percent of the articles, and "woman," which was included in 53 percent of the articles. [...] Like race, gender is an aspect of identity. And, as in the case of racial identity, gender identity is constructed, in part, through interactions in the social world. As a subordinating act, rape gives gender its meaning. In the context of the jogger coverage, the suspects' race is privileged over gender oppression/subordination as a feature of the coverage. In the analysis, the "black and Latino" race of the suspects cannot be separated from the act of rape.[7] Thus, the term "rape" also becomes associated with race, either the jogger's or the suspects'.

However, the concept of gender did not appear to dominate the coverage in a story purportedly about a rape incident. The jogger was a raped woman and as such her identity was marked by this vulnerability, which the media treated as something that warranted protection. Media organizations, in general, including those incorporated in my study, withheld publication of the jogger's name to protect her privacy. This is common practice when reporting cases of rape. However, the *Amsterdam News*, a Harlem-based black-owned and -run newspaper, published the jogger's name, to much criticism from the mainstream press. Journalist Timothy Sullivan (1992) noted in his book about the case that the *Amsterdam News* named the jogger because mainstream papers had identified the black and Latino underage suspects by name and address, a deviation from common practice concerning young people accused of committing crimes.

The significant point here is that the media appeared to use some type of hierarchy to determine who in the jogger case warranted protection. While it initially appeared that the issue of protection revolved around the identity category "raped woman," there may have been other factors operating. The person who was raped did not become known to the public as a "raped woman"; she became known as the "jogger." Additionally, other women who were raped around that time were not brought significantly into the coverage of the Central Park incident. In the context of my study, the term "jogger" is one of the indicators of class. In the coverage, it was the most frequently used indicator of class, appearing in 95 percent of all the articles in the sample and in 99 percent of all the stories in Time Periods 3 and 4 (the post-trial coverage). [...]

Kristin Bumiller (2008) argues that the jogger became an iconic symbol within the movement against sexual violence, but she was a different type of symbol for the mainstream press. My content analysis suggests that, within the media, the jogger was not an iconic representation of crimes against women, because the rape culture in U.S. society was not an element of the coverage. Although the media had the opportunity to associate the attack with the agenda of the women's movement, they chose to use the jogger to deliver a different message.

The jogger was the iconic representation of an attack against an important societal and economic institution. Male-dominated corporate America, the physical representation of capitalism, was being symbolically projected in the mainstream media as vulnerable to disruption, and low-income, young black males were presented as the biggest threat to the behemoth system undergirding corporate America. While class and gender references constituted the most frequently used language in the jogger coverage, in the era of color blindness class and gender as concepts were used to mask a racist attack against young black males. Black male sexuality has historically been a symbol of danger in U.S. society, and it has typically been presented as a danger specifically to white women. Near the end of the twentieth century, as the mainstream grew more inclusive, however, those managing the mainstream boundaries appeared to be ensuring that black masculinity would be limited in mainstream spaces.

"Science" Reshapes the Society

This would not be the first time black males were represented as a threat to society. There is a long history in U.S. culture, from the days of early America, of constructing associations between the black or nonwhite "race" and savagery (Fredrickson 1971a) and doing so with the help of "science" (Banton 2009; Jordan 1968). This new moral crusade also received its imprimatur from academia.[8] Theories about a black subculture of violence had developed from the late 1960s, when the moral crusade began (Wolfgang 1983; Wolfgang and Ferracuti 1967), and this work was used by others to develop newer theories about the propensity for violence among low-income urban black males.

The message in the media coverage of the jogger case, coming amidst the trend of rising youth violence, seemed to take hold of the imaginations of important members of the academic and governmental elites. Some in academic circles returned to "scientific analysis" to further develop the 1960s conceptualizations of black and Latino youths as innately violent. In the late 1980s, the research of political scientist John J. Dilulio Jr. (1989: 35) blamed the dismal life conditions of poor people of color in urban areas on "the large numbers of chronic and predatory street criminals." By 1995, he had constructed his notion of the "super-predator," a category of juvenile criminals who supposedly would be more deadly than anything witnessed before in the United States (Dilulio 1995).[9] Dilulio (1995) based his conclusions on (1) old birth-cohort studies of 10,000 Philadelphia boys born in 1945 (Wolfgang 1983)[10] and (2) research by contemporary criminologists that extrapolated from the birth-cohort studies to predict the number of juvenile offenders in the future (J. Q. Wilson 1995). Dilulio stated that of the boys between ten and eighteen years old in the birth-cohort studies, "more than one-third had at least one recorded arrest by the time they were 18" (1995: 31). He also noted that "two-thirds of all the violent crimes committed by the cohort" were committed by about 6 percent of the boys (Dilulio 1995: 31). The findings of the birth-cohort study, along with projections of an unchanging rate of delinquency led Dilulio to concur with predictions by James Q. Wilson and other criminologists that, given the birth rates of the time, an "additional 500,000 boys who will be 14 to 17 years old in the year 2000 will mean at least 30,000 more murderers, rapists and muggers on the streets than we have today" (Dilulio 1995: 31).

Dilulio (1995) predicted that this newly expanded group of "super-predators" would be much more dangerous than earlier groups because they were being raised in a state of moral poverty, which he defined as follows:

> [It] is the poverty of being without loving, capable, responsible adults who teach you right from wrong. It is the poverty of being without parents and other authorities who habituate you to feel joy at others' joy, pain at others' pain, happiness when you do right, remorse when you do wrong. It is the poverty of growing up in the virtual absence of people who teach morality by their own everyday example and who insist that you follow suit.
>
> In the extreme, moral poverty is the poverty of growing up surrounded by deviant, delinquent, and criminal adults in abusive, violence-ridden, fatherless, Godless and jobless settings. In sum, whatever their material circumstances, kids of whatever race, creed or color are most likely to become criminally depraved when they are morally deprived ... .
>
> The abject moral poverty that creates superpredators begins very early in life in homes where unconditional love is nowhere but unmerciful abuse is common. (Dilulio 1995: 31)

The message here was clear: The rising rate of youth violence was unavoidable and our society had better be prepared for it. The youth who were primarily targeted in Dilulio's (1995) declaration were black and Latino young males living in urban areas.

At the nexus of research and public policy, DiIulio's work was quite influential. He wrote, along with William Bennett and John P. Walters, *Body Count: Moral Poverty ... And How to Win America's War against Crime and Drugs,* about the centrality of drug abuse to crime (Bennett, DiIulio, and Walters 1996). Given his access to high-level policy makers (including testimony before Congress) and the national media attention his ideas received in *Time* and *Newsweek* (Annin 1996; Zoglin, Allis, and Kamlani 1996), it is no surprise that DiIulio's work also had a dramatic effect on policies affecting juveniles (Keenan 2005). This work shaped policy by way of contributing to state and federal authorities' reliance on incarceration as a means of addressing crime (Pager 2007). Years later, DiIulio would recant his theory of the rise of the "super-predator" (Becker 2001), but that came after it had already buttressed the transformation of juvenile justice laws, supporting the use of more extreme law enforcement methods—including imprisonment in adult facilities—for young offenders (Hancock 2003; Keenan 2005). In 2012, DiIulio went so far as to join in a friend of the court brief filed with the U.S. Supreme Court in two cases involving harsh sentencing of juveniles.[11] The brief argued, in part, that the "super-predator" theory had no validity.

Although DiIulio had been renouncing his own theory publicly since 2001 (Becker 2001), as recently as 2005, his colleague William Bennett continued to promulgate biological correlations between race and crime. While in conversation with a caller to his syndicated radio talk show, Bennett offered a "hypothetical proposition" for reducing crime—"Abort every black baby" in the country—then immediately countered that this solution to crime was "morally reprehensible" (CNN 2005). Underlying Bennett's comment, however, is the assertion that there is likely a bio-logical association between race and crime.

Society's response to the growing drug problem in the United States was to construct asso-ciations between race and crime. These associations have become much more salient because research that draws connections among race, crime, and youth has been given a great deal of attention in the media. Media language has used such connections to essentially form a symbolic framework that allows for the reification of associations among race, crime, and youth.

Reifying Racial Meaning in the Criminal Justice System

The moral panic in which the Central Park jogger's rape was enveloped had already embraced increased rates of incarceration as a solution to the problems of crime in general and drug crimes in particular. The sensationalized coverage of the rape exacerbated this approach; as some juvenile justice advocates noted (Ryan and Ziedenberg 2007), it intensified the panic, leading to a transformation in the juvenile justice system.[12] Of the six young suspects charged with the jogger's rape, five were tried in adult court (the sixth entered a plea bargain), but five were sentenced as juveniles. In my content analysis of the press reports during Time Period 2, the legal phase of the coverage, one of the most curious findings was the sharply diminished use of words or terms that served as racial indicators [...]. In Time Period 1, during the construction

Table 4.1   Percentages of Articles that Included at Least One Indicator for Each of the Major Concepts of Coverage, by Time Period.

CONCEPT	TIME PERIOD 1: APR 21, 1989–JUN 9, 1989	TIME PERIOD 2: JUN 10, 1989–MAR 14, 1991	TIME PERIODS 3 AND 4: MAR 15, 1991–DEC 31, 2003
Race	67.3	49.2	78.9
Violence	96.4	92.5	92.1
Class	96.4	96.7	100.0
Gender	98.2	93.2	94.7
Age	89.1	74.2	89.5
Victimhood	63.6	36.7	36.5
Sample size	N = 55	N = 120	N = 76

of the narrative, 67 percent of the articles included at least one indicator for race. This was a relatively low frequency of use for racial indicators, considering that so many perceived the case to be about race. Even more surprisingly, however, during the second time period (the legal phase), the proportion of articles with at least one racial indicator fell to 49 percent. This was a decrease of 18 percentage points in the use of indicators of racial categorical groupings. (See Table 4.1.) What could account for such a steep decline?

It appears that, for media content producers, when the legal system was part of the subject of press reports, representations of black and Latino racial groupings[13] were less important as an explicit feature of the coverage. This may have been the case because race, particularly black racial identity, was becoming much more associated with the criminal justice system. New anticrime measures had vastly increased the rate of incarceration in the United States for all people (Mauer and King 2007: 2; Pager 2007), but incarceration of African Americans was disproportionately high relative to their rate of arrest (Mauer and King 2007: 2; Pager 2007; Wacquant 2002). This disparity suggests that the moral panic that drove the War on Drugs had transformed the criminal justice system into a system of mass incarceration for black males, and had so united perceptions of "criminal" and "black race" that the societal meaning assigned to members of this racial group had been transformed. Thus, the War on Drugs greatly exacerbated the marginalization of people in a social location that included black race, lower income, male gender, and conviction for a felony. Sociologists Devah Pager (2007) and Loïc Wacquant (2002) and critical race scholar Michelle Alexander (2010) have come to similar conclusions in recent studies. Wacquant (2002) argues that the increasing levels of incarceration of African Americans have come to represent one of four "peculiar institutions" (the others being slavery, Jim Crow, and the construction of the ghettos) that have confined blacks over the course of U.S. history. Given the way in which the War on Drugs criminalized blacks, and the attendant increase in rates of incarceration of blacks, the black racial grouping became closely associated with people ensnared by the criminal justice system. This close association between "black race" and "subjects in the criminal justice system," which was supported by the results of my content analysis, came shortly after the period in U.S. history when blacks for the first time began to outnumber whites in the national inmate population.[14]

Incorporating Juveniles into the System of Mass Incarceration

By the time the Central Park jogger story broke, public discourse had been primed with these notions of an association—possibly biological but certainly cultural—between race and crime. One of the greatest ironies and injustices of the jogger case is that the six accused teens were in fact innocent. Media sensationalism in the coverage of the story has been blamed for heightening the atmosphere of fear in society. In the wake of the case, there was a ramping up of juvenile justice laws, beginning in the period 1992–1999, in which most states in the United States passed laws designed to try more juveniles as adults (Keenan 2005; Ryan and Ziedenberg 2007).[15] After spiking in the mid-1990s, rates of juvenile crime have declined "for a dozen years to a 30-year low" (Ryan and Ziedenberg 2007: 4).

Following the attack on the jogger and the trials of the defendants, states across the nation expanded the scope of their juvenile justice laws by changing the boundaries of jurisdiction for juvenile courts. Between 1992 and 1997, forty-four states put new laws on the books or expanded existing laws that allowed juveniles to be tried as adults in criminal court, according to a report published by the U.S. Department of Justice, Office of Juvenile Justice and Delinquency Prevention (Snyder and Sickmund 1999). Academics and policy makers at the highest levels of government provided a rationale for these changes through the construction of the now-defunct theory of the "super-predator" (DiIulio 1995; Krajicek 1999). The jogger case seemed to add to the empirical evidence needed to justify the racial project that right-wing policy makers began in the wake of the social movements of the 1960s. The problem, of course, is that the case against the suspects in the jogger attack itself was constructed; the boys were innocent.

The transformation of the juvenile justice system in the wake of the jogger case has had a disproportionate impact on black and Latino youths in the United States, forever ensnaring them in this nation's system of mass incarceration. According to juvenile justice advocates, approximately 200,000 youths are prosecuted in adult courts annually (Ryan and Ziedenberg 2007). Although many of these minors do not end up in adult prisons, thirty-one states now have laws that require that young people tried once in juvenile court must be tried for subsequent offenses in adult criminal court. These changes in juvenile justice laws suggests a possible impact of media coverage of youth on U.S. social structure. The disproportionate impact on black and Latino youths indicates how media associations of race, youth, and crime have become reified in the social structure.

While juvenile justice advocates are fighting for changes in the system, it is important to note the effectiveness of these laws. The changes have become institutionalized as crime prevention and reduction measures. However, researcher Jeffrey A. Butts (2012) found that there is no relationship between the placement of juveniles in the adult or criminal court system and a reduction in violent crime. He noted:

> At first glance, it may appear that the greater use of transfer lowered violent youth crime, but this argument is refuted by a simple analysis of crime trends. In the six states that allow fair comparisons (i.e., where all juveniles ages 16–19 are originally subject to juvenile court jurisdiction and sufficient data exist for the calculations), the use of criminal court transfer bears no relationship to changes in juvenile violence. (Butts 2012)

States have been increasing prosecutorial power or have created laws that enable them to bypass family court and transfer youthful offenders to criminal court. According to Butts (2012), "entire classes of young offenders are transferred without the involvement of the court."

The reification of associations of race, youth, and crime in the social structure is dialectically related to the mainstream media renditions that normalize the marginalization of black and Latino youths, particularly male youths, from the mainstream. They stand apart, distinct from categorical groupings of other youths, vulnerable but despised.

Notes

1 Mentioning the attack on the Central Park jogger and the murder Michael Griffith in the same context suggests that even at the federal level there was an attempt to create moral equivalence between the two incidents and to suggest that both were possibly symbolic of the perils of racial border crossings.

2 Hall et al. (1978) also credit a conservative backlash, starting in the 1960s in Great Britain, as part of the reason for that moral panic around muggings.

3 At the time of Robert Stutman's retirement in 1990, a New York Times report (Kerr 1990) stated that he was critical of U.S. drug policies because of the meager spending on drug treatment and education.

4 Although the idea of race as a social construction has been the dominant paradigm, biologically based ideas of race still existed and continue to exist. In science, when new paradigms emerge, followers of the old theories oft en continue to try to prove the worth of the old paradigm. See Kuhn 1962.

5 The findings from my content analysis point to the ways in which media producers conceptualize the world outside their institutional doors.

6   This does not make class the most important concept in the coverage. In the context of media systems, analyses that rely on frequencies will not indicate the degree or level of importance. In media, importance is determined by prominent placement of stories. Th erefore, the frequency of inclusion of indicators for the concept of class does not determine how important class was to the media content makers. Krippendorff (2004: 195) notes that in content analyses "simple frequencies say nothing about relationships between content variables." Additional analysis would be needed to determine the relationships between the concepts and prominent placement in media.

7   Interracial rapes are more frequently covered by the media than rapes in which the perpetrator and victim are from the same racial category.

8   See also note 4 above.

9   See also Krajicek 1999 on the history of Dilulio's concept of the "super-predator." Satcher (2001) argues in his study on youth violence that the notion of a "super-predator" is one of the "myths" about young people and violence.

10   Marvin E. Wolfgang's (1983) birth-cohort studies form the basis of all of this work by John J. Dilulio Jr. and James Q. Wilson.

11   In what was essentially a repudiation of their earlier work, Dilulio and several prominent criminologists who had supported the "super-predator" theory joined a 2012 friend of the court brief supporting the petitioners in two cases heard together in which the U.S. Supreme Court would be ruling on the "constitutionality of sentences of life without parole for juveniles convicted of homicide off enses, including felony homicide" (p. 2). Th e brief stated that "Empirical research that has analyzed the increase in violent crime ... demonstrates that the juvenile superpredator was a myth and the predictions of future youth violence were baseless" (p. 8). See U.S. Supreme Court brief in the cases of petitioners Kuntrell Jackson v. Ray Hobbs, Director, Arkansas Department of Corrections, and Evan Miller v. Alabama, 10-9647 and 10-9646, amici curiae brief fi led by Carl Micarelli, Counsel of Record, January 17, 2012.

12   Ryan and Ziedenberg (2007: 3) directly cite the Central Park jogger case in their report. "Sometimes all it takes is one case to change the course of public opinion and national policy. Th e Central Park Jogger case did just that." Th eir conclusions are not scientifi cally drawn, and the organization they produced their study for—Campaign for Youth Justice—is engaged in a national campaign to end youth incarceration in adult facilities across the nation.

13   All but two of the eighteen racial words or terms refer to black and Latino race.

14   Wacquant (2002) argues that mass incarceration operates like slavery as an institution that defi nes blacks in the United States. He noted that the inmate population in the United States was predominantly white until 1988.

15   See also the U.S. Supreme Court brief cited in note 11 for this chapter.

References

Alexander, Michelle. 2010. *The New Jim Crow: Mass Incarceration in the Age of Color-blindness*. New York: New Press.

Alvarez, Lizette. 1990b. "DNA Prints Fail to ID Jogger's Attackers." *New York Daily News,* July 14, p. 3.

Annin, Peter. 1996. "Superpredators Arrive: Should We Cage the New Breed of Vicious Kids?" *Newsweek,* January 22, p. 57.

Banton, Michael. 2009. "The Idiom of Race: A Critique of Presentation." In *Theories of Race and Racism: A Reader.* Rev. ed. Edited by Les Back and John Solomos. New York: Routledge.

Becker, Elizabeth. 2001. "As Ex-Theorist on Young 'Superpredators,' Bush Aide Has Regrets." *New York Times,* February 9, p. A19.

Bennett, William. 1989. "National Drug Control Strategy." Office of National Drug Control Policy, September 5. Washington, DC: The White House.

Bennett, William J., John J. DiIulio Jr., and John P. Walters. 1996. *Body Count: Moral Poverty ... And How to Win America's War against Crime and Drugs.* New York: Simon and Schuster.

Berke, Richard L. 1989. "Bennett Asks Tough Drug Fight, Declaring Crack Biggest Problem." *New York Times,* August 1, p. A14. Available at http://www.nytimes.com/1989/08/01/us/bennett-asks-tougher-drug-fight-declaring-crack-biggest-problem.html?scp=1&sq=William+Bennett&st=nyt.

Bourgois, Philippe. 1995. *In Search of Respect: Selling Crack in El Barrio.* New York: Cambridge University Press.

Bumiller, Kristin. 2008. *In an Abusive State: How Neoliberalism Appropriated the Feminist Movement against Sexual Violence.* Durham, NC: Duke University Press.

Bush, George H.W. 1989. "Address to the Nation on the National Drug Control Strategy." Public Papers from the George Bush Presidential Library and Museum, September 5. Available at bushlibrary.tamu.edu/research/public_papers.php?id=863&year=&month=.

Butts, Jeffrey A. 2012. "Transfer of Juveniles to Criminal Court Is Not Correlated with Falling Youth Violence." *Research and Evaluation Data Bits,* no. 2012–05. New York: Research and Evaluation Center, John Jay College of Criminal Justice, City University of New York. Available at http://johnjayresearch.org/wp-content/uploads/2012/03/databit2012_05.pdf.

Chang, Jeff. 2005. *Can't Stop Won't Stop: A History of the Hip-Hop Generation.* New York: Picador/St. Martin's Press.

CNN. 2005. "Bennett under Fire for Remarks on Blacks, Crime." *CNN.com,* September 30. Available at http://www.cnn.com/2005/POLITICS/09/30/bennett.comments.

Cohen, Stanley. 2002. *Folk Devils and Moral Panics: Thirtieth Anniversary Edition.* 3rd ed. London: Taylor and Francis.

DiIulio, John J., Jr. 1989. "The Underclass: III. The Impact of Inner-City Crime." *Public Interest* 96 (Summer): 28–46.

———. 1995. "Moral Poverty: The Coming of the Super-predators Should Scare Us into Wanting to Get to the Root Causes of Crime a Lot Faster." *Chicago Tribune,* December 15, p. 31.

Fredrickson, George. 1971a. *The Black Image in the White Mind: Debate on Afro-American Character and Destiny, 1817–1914.* New York: Harper and Row.

Goodman, James. 1995. *Stories of Scottsboro.* New York: Knopf Doubleday.

Hall, Stuart, Chas Critcher, Tony Jefferson, John Clarke, and Brian Roberts. 1978. *Policing the Crisis: Mugging, the State, and Law and Order.* London: MacMillan.

Hancock, LynNell. 2003. "Wolf Pack: The Press and the Central Park Jogger." *Columbia Journalism Review,* January/February 2003. Available at http://www.cjr.org/archives.asp?url=/01/3/hancock.asp.

Herbert, Bob. 1990. "A Case that Stunned the City: Park Rape Scene Is Still Jarring." *New York Daily News,* June 26, p. 4.

Houck, Davis, and Matthew Grindy. 2008. *Emmett Till and the Mississippi Press*. Jackson: University of Mississippi Press.

Isikoff, Michael. 1989. "Drug Buy Set Up for Bush Speech: DEA Lured Seller to Lafayette Park." *Washington Post*, September 22, p. A1.

Jordan, Winthrop D. 1968. *White over Black: American Attitudes toward the Negro, 1550–1812*. Durham: University of North Carolina Press.

Keenan, Kevin. 2005. *Invasion of Privacy: A Reference Handbook*. Santa Barbara, CA: ABC-CLIO.

Krajicek, David. 1999. "'Super-Predators': The Making of a Myth." *Youth Today* 8 (April): 4.

Mauer, Mark, and Ryan King. 2007. *A 25-Year Quagmire: The War on Drugs and Its Impact on American Society*. Washington, DC: The Sentencing Project.

Murch, Donna. 2010. *Living for the City*. Raleigh: University of North Carolina Press.

Pager, Devah. 2007. *Marked: Race, Crime, and Finding Work in an Era of Mass Incarceration*. Chicago: University of Chicago Press.

Reinarman, Craig, and Harry G. Levine. [1997] 2006. "The Crack Attack: Politics and Media in the Crack Scare." In *Sociology: Exploring the Architecture of Everyday Life Readings*, edited by David M. Newman and Jodi O'Brien, 47–66. Thousand Oaks, CA: Pine Forge Press.

Ryan, Liz, and Jason Ziedenberg. 2007. "The Consequences Aren't Minor: The Impact of Trying Youth as Adults and Strategies for Reform." *Campaign for Youth Justice Report*, March. Washington, DC: Campaign for Youth Justice. Executive Summary available at http://www.campaign4youthjustice.org/Downloads/NationalReportsArticles/JPI014-Consequences_exec.pdf.

Satcher, David. 2001. *Surgeon General Report*. Washington, DC: U.S. Department of Health and Human Services. Available at http://www.ncbi.nlm.nih.gov/books/NBK 44297/#A12312.

Snyder, Howard, and Melissa Sickmund. 1999. "Juvenile Offenders and Victims: 1999 National Report." Washington, DC: Office of Juvenile Justice and Delinquency Prevention, U.S. Department of Justice. Available at https://www.ncjrs.gov/html/ojjdp/ nationalreport99/toc.html.

Sullivan, Timothy. 1992. *Unequal Verdicts: The Central Park Jogger Trials*. New York: American Lawyer Books/Simon & Schuster.

Wacquant, Loïc. 2002. "From Slavery to Mass Incarceration: Rethinking the 'Race Question' in the US." *New Left Review* 13 (Jan–Feb): 41–60.

Weinraub, Bernard. 1989. "President Unveils $1.2 Billion Plan to Battle Crime." *New York Times*, May 16, p. A1.

Welch, Michael, Eric Price, and Nana Yankey. 2002. "Moral Panic over Youth Violence: Wilding and the Manufacture of Menace in the Media." *Youth and Society* 34:3.

———. 2004. "Youth Violence and Race in the Media: The Emergence of 'Wilding' as an Invention of the Press." *Race, Gender and Class* 11:2.

Wolfgang, Marvin E. 1983. "Delinquency in Two Birth Cohorts." *American Behavioral Scientist* 27 (1): 75–86.

Wolfgang, Marvin E., and Franco Ferracuti. 1967. *The Subculture of Violence: Towards an Integrated Theory in Criminology*. London: Tavistock Publications.

Zoglin, Richard, Sam Allis, and Ratu Kamlani. 1996. "Now for the Bad News: A Teenage Time Bomb." *Time*, January 15, p. 52.

Post-Reading Questions

1   What is your concept of "wilding"? What does the term suggest about human nature? Are there any other behaviors that we might automatically associate with this term?

2   Where does the concept of a "moral panic" originate in criminal justice research? What is its connection to the term "wilding"?

3   In what ways has the war on crime and the war on drugs been highly politicized?

4   To what extent is a crime a function of one's social class? Is social class more salient than one's race or some other variable? Why or why not?

5   What are the four "peculiar institutions" referred to by Wacquant (2012)? In what ways have these intersected to create the current carceral state?

Reference

Wacquant, L. (2012). Probing the meta-prison. In J. I. Ross (Ed.), *The globalization of supermax prisons* (pp. ix–xiv). New Brunswick, NJ: Rutgers University Press.

PART II

DIVERSITY AND CRIMINOLOGICAL THEORY

"ISN'T IT AMAZING THAT WE ARE ALL MADE IN GOD'S IMAGE, AND YET THERE IS SO MUCH DIVERSITY AMONG HIS PEOPLE?"

– *Desmond Tutu*

Toward a Theory of Race, Crime, and Urban Inequality

Robert J. Sampson and William Julius Wilson

Our purpose in this [reading] is to address one of the central yet difficult issues facing criminology—race and violent crime. The centrality of the issue is seen on several fronts: the leading cause of death among young black males is homicide (Fingerhut and Kleinman 1990, 3292), and the lifetime risk of being murdered is as high as 1 in 21 for black males, compared with only 1 in 131 for white males (U.S. Department of Justice 1985). Although rates of violence have been higher for blacks than whites at least since the 1950s (Jencks 1991), record increases in homicide since the mid-1980s in cities such as New York, Chicago, and Philadelphia also appear racially selective (Hinds 1990; James 1991; Recktenwald and Morrison 1990). For example, while white rates remained stable, the rate of death from firearms among young black males more than doubled from 1984 to 1988 alone (Fingerhut et al. 1991). These differentials help explain recent estimates that a resident of rural Bangladesh has a greater chance of surviving to age 40 than does a black male in Harlem (McCord and Freeman 1990). Moreover, the so-called drug war and the resulting surge in prison populations in the past decade have taken their toll disproportionately on the minority community (Mauer 1990). Overall, the evidence is clear that African-Americans face dismal and worsening odds when it comes to crime in the streets and the risk of incarceration.

Despite these facts, the discussion of race and crime is mired in an unproductive mix of controversy and silence. At the same time that articles on age and gender abound, criminologists are loath to speak openly on race and crime for fear of being misunderstood or labeled racist. This situation is not unique, for until recently scholars of urban poverty also consciously avoided discussion of race and social dislocations in the inner city lest they be accused of blaming the victim (see W. J. Wilson 1987). And when the topic is broached, criminologists have reduced the race–crime debate to simplistic arguments about culture versus social structure. On the one side, structuralists argue for the primacy of "relative deprivation" to understand black crime (e.g., Blau and Blau 1982), even though the evidence on social class and crime is weak at best. On the other side, cultural theorists tend to focus on an indigenous culture of violence in black ghettos (e.g., Wolfgang and Ferracuti 1967), even though the evidence there is weak too.

Still others engage in subterfuge, denying race-related differentials in violence and focusing instead on police bias and the alleged invalidity of official crime statistics (e.g., Stark 1990). This in spite of evidence not only from death records but also from survey reports showing that blacks are disproportionately victimized by, and involved in, criminal violence (Hindelang 1976, 1978). Hence, much like the silence on race and inner-city social dislocations engendered by the vociferous attacks on the Moynihan Report in the 1960s, criminologists have, with few exceptions (e.g., Hawkins 1986; Hindelang 1978; Katz 1988), abdicated serious scholarly debate on race and crime.

In an attempt to break this stalemate we advance in this [reading] a theoretical strategy that incorporates both structural and cultural arguments regarding race, crime, and inequality in American cities. In contrast to psychologically based relative deprivation theories and the subculture of violence, we view the race and crime linkage from contextual lenses that highlight the very different ecological contexts that blacks and whites reside in—regardless of individual characteristics. The basic thesis is that macrosocial patterns of residential inequality give rise to the social isolation and ecological concentration of the truly disadvantaged, which in turn leads to structural barriers and cultural adaptations that undermine social organization and hence the control of crime. This thesis is grounded in what is actually an old idea in criminology that has been overlooked in the race and crime debate—the importance of communities.

The Community Structure of Race and Crime

Unlike the dominant tradition in criminology that seeks to distinguish offenders from nonoffenders, the macrosocial or community level of explanation asks what it is about community structures and cultures that produce differential rates of crime (Bursik 1988; Byrne and Sampson 1986; Short 1985). As such, the goal of macrolevel research is not to explain individual involvement in criminal behavior but to isolate characteristics of communities, cities, or even societies that lead to high rates of criminality (Byrne and Sampson 1986; Short 1985). From this viewpoint the "ecological fallacy"—inferring individual-level relations based on aggregate data—is not at issue because the unit of explanation and analysis is the community.

The Chicago School research of Clifford Shaw and Henry McKay spearheaded the community-level approach of modern American studies of ecology and crime. In their classic work *Juvenile Delinquency and Urban Areas*, Shaw and McKay (1942) argued that three structural factors—low economic status, ethnic heterogeneity, and residential mobility—led to the disruption of local community social organization, which in turn accounted for variations in crime and delinquency rates (for more details see Kornhauser 1978).

Arguably the most significant aspect of Shaw and McKay's research, however, was their demonstration that high rates of delinquency persisted in certain areas over many years, regardless of population turnover. More than any other, this finding led them to reject individualistic explanations of delinquency and focus instead on the processes by which delinquent and criminal patterns of behavior were transmitted across generations in areas of social disorganization and weak social controls (1942; 1969, 320). This community-level orientation led them to an explicit contextual interpretation of correlations between race/ethnicity and delinquency rates. Their logic was set forth in a rejoinder to a critique in 1949 by Jonassen, who had argued that ethnicity had direct effects on delinquency. Shaw and McKay countered:

> The important fact about rates of delinquency for Negro boys is that they, too, vary by type of area. They are higher than the rates for white boys, but it cannot be said that they are higher than rates for white boys in comparable areas, since it is impossible to reproduce in white communities the circumstances under which Negro children live. Even if it were possible to parallel the low economic status and the inadequacy of institutions in the white community, it would not be possible to reproduce the effects of segregation and the barriers to upward mobility (1949, 614).

Shaw and McKay's insight almost a half century ago raises two interesting questions still relevant today. First, to what extent do black rates of crime vary by type of ecological area? Second, is it possible to reproduce in white communities the structural circumstances in which many blacks live? The first question is crucial, for it signals that blacks are not a homogeneous group any more than whites are: Indeed, it is racial stereotyping that assigns to blacks a distinct or homogeneous character, allowing simplistic comparisons of black-white group differences in crime. As Shaw and McKay recognized, the key point is that there is heterogeneity among blacks in crime rates that correspond to community context. To the extent that the causes of black crime are not unique, its rate should thus vary with specific ecological conditions in the same way that the white crime rate does. As we shall now see, recent evidence weighs in Shaw and McKay's favor.

Are the Causes of Black Crime Unique?

Disentangling the contextual basis for race and crime requires racial disaggregation of both the crime rate and the explanatory variables of theoretical interest. This approach was used in recent research that examined racially disaggregated rates of homicide and robbery by juveniles and adults in over 150 U.S. cities in 1980 (Sampson 1987). Substantively, the theory explored the effects of black male joblessness and economic deprivation on violent crime as mediated by black family disruption. The results supported the main hypothesis and showed that the scarcity of employed black males relative to black females was directly related to the prevalence of families headed by women in black communities (W. J. Wilson 1987). In turn, black family disruption was substantially related to rates of black murder and robbery, especially by juveniles (see also Messner and Sampson 1991). These effects were independent of income, region, density, city size, and welfare benefits.

The finding that family disruption had stronger effects on juvenile violence than on adult violence, in conjunction with the inconsistent findings of previous research on individual-level delinquency and broken homes, supports the idea that the effects of family structure are related to macro-level patterns of social control and guardianship, especially for youth and their peers (Sampson and Groves 1989). Moreover, the results suggest why unemployment and economic deprivation have had weak or inconsistent direct effects on violence rates in past research—joblessness and poverty appear to exert much of their influence indirectly through family disruption.

Despite a tremendous difference in mean levels of family disruption among black and white communities, the percentage of white families headed by a female also had a large positive effect on white juvenile and white adult violence. In fact, the predictors of white robbery were shown to be in large part identical in sign and magnitude to those for blacks. Therefore, the effect of black family disruption on black crime was independent of commonly cited alternative explanations (e.g., region, density, age composition) and could not be attributed to unique cultural factors within the black community given the similar effect of white family disruption on white crime.

To be clear, we are not dismissing the relevance of culture. As discussed more below, our argument is that if cultural influences exist, they vary systematically with structural features of the urban environment. How else can we make sense of the systematic variations within race—for example, if a uniform subculture of violence explains black crime, are we to assume that this subculture is three times as potent in, say, New York as in Chicago (where black homicide differs by a factor of three)? In San Francisco as in Baltimore (3:1 ratio)? These distinct variations exist even at the state level. For example, rates of black homicide in California are triple those in Maryland (Wilbanks 1986). Must whites then be part of the black subculture of violence in California, given that white homicide rates are also more than triple the rates for whites in Maryland? We think not. The sources of violent crime appear to be remarkably invariant across race and rooted instead in the structural differences among communities, cities, and states in economic and family organization.

The Ecological Concentration of Race and Social Dislocations

Having demonstrated the similarity of black-white variations by ecological context, we turn to the second logical question. To what extent are blacks as a group differentially exposed to criminogenic structural conditions? More than 40 years after Shaw and McKay's assessment of race and urban ecology, we still cannot say that blacks and whites share a similar environment—especially with regard to concentrated urban poverty. Consider the following. Although approximately 70 percent of all poor non-Hispanic whites lived in non-poverty areas in the ten largest U.S. central cities (as determined by the 1970 census) in 1980, only 16 percent of poor blacks did. Moreover, whereas less than 7 percent of poor whites lived in extreme poverty or ghetto areas, 38 percent of poor blacks lived in such areas (W. J. Wilson et al. 1988, 130). In the nation's largest city, New York, 70 percent of poor blacks live in poverty neighborhoods; by contrast, 70 percent of poor whites live in non-poverty neighborhoods (Sullivan 1989, 230). Potentially even more important, the majority of poor blacks live in communities characterized by high rates of family disruption. Poor whites, even those from "broken homes," live in areas of relative family stability (Sampson 1987; Sullivan 1989).

The combination of urban poverty and family disruption concentrated by race is particularly severe. As an example, we examined race-specific census data on the 171 largest cities in the United States as of 1980. To get some idea of concentrated social dislocations by race, we selected cities where the proportion of blacks living in poverty was equal to or less than the proportion of whites, and where the proportion of black families with children headed by a single parent was equal to or less than that for white families. Although we knew that the average national rate of family disruption and poverty among blacks was two to four times higher than among whites, the number of distinct ecological contexts in which blacks achieve equality to whites is striking. In not one city over 100,000 in the United States do blacks live in ecological equality with whites when it comes to these basic features of economic and family organization. Accordingly, racial differences in poverty and family disruption are so strong that the "worst" urban contexts in which whites reside are considerably better than the average context of black communities (Sampson 1987, 354).

Taken as a whole, these patterns underscore what W. J. Wilson (1987) has labeled "concentration effects," that is, the effects of living in a neighborhood that is overwhelmingly impoverished. These concentration effects, reflected in a range of outcomes from degree of labor force attachment to social deviance, are created by the constraints and opportunities that the residents of inner-city neighborhoods face in terms of access to jobs and job networks, involvement in quality schools, availability of marriageable partners, and exposure to conventional role models.

The social transformation of the inner city in recent decades has resulted in an increased concentration of the most disadvantaged segments of the urban black population—especially poor, female-headed families with children. Whereas one of every five poor blacks resided in ghetto or extreme poverty areas in 1970, by 1980 nearly two out of every five did so (W. J. Wilson et al. 1988, 131). This change has been fueled by several macrostructural forces. In particular, urban minorities have been vulnerable to structural economic changes related to the deindustrialization of central cities (e.g., the shift from goods-producing to service-producing industries; increasing polarization of the labor market into low-wage and high-wage sectors; and relocation of manufacturing out of the inner city). The exodus of middle-and upper-income black families from the inner city has also removed an important social buffer that could potentially deflect the full impact of prolonged joblessness and industrial transformation. This thesis is based on the assumption that the basic institutions of an area (churches, schools, stores, recreational facilities, etc.) are more likely to remain viable if the core of their support comes from more economically stable families in inner-city neighborhoods (W. J. Wilson 1987, 56). The social milieu of increasing stratification among blacks differs significantly from the environment that existed in inner cities in previous decades (see also Hagedorn 1988).

Black inner-city neighborhoods have also disproportionately suffered severe population and housing loss of the sort identified by Shaw and McKay (1942) as disrupting the social and institutional order. Skogan (1986, 206) has noted how urban renewal and forced migration contributed to the wholesale uprooting of many urban black communities, especially the extent to which freeway networks driven through the hearts of many cities in the 1950s destroyed viable, low-income communities. For example, in Atlanta one in six residents was dislocated by urban renewal; the great majority of those dislocated were poor blacks (Logan and Molotch 1987, 114). Nationwide, fully 20 percent of all central-city housing units occupied by blacks were lost in the period 1960–70 alone. As Logan and Molotch (1987, 114) observe, this displacement does not even include that brought about by more routine market forces (evictions, rent increases, commercial development).

Of course, no discussion of concentration effects is complete without recognizing the negative consequences of deliberate policy decisions to concentrate minorities and the poor in public housing. Opposition from organized community groups to the building of public housing in their neighborhoods, de facto federal policy to tolerate extensive segregation against blacks in urban housing markets, and the decision by local governments to neglect the rehabilitation of existing residential units (many of them single-family homes), have led to massive, segregated housing projects that have become ghettos for the minorities and disadvantaged (see also Sampson 1990). The cumulative result is that, even given the same objective socioeconomic status, blacks and whites face vastly different environments in which to live, work, and raise their children. As Bickford and Massey (1991, 1035) have argued, public housing is a federally funded, physically permanent institution for the isolation of black families by race and class and must therefore be considered an important structural constraint on ecological area of residence.

In short, the foregoing discussion suggests that macrostructural factors—both historic and contemporary—have combined to concentrate urban black poverty and family disruption in the inner city. These factors include but are not limited to racial segregation, structural economic transformation and black male joblessness, class-linked out-migration from the inner city, and housing discrimination. It is important to emphasize that when segregation and concentrated poverty represent structural constraints embodied in public policy and historical patterns of racial subjugation, notions that individual differences (or self-selection) explain community-level effects on violence are considerably weakened (see Sampson and Lauritsen 1994).

Implications

The consequences of these differential ecological distributions by race raise the substantively plausible hypothesis that correlations of race and crime may be systematically confounded with important differences in community contexts. As Testa has argued with respect to escape from poverty:

> Simple comparisons between poor whites and poor blacks would be confounded with the fact that poor whites reside in areas which are eco-logically and economically very different from poor blacks. Any observed relationships involving race would reflect, to some unknown degree, the relatively superior ecological niche many poor whites occupy with respect to jobs, marriage opportunities, and exposure to conventional role models (quoted in W. J. Wilson 1987: 58–60).

Regardless of a black's individual-level family or economic situation, the average community of residence thus differs dramatically from that of a similarly situated white (Sampson 1987). For example, regardless of whether a black juvenile is raised in an intact or single-parent family, or a rich or poor home, he or she will not likely grow up in a community context similar to that of whites with regard to family structure and income. Reductionist interpretations of race and social class camouflage this key point.

In fact, a community conceptualization exposes the "individualistic fallacy"—the often-invoked assumption that individual-level causal relations necessarily generate individual-level correlations. Research conducted at the individual level rarely questions whether obtained results might be spurious and confounded with community-level processes. In the present case, it is commonplace to search for individual-level (e.g., constitutional) or group-level (e.g., social class) explanations for the link between race and violence. In our opinion these efforts have largely failed, and so we highlight contextual sources of the race-violence link among individuals. More specifically, we posit that the most important determinant of the relationship between race and crime is the differential distribution of blacks in communities characterized by (1) *structural social disorganization* and (2) *cultural social isolation*, both of which stem from the concentration of poverty, family disruption, and residential instability.

Before explicating the theoretical dimensions of social disorganization, we must also expose what may be termed the "materialist fallacy"—that economic (or materialist) causes necessarily produce economic motivations. Owing largely to Merton's (1938) famous dictum about social structure and anomie, criminologists have assumed that if economic structural factors (e.g., poverty) are causally relevant it must be through the motivation to commit acquisitive crimes. Indeed, "strain" theory was so named to capture the hypothesized pressure on members of the lower classes to commit crime in their pursuit of the American dream. But as is well known, strain or materialist theories have not fared well empirically (Kornhauser 1978). The image of the offender stealing to survive flourishes only as a straw man, knocked down most recently by Jack Katz, who argues that materialist theory is nothing more than "twentieth-century sentimentality about crime" (1988, 314). Assuming, however, that those who posit the relevance of economic structure for crime rely on motivational pressure as an explanatory concept, is itself a fallacy. The theory of social disorganization does see relevance in the ecological concentration of poverty, but not for the materialist reasons Katz (1988) presupposes. Rather, the conceptualization we now explicate rests on the fundamental properties of structural and cultural organization.

The Structure of Social (Dis)Organization

In their original formulation Shaw and McKay held that low economic status, ethnic heterogeneity, and residential mobility led to the disruption of community social organization, which in turn accounted for variations in crime and delinquency rates (1942; 1969). As recently extended by Kornhauser (1978), Bursik (1988), and Sampson and Groves (1989), the concept of social disorganization may be seen as the inability of a community structure to realize the common values of its residents and maintain effective social controls. The *structural* dimensions of community social disorganization refer to the prevalence and interdependence of social networks in a community—both informal (e.g., the density of acquaintanceship; intergenerational kinship ties; level of anonymity) and formal (e.g., organizational participation; institutional stability)—and in the span of collective supervision that the community directs toward local problems.

This social-disorganization approach is grounded in what Kasarda and Janowitz (1974, 329) call the "systemic" model, where the local community is viewed as a complex system of friendship and kinship networks, and formal and informal associational ties are rooted in family life and ongoing socialization processes (see also Sampson 1991). From this view social organization and social disorganization are seen as different ends of the same continuum of systemic networks of community social control. As Bursik (1988) notes, when formulated in this way, social disorganization is clearly separable not only from the processes that may lead to it (e.g., poverty, residential mobility), but also from the degree of criminal behavior that may be a result. This conceptualization also goes beyond the traditional account of community as a strictly geographical or spatial phenomenon by focusing on the social and organizational networks of local residents (see Leighton 1988).

Evidence favoring social-disorganization theory is available with respect both to its structural antecedents and to mediating processes. In a recent paper, Sampson and Lauritsen (1994) reviewed in depth the empirical literature on individual, situational, and community-level sources of interpersonal violence (i.e., assault, homicide, robbery, and rape). This assessment revealed that community-level research conducted in the past twenty years has largely supported the original Shaw and McKay model in terms of the exogenous correlates of poverty, residential mobility, and heterogeneity. What appears to be especially salient is the *interaction* of poverty and mobility. As anticipated by Shaw and McKay (1942) and Kornhauser (1978), several studies indicate that the effect of poverty is most pronounced in neighborhoods of high residential instability (see Sampson and Lauritsen 1994).

In addition, recent research has established that crime rates are positively linked to community-level variations in urbanization (e.g., population and housing density), family disruption (e.g., percentage of single-parent households), opportunity structures for predatory crime (e.g., density of convenience stores), and rates of community change and population turnover (see also Bursik 1988; Byrne and Sampson 1986; Reiss 1986). As hypothesized by Sampson and Groves (1989), family disruption, urbanization, and the anonymity accompanying rapid population change all undercut the capacity of a community to exercise informal social control, especially of teenage peer groups in public spaces.

Land et al. (1990) have also shown the relevance of *resource deprivation, family dissolution,* and *urbanization* (density, population size) for explaining homicide rates across cities, metropolitan areas, and states from 1960 to 1980. In particular, their factor of resource deprivation/affluence included three income variables—median income, the percentage of families below the poverty line, and the Gini index of income inequality—in addition to the percentage of population that is black and the percentage of children not living with both parents. This coalescence of structural conditions with race supports the concept of concentration effects (W. J. Wilson 1987) and is consistent with Taylor and Covington's finding (1988) that increasing entrenchment of ghetto poverty was associated with large increases in violence. In these two studies the correlation among structural indices was not seen merely as a statistical nuisance (i.e., as multicolinearity), but as a predictable substantive outcome. Moreover, the Land et al. (1990) results support Wilson's argument that concentration effects grew more severe from 1970 to 1980 in large cities. Urban disadvantage thus appears to be increasing in ecological concentration.

It is much more difficult to study the intervening mechanisms of social disorganization directly, but at least two recent studies provide empirical support for the theory's structural dimensions. First, Taylor et al. (1984) examined variations in violent crime (e.g., mugging, assault, murder, rape) across sixty-three street blocks in Baltimore in 1978. Based on interviews with 687 household respondents, Taylor et al. (1984, 316) constructed block-level measures of the proportion of respondents who belonged to an organization to which coresidents also belonged, and the proportion of respondents who felt responsible for what happened in the area surrounding their home. Both of these dimensions of informal social control were significantly and negatively related to community-level variations in crime, exclusive of other ecological factors (1984, 320). These results support the social-disorganization hypothesis that levels of organizational participation and informal social control—especially of public activities by neighborhood youth—inhibit community-level rates of violence.

Second, Sampson and Groves's analysis of the British Crime Survey in 1982 and 1984 showed that the prevalence of unsupervised teenage peer groups in a community had the largest effects on rates of robbery and violence by strangers. The density of local friendship networks—measured by the proportion of residents with half or more of their friends living in the neighborhood—also had a significant negative effect on robbery rates. Further, the level of organizational participation by residents had significant inverse effects on both robbery and stranger violence (Sampson and Groves 1989, 789). These results suggest that communities characterized by sparse friendship networks, unsupervised teenage peer groups, and low organizational participation foster increased crime rates (see also Anderson 1990).

Variations in these structural dimensions of community social disorganization also transmitted in large part the effects of community socioeconomic status, residential mobility, ethnic heterogeneity, and family disruption in a theoretically consistent manner. For example, mobility had significant inverse effects on friendship networks, family disruption was the largest predictor of unsupervised peer groups, and socioeconomic status had a significant positive effect on organizational participation in 1982. When combined with the results of research on gang delinquency, which point to the salience of informal and formal community structures in controlling the formation of gangs (Short and Strodtbeck 1965; Sullivan 1989; Thrasher 1963), the empirical data suggest that the structural elements of social disorganization have relevance for explaining macrolevel variations in crime.

Further Modifications

To be sure, social-disorganization theory as *traditionally conceptualized* is hampered by a restricted view of community that fails to account for the larger political and structural forces shaping communities. As suggested earlier, many community characteristics hypothesized to underlie crime rates, such as residential instability, concentration of poor, female-headed families with children, multiunit housing projects, and disrupted social networks, appear to stem directly from planned governmental policies at local, state, and federal levels. We thus depart from the natural market assumptions of the Chicago School ecologists by incorporating the political economy of place (Logan and Molotch 1987), along with macrostructural transformations and historical forces, into our conceptualization of community-level social organization.

Take, for example, municipal code enforcement and local governmental policies toward neighborhood deterioration. In *Making the Second Ghetto: Race and Housing in Chicago, 1940–1960*, Hirsch (1983) documents in great detail how lax enforcement of city housing codes played a major role in accelerating the deterioration of inner-city Chicago neighborhoods. More recently, Daley and Mieslin (1988) have argued that inadequate city policies on code enforcement and repair of city properties contributed to the systematic decline of New York City's housing stock, and consequently, entire neighborhoods. When considered with the practices of redlining and disinvestment by banks and "block-busting" by real estate agents (Skogan 1986), local policies toward code enforcement—that on the surface are far removed from crime—have in all likelihood contributed to crime through neighborhood deterioration, forced migration, and instability.

Decisions to withdraw city municipal services for public health and fire safety—presumably made with little if any thought to crime and violence—also appear to have been salient in the social disintegration of poor communities. As Wallace and Wallace (1990) argue based on an analysis of the "planned shrinkage" of New York City fire and health services in recent decades: "The consequences of withdrawing municipal services from poor neighborhoods, the resulting outbreaks of contagious urban decay and forced migration which shred essential social networks and cause social disintegration, have become a highly significant contributor to decline in public health among the poor" (1990, 427). The loss of social integration and networks from planned shrinkage of services may increase behavioral patterns of violence that may themselves become "convoluted with processes of urban decay likely to further disrupt social networks and cause further social disintegration" (1990, 427). This pattern of destabilizing feedback (see Skogan 1986) appears central to an understanding of the role of governmental policies in fostering the downward spiral of high crime areas. As Wacquant has recently argued, federal U.S. policy seems to favor "the institutional desertification of the urban core" (1991, 36).

Decisions by government to provide public housing paint a similar picture. Bursik (1989) has shown that the planned construction of new public housing projects in Chicago in the 1970s was associated with increased rates of population turnover, which in turn were related to increases in crime. More generally, we have already noted how the disruption of urban renewal contributed disproportionately to housing loss among poor blacks.

Boiled down to its essentials, then, our theoretical framework linking social-disorganization theory with research on urban poverty and political economy suggests that macrosocial forces (e.g., segregation, migration, housing discrimination, structural transformation of the economy) interact with local community-level factors (e.g., residential turnover, concentrated poverty, family disruption) to impede social organization. This is a distinctly sociological viewpoint, for it focuses attention on the proximate structural characteristics and mediating processes of community social organization that help explain crime, while also recognizing the larger historical, social, and political forces shaping local communities.

Social Isolation and Community Culture

Although social-disorganization theory is primarily structural in nature, it also focuses on how the ecological segregation of communities gives rise to what Kornhauser (1978, 75) terms *cultural disorganization*—the attenuation of societal cultural values. Poverty, heterogeneity, anonymity, mutual distrust, institutional instability, and other structural features of urban communities are hypothesized to impede communication and obstruct the quest for common values, thereby fostering cultural diversity with respect to nondelinquent values. For example, an important component of Shaw and McKay's theory was that disorganized communities spawned delinquent gangs with their own subcultures and norms perpetuated through cultural transmission.

Despite their relative infrequency, ethnographic studies generally support the notion that structurally disorganized communities are conducive to the emergence of cultural value systems and attitudes that seem to legitimate, or at least provide a basis of tolerance for, crime and deviance. For example, Suttles's (1968) account of the social order of a Chicago neighborhood characterized by poverty and heterogeneity supports Thrasher's (1963) emphasis on age, sex, ethnicity, and territory as markers for the ordered segmentation of slum culture. Suttles found that single-sex, age-graded primary groups of the same ethnicity and territory emerged in response to threats of conflict and community-wide disorder and mistrust. Although the community subcultures Suttles discovered were provincial, tentative, and incomplete (Kornhauser 1978, 18), they nonetheless undermined societal values against delinquency and violence. Similarly, Anderson's (1978) ethnography of a bar in Chicago's South-side black ghetto shows how primary values coexisted alongside residual values associated with deviant subcultures (e.g., hoodlums), such as "toughness," "getting big money," "going for bad," and "having fun" (1978, 129–30; 152–58). In Anderson's analysis, lower-class residents do not so much "stretch" mainstream values as "create their own particular standards of social conduct along variant lines open to them" (1978, 210). In this context the use of violence is not valued as a primary goal but is nonetheless expected and tolerated as a fact of life (1978, 134). Much like Rainwater (1970), Suttles (1968), and Horowitz (1987), Anderson suggests that in certain community contexts the wider cultural values are simply not relevant—they become "unviable."

Whether community subcultures are authentic or merely "shadow cultures" (Liebow 1967) cannot be resolved here (see also Kornhauser 1978). But that seems less important than acknowledging that community contexts seem to shape what can be termed *cognitive landscapes* or ecologically structured norms (e.g., normative ecologies) regarding appropriate standards and expectations of conduct. That is, in structurally disorganized slum communities it appears that a system of values emerges in which crime, disorder, and drug use are less than fervently condemned and hence expected as part of everyday life. These ecologically structured social perceptions and tolerances in turn appear to influence the probability of criminal outcomes and harmful deviant behavior (e.g., drug use by pregnant women). In this regard Kornhauser's attack on subcultural theories misses the point. By attempting to assess whether subcultural values are authentic in some deep, almost quasi-religious sense (1978, 1–20), she loses sight of the processes by which cognitive landscapes rooted in social ecology may influence everyday behavior. Indeed, the idea that dominant values become existentially irrelevant in certain community contexts is a powerful one, albeit one that has not had the research exploitation it deserves (cf. Katz 1988).

A renewed appreciation for the role of cultural adaptations is congruent with the notion of *social isolation*—defined as the lack of contact or of sustained interaction with individuals and institutions that represent mainstream society (W. J. Wilson 1987, 60). According to this line of reasoning, the social isolation fostered by the ecological concentration of urban poverty deprives residents not only of resources and conventional role models, but also of cultural learning from mainstream social networks that facilitate social and economic advancement in modern industrial society (W. J. Wilson 1991). Social isolation is specifically distinguished from the culture of poverty by virtue of its focus on adaptations to constraints and opportunities rather than internalization of norms.

As Ulf Hannerz noted in his seminal work *Soulside*, it is thus possible to recognize the importance of macrostructural constraints—that is, avoid the extreme notions of the culture of poverty or culture of violence, and yet see the "merits of a more subtle kind of cultural analysis" (1969, 182). One could hypothesize a difference, on the one hand, between a jobless family whose mobility is impeded by the macrostructural constraints in the economy and the larger society but nonetheless lives in an area with a relatively low rate of poverty, and on the other hand, a jobless family that lives in an inner-city ghetto neighborhood that is influenced not only by these same constraints but also by the behavior of other jobless families in the neighborhood (Hannerz 1969, 184; W. J. Wilson 1991). The latter influence is one of culture—the extent to which individuals follow their inclinations as they have been developed by learning or influence from other members of the community (Hannerz 1969).

Ghetto-specific practices such as an overt emphasis on sexuality and macho values, idleness, and public drinking are often denounced by those who reside in inner-city ghetto neighborhoods. But because such practices occur much more frequently there than in middle-class society, largely because of social organizational forces, the transmission of these modes of behavior by precept, as in role modeling, is more easily facilitated (Hannerz 1969). For example, youngsters are more likely to see violence as a way of life in inner-city ghetto neighborhoods. They are more likely to witness violent acts, to be taught to be violent by exhortation, and to have role models who do not adequately control their own violent impulses or restrain their own anger. Accordingly, given the availability of and easy access to firearms, knives, and other weapons, adolescent experiments with macho behavior often have deadly consequences (Prothrow-Stith 1991).

The concept of social isolation captures this process by implying that contact between groups of different class and/or racial backgrounds either is lacking or has become increasingly intermittent, and that the nature of this contact enhances effects of living in a highly concentrated poverty area. Unlike the concept of the culture of violence, then, social isolation does not mean that ghetto-specific practices become internalized, take on a life of their own, and therefore continue to influence behavior no matter what the contextual environment. Rather, it suggests that reducing structural inequality would not only decrease the frequency of these practices; it would also make their transmission by precept less efficient. So in this sense we advocate a renewed appreciation for the ecology of culture, but not the monolithic and hence noncontextual culture implied by the subculture of poverty and violence.

Discussion

Rejecting both the "individualistic" and "materialist" fallacies, we have attempted to delineate a theoretical strategy that incorporates both structural and cultural arguments regarding race, crime, and urban inequality in American cities. Drawing on insights from social-disorganization theory and recent research on urban poverty, we believe this strategy provides new ways of thinking about race and crime. First and foremost, our perspective views the link between race and crime through contextual lenses that highlight the very different ecological contexts in which blacks and whites reside—regardless of individual characteristics. Second, we emphasize that crime rates among blacks nonetheless vary by ecological characteristics, just as they do for whites. Taken together, these facts suggest a powerful role for community context in explaining race and crime.

Our community-level explanation also departs from conventional wisdom. Rather than attributing to acts of crime a purely economic motive springing from relative deprivation—an individual-level psychological concept—we focus on the mediating dimensions of community social organization to understand variations in crime across areas. Moreover, we acknowledge and try to specify the macrosocial forces that contribute to the social organization of local communities. Implicit in this attempt is the incorporation of the political economy of place and the role of urban inequality in generating racial differences in community structure. As Wacquant observes, American urban poverty is "preeminently a *racial poverty* ... rooted in the *ghetto* as a historically specific social form and mechanism of racial domination" (1991, 36, emphasis in original). This intersection of race, place, and poverty goes to the heart of our theoretical concerns with societal and community organization.

Furthermore, we incorporate culture into our theory in the form of social isolation and ecological landscapes that shape perceptions and cultural patterns of learning. This culture is not seen as inevitably tied to race, but more to the varying structural contexts produced by residential and macroeconomic change, concentrated poverty, family instability, and intervening patterns of social disorganization. Perhaps controversially, then, we differ from the recent wave of structuralist research on the culture of violence (for a review see Sampson and Lauritsen 1994). In an interesting methodological sleight of hand, scholars have dismissed the relevance of culture based on the analysis of census data that provide no measures of culture whatsoever (see especially Blau and Blau 1982). We believe structural criminologists have too quickly dismissed the role of values, norms, and learning as they interact with concentrated poverty and social isolation. In our view, macrosocial patterns of residential inequality give rise to the social isolation and concentration of the truly disadvantaged, engendering cultural adaptations that undermine social organization.

Finally, our conceptualization suggests that the roots of urban violence among today's 15- to 21 year-old cohort may stem from childhood socialization that took place in the late 1970s and early 1980s. Consider that this cohort was born between 1970 and 1976 and spent its childhood in the context of a rapidly changing urban environment unlike that of any previous point in U.S. history. As documented in detail by W. J. Wilson (1987), the concentration of urban poverty and other social dislocations began increasing sharply in about 1970 and continued unabated through the decade and into the 1980s. As but one example, the proportion of black families headed by women increased by over 50 percent from 1970 to 1984 alone (W. J. Wilson 1987, 26). Large increases were also seen in the ecological concentration of ghetto poverty, racial segregation, population turnover, and joblessness. These social dislocations were, by comparison, relatively stable in earlier decades. Therefore, the logic of our theoretical model suggests that the profound changes in the urban structure of minority communities in the 1970s may hold the key to understanding recent increases in violence.

Conclusion

By recasting traditional race and poverty arguments in a contextual framework that incorporates both structural and cultural concepts, we seek to generate empirical and theoretical ideas that may guide further research. The unique value of a community-level perspective is that it leads away from a simple "kinds of people" analysis to a focus on how social characteristics of collectivities foster violence. On the basis of our theoretical framework, we conclude that community-level factors such as the *ecological concentration of ghetto poverty, racial segregation, residential mobility* and population turnover, *family disruption*, and the dimensions of local *social organization* (e.g., density of friendship/acquaintanceship, social resources, intergenerational links, control of street-corner peer groups, organizational participation) are fruitful areas of future inquiry, especially as they are affected by macrolevel public policies regarding housing, municipal services, and employment. In other words, our framework suggests the need to take a renewed look at social policies that focus on prevention. We do not need more after-the-fact (reactive) approaches that ignore the structural context of crime and the social organization of inner cities.

References

Anderson, E. (1978). *A place in the corner*. Chicago: University of Chicago Press.

Anderson, E. (1990). *Streetwise: Race, class and change in an urban community*. Chicago: University of Chicago Press.

Bickford, A., & Massey, D. (1991). Segregation in the second ghetto: racial and ethnic segregation in American public housing, 1977. *Social Forces, 69*, 1011–1036.

Blau, J. R., & Blau, P. M. (1982). The cost of inequality: Metropolitan structure and violent crime. *American Sociological Review, 47*, 114–129.

Bursik, R. J., Jr. (1988). Social disorganization and theories of crime and delinquency: Conflict and consensus. In S. Messner, M. Krohn, & A. Liska (Eds.), *Theoretical integration in the study of deviance and crime*. Albany, NY: State University of New York Press.

Byrne, J., & Sampson, R. J. (1986). Key issues in the social ecology of crime. In J. Byrne & R. J. Sampson (Eds.), *The social ecology of crime*. New York: Springer-Verlag.

Daley, S., & Mieslin, R. (1988). New York City, the landlord: A decade of housing decay. *New York Times*, February 8.

Fingerhut, L. A., & Kleinman, J. C. (1990). International and interstate comparisons if homicide among young males. *Journal of the American Medical Association, 263*, 3292–3295.

Fingerhut, L. A., Kleinman, J., Godfrey, E., & Rosenberg, H. (1991). Firearms mortality among children, youth, and young adults, 1–34 years if age, trends and current status: United states, 1979–88. *Monthly Vital Statistics Report, 39*, 11, 1–16.

Hagedorn, J. (1988). *People and folks: Gangs, crime and the underclass in a rustbelt city*. Chicago: Lake View Press.

Hannerz, U. (1969). *Soulside: Inquiries into ghetto culture and community*. New York: Columbia University Press.

Hawkins, D. (Ed.). (1986). Homicide among Black Americans. Lanham, MD: University Press of America.

Hindelang, M. J. (1976). *Criminal victimization in eight American cities*. Cambridge, MA: Ballinger.

Hindelang, M. J. (1978). Race and involvement in common law personal crimes. *American Sociological Review, 43*, 93–109.

Hinds, M. (1990). Number of killings soars in big cities across U.S. *New York Times*, July 18, 1.

Hirsch, A. (1983). *Making the second ghetto: Race and housing in Chicago*, 1940–1960. Chicago: University of Chicago Press.

Horowitz, R. (1987). Community tolerance of gang violence. *Social Problems, 34*, 437–450.

James, G. (1991). New York killings set record in 1990. *New York Times*, A14.

Jencks, C. (1991). Is violent crime increasing? *The American Prospect, Winter*, 98–109.

Jonassen, C. (1949). A reevaluation and critique of the logic and some methods of Shaw and McKay. *American Sociological Review, 14*, 608–614.

Kasarda, J., & Janowitz, M. (1974). Community attachment in mass society. *American Sociological Review*, 39, 328–339.

Katz, J. (1988). *Seductions of crime: The sensual and moral attractions of doing evil*. New York: Basic Books.

Kornhauser, R. (1978). *Social sources of delinquency*. Chicago: University of Chicago Press.

Land, K., McCall, P., & Cohen, L. (1990). Structural covariates of homicide rates: Are there any invariances across time and space? *American Journal of Sociology*, 95, 922–963.

Leighton, B. (1988). The community concept in criminology: Toward a social network approach. *Journal of Research in Crime and Delinquency, 25*, 351–374.

Liebow, E. (1967). *Tally's corner*. Boston: Little, Brown.

Logan, J., & Molotch, H. (1987). *Urban fortunes: The political economy of place*. Berkeley: University of California Press.

McCord, M., & Freeman, H. (1990). Excess mortality in Harlem. *New England Journal of Medicine, 322*, 173–175.

Mauer, M. (1990). *Young Black men and the criminal justice system: A growing national problem*. Washington, DC: The Sentencing Project.

Merton, R. (1938). Social structure and anomie. *American Sociological Review, 3*, 672–682.

Messner, S., & Sampson, R. (1991). The sex ratio, family disruption, and the rates of violent crime: The paradox of demographic structure. *Social Forces, 69*, 693–714.

Prothrow-Stith, D. (1991). *Deadly consequences.* New York: Harper Collins.

Rainwater, L. (1970). *Behind ghetto walls: Black families in a federal slum.* Chicago: Aldine.

Recktenwald, W., & Morrison, B. (1990). *Guns, gangs, drugs make a deadly combination.* Chicago Tribune, July 1, Section 2, 1.

Reiss, A. J., Jr. (1986). Why are communities important in understanding crime? In A. J. Reiss, Jr., & M. Tonry (Eds.), *Communities and crime.* Chicago: University of Chicago Press.

Sampson, R. J. (1987). Urban Black violence: The effect of male joblessness and family disruption. *American Journal of Sociology, 93,* 348–382.

Sampson, R. J. (1990). The impact of housing policies on community social disorganization and crime. *Bulletin of the New York Academy of Medicine, 66,* 526–533.

Sampson, R. J. (1991). Linking the micro and macrolevel dimensions of community social organization. *Social Forces, 70,* 43–64.

Sampson, R. J., & Groves, W. B. (1989). Community structure and crime: Testing social-disorganization theory. *American Journal of Sociology, 94,* 774–802.

Sampson, R. J., & Lauritsen, J. (1994). Violent victimization and offending: Individual, situational, and community-level risk factors. In A. J. Reiss, Jr., & J. Roth (Eds.), *Understanding and preventing violence: Social Influences, Vol. 3,* Committee on Law and Justice, National Research Council. Washington, DC: National Academy Press.

Shaw, C., & McKay, H. (1942). *Juvenile delinquency and urban areas.* Chicago: University of Chicago Press.

Shaw, C., & McKay, H. (1969). *Juvenile delinquency and urban areas (rev. ed.).* Chicago: University of Chicago Press.

Short, J. F., Jr. (1985). The level of explanation problem in criminology. In R. Meir (Ed.), *Theoretical methods in criminology.* Beverly Hills: Sage Publications.

Short, J. F., Jr., & Strodtbeck, F. L. (1965). *Group process and gang delinquency.* Chicago: University of Chicago Press.

Skogan, W. (1986). Fear of crime and neighborhood change. In A. J. Reiss, Jr., & M. Tonry. (Eds.), *Communities and crime.* Chicago: University of Chicago Press.

Stark, E. (1990). The myth of Black violence. *New York Times,* July 18, A21.

Sullivan, M. (1989). *Getting paid: Youth crime and work in the inner city.* Ithaca, NY: Cornell University Press.

Suttles, G. (1968). *The social order of the slum.* Chicago: University of Chicago Press.

Taylor, R., Gottfredson, S., & Brower, S. (1984). *Black crime and fear: Defensible space, local social ties, and territorial functioning.* Journal of Research and Crime and Delinquency, 21, 303–331.

Taylor, R., & Covington, J. (1988). Neighborhood changes in ecology and violence. *Criminology, 26,* 553–590.

Thrasher, F. (1963). *The gang: A study of 1,313 gangs in Chicago (rev. ed.).* Chicago: University of Chicago Press.

U.S. Department of Justice. (1985). *The risk of violent crime.* Washington, DC: Government Printing Office.

Wacquant, L. (1991). *The specificity of ghetto poverty: A comparative analysis of race, class, and urban exclusion in Chicago's Black belt and the Parisian Red Belt.* Paper presented at the Chicago Urban Poverty and Family Life Conference, University of Chicago.

Wallace, R., & Wallace, D. (1990). *Origins of public health collapse in New York City: The dynamics of planned shrinkage, contagious urban decay and social disintegration.* Bulletin of the New York Academy of Medicine, 66, 391–434.

Wilbanks, W. (1986). Criminal homicide offenders in the U.S. In D. Hawkins (Ed.), *Homicide among Black Americans.* Lanham, MD: University Press of America.

Wilson, W. J. (1987). *The truly disadvantaged: The inner city, the underclass, and public policy.* Chicago: University of Chicago Press.

Wilson, W. J. (1991). Studying inner city social dislocations: The challenge of public agenda research. *American Sociological Review, 56,* 1–14.

Wilson, W. J., & Aponte, R., Kirschenman, J., & Wacquant, L. (1988). The ghetto underclass and the changing structure of American poverty. In F. Harris & R. Wilkins (Eds.), *Quiet riots: Race and poverty in the United States.* New York: Pantheon.

Wolfgang, M., & Ferracuti, F. (1967). *The subculture of violence.* London: Tavistock.

Post-Reading Questions

1   In your estimate, what is it about diverse community structures and cultures that produce differential rates of crime?

2   What are some basic differences between individualistic and materialist fallacies of crime?

3   What have been some of the barriers researchers encounter in the sociological study of race and violent crime? How did Shaw and McKay's community-level approach help overcome these barriers?

4   Why did the authors focus on geographic and community structures over cultural influence in the study of race and crime?

5   What factors seem to account for the higher violent crime rates among Blacks in the inner city? Why do general economic downturns hit these inner city areas harder than suburban or rural environments?

Rethinking Subculture and Subcultural Theory in the Study of Youth Crime—A Theoretical Discourse

Chijioke J. Nwalozie

Meaning of Subculture(s)

One of the assumptions about "subculture" is the lower, subordinate, or deviant status of social groups labelled as such. These labelled groupings are distinguished by their class, ethnicity, language, poor and working class situations (Cutler, 2006); age or generation (Maira, 1999). These cultural and socio-structural variables make subcultures relatively homogeneous (Epstein, 2002). That is to say, subcultures must bear specific and similar cultural identities to qualify for the name, and they must also be particular to certain societies that labelled them as such. In most cases reference must be made to the Anglo/American youth subcultures, which dominated the whole idea of subculture and subcultural theory for many decades.

Phil Cohen (1972:23), one of the most influential British subcultural scholars describes subculture (s):

> as so many variations on a central theme—the contradiction, at an
> ideological level, between traditional working class Puritanism,
> and the new hedonism of consumption; at an economic level,
> between the future as part of the socially mobile elite, or as
> part of the new lumpen. Mods, Parkers, Skinheads, Crombies, all
> represent, in their different ways, an attempt to retrieve some

of the socially cohesive elements destroyed in their parent culture, and to combine these with elements selected from other class fractions.

Cohen has clearly indicated that subculture has many varied ways of describing it, which seem contradictory. Irrespective of all these different patterns, the overriding principle is the struggle of the membership to aim at solving the problem created by the dominant culture, which apparently has been considered the main object of subcultural formation. As Newburn (2013) argues, the emergence of subculture is not just to respond to human material conditions, but far beyond that, they also represent a symbolic appraisal of the parent culture in which "style" was considered a form of resistance. Similarly, Jones (2013) stresses that the subcultural activity of youths is a manifesatation of political reaction to the dominant culture from which such youths consided themselves excluded.

Since the 1990s, the term subculture has been used in a much broader perspective to explain any group of people who adjust to norms of behaviour, values, beliefs, consumption patterns, and lifestyle choices that are distinct from those of the dominant mainstream culture (Cutler, 2006). According to Gelder (2005: 1):

> Subcultures are groups of people that are in some way represented as non-normative and/or marginal through their particular interests and practices, through what they are, what they do, and where they do it. They may represent themselves in this way; since subcultures are usually aware of their differences, bemoaning them, relishing them, exploiting them, and so on. But they will also be represented like this by others, who in response can bring an entire apparatus of social classification and regulation to bear upon them.

Gelder's definition takes into account the distinctiveness between the groups themselves on the one hand; and mainstream society on the other. The groups feel marginalized because of their life situation, hence they decide to exhibit negative behaviour. Gelder also reveals how the entire society views these groups, and especially the way they categorize and isolate them as "subcultures". Yet subcultures share elements of the main culture, while at the same time different from it (Brake, 1987: 6).

In the generic sense, the term subculture could be applied to any group of individuals whose behaviour differs from the rest of society. For example, we hear about occupational subculture (Trice, 1993; Downes, 1966; Brake, 1985); religious subculture (Gay & Ellison, 1993); consumer subculture (Schouten & Mcalexander, 1995); drug subculture (Cutler, 2006; Cohen & Sas, 1994), immigrant subculture (Brake, 1987); internet or cybercrime subculture (Adeniran, 2008; Kahn & Kellner, 2006), police subculture (Waddington, 1999; Blumenstein et al, 2012), and so on. This wider description of subculture has come to the attention of some scholars (Weinzierl &

Muggleton, 2006; Cutler, 2006) who query its utility, hence their call for a reconceptualisation or replacement of the term. This new conceptualisation, it is argued, captures the changing sensibilities and practices of subcultural forms (Weinzierl & Muggleton, 2006) in relation to youth groups who are now being referred to as "channels or subchannels"; "temporary substream networks"; "neo-tribes" and "clubculture" (see Weinzierl & Muggleton, 2006).

While this reconceptualisation project does not receive the outright approval of scholars like Hodkinson (2002), it is apparent that some of these confusions can be clarified once there is a recognition that different concepts are often used to abstract varied aspects of social reality, and that they can be used interchangeably with subculture to refer to a variety of youth cultural formations (see Weinzierl & Muggleton, 2006), that may have either a criminal or non-criminal connotation. A criminal group of youths is indicative of criminal subculture, which bears on the dominant culture. Therefore, a reconceptualised idea of subculture must have "relative distinctiveness", provide a sense of "identity", a level of "commitment", and the relative "autonomy" to operate (see Hall & Jefferson, 2006; Hodkinson, 2002).

Evolution of Subcultural Theory and Theorists

Subcultural theory and theorists have a unique Western origin. For more than half a century, subcultural theory has increasingly influenced the study of youth crime (Young, 2010). In doing so, it has developed two waves on the two sides of the Atlantic—a liberal or structural-functionalist American current of the 1950s and 1960s; and a Marxist British version of the late 1970s (see Young, 2010; Newburn, 2007; Blackman, 2005). The former started at the Chicago School, while the latter originated from the Birmingham Centre for Contemporary Cultural Studies, University of Birmingham (CCCS) (see Young, 2010).

In 1892, the University of Chicago decided to establish a Department of Sociology, with Albion Small as its founding head. Since then the School has had a great influence on criminological thought (Newburn, 2013). By the 1930s, the Department was already actively vibrant in ethnographic studies. Eminent scholars like Walter Recless, Fredrick Trasher, Everett Hughes, Robert Park, Edwin Sutherland, Clifford Shaw, Henry Mckay, Louis Wirth and Gerald Suttles engaged in the study of immigrant and minority communities, the city's entire population and their criminal behaviours (Newburn, 2013). These scholars came to a conclusion that crime is necessarily a social problem rather than an individual pathological issue (Lilly et al, 2011). As Short (2002) admits, the best Chicago legacy to criminology which has evolved, is still evolving, and hopefully will continue to evolve is the project on Human Development in Chicago Neighbourhoods, which has led to the study of different aspects of crime and delinquency affecting the area, not excluding the youth groups who may come together to form subculture(s).

The Chicago School first used the concept "subculture" in their explanation of delinquency (see for example Cohen, 1955; Miller, 1958; Cloward & Ohlin, 1960). Cohen (1955) went as far as developing Merton's anomic propositions in his seminal work, *Delinquent Boys*. He argued that a large group of male adolescents had developed a culture, with its norms, values, and expectations contrary to the dominant culture. This subculture emerged when youths from lower socio-economic status families struggled to achieve success. When compared to youths from middle class society, those from the lower class had disadvantaged academic backgrounds. Their inability to achieve success brought about their involvement in a subculture where they could find success and status enhancement. So, this subculture refused middle class values such as academic achievement, courtesy and delayed gratification (see also Nihart et al, 2005). Cohen concludes that this delinquent subculture is "non-utilitarian", "malicious" and "negativistic" (Cohen, 1955: 25) because it is used by status-frustrated youths as a hit-back mechanism (Macdonald, 2001: 33). Therefore, from the point of view of the youths themselves, their conduct is to be considered as meaningful (see Clubb, 2001).

Miller (1958) further developed the work of Cohen by identifying what he refers to as "focal concerns" of the lower class culture. He uses "focal concerns" in preference to "value"; and they include: trouble, toughness, smartness, excitement, fate and autonomy. Apparently, the "focal concerns" are a reflection of working class traditions rather than working class frustrations (see also Macdonald, 2001: 34). For Miller, middle-class norms and values are not subculturally relevant. What is relevant, he argues, is that members of the subculture conform to the distinctive value system of their own working class culture (see also Macdonald, 2001: 33). This implies that people's circumstances in life may push them to adopt certain measures or patterns of behaviour, which may be beneficial or not. Miller put this question: why is the commission of crimes a customary feature of gangs? His answer is: street youths are motivated to commit crime by the desire to achieve ends, status, or conditions which are valued, and to avoid those that are disvalued within their most meaningful cultural milieu, through those culturally available avenues which appear as the most feasible means of achieving those ends (Miller, 1958: 17).

Cloward and Ohlin (1960) improved on the groundwork established by both Cohen and Miller, namely the kind of environment that gave rise to delinquent youths (see also Nihart et al, 2005). As Cloward and Ohlin (1960: 86) maintain, adolescents who form delinquent subcultures, have internalized an emphasis upon conformist goals. Drawing on Merton's (1938) anomie-strain theory and Shaw and Mckay's (1942) social disorganisation theory, Cloward and Ohlin argued that lower class boys were faced with inadequacies of lawful avenues of access to these goals and unable to revise their ambitions downward, they experienced severe disappointments, hence their involvement in higher levels of delinquency than middle and upper class youths (see also Nihart et al, 2005). Thus, unfavourable and disappointing expectation in life could determine delinquent behaviour as a viable option. Finally, Cloward and Ohlin outlined three typologies of deviant subculture namely: criminal, conflict, and retreatist.

British subcultural studies which flourished in the 1970s, was mostly pioneered by the CCCS, which earlier started in 1964, with the appointment of Richard Hoggart as its founding Director. Hoggart's influential work, *The Uses of Literacy* (1957) and Raymond William's work, *Culture and*

Society (1958) became the foundational texts for British subcultural studies (Newburn, 2013). This year marks the 50th anniversary of the CCCS 1964–2014, and all this while, the CCCS has been fully involved in the study of popular culture and its impact on society. Like the Chicago School, the early Birmingham School focused on the link between the "deviant" sensibilities of youth "gangs" and the localities from which such gangs emerged (Bennett, 1999). Ecological studies of various parts of post-war Britain[1] found poverty as the main cause of delinquency, especially when combined with the absence of the father figure. In the 1950s, the absent or working mother came in for criticism. Child-rearing practices were compared, and working class life was seen as divided into "the rough" and "the respectable". Delinquency was found to have local traditions and values in underprivileged areas of Liverpool and London (see Brake, 1987: 59). An extreme situation was such that the so called "respectable" working class had no other option than to accept minor office jobs. This was because the working class became polarised following the replacement of the traditional skilled work with automation and machinery (Jones, 2013).

With the publication of the CCCS research, British studies of youth culture experienced two fundamental changes. Firstly, emphasis shifted from the study of youth gangs to style-based youth cultures, such as Teddy boys, Mods, Rockers and Skinheads, which from the 1950s onwards rapidly became an essential feature of everyday British social life. Secondly, in keeping with the central hypothesis of the CCCS, as noted above, the "local" focus of earlier youth studies was given up completely in favour of a subcultural model of explanation (Bennett, 1999). The initial Chicago School's premise that subcultures are critical to an understanding of deviance as normal behaviour in the face of particular social circumstances was reworked by the Birmingham School in their most influential work, *Resistance Through Rituals (1976)*, to account for the style-centred youth cultures of post-war Britain. According to the CCCS, the deviant behaviour of such youth "subcultures" had to be understood as the collective reaction of youths themselves, or rather working-class youths, to structural changes taking place in British post-war society (Bennett, 1999).

In his assessment of the two subcultural waves mentioned above, Cohen (1980: vi) said: "Both work with the same "problematic" ... growing up in a class society; both identify the same vulnerable group: the urban male working-class late adolescents; both see delinquency as a collective solution to a structurally imposed problem" in the polity. These subcultures are known for their cultural identities (such as common language, code of dressing, and music) shared by popular subcultural groups like Teddy boys, Punks, and Hip hops. These cultural identities mark them out and distinguish them from any other group or groups. Such identities present what their behaviours look like among their memberships, which they exhibit with interest and at times frustrations. Their behaviours may be criminal and noncriminal, but apparently criminal behaviours are easily identifiable among youth subcultures. It is on this note that subcultural theorists have always insisted that they are better placed to explain criminal behaviour (Blackman, 2005), and no study of youth delinquency can easily be undertaken without recourse to many of their insights (Newburn, 2007). This is because subcultural theorists tend to consider the general nature of delinquency with an emphasis on youth gangs and groups instead of the individual deviant (Newburn, 2007). Thus, they place the group in the context of the entire society (see Young, 2010).

Delinquency is not about something individualistic, but refers to "gangs of boys doing things together, their actions deriving their meaning and flavour from the fact of togetherness and governed by a set of common understanding, common sentiments and common loyalties" (Cohen 1955: 178 cited in Gelder, 2005: 21). To be involved in group delinquency also implies that the individual takes delight and relief in the protective and sympathetic comfort of the group as he shares his experience of facing common tasks with them (Walsh, 1986). It is usually the group's decision to get involved in crime, and acts in like manner. Even though the boundaries may not be well defined and the membership not specified nor does the degree of commitment, yet the subculture constitutes a definitive human association for those involved in it. It does not only involve a group of people but also a network of symbols, meaning and knowledge, which are linked with style that emerge in the day-to-day dynamics of criminal events and criminal subcultures (Ferrell, 1995).

In subcultural theory, deviant subcultures are construed not as pathological groupings of maladjusted people deficient of culture, instead they are understood as meaningful attempts to resolve problems faced by the people concerned (Young, 2010; see also Brake, 1985). As Cohen (1955) argues, all human action, not excluding delinquency, is an ongoing process of problem solving. Such problems may be located in the political, cultural, social and economic structures of mainstream society. Any attempt not to solve these problems is normally resisted, even with impunity, by the subcultural group involved.

Wolfgang and Ferracuti (1967) dealt with the issue of subculture in their seminal work, *Subculture of Violence*. They argue that the subculture is secluded and opposed to the dominant group due to the latter's shared values which its members have learnt and adopted overtime. Such values create total disintegration and at times open aggression against the dominant group. It is also their view that violent crimes such as homicide, rape, robbery, and aggravated assault emanate from the subculture overpopulated by male youths (1967: 298).

Contemporary criminologists have invoked the principles of subcultural theorisation in their various studies of youth offending, including armed robbery. For example, Jacobs and Wright (1999) interviewed 86 active armed robbers in St Louis Missouri (USA), on the impact of "street culture" on an offender's decision to engage in armed robbery. They conclude that "street culture subsumes a number of powerful conduct norms, including but not limited to the hedonistic pursuit of sensory stimulation, disdain for conventional living, lack of future orientation, and persistent eschewal of responsibility" (Jacobs & Wright, 1999: 165).

Anderson's (1994) most influential work, *Code of the Street*, reveals a somewhat disparity existing between two opposing camps. First, there is the inner city poor black American youths who get involved in criminal activities like mugging, robbery and so on, through formation of street codes as their moral guide for agressive and violent criminal behaviour. Although Anderson did not refer to them as "subculture" but it is implicit, given their way of life. Reocurring variables in society such as social injustice, poverty and inequality may have motivated these youths to create their own group independent of the mainstream community. Anderson (1994) talks about another group known as "decent family" who are middle class oriented, and aligned to mainstream society. He argues that while families with a decency orientation are normally opposed to the values of the street code; they often reluctantly encourage their children's familiarity with it to enable them negotiate the inner-city environment. This largely helps to prevent violent clashes between the two competing camps.

Anderson's (1994) street youths have their code of dressing and manner of behaviour which make them quite distinct from the rest of society. They see themselves as victims of the larger society and so exhibit a differential attitude to law enforcement agencies and mainstream culture because they feel nothing is being done to support them in alleviatiating their social problems. It is this aversion to the norms of mainstream society that makes them a deviant subculture. In essence, criminal behaviour is often predicated on subcultural behaviour (Ferrell, 1995; 1999). However, not all subcultures are deviant or criminal-oriented. For example, Cohen & Sas (1994) in their study of cocaine use in Amsterdam identified a large pool of experienced community based cocaine users as non-deviant, as opposed to treatment clients, prison inmates, or prostitutes.

Criticisms of Subculture and Subcultural Theory

To begin with, the notion of subculture has never really been adequately defined. Even when definitions are attempted, they are generically driven and without any connection with youth delinquency, which the concept purports to be addressing. As Bennett (1999: 599) stresses, "the problems of using 'subculture' is that it has sometimes been applied inexactly, becoming little more than a convenient 'catch-all' term for any aspect of social life in which young people, style and music intersect". It is little wonder that "subculture" has been used as an ad hoc concept whenever a writer wishes to emphasize the normative aspects of behaviour contrary to some general standard. The result has been a blurring of the meaning of the term, confusion with other terms, and a failure frequently to distinguish between two levels of social causation (see Yinger, 1960: 625–6 cited in Jenks, 2005: 7). Arguably, though, the random use of the term "subculture" to apply to those who live oppositional to the mainstream society as those who have no positive ideals to pursue, makes them all the more isolated from the larger society. On this view, their marginalization is simply intensified by their designation as a "subculture" (Jenks, 2005: 130), which becomes a sort of "label" on the group. Yet subcultural theory is obviously different from labelling theory.

Subcultural theory fails to clearly distinguish between "subcultures" and "gangs". Every so often, it tries to merge the two together in the name of studying deviant criminal groups. For example, Walsh (1986: 19) makes this merger by arguing that the concept of "gang" and "subculture" are conventionally used to explain the cultural enclave in which the apprenticeship process occurs, stressing group support, both physical and in the sense of shared guilt or blame after events. In doing so, he begs the question about the authenticity of the so-called "subcultures". It is important to stress that both concepts are different in every respect. Gangs are informally-structured "near groups" made up of a closely connected core with a looser network of peripheral members; whereas subcultures are the cluster of actions, values, style, imagery and lifestyles which through media reportage, extend beyond a neighbourhood to form a complex relationship with other larger cultures to form a symbolic pseudo-community (Brake, 1987). This distinction is obviously important if we are to avoid the misrepresentation of subculture as almost anything any person may conjecture. Otherwise, looking at the formal and substantive elements of "subculture", if the term were to be introduced for the first time now, it would be dismissed as inadequate (Clark 1974 cited in Brake, 1987) in the sense that every group may be regarded as subculture.

The subcultural approach is notoriously "overly deterministic" in its emphasis on the "peer group" or "gangs" or rather "group criminality"; but it tends to be silent about the place of "personal choice" and "free will" in criminal behaviour (Clubb, 2001). Being in a subculture or gang makes delinquent activity more likely by actively promoting it, nevertheless, this does not make deviant behaviour obligatory. Crime can still be committed for personal reasons rather that as a group requirement (Clubb, 2001; Williams, 1997). Crime causation is a matter for the individual to deal with without much concern for the group (Clubb, 2001). This also has been a favourable argument for Merton's anomie theory. However, according to Sutherland and Cressey's differential association theory (1978), the values which encourage peers to commit crime are learnt alongside the techniques to commit crime. When peers behave contrary to the group, they break away from the group's solidarity. Group solidarity is a formidable and pivotal force as far as the subculture is concerned. Therefore, being overly deterministic is a subcultural "complacency" to perpetuate criminal behaviour among youths.

The claim of subcultural theorists to be better placed in the study of youth delinquency is overexaggerated, and indeed a monopolistic way of denying other theorists such as strain, control and labelling, their contribution to youth crime. Whereas subcultural theorists have a stake in explaining group delinquency, they are deficient in understanding individual criminality. Group criminality presupposes individual criminality, which may degenerate into peer delinquency in the form of a subculture.

Subcultural theorists claim that deviance could be better comprehended in social and political settings, but not as something drawn from biology or psychology (Newburn, 2007). In this connection, they visualise crime as something found around a people's culture; (see Ferrell, 1999), but at the same time dissociating themselves from the classical theorisation of criminal behaviour as something "inborn" in people. Thus, subcultural theorists seem to delve into argumentum petitio principii (argument in a circle), and so lack the ability of a convincing hypothesis.

The issue of a group's homogeneity makes subcultural formation utterly "selective" and strictly pro-western. Whereas it is utterly unnecessary to look for a homogeneous youth criminal population before grouping them into a subcultural form, but youths of different age brackets and multi-ethnic or multi-tribal backgrounds can still coalesce as a subculture to address what they perceive as youth problems in the polity. Considering this line of thought as somewhat credible, subcultures can then cut across national and continental frontiers so as to be better understood and defined appropriately.

There has been a consistent attack on subcultural theory for having only one vulnerable group of people in mind, that is urban male working class late adolescents (see for example Macdonald, 2001). This position of criminologists from both sides of the Atlantic has overdominated subcultural studies with a stereotype of the youthful offender. An all-important question is: why has a particular group of individuals remained the focus of subcultural theorists as those that can be associated with delinquency? Subcultural theorists should make a leap and extend their studies to various groups of youths in post-modern societies so as to understand the dynamics of youth delinquency. Criminologists from Africa, for example, must now rise to the challenge of creating their own school of subcultural studies instead of depending on the sort of "benchmark" set by both the Chicago and Birmingham Schools as a parameter for subcultural studies.

As part of that Western formulation, scholars (Redhead, 1990; Melechi, 1993; Miles, 1995; Malbond, 1998; Muggleton, 1997; Bennett, 2000) have argued that subcultures were created by subcultural theorists, not vice versa. That is to say, subcultural theorists determine what subcultures should necessarily represent. They label them with specific nomenclatures for easy identification. For instance, American theorists would answer the question about the delinquent by referring to the "delinquent subculture" involving coded honours based on "Rep" and the mobilisation of violence (Young, 2010). British theorists would talk about the Teds, Punks, Mods, and so on, by clearly defining their styles, thereby ignoring the lack of clarity of the actors involved (Young, 2010). In this sense, subcultural theory may be accused of being over-dominated by Western criminologists, and indeed so, especially American and British scholars, to an extent that any study of youth subcultures elsewhere must be influenced by studies from either or both countries. The danger is that subcultural theorists from both sides of the Atlantic end up glamorising delinquents by "popularising" them as Rep, Mods, Teds, Hip hops etc, with the end result that the criminal behaviours of youth subcultures are downplayed and accepted as part of the acclaimed "popular culture" where every behaviour is acceepted as part of the societal norm.

Subcultures are male-dominated so much so that an emphasis on "maleness" is seen as a panacea for an identity that has been weakened by structural features (Brake, 1987). Perhaps the invisibility of girls' subculture is because the very term "subculture" has right from the beginning, acquired such consistently masculine overtones (McRobbie and Garber, 2005). In this connection, men are regarded as more criminally-minded than women, hence the "absence of girls from the whole of literature in this area is quite striking and demands explanation" (McRobbie & Garber, 1976: 209), and very little seems to have been written about the involvement of girls in group delinquency (McRobbie and Garber, 2005); but whenever they are acknowledged in the literature, the focus tends to shift to their sexual attractiveness, thereby neglecting the holistic study of female group delinquency, which supposedly is a crucial element of research that can explore the gender divide in offending.

Subcultural theory has been accused of over-prediction with regard to delinquency. For example, among the poorest working class communities, crime is not ever-present in all individuals (see Newburn, 2007), yet subcultural theory makes a blanket assumption of criminalising everybody. In addition to that, critics maintain that subcultural theory is unnecessarily over-rational in an attempt to grant human actors a sense of making their history in a determinate world. Consequent to that is an unreflective bouncing off the conditions that beset such people (Young, 2010) hence the freedom to drift (Matza, 1964) into crime. For instance, the robber continues to rob, the alcoholic continues to drink and get drunk (see Young, 2010), so much so that a culture of crime is developed and animated.

The problem of subcultural theorisation is such that tends to split up a whole society when it talks about "deviants", perhaps suggesting there are also non-deviants. This makes the deviants to claim a moral high ground for their actions, but at the same time finding faults with the mainstream society. Arguably, for the deviant, the mainstream is seen as deviant; whereas for the mainstream, the subculture is the deviant. This war of words is aimed at criminalising either side which might end up breeding anger and dissention between the mainstream and the subculture. In the end it is still the deviant subculture that appears to bear the label "subculture". According to Jenks (2005: 129) "the idea of subculture can be employed to valorise the underdog, radicalize the dispossesed, give voice to the inarticulate but equally to marginalize and contain the deviant or non-mainstream".

If by subculture we are referring to the well-known theory of the 1950s and 1970s, then it might not be feasible to employ it in the explanation of youth crime in Africa where age, state of origin, tribe, and geo-political zone do not fit with the homogeneous nature of subculture. Although cultural identities may be crucial to any subcultural formation, they seem to have been overemphasized by the theory, thereby overshadowing the study of criminal behaviour of youth subcultures.

Even if subculture remains the best way to explain more unconventional aspects of youth culture, it does not seem to offer much help for an understanding of the wide range of youth groups in the post-modern world (Cutler, 2006). By that weakness, subcultural theory has probably now, "run its course" (Jenks 2005: 145), become "superfluous" and "no longer relevant" (Chaney 2004: 36) and fails to provide "a useful description of young people's social world or their experiences" (Karvonen et al, 2001: 393) in relation to crime. Therefore the concept requires a rethink in relation to youth crime.

Rethinking Subculture and Subcultural Theory: Is Post-subculture the Panacea?

Subculture has been considered a redundant conceptual framework (Bennett, 2011). However opinions vary as to the reason(s) for this, but a somewhat generally held opinion is that the cultural identities of youths had become more reflexive, fluid and fragmented as a result of an ever increasing flow of cultural commodities, images and texts through which more individualised identity projects and notions of self could be fashioned (Bennett, 2011). Implicitly, cultural identities of youths have the tendency of emerging from isolationism and specific grouping to an overarching youth groups who are not so much concerned with specified cultural identities. In short, what might resultantly happen is a subcultural transmigration, cutting across cultures and countries, thus making subcultural groups less homogeneous.

Rethinking subculture brings about a rebranding of the concept, which Readhead (1990) initiated in the post-subculture project; an idea that was later modernised by Muggleton (2000). This post-modern perspective was expected to fill the gap created by subcultural theory, and or even to make-up for its limitations. Accordingly, Weinzierl and Muggleton (2006) attempted to get rid of the whole theoretical apparatus of the CCCS and create a new framework for the analysis of contemporary subcultural phenomena. Post-subcultural theory then came about as a more vehement rejection of the "theoretical orthodoxies of the CCCS". It wanted an outright annihilation of previous conceptions of subculture, going so far as to argue that the term itself is no longer a useful description of the complex relationships between "post-subcultural formations" and the dominant culture with which they interact (Philpot, 2008).

Whereas post-subcultural theory seems to contribute much to the understanding of the cultural dynamics, which inform youth's everyday appropriation of music, style and associated objects, images and texts (Bennett, 2011), it is loose to proffer a unified set of alternative, analytical and empirical concepts for the study of youth culture. On its part, subculture can be discredited for adopting a naive and essentially celebratory standpoint concerning the role of the cultural industries in shaping the identities and lifestyle of youths (Bennett, 2011). Since subculture is deemed unfit, postsubculture becomes a mere transformation of subculture in name, which failed to transform an understanding of youth cultural life. Some scholars (Shildrick and MacDonald, 2006: 4) argue that empirically, post-subcultural studies tend to ignore the youth cultural lives and identities of less advantaged young people and that, theoretically, they aim at under-playing the potential significance of class and other social inequalities in contemporary youth culture. Any neglect or total rejection of these variables is detrimental to the proper understanding of the concepual framework—subculture.

Rethinking subculture and subcultural theory implies seeking alternative ways of using the concept and theory to address youth criminal activity globally. Rather than employ alternative terminologies such as post-subculture, which eventually became counter-productive and indeed repetitious of the classic subculture, a persuasive suggestion is that the useage of subculture and subcultural theory be widened to embrace a universal explanation of youth criminal life. The notion of globalization or rather the world being a "global village", coupled with modern technology, may have a major role to play here, in the sense that youths of nowadays are far more informed by the social media networks to behave in similar ways. When in 1964, Marshall Mcluhan, a renowned American Communications expert came up with the concept "global village", he envisaged or rather predicted the world's culture would sooner or later shrink or even expand as a result of a perverse technological savvy society, which may have exposed itself to instantaneous sharing of culture (Dixon, 2009). Since the Internet is the fastest mechanism for culture sharing, and of course, the Anglo-American societies also dominate the traffic; they also possess an overpowering influence on cultural identities, and tend to influence other societies aound the world. In his study of the Canadian youth culture, Brake (1985) argued that many of their cultural forms were "borrowed" rather than "authentic". For instance, the use of hip-hop by black Canadian youths from the Afro-American culture, or the borrowing of punk hairstyle from England by white youths. These identities are expressed through the use of clothing or the consumption of particular commodities rather than being substantively derived from aboriginal or class-based experiences. This can technically be described as hybridity which "... denotes a wide register of multiple identity, crossover, pick-'n'-mix, boundary-crossing experiences and styles", reflecting increased migration, mobility and global multiculturalism" (Pieterse, 2001: 221).

Youths who are likely to engage in culture hybridization, may not necessarily be affiliated to a specific or known subcultural group but have the proclivity making either a good or bad impression in the environment they find themselves. A closer look at events of the recent uprisings and revolutions that brought about regime changes in some parts of the world, especially the Arab Spring, shows they were ochestrated by youths of those countries, who though behaved deviantly and violently too, and could as well be regarded as subcultures. They were simply motivated by what they saw other youths within the region did to address their looming societal problems. This tends to affirm that the laten function of a subculture is to express and resolve, albeit "magically" the contradictions which appear in the parent culture (Cohen, 1972: 23). The summation is that youths in various societies are not immuned from behaving alike for the reason that culture contact or interaction may bring about culture influence and or change.

Admittedly, cultural differences still abound, but the concept and theory of subculture should be open to address all deviant youths (male and female alike) of different cultures and societies, for the reason that, as earlier mentioned, variables such as age, sex, and peer group are universally invariant in predicting crime (see also LaFree, 1998; Warr, 2006) and other forms of deviant behaviours. Therefore then, when a group of youths in any culture or nationality behave contrary to the conventional norms of that society, they should qualify for the name "subculture", whether or not they possess cultural identities. Even so, considering the global nature of society, cultural identities are becoming far more individualistic and seem to be loosing their specificity to a group; and may not say much about them because anybody can develop any type of identity, which may not necessarily infer that they belong to a subculture. For example, the "Mohican" hairstyle was mainly associated with members of the warlike tribe of the North American Indians, but later taken up by the "punk culture" in Britain, who were anti-establishment at the time. These punks appeared to contradict all the codes their parents believed in and grew up with.

Secondly, the "Skinheads" of the 1970s Britain, were associated with white supremacy and racism, but later metamorphosed into different "political subcultures" which tend to possess racist connotations, such as the National Front (NF) British National Party (BNP) and the English

Defence League (EDL). It is very striking that the styles exhibited by the punks and skinheads have become common fashion to some ordinary youths namely, Irish Travellers (Gypsies), Footballers, Artistes, children and others, in many parts of the world, including Africa. The ideology is just people wishing to have a hairstyle of their choice, and again the issue of individualism is under-scored. The solution to their problem is far more expressed via style rather than involvement in criminal activity; hence the style of each subculture involves the creation of identities and images built upon objects adopted or borrowed from other cultures and eras (Newburn, 2013). By identifying them as subculture helps to break barriers and broaden the concept so as to allow for inclusivity of youths from different parts of the world.

Conclusion

The American and British understanding of subculture and subcultural theory has weakened both the concept and theory in accounting for a wider youth criminal behaviour because it refers to a selection of western youths with specific cultural identities such as language, music and style. Moreover, the usefulness of subcultural theory in the explanation of youth crime requires thorough scrutiny, in the sense that, rather than place emphasis on the explanation of youth crime, theorists tend to be trapped in the promotion of popular culture and glamorization of youth criminal activity. It has earlier been noted that with little or no attention paid to female youth subculture, subcultural theory tries to exhibit its unviability to fully offer explanation for the involvement of both male and female youths in crime.

The selfish claim of subcultural dominance in the study of youth crime for most part of the twentieth century, makes other criminological theories unimportant and irrelevant. Its self-acclaimed position as a specialized theory for the explanation of criminal behaviour of youths makes it ambitiously egoistic and monopolistic.

However, the employment of "post-subculture" for a change has failed to bring about any improvement on subculture, rather it only established catch phrases which are not far from what is already known about subculture. It was thought that an ascent to post-subculture could solve the problem created by subculture but the difference that exists between both concepts remains vague. What is found to be clear is the rebranding from "subculture to post-subculture". The propounders of postsubcultural theory being disciples of the CCCS, still maintain the CCCS' understanding of subculture, which is the obvious "male urban working class youths of post-World War II Britain".

With that in mind, it is apparently that both subcultural and post-subcultural studies are in the same continuum, and as such, the obvious and inherent limitations of subcultural and post-subcultural theories call for a rethink, which would among other things champion the withdrawal from an over emphasis on specific cultural identies as found in the Anglo/American subcultures and focus more on a broader or rather holistic explanation of the criminal behaviour of both male and female youth subcultures in virtually other societies. That is to say, any behaviour of youths that is anti-mainstream society is to be regarded as subcultural behaviour.

Nevertheless, credit should be accorded both the Chicago School and the CCCS for their interest in the study of youth criminality in both sides of the Atlantic. Yet, both theories are seemingly unprepared to move further afield into the wider domain or rather global explanation of youth cultural life. Although no one theory may account for the global explanation of crime, but this paper makes the case that subcultural theory should demonstrate a somewhat inclusivity of other youths from other backgrounds and cultures. That is to say, with the globalization of youth culture, aided by the digital age, youth subcultures can emerge in varied styles, from any mainstream society, as a deviant or criminal group, who may not just be suffering from status fraustration as the Chicago School would claim, but far beyond that, who are poised to seeking answers to address their generational problems.

Note

1   Thanks to scholars like Mays (1954); Morris (1957); Kerr (1958) for conducting such studies.

References

Adeniran, A. I. (2008) 'The Internet and Emergence of Yahooboys Subculture in Nigeria'. International Journal of Cyber Criminology, 2, 2, 368–381.

Anderson, E. (1994) The Code of the Streets, The Atlantic Monthly, 273,(5), Research Library, 80–94.

Bennett, A. (1999) 'Subcultures or Neo-tribes? Rethinking the Relationship between Youth, Style and Musical Taste'. Sociology, 33, 3, 599–617.

Bennett, A. (2011)'The Post-subcultural Turn: Some Reflections 10 Years On'. Journal of Youth Studies, 14, 5, 493–506.

Bennett, A. (2000) Popular Music and Youth Culture: Music Identity and Place, London, Macmillan.

Blackman, S. (2005) 'Youth Subcultural Theory: A Critical Engagement with the Concept, its Origins and Politics, from the Chicago School to Postmodernism'. Journal of Youth Studies, 8, 1–20.

Blumenstein, L., Fridell, L. & Jones, S. (2012) 'The Link Between Traditional Police Subculture and Police Intimate Partner Violence', Policing: An International Journal of Police Strategies & Management, 35, (1), 147–164

Brake, M. (1985) Comparative Youth Culture: The Sociology of Youth Culture and Youth Subcultures in America, Britain and Canada, London, Routledge and Kegan Paul.

Chaney, D. (2004) 'Fragmented Culture and Subcultures'. In A. Bennett, & K. Khan-Harris. (Eds.), After Subculture, London, Palgrave.

Cloward, R. A. & Ohlin, L. E. (1960) Delinquency and Opportunity, New York, Free Press.

Clubb, S. (2001) What Do You Think is the Principal and Principal Weakness of Subcultural Theories? www.scottishlaw.org.uk.

Cohen, A. K. (1955) Delinquent Boys, New York, Free Press.

Cohen, P. (1972) "Subcultural Conflict and Working Class Community" in S. Hall, D. Hobson, A Lowe, and P. Willis (Eds.) Culture, Media, Language, London, Hutchinson.

Cohen, P. & Sas, A. (1994) 'Cocaine Use in Amsterdam in Non-Deviant Subcultures'. Addiction Reseaech, 2, 1, 71–79.

Cohen, S. (1980) Folk Devils and Moral Panics, London, Routledge.

Cutler, C. (2006) Subcultures and Counter Cultures, Stony Brook University, Stony Brook, New York.

Dixon, V.K. (2009) Understanding the Implications of a Global Village, Student Pulse, The Student International Journal, 1, 11, 1–2.

Downes, D. & Rock, P. E. (2007) Understanding Deviance, Oxford, Oxford University Press.

Epstein, J. S. (2002) Youth Culture: Identity in a Postmodern World. Malden, Massachussetts.

Gay, D. A. & Ellison, C. G. (1993) 'Religious Subcultures and Political Tolerance: Do Denominations Still Matter'. Review of Religious Research, 34, 4, 311–332.

Gelder, K. (2005) 'Introduction to Part One'. In K. Gelder (Ed.), The Subcultures Reader. Second Edition, London, Routledge.

Hall, S. & Jefferson, T. (2006) 'Once More Around and Through Subcultures' In S. Hall & T. Jefferson (Eds.), Resistance Through Rituals: Youth Subcultures in Post-war Britain. Oxford, Routledge.

Hodkinson, P. (2002) Goth: Identity, Style and Subculture. Oxford, Berg.

Jacobs, B. A. & Wright, R. (1999) 'Stick-up, Street Culture, and Offender Motivation'. Criminology, 37, 149–174.

Jenks, C. (2005) Subcultures: The Fragmentation of the Social. London, Sage.

Jones, S. (2013) Criminology, 5th Edition, Oxford, Oxford University Press.

Kahn, R. & Kellner, D. (2006) 'Internet Subcultures and Opposition Politics', In D. Muggleton & R. Weinzierl (Eds.), The Post-subcultural Reader. Oxford, Berg Publishers.

Karvonen, S., West, P., Sweeting, H., Rahkonen, O. & Young, R. (2001) Lifestyle, Social Class and Health-Related Behaviour: A Cross-Cultural Comparison of 15 Year Olds in Glasgow and Helsinki'. Journal of Youth Studies, 4: 393–413.

Lafree, G. (1998) Losing Legitimacy: Street Crime and the Decline of Social Institutions in America, Colorado, Westview Press.

Lilly, R. J., Cullen, F. T. & Ball, R. A. (2011) Criminological Theory: Context and Consequences, Thousand Oakes, Sage.

Macdonald, N. (2001) The Graffiti Subculture: Youth, Masculinity and Identity in London and New York. Basingstoke, Palgrave.

Maira, S. (1999) 'Identity Dub: The Paradoxes of an Indian American Youth Subculture (New York Mix). Cultural Anthropology, 14, 1, 26–60.

Malbond, B. (1998) 'Clubbing: Consumption, Identity and the Spatial Practice of Every-night Life'. In T. Skelton & G. Valentine (Eds.), Cool Places: Geographies of Youth Culture. London, Routledge.

Marenin, O. (1987) 'The Anini Saga: Armed Robbery and the Reproduction of Ideology in Nigeria'. The Journal of Modern African Studies, 25, 259–281.

Matza, D. (1964) Delinquency and Drift, New York, Wiley.

McRobbie, A. & Garber, J. (1976) 'Girls and Subcultures: An Exploration'. In S. Hall & T. Jefferson (Eds.), Resistance Through Rituals. London, Hutchinson.

McRobbie, A. & Garber, J. (2005) 'Girls and Subcultures [1977]'. In K. Gelder (Ed.), Second Edition, London, Routledge.

Melechi, A. (1993) 'The Ecstacy of Disappearance'. In S. Readhead (Ed.), Rave Off. Avebury, Aldershot.

Merton, R. K. (1938) 'Social Structure and Anomie'. American Sociological Review, 3, 672–682.

Miles, S. (1995) 'Towards an Understanding of the Relationship between Youth Identities and Consumer Culture'. Youth and Policy, 51, 35–45.

Miller, W. B. (1958) 'Lower Class Culture as a Generating Milieu of Gang Delinquency'. Journal of Social Issues, 14, 5–19.

Muggleton, D. (1997) 'The Post-subculturalists'. In S. Redhead (Ed.), The Club Culture Reader. Oxford, Blackwell.

Muggleton, D., 2000. Inside Subculture: The Postmodern Meaning of Style. Oxford: Berg.

Newburn, T. (2007) Criminology, Cullompton, Devon, Willan Publishing.

Newburn, T. (2013) Criminology, Second Edition, Abingdon, Oxon, Routledge.

Newman, G. and Howard, G. J. (2001), 'Varieties of Comparative Criminology,' Comparative Sociology, Brill Academic Publishers.

Nihart, T., Lersch, K. M., Sellers, C. & Mieczkowski, T. (2005) 'Kids, Cops, Parents and Teachers: Exploring Juvenile Attitudes Toward Authority Figures'. Western Criminology Review, 6, 1–11.

Philpot, J. (2008) Reevaluating Subculture: Pro-Life Youth and the Rhetoric of Resistance, A Thesis Submitted to the Graduate College of Bowling Green State University in Partial Fulfillment of the Requirements for the Degree of Master of Arts, August 2008.

Pieterse, J. N. (2001) 'Hybridity, So What? The Anti-Hybridity Backlash and the Riddles of Recognition', Theory, Culture and Society, 18, (2) 219–245.

Redhead, S. (1990) The End of the Century Party: Youth and Pop Towards 2000, Manchester, University of Manchester Press.

Schouten, J. W. & Mcalexander, J. H. (1995) 'Subculture of Consumption: An Ethnography of the New Bikers'. Journal of Consumer Research, 22, 43–61.

Shaw, C. R. & Mckay, H. D. (1942) Juvenile Delinquency in Urban Areas, Chicago, University of Chicago Press.

Shildrick, T. A. and MacDonald, R. (2006) 'In Defence of Subculture: Young People, Leisure and Social Divisions', Journal of Youth Studies, 9 (2), 125–140.

Short, J.F. (2002) Criminology, the Chicago School, and Sociological Theory, Crime Law and Sociological Theory, 37, 107–115

Sutherland, E. & Cressey, D. (1978) Criminology, Philadelphia, Lippincott.

Trice, M. T. (1993) Occupational Subcultures in the Work Place. Ithaca, New York, ILR Press.

Waddington, P. A. J. (1999) 'Police (Canteen) Subculture: An Appreciation', British Journal of Criminology, 39 (2), 287–309.

Walsh, D. (1986) Heavy Business: Commercial Burglary and Robbery, London, Routledge & Kegan Paul.

Warr, M. (2006) Companions in Crime: The Social Aspects of Criminal Conduct, Cambridge, Cambridge University Press.

Weinzierl, R. & Muggleton, D. (2006) 'What is Post-subcultural Studies', Anyway? In D. Muggleton & R. Weinzierl (Eds.), The Post-subcultural Reader. Oxford, Berg Publishers.

Williams, K. (1997) Textbook on Criminology. Blackstone Press Ltd.

Wolfgang, M. E. & Ferracuti, F. (1967) The Subculture of Violence: Towards an Integrated Theory in Criminology, London, Tavistock Publications.

Young, J. (2010) 'Subcultural Theories: Virtues and Vices'. In R. Agnew & J. Kaufman (Eds.), Anomie, Strain and Subcultural Theories of Crime. Farnham, Ashgate.

Post-Reading Questions

1   What are some of the ways the term "subculture" has been used? What is your concept of a subculture?

2   In what ways has subcultural theory influenced the study of youth crime?

3   According to our the authors, what are some common criticisms of subculture and subcultural theory? Which of these criticisms do you regard as most valid?

4   Why do the authors argue that the subcultural approach to crime and delinquency is "overly deterministic"?

5   According to the authors, what are the implications of rethinking subculture and subcultural theory?

A Vision of Race, Crime, and Justice Through the Lens of Critical Race Theory

Lee E. Ross

Introduction

This chapter presents an overview of critical race theory and its application to select areas of race, crime, and justice. Critical race theory concerns the study and transformation of relationships among race, racism, and power. Unlike traditional civil rights, which embraces incrementalism and systematic progress, critical race theory questions the very foundations of the legal order. In examining the dynamics of race, crime, and justice, this [reading] applies various themes and terminologies— such as interest convergence, legal indeterminacy, and first person narratives—to assess their potential to inform and facilitate an understanding of racial disparities in American criminal justice systems.

What is Critical Race Theory?

Over the last three decades, the fields of legal studies, criminology, and education have witnessed a number of exciting theoretical developments. Few have been as promising and insightful as critical race theory (CRT). This theory concerns the study and transformation of relationships among race, racism, and power. Unlike traditional civil rights, which embraces incrementalism and systematic progress, critical race theory questions the very foundations of the legal order, including equality theory, legal reasoning, enlightenment rationalism, and neutral principles of constitutional law (Delgado and Stefani, 2001: 3). Over the course of its development, critical race theory has assumed many operational definitions. Matsuda (2002) characterizes it as:

> The work of progressive legal scholars of color who are attempting to develop a jurisprudence that accounts for the role of racism in American law and that works toward the elimination of racism as part of a larger goal of eliminating all forms of subordination.
>
> (p. 331)

Today, hundreds of American legal academics consider themselves critical race theorists; they teach courses and write articles and books about race, civil rights, and constitutional law from this perspective. Interestingly, critical race theory, which began as a movement in law (as critical legal studies), has a prominent place in the field of education. For example, critical race theorists explore a variety of issues such as school discipline and hierarchy, controversies over curriculum and history, intelligence, and achievement testing. In the process, critical race theorists have influenced other disciplines as well. In the field of political science, for instance, researchers have pondered voting strategies.

Critics allege that the core claim of both critical race theory and feminist jurisprudence is that law is merely a mask for white male power relations (see MacDonald, 1995). The law, critics further claim, is virtually indistinguishable from politics. Moreover, the purported objectivity and neutrality of legal reasoning is a sham (MacDonald, 1995). These ideals have emerged with feminist insights into the relationships of power and the construction of social roles, a concern for addressing historic wrongs, and sympathetic understandings of notions of nationalism and group empowerment. Equally important, critical race theory contains an academic dimension as it attempts to both understand our social situation and to change it. It sets out not only to ascertain how society organizes itself along racial lines and hierarchies, but also to transform it for the better.

Conceived by critical legal studies, pioneers in the area of critical race theory included the likes of Derrick Bell, Alan Freeman, and Richard Delgado. Confronting the reality of a fading Civil Rights Movement, these men recognized that overt practices of racism often times yielded to more subtle and covert forms of racism that rendered it far more difficult to discern. Imagine placing a white jellybean into a jar of other white jellybeans, shaking the jar up and finding it later on. The difficulty is that all the jellybeans, like racism, look ordinarily similar: virtually indistinguishable from one another. For critical race theorists, so too is racism. Its ordinariness and prevalence renders it harder to recognize—much less address. Consequently, formal rules that demand color-blind treatment will enable remedies to only the most flagrant forms of racism (i.e., the black jellybean).

The idea that racism and sexism are limited phenomena perpetuated by a few intentional bad actors is one of the most destructive myths of all. Discrimination, according to Hayman (1997), results simply from bureaucratic practices, from the unthinking repetition of the ordinary ways of operating in the world. The modern, righteously indignant and seemingly egalitarian calls for a color-blind society ignore the history and tradition of our treatment of race in America (Levitt, 1999). At the heart of the myth of merit is the [Achilles heel] of purposeful discrimination: if only we can eradicate intentional, malicious discrimination, the market, freed from discrimination, will guarantee equality of opportunity.

Among a myriad of themes commonly used by scholars to promote discussions of critical race theory, most begin with an exploration of racism itself. For critical race theorists, racism is ordinary, not aberrational—"normal science." Racism, forever alive and well, manifests itself though various disparities within nearly every sector of society, whether in the prison system, the banking and lending industry, the educational system, or within a healthcare industry where racial disparities in longevity, diabetes, and infant mortality rates are readily apparent.

Mortgage redlining practices that deny low-cost loans to anyone wanting to buy a house in the black part of town would be a prime example (Delgado and Stefancic, 2001). For the most part, critical race theory rejects the idea that extremist individuals perpetuate racism today and theorize instead that societal systems are to blame for the continuation of racism. For Valdes *et al.* (2002: 2), "critical race theory describes and critiques not a world of bad actors, wronged victims, and innocent bystanders, but a world in which all of us are more or less complicit in sociological webs of domination and subordination." Regarding the purpose of the law, Delgado theorizes that critical race theory exposes "traditional claims of legal neutrality, objectivity, color-blindness, and meritocracy" as camouflages for the self-interest of dominant groups in American society (cited from Ladson-Billings and Tate, 1995: 52). Overall, critical race theory acknowledges the inextricable racialized subordination based on gender, class, immigration status, surname, phenotype, accent and sexuality (Crenshaw, 1989; Valdes *et al.*, 2002).

While membership and identity in the CRT movement was minimal, the spirit of European philosophers, theorists, and American activists imparted both vision and inspiration. European influences included important figures like Antonio Gramsci and Jacques Derrida. The American tradition is exemplified by such figures as Sojourner Truth, Frederick Douglass, W. E. B. DuBois, César Chávez, Martin Luther King Jr., and the Black Panther and Chicano Movements of the sixties and early seventies. Critical race theory is also credited with various spin-off movements that include an emerging Asian American jurisprudence, a powerful Latino-critical *(LatCrit)* contingent, a spirited queer-crit interest group, and Native American scholars who address indigenous people's rights, sovereignty, and land claims.

In The Beginning

Organizationally, critical race theory came into being either at UC-Berkeley or at Harvard University. One version suggests that students at Harvard University were disgruntled that a prominent civil rights lawyer, Jack Greenberg, was hired to replace Derrick Bell, an African-American law professor who left to take a deans position elsewhere (see Delgado and Stetancic, 2005). Students, upset at these developments, boycotted the class taught by Greenberg and started their own alternative course which met on Saturday mornings. Various guest speakers were brought in, including Charles Lawrence, author of a famous article on unconscious racism, and Richard Delgado, who spoke about imperial racism. Student organizers of the Saturday series included Kimberly Crenshaw and Mara Matsuda, who went on to become law professors and major architects for critical race theory (Delgado and Stefancic, 2005: p. 4). At the same time, a similar movement took place on the west coast at UC-Berkeley in the form of high profile speakers, student sit-ins, and rallies to hire more professors of color. In 1989, the first ever critical race theory workshop was convened in Madison, Wisconsin.

Types of Racism

Britannica Encyclopedia defines racism as "any action, practice, or belief that reflects the racial worldview-the ideology that humans are divided into separate and exclusive biological entities called "races," and that there is a causal link between inherited physical traits and traits of personality, intellect, morality, and other cultural behavioral features, that some "races" are innately superior to others. To the contrary, *Social Construction Thesis* holds that race and races are products of social thought and relations. Organizations and institutions that practice racism discriminate against, and marginalize a class of people who share a common racial designation. The term "racism" is usually applied to the dominant group in a society, because it is that group which has the means to oppress others, but readily applies to any individual or group(s), regardless of social status or dominance. Consequently, inequalities are a logical and predictable result of a racialized society where discussions of race and racism continue to be muted and marginalized (Ladson-Billings and Tate, 1995).

When we speak of racism, we think of Wellman's (1977) definition of "culturally sanctioned beliefs which, regardless of the intentions involved, defend advantages whites have because of the subordinated positions of racial minorities." We must therefore contend with the "problem facing White people [of coming] to grips with the demands made by Blacks and Whites while at the same time avoiding the possibility of institutional challenge and reorganization that might affect them" (Wellman, 1977: 42).

According to Nobel Laureate Toni Morrison, race has become metaphorical—a way of referring to and disguising forces, events, classes, and expressions of social decay and economic division far more threatening to the body politic than "biological race" (Morrison, 1993: 63). For Omi and Winant (1994), the paradigm of race has been conflated with notions of ethnicity, class, and nation. Moreover, theories of race—of it meaning, its transformations, and the significance of racial events—have never been a top priority in social science. In the U.S., although the "founding fathers" of American sociology were explicitly concerned with the state of domestic race relations, racial theory remained one of the least developed fields of sociological inquiry (p. 9).

Barbara Field (1990), a historian from Columbia University, argued in *Slavery, Race, and Ideology in the United States of America,* that 'racism' is a 'historical phenomenon', which does not explain racial ideology (p. 100). She suggests that investigators should consider the term to be an American rhetorical device with a historical explanation—but not as an explanation in itself. Much like the notion of reification, where concepts used to represent reality are regarded as real, using race as a word with real meaning is a common error.

There are two, closely related, forms of racism: individuals acting against other individuals, and acts by a total community against another community. These are called individual and institutional racism. Individual racism consists of both overt and covert acts by individuals, which can directly cause death, injury or the violent destruction of property. Institutional racism on the other hand is more covert and subtle, less identifiable in terms of specific individuals committing the acts, but no less destructive. It often originates in the operation of established and respected forces in the society, and thus frequently receives far less public condemnation than the first type. In furtherance of this discussion, the next section introduces readers to important themes related to critical race theory. Given the scope of the [reading], however, these themes are limited to those most relevant toward issues of race, crime, and justice.

Legal Indeterminacy

Critical legal studies, a prelude to critical race theory, distinguishes itself from other theoretical perspectives with its ideal of legal indeterminacy—the idea that not every legal case has *one* correct outcome. A given body of legal doctrine is said to be "indeterminate" by demonstrating that every legal rule in that body of legal doctrine is opposed by a counter rule that can be used in a process of legal reasoning. According to Delgado and Stefancic (2001: 5), one can decide most legal cases either way by emphasizing one line of authority over another, or interpreting one fact differently from the way one's adversary does. In terms of legal theory, the following question sums up the indeterminacy debate quite nicely: Can the law constrain the results reached by adjudicators in legal disputes? This question has generated tremendous discussion among scholars. Some members of the critical legal studies movement—primarily legal academics in the United States—argued that the answer to this question is "no." In other words, disputes cannot be resolved with clear answers and, thus, there is at least some amount of uncertainty in legal reasoning and its application to disputes.

The indeterminacy thesis, in its strongest form, is the proposition that a judge can "square" any result in a particular case with the existing legal materials using legitimate legal arguments (see Solum, 1987). To paraphrase Solum (1987), the existing body of legal doctrines—statutes, administrative regulations, and court decisions—permits a judge to justify any desired result in any particular case. Put another way, the idea is that a competent adjudicator can square a decision in favor of either side in any given lawsuit with the existing body of legal rules. Hence, the expression, "square the deal." Closely related to this line of thought is the *theory of judicial shamanism*: a postmodern analytical approach to judicial reasoning. It broadens the constitutional atheism proclaimed by the Critical Legal Studies movement (CLS) with the suggestion that judicial reasoning is a contemporary form of shamanism.

Criminal Law and Legal Indeterminacy

Constant reminders of legal indeterminacy can be witnessed in an examination of criminal procedure throughout various aspects of American criminal justice systems. In the 1985 Supreme Court case of *Tennessee v. Garner,* the Court held that the police might not invariably use deadly force on a fleeing suspect, even though they have probable cause to authorize an arrest (a "seizure" of the person under the Fourth Amendment). As life is a distinct fundamental right— quite apart from the liberty and privacy interests ordinarily associated with Fourth Amendment safeguards—the Court refused to authorize the use of deadly force in the absence of any threat to the police or the public. Civil libertarians embraced this decision, but with guarded optimism, given a lack of compelling reasons to have prevented the court from ruling otherwise. Law, after all—even in its finest hour—is a function of time, place, and circumstance.

Yet, the circumstances surrounding the *Garner* case were ripe for constitutional protections. Thus, the court ruled that whenever an officer restrains the freedom of a person to walk away, the officer has seized that person. When considering whether the seizure was constitutional, the specter of legal indeterminacy surfaces. To determine the constitutionality of a seizure [the court] must balance the nature and quality of the intrusion on the individual's Fourth Amendment interests against the importance of the governmental interests alleged to justify the intrusion. In other words, reasonableness depends on not only *when* a seizure is made, but also *how* it is carried out. In an earlier case, *Bell v. Wolfish* (1979), the court ruled that the test of reasonableness under the Fourth Amendment [was] *not capable of precise definition or mechanical application.* Even more uncertain (and indeterminate) is that the "reasonableness" of a particular use of force must be judged from the perspective of a reasonable officer on the scene, rather than with the 20/20 vision of academic or scholarly hindsight.

In contrast, one need only consider the current atmosphere of increased government surveillance under the guise and rubric of national security since the events of 9–11. Assume for the moment that Garner was a suspected terrorist in possession of an incendiary device. He refuses to halt when ordered by police and deadly force was used to make his arrest. We soon realize there is little to prevent a court from validating police use of deadly force on a 'fleeing terrorist.' Hence, the indeterminacy thesis serves as an unpleasant reminder of the precariousness of criminal law. In this example, some would argue that the climate and circumstance makes the use of deadly force perfectly reasonable. Nonetheless, this hypothetical illustrates that the court could have ruled either way. This is what breathes new life into the *theory of legal indeterminacy*.

Closely related to this concept is the notion of suspending the constitution when the rights of individuals potentially conflict with the interests of government. Under the United States Patriot Act, for instance, the government has the power to access one's medical records, tax records, information about books borrowed from libraries—all without probable cause. It also has the potential to allow the government to break into your home and conduct secret searches without telling you for weeks, months, or indefinitely. Axioms that have stood the test of time, such as "tough cases make bad law," suggest that the theory of legal indeterminacy is alive and well where contrary rulings, dripping with contempt for *stare decisis and precedent law,* can be expected. After all, the states' compelling interest is arguably greater than a citizen's civil right.

Giorgio Agamben (2005) underscores this point further in the book *State of Exception* where he described a situation, in which a domestic or international crisis creates a pretext for the suspension of some aspect of the juridical order. A state of exception often implies a suspension of judicial oversight of civil liberties and the use of summary judgment against civilians by members of the military or executive. For some scholars, the state of exception is a legitimate part of positive law because it is based on necessity, a fundamental source of law. Similar to the individual's claim of self-defense in criminal law, the polity has a right to self-defense when its sovereignty is threatened. Consequently, when government exercises this right, it might involve a technical violation of existing statutes *(legge)* but it does so in the name of upholding the juridical order *(diritto)*. Supposedly, the end justifies the means.

On the other hand, some regard the assumed legitimacy of dictatorial action (in times of crisis) a matter of interpretation. Carl Schmitt (2005), in *Political Theology and Dictatorship,* emphasizes that declaring a state of exception is the prerogative of the sovereign and therefore essentially extra-juridical. For Schmitt (2005), however, while the state of exception always involves the suspension of the law, it serves two different purposes: commissarial and sovereign. A "commissarial dictatorship" aims at restoring the existing constitution and a "sovereign dictatorship" constitutes a new juridical order. Thus, the state of exception is a violation of law that expresses the more fundamental logic of politics itself.

The principle of legal indeterminacy is also seen in the 1987 death penalty case of *McCleskey v. Kemp*. Here, the Supreme Court, by a 5–4 vote, rejected an equal protection and Eighth Amendment (cruel and unusual punishment) challenge to a Georgia death penalty statute that raised this issue. The challenge was based on a state-of-the-art statistical study showing that murderers of white people were 4.3 times more likely to get the death penalty than comparable murderers of blacks. Put simply, the study showed that Georgia's capital case prosecutors and juries valued white lives far more than black lives. However, Justice Lewis Powell, the author of *McCleskey* and the swing vote in the case, was unimpressed with these statistics. In his view, if Georgia's death penalty really was [racially] discriminatory, the statistical study would have shown that a disproportionate number of Georgia's death penalty defendants were black. Powell took considerable comfort in the fact that, instead, the only significant racial disparity in the Georgia system correlated not with the race of capital defendants, but rather with the race of their victims (Lazarus, 2001). Yet, it is clear that the philosophy of critical race theorists would suggest that the court could have ruled otherwise. Moreover, deficient legal reasoning in the absence of compelling arguments leaves the door open for reversal.

Interest Convergence

Interest convergence (or material determinism) adds a further dimension to critical race theory. Here, racism is endowed with the propensity to advance the interests of whites in both a material and psychic manner. Therefore, it is not surprising that large segments of society have little interest in eradicating it (see Delgado and Stefancic, 2001).

In a classic article, Derrick Bell (1980) argued that civil rights advances for blacks tended to coincide with changing economic conditions and self-interest of elite whites. Using the famous 1954 case of *Brown v. Board of Education of Topeka Kansas* as an example, he suggested that sympathy, mercy, and evolving standards of social decency did not fully explain the U.S. Supreme Court's sudden decision in favor of school integration. Rather, Bell thought that world and domestic considerations—not oral qualms over the plight of blacks—precipitated this path breaking decision (cited from Delgado and Stefani, 2001: 19). Given the climate at that time, Bell regarded the *Brown* decision as somewhat of a concession, where cooperation and national survival took precedence over racism. In describing conditions that led up to this decision, Bell asserts:

> During that period, as well, the United States was locked in a Cold War, a titanic struggle with the forces on international communism for the loyalties of the uncommitted Third World, much of which was black, brown, or Asian. It would ill serve the U.S. interests if the world press continued to carry stories of lynchings, racists sheriffs, or murders like that of Emmett Till. It was time for the United States to soften its stance toward domestic minorities. The interest of whites and blacks, for a brief moment, converged.
> (cited from Delgado and Stefancic, 2001: p. 19)

Subsequent research and the passage of time offered further testimony to the validity of his claims. For instance, despite the gallantry and performance of blacks during the Korean War, they eventually returned home to conditions of racial segregation and continued Jim Crow practices. In spite of noble attempts to eradicate segregated schools and to insure equal access to quality education, the *Brown* decision did not meet with the successes it had envisioned. Once handed down, the African-American community, along with forward-thinking white Americans, placed sufficient pressure on the legal and political system to bring an end to state-supported segregation in all public facilities within twenty years through the Civil Rights Movement, led by Dr. Martin Luther King, Jr. The nation paid a high price for its moral conversion, however, in the form of riots, assassinations, and additional government programs to enforce the Court's decision, such as court-ordered busing and affirmative action programs.

Today, students of color are more segregated than ever before in the educational system (see Orfield, 1988). Instead of providing for better educational opportunities, school desegregation has meant increased white flight along with a loss of African-American teaching and administrative positions (Ladson-Billings and Tate, 1995: 56). Over the last thirty years, for instance, various institutions of higher education have provided unpleasant reminders in their challenges to college admission policies based on race-based affirmative action as some view it as a form of reverse discrimination. Ironically, those advocating the elimination of race-based affirmative action policies argue that it would lead to legislation that fosters a color-blind society—the exact antithesis of what critical race theory espouses. Critical race theorists, after all, do not seek a color-blind society endowed with mythical notions of equality before the law. They recognized that legislation espousing a colorblind society carries with it a potential double-edged sword. Moreover, Crenshaw (1988: 1331) argued:

> The civil rights community ... must come to grips with the fact that antidiscrimination discourse is fundamentally ambiguous and can accommodate conservative as well as liberal views of race and equality ... [a]ntidiscrimination law presents an ongoing ideological struggle in which occasional winners harness the moral, coercive, consensual power of law. Nonetheless, the victories it offers can be ephemeral and the risks of engagement substantial.
>
> (cited from Ladson-Billings and Tate, 1995: 56)

Ladson-Billings (1998) builds an even stronger case for interest convergence by depicting what transpired in the state of Arizona over the Martin Luther King, Jr. Holiday commemoration. Originally, the state of Arizona insisted that the King Holiday was too costly and therefore failed to recognize it for state workers and agencies. When members of professional sports organizations (i.e., the National Basketball Association, and the National Football League) threatened to boycott sporting events held in Arizona, the state literally changed its position overnight. Fearing a loss of revenue that a boycott would produce, the states interests (in protecting the revenue) converged with that of the African American community to honor Dr. King.

Interest Convergence in Criminal Justice System

Perhaps similar claims can be made in the criminal justice arena when considering other landmark decisions, such as the U.S. Supreme Court decision in *Powell v. Alabama,* commonly referred to as the Scottsboro case. Here, nine black men (and boys) were accused of raping two white women on a freight train near Paint Rock, Alabama. They were arrested on March 25, 1931, tried without adequate counsel, and hastily convicted based on shallow evidence. All but one was sentenced to death. Ultimately, the Supreme Court, by a vote of 7–2, reversed the convictions because the state of Alabama failed to provide adequate assistance of counsel as required by the Sixth Amendment and the due process clause of the 14th Amendment.

This decision, and other less publicized ones spanning from 1910 to 1940 became the pillars of the judicial reforms, which would constitute the due process revolution in American law and criminal procedure (cited from Hawkins *et al.,* 2003: 437). While the court specified a clear mandate to provide attorneys to those accused of capital crimes (rape and murder at that time), this case too, provides a prime example of other constitutional gains that have gradually eroded through the passage of time. For instance, once counsel is appointed, are constitutional rights somehow violated in cases where counsel is proven incompetent or ineffective? Citing numerous examples of incompetent counsel in recent death penalty cases and inequities in the imposition of capital punishment in America, the American Civil Liberties Union (ACLU, 2003) has called upon the United States Congress to ensure effective legal representation for all defendants facing possible execution. Their request was made with knowledge of a Texas man convicted in a state court for the stabbing to death of his companion. He was given a new trial after a federal judge discovered that the defendant's lawyer had slept through the bulk of the original trial. The federal court judge is paraphrased as saying: sleeping counsel is equivalent to no counsel at all. Adding further context, a recent report on indigent defense by the Texas Defender Service found that judges often appointed defense attorneys—not based on their competence or experience—but rather, their reputation for rapidly moving cases through the system. The importance of this cannot be over-stated as the study concluded that death row prisoners "face a one-in-three chance of being executed without having the case properly investigated by a competent attorney or without having any claims of innocence or unfairness heard" (ACLU, 2003).

Miranda Revisited

Other examples of an erosion of rights relate to one's Fifth Amendment rights while held incommunicado and interrogated by police. In *Miranda v. Arizona,* a 1966 ruling, the Court held that criminal suspects must be informed of their right to consult with an attorney and of their right against self-incrimination prior to questioning by police. Nearly 40 years later in 2003 the United States Supreme Court ruled 6–3 to eliminate the universality of having to read Miranda rights before interrogation. Consequently, police could aggressively question a person without first apprising them of their constitutional protections. This ruling resulted from a 1977 incident in which an officer, Oliverio Martinez, was shot five times by Oxnard, California police who allegedly violated his Fifth Amendment rights when questioning him. While awaiting emergency treatment for his injuries, Martinez was interrogated at length without being read his Miranda rights. In the hospital, officers continued to interrogate him. Martinez who was in pain, had stated that he did not want to answer, and had begged the officer to stop his questioning. Mel Lipman, president of the American Humanist Association, regards this is a serious problem. He adds: "if Miranda rights are not needed in questioning, it is possible that future witnesses will be committing a crime by simply pleading for their silence" (American Humanist Association, 2003). Some regard this decision as a significant infringement of Fifth Amendment protections, further eroding basic civil liberties, given its potential to promote hostile and coercive actions to obtain information.

Additional Themes

Differential racialization and first person narrative, alongside intersectionality and anti-essentialism provide additional insights into the nature and study of critical race theory. A brief mentioning of each is essential—but an in-depth exploration of each is beyond the scope of this [reading]. Nonetheless, differential racialization suggests that the dominant society racializes different minority groups at different times in response to shifting needs such as the labor market. Throughout American history, labor market forces have dictated the need and status of Blacks, Mexicans, Asians and other persons of color. Closely related to this is that popular images and stereotypes of People of Color have also changed through time; sometimes depicted as happy-go-lucky, while at other times seen as menacing and brutish.

For more than 125 years, the U.S. Census Bureau has played a vital role in racial classification, often exceeding the black/white binary. When the question of race was first asked in 1890, there were almost 16 categories ranging from black to white. Ladson-Billings (2005: 116) speaks to this issue in the following manner:

> Asians were phenotypically determined to be White. In the Lemon Grove School District Incident, Mexican American parents won their suit against having their children sent to a segregated school because they were categorized as White, and for a short period, the Cherokee Indians were considered White as they worked hard to assimilate in U.S. Society.

Perhaps more obvious are the events of 9–11 that have resulted in the differential racialization of Arabs and Moslems, regarded by some as more deserving of suspicion and government surveillance than others. Ironically, African-Americans appear to embrace the "focus on others" as a welcomed reprieve, given their historical (and continued) victimizations from racial profiling under the familiar adage of "diving while black." In economic terms, some groups (i.e., migrant workers and other laborers) are highly sought after, despite their perceived illegal immigrant status. In the twinkling of an eye, migrant workers are potentially racialized in response to shifting needs in the labor market. In some parts of the United States, migrant labor is valued and accepted, especially within cheap labor industries (i.e., farming, building, and house cleaning). As the political winds change, however, public perceptions tend to blow in a different direction. Clouded by suspicions of involvement in terrorist related activities or failure to provide adequate documentation, migrant workers are potentially transformed into "illegal immigrants." Similar practices are portrayed, for instance, in the continued reliance on Asian professionals to sustain some American economies, such as the computer industry. Most troubling, however, is the potential of racialization to "divide and conquer" the oppressed.

Contemporary examples of differential racialization resemble instances where white families adopt transracially. No longer a white family by virtue of their child(ren), they become racialized others. Other examples of racialization are alluded to by Ladson-Billings (1998: 11) in relation to the infamous O. J. Simpson trial:

> The criminal trial jury was repeatedly identified as the "Black" jury despite the presence of one White and one Latino juror. However, the majority White civil case jury was not given a racial designation. When whites are exempted from racial designations and become "families," "jurors," "students," teacher," etc. their ability to apply a CRT analytical rubric is limited.

Intersectionality

Other important concepts of critical race theory include intersectionality and anti-essentialism, which suggest that no person has a single, easily stated, unitary identity. Rather, everyone has potentially conflicting, overlapping identities, loyalties, and allegiances, which makes claims of discrimination unusually difficult to sustain in a court of law. The complexity of this concept is portrayed through and examination of hate crime legislation which promotes stiffer punishments for crimes motivated by hate. According to the Dictionary of Sociology (1998), hate crimes—or bias motivated crimes—are defined as "crimes committed out of racial, religious, or sexual prejudice, which target minority groups, and which often violate anti-discrimination laws." Such crimes are usually crimes of violence motivated against (for example) women, Jews, Blacks, or gays. In Great Britain, however, the definition of a hate crime incident, is exceedingly flexible and depends largely on the subjective perception of the victim. Hence, "anyone can be a victim of hate crime if they believe themselves to be so," even those historically regarded as proverbial offenders (Hall, 2005: 11).

In terms of critical race theory, hate crimes based on race are easily disguised in the midst of other relevant demographics, such as gender. Take for instance a Black lesbian who is physically attacked by a white male after voicing atheistic beliefs while drinking at a local bar. The question might become: what motivated the attack? Was it her race, gender, sexual orientation, her non-religious beliefs, or some combination of these? Was she a victim of a hate crime? Given the intersectionality and anti-essentialism of her identity (in general), the practicality of hate crime legislation, despite good intentions, is severely undermined. A CRT analysis, on the other hand, would explore the nature of the threat, including its meaning and intent. More potently, it requires an examination of the social context that lead to disparate treatment and outcomes.

First Person Narrative

Everyone loves a good story and the last theme [...] entails how stories (i.e., first person narratives) are utilized by unique People of Color. Critical race theory recognizes that the experiential knowledge of People of Color as legitimate, appropriate, and critical to understanding, analyzing and teaching about racial subordination (cited from Yosso, 2005). Drawing explicitly on the lived experiences of People of Color, Critical race theory includes various methods, such as storytelling, family histories, biographies, scenarios, parables, *cuentos, testiminios,* chronicles and narratives (Yosso, 2005: 74).

Delgado and Stefancic (2001) defined counter-story-telling as "a method of telling a story that aims to cast doubt on the validity of accepted premises as myths, especially ones held by the majority" (p. 144). Historically, story telling has been a kind of medicine to heal the wounds of pain caused by racial oppression. The story of one's condition leads to the realization of how one came to be oppressed and subjugated, thus allowing one to stop inflicting mental violence on oneself (Ladson-Billings, 1998: 14). This concept maintains that because of their different histories and experiences with oppression, Black, Indian, Asian, and Latino/a writers and thinkers may be able to communicate to their white counterparts matters that the whites are unlikely to know.

Well-told stories describing the reality of black and brown lives can help readers bridge the gap between their worlds and those of others. Engaging stories can foster an understanding of what life is like for others, and invite readers into a new and unfamiliar world. For instance, it is often pointed out that white-collar and corporate/industrial crime—perpetuated mostly by whites—causes more personal injury, death, and property loss than all street crime combined, even on a per capita basis (see Delgado and Stefani, 2001: 43). Historically, though, the bulk of criminal justice resources is targeted toward street crime and the processing of offenders stereotypically perceived as dangerous. That is a belief that often translates into policy. In this context, preconceptions and myths, for example about black criminality, shape mindset—the bundle of received wisdoms, stock stories, and suppositions that allocate suspicion, place the burden of proof on one party or the other, and tell us in cases of divided evidence what really happened. Critical race theorists use counter stories to challenge, displace, or mock these pernicious narratives and beliefs. The primary reason, then, that stories, or narratives, are deemed important among CRT scholars is they add necessary contextual contours to the seeming "objectivity" of positivist perspectives. It does so in a manner that reveals the contingency, cruelty, and self-serving notions of these presuppositions.

Criminal Justice Through the Lens of Critical Race Theory

Why is a CRT perspective important to incorporate into our understanding of criminal justice system practices? Given the current practices and conditions of justice systems world-wide, an application of CRT principles enable readers to examine social reality through a different lens when addressing perceived injustices. According to Yasso (2005: 75): looking through a CRT lens means analyzing deficit theorizing and data that they may be limited by its omission of the voices of People of Color. Such deficit informed research often 'sees' deprivation in Communities of Color. Indeed, one of the most prevalent forms of contemporary racism in U.S. school systems and other systems is deficit thinking. *Deficit thinking* refers to the notion that students (particularly those of low-income, racial/ethnic minority background) fail in school because such students and their families have internal defects (deficits) that thwart the learning process (Valencia, 1997). Examples of this include notions of educability; unmotivated; inadequate family support. Moreover, deficit thinking, an endogenous theory, "blames the victim" rather than examining how the schools are structured to prevent certain students from learning (see also Crenshaw, 1993).

Similar remnants of deficit thinking are evidenced in the criminal justice system by widely held perceptions and treatment of criminal offenders, many of whom are viewed as beyond rehabilitation and psychopathic. Traditionally, affective and interpersonal traits such as egocentricity, deceit, shallow affect, manipulativeness, selfishness, and lack of empathy, guilt or remorse, have played a central role in the conceptualization and diagnosis of psychopathy (see Widiger and Corbitt, 1996). Defined as a person with an antisocial personality disorder, psychopaths tend to manifest aggressive, perverted, criminal, or amoral behavior without empathy or remorse. Personality characteristics of psychopaths are highly correlated with the *DSM-IV-R* classifications of antisocial personality disorder (APD). The field of Criminology tends to treat APD as so synonymous, in fact, with criminal behavior that practically all convicted criminals (65–75%) have this deficit (see Hare, 1996; McCord, 1964).

In terms of critical race theory, the failure to differentiate between psychopathy and APD can have serious consequences for clinicians and for society. For example, most jurisdictions consider psychopathy as an aggravating rather than a mitigating factor in determining criminal responsibility. In some states, an offender convicted of first-degree murder and diagnosed as psychopathic is likely to receive the death penalty on the ground that psychopaths are cold-blooded, remorseless, untreatable and almost certain to re-offend (see Meloy, 1990). Given the existing racial disparities in arrests, prosecution, conviction, and sentencing rates, these classifications serve to perpetuate common stereotypes of what criminals look like and what the types of punishments they "deserve." Most damaging, however, is the potential of these diagnoses to exacerbate racial disparities in the imposition of the death sentences where racial disparities are already exceedingly pronounced.

Building on the work of radical criminologists, it is no surprise that critical race theorists believe the disproportionate criminalization of African-Americans and other Persons of Color is a product, in large part, of the way we define crime. Many lethal acts, such as marketing defective automobiles, alcohol, and pharmaceuticals or waging undeclared wars, are not considered crimes at all (Delgado and Stefancic, 2001: 113). By the same token, many things that young black men and Latino men are prone to do, such as congregating on street corners, cruising in low-riders (drop tops), or scrawling graffiti in public places, are energetically policed. Critical race theorists are concerned that racial profiling that targets certain minority youth because they are viewed as more likely involved in crime or perpetrators of crime. Both practices tend to penalize law-abiding people of color and alienate youths.

Along more radical lines, some critical race theorists urge jury nullification to combat the disproportionate incarceration of young black men (see Butler, 1995). In jury nullification, the jury—usually containing some black jurors—exercises its discretion to acquit black defendants if they thought the case was racially motivated (such as the perception that an arresting officer was racist), or if they thought it useless to send a *non-violent* offender to jail. The power of jurors to nullify verdicts derived from English Common law, which gave citizens the discretionary power to correct what they perceived as unjust laws and punishments. In a highly referenced American case one judge, well versed in critical race theory, applied a similar analysis in the case of a black defendant. Under a three-strikes-and-you are out type of law, the judge was required to sentence the man to a long term. On noticing that two of his previous offenses had been automobile-connected, the judge declined to do so. Reasoning that racial profiling by the police causes black motorists to be pulled over more frequently than whites, she concluded that the defendant's two prior convictions had likely been tainted by racism. Consequently, she sentenced him to the shorter term appropriate as a repeat offender (Delgado and Stefancic, 2001: 115).

In a similar context, Butler (1995) proposed that one way to remedy injustices in the criminal justice system is to apply principles of affirmative action to the criminal law. Similar to the concept of jury nullification, he advocated that only black juries deliberate on cases involving both black offenders and black victims. Likewise, only an all black jury should decide the fate of a black murderer facing a potential death sentence. There have been noted objections to this approach. Kennedy (1997: 299) for instance, characterizes Butler's approach as "profoundly misleading and that problems of the criminal justice system require judicious attention—not a campaign of defiant sabotage." According to Kennedy (1997), a campaign of jury nullification could actually backfire as there is nothing to prevent White jurors from doing the same thing in cases involving White-on-Black crime. Criticisms of this nature, regarding the utility of critical race theory, are but a microcosm of even broader concerns that are outlined below.

A Critique of Critical Race Theory

The themes of critical race theory have circulated for nearly 30 years, encompassing powerful notions, like the centrality and intersectionality of race and racism, the challenge to the dominant ideology, commitment to social justice, and the promotion of an interdisciplinary perspective. This section entails a critical review of the contemporary status of critical race theory and problems it has encountered along the way toward achieving acceptance before a skeptical and often times defensive audience. We begin with Solorzano and Villipando (1998), who expressed doubts that critical race theory had achieved its goals, especially in its ability to understand forms of subtle discrimination. They assert:

> indeed, we know very little about whom, where, and how these microaggressions are initiated and responded to. Without careful documentation and analysis, these racial and gender microaggressions can easily be ignored or downplayed.
>
> (1998: 132)

Just as other theories are inadequate toward explaining many disparities in the arena of race, crime, and justice, critical race theory also has its shortcomings, not the least of which is proving racism. Part of the problem is that evidence of racism in the criminal justice system is often measured by historical standards of positivism. Yet, positivistic approaches are woefully inadequate at discerning more subtle and hidden forms of racism. Critical race theory appears to use a different standard of measurement to capture the experiences and perceptions of oppressed people who are typical victims of social injustice.

Levitt (1999), in a classic essay, explores the increasing intolerance that critical theorists—particularly critical race theorists—face in response to their call for inclusion in society's collective decision-making. Typically, most of the opposition and critical reviews derive from conservatives. Take George Will (1996) for instance, who accuses critical race theorists of "playing the race card." Or Rosen (1996), in his assertion that some critical race scholars indulge in "a vulgar racial essentialism," and that [t]he rhetoric of the movement is already reverberating beyond the lecture hall and seminar room. In harsher terms, Judge Richard Posner of the United States Court of Appeals labels critical race theorists and postmodernists as the "lunatic core" of radical legal egalitarianism. Interestingly, Posner (1997) is less harsh on selected critical legal studies and radical feminist scholars, who simply "have plenty of goofy ideas and irresponsible dicta" (cited from Levitt, 1999). Compounding the case against critical race theorist are the likes of those who claim that critical race scholarship "fails the test for rational discourse."

Highly judgmental and less tolerant of critical race theory; Farber and Sherry (1997) refer to CRT scholars as "radical multiculturalists" whose arguments are "beyond all reason." Radical multiculturalism, Farber and Sherry diagnose, is "a paranoid mode of thought that sees behind every social institution nothing but the tracks of white supremacy and male oppression" (p. 132). This sentiment sufficiently describes the attitudes of many who reject CRT premises.

Regarded by some as radical scholarship, traditionalist fear that critical race theory tends to distort public discourse (Farber and Sherry, 1997). They characterize critical race theorists in the following manner:

> ... [T]heir disdain for standards, objectivity, and truths leads [the] radical scholars to indulge in a form of writing that is blatantly subjective. Instead of offering theoretical or doctrinal analysis, radical multiculturalists tell stories. These stories are intended to "explode the dominant myths or received knowledge, disrupt the established order, shatter complacency, and seduce the reader".
>
> (p. 24)

An Assault on Story-Telling

Clearly, some themes of critical race theory are more scrutinized than others. "Story-telling" has become the poster child of illegitimacy and scrutiny, given its challenge to traditional notions of epistemology that looks at how one knows reality. For scientists, the way of knowing reality is via the scientific method. Traditionalists claim that story telling is inherently problematic because stories cannot be verified, are inevitably subjective, and may be atypical of real world experiences. Moreover, narrative methodology "reject[s] the linearity, abstraction, and scientific objectivity of rational argument" (Levitt, 1999). Therefore, for the traditionalists, storytelling is neither legal nor academic, and threatens the credibility of the scholarly enterprise. As stories are unrepresentative or atypical, they are of limited value. Levitt (1999), raises the following concerns:

> ... [R]ather than relying solely on legal or interdisciplinary authorities, empirical data, or rigorous analysis, legal scholars have begun to offer stories, often about their own real or imagined experiences ... . Often the story recounts how the author was mistreated because of race, gender, or sexual orientation.

Yet story telling is defended by many critical race theorists who regard it as exceedingly useful and undeniably powerful in its effect. Fearing that some are missing the point, Murray (1996) asserts: "at hand is an attempt to transform the meritocratic ideal by including what has been up to now excluded: the valuable, concrete, lived experiences of oppressed peoples." For Levitt (1999), the problem is not story telling, *per se,* but a lack of dialogue. She reminds readers that using narrative to move toward inquiry is not only an obligation owed by a storyteller; it is an obligation due by a reader. This obligation on readers includes distinguishing metaphorical stories from stories of actual experience, and asking different purpose and credibility questions with respect to made-up stories, once-upon-a time stories, parables, and accounts offered as factual renditions of events. Thus, critical race theory acknowledges an interactive relationship between the researcher and the participants (Guba and Lincoln, 1994).

Summary and Conclusion

This [reading] attempted to spell out the potential of critical race theory as an analytic tool in criminology and criminal justice regarding issues of race, crime, and justice. A critical race theoretical perspectives is regarded are more appropriate than competing perspectives, such as conflict theory, which maintains that the fundamental causes of crime are the social and economic forces operating within society. Moreover, the criminal justice system and criminal law are thought to be operating on behalf of rich and powerful social elites, with resulting policies aimed at controlling the poor. The inability of Conflict Theory to address more subtle and covert forms of racism, however, is a severe limitation on it usefulness.

Critical race theory, on the other hand, challenges us to view race and racism through the lens of People of Color while providing ways of systematizing the search for knowledge (Delgado and Stefancic, 2005). In the process, it helps avoid the search for easy answers, focuses attention on social construction and mindset, asks us to attend to the material factors underlying race and racism, and goes beyond the ordinariness of racist action and treatment (Delgado and Stefancic, 2005). In the now famous words of Justice Blackmun in his dissenting opinion in the *Bakke* case, "[I]n order to get beyond racism, we must first take account of race. There is no other way. And in order to treat some people equally, we must treat them differently." Race continues to play a significant role in explaining inequality, discrimination, and disparities in American justice systems. One way to understand and appreciate the dynamic intersection between issues of race, crime, and justice is through an examination and appreciation of critical race theory.

References

Agamben, G. (2005). *State of Exception*. Chicago: University of Chicago Press.

American Civil Liberties Union (2003). Inadequate Representation. Retrieved on 10/16/2006, from http//www.aclu.org/capital/unequal/10390pub20031008.html

American Humanist Association (2003). Retrieved on 10/18/2006, from (http://www.americanhumanist.org/press/FifthAmendment053003.html).

Bell, D. (1980). *Brown* and the Interest Convergence Dilemma. In D. Bell (ed.), *Shades of Brown: New Perspectives on School Desegregation* (pp. 90–106). New York: Teachers College Press.

Butler, P. (1995). Racially based jury nullification: Black power in the criminal justice system," *Yale Law Journal,* 105: 677.

Crenshaw, K. (1993). Race, reform, and retrenchment: Transformation and legitimation in antidiscrimination law. *Harvard Law Review,* 101(7): 1331–1387.

Crenshaw, K. (1989). Demarginalizing the intersection between race and sex: A black feminist critique of antidiscrimination doctrine, Feminist theory and antiracist politics. *University of Chicago Law Forum,* pp. 139–167.

Crenshaw, K. (1993). Mapping the margins: Intersectionality, identity politics and the violence against women of color. *Standford Law Review,* 43: 1241–1299.

Delgado, R. and Stefancic, J. (2001). *Critical Race Theory: An Introduction,* New York: New York University Press.

Delgado, R. and Stefancic, J. (2005). The role of critical race theory in understanding race, crime, and justice issues. Paper presented at John Jay College of Criminal Justice, CUNY (December 13, 2005).

Dictionary of Sociology (1998). Originally published by Oxford University Press.

Darber, D. and Sherry, S. (1997). Beyond all reason: The radical assault on truth in American Law. New York: Oxford University Press.

Field, B. (1990). *Slavery, Race, and Ideology in the United States of America.* New York: Bantam Books.

Guba, G. and Lincoln, Y. S. (1994). Competing paradigms in qualitative research. In N. K. Denzin and Y. S. Lincoln (eds), Handbook of qualitative research (pp. 105–117). Thousand Oaks, CA: SAGE.

Hall, N. (2005). *Hate Crime.* Portland, Oregon: Wilan Publishing.

Hare, R. (1996). Psychopathy: A clinical construct whose time has come. *Criminal Justice and Behavior* 23: 25–54.

Hawkins, D. F., Myers, S. L. and Stone, R. N. (eds) (2003). *Crime Control and Social Justice: The Delicate Balance.* Westport, Connecticut: Greenwood Press.

Hayman, R. Jr. (1997). *The Smart Culture: Society, Intelligence, and Law.* New York: New York University Press.

Kennedy, R. (1997). *Race, Crime and the Law.* New York: Vintage Books.

Ladson-Billings, G. (1998). Just what is critical race theory and what is it doing in a *nice* field like education? *Qualitative Studies in Education,* 1(11): 7–24.

Ladson-Billings, G. (2005). The evolving role of critical race theory in educational scholarship. *Race, Ethnicity and Education,* 1(8): 115–119.

Ladson-Billings, G. and Tate, W. F. (1995). Towards a critical theory of education. *Teachers College Record,* 97(1): 47–68.

Lazarus, E. (2001). The coming era of federal executions? Legal Challenges we can expect if more federal defendants share McVeigh's fate. Retrieved on 2/16/2007, from http://writ.news.findlaw.com/lazarus/20010123.html

Levitt, N. (1999). Critical of race theory; Race, reason, merit, and civility. *Georgetown Law Journal,* 87(3): 795–822. Avialable at: http://workers.bepress.com/nancy-lerit/16

MacDonald, H. (1995). Law school humbug. *The City Journal.* Retrieved 11/21/2006, from http://www.city-journal.org/html/5_4_a2.html on 10/2006

Matsuda, M. J. (2002). I and Thou and We and the Way to Peace. *Issues in Legal Scholarship,* The origins and Fate of Antisubordination Theory: Article 6 http://www.bepress.com/ils/iss2/art6

McCord, W. J. (1964). *The Psychopath: An Essay on the Criminal Mind.* Princeton: Van Nostrand.

Meloy, J. R. (1990). *Symposium on the Psychopath and the Death Penalty.* American Academy of Psychiatry and the Law, 21st Annual Meeting. October 27, 1990; San Diego. Retrieved on 2/4/2007, from www.psychiatrictimes.com/p960239.html

Morrison, T. (1993). *Playing in the Dark.* Random House.

Murray, Y. M. (1996). Merit-teaching. *Hastings Constitutional Law Quarterly,* 1073(23): 1080–1081.

Omi, M. and Winant, H. (1994). *Racial Formation in the Unite States: 1960s to 1990s.* New York: Routledge Publishing.

Orfield, G. (1988). The growth and concentration of Hispanic enrollment and the future of American education. Presented at *National Council of La Raza Conference,* Albuquerque, NM.

Posner, R. (1997). The Skin Trade, *New Republic,* October 13, p. 40.

Rosen, J. (1996). The bloods and the crits: O. J. Simpson, critical race theory, the law, and the triumph of color in America, *New Republic,* December 9, p. 27.

Schmitt, C. (2005). *Political Theology* and *Dictatorship.* Chicago: University of Chicago Press. Retrieved on 10/18/2006, from http://muse.jhu.edu/journals/theory_and_event/v009/9.2kohn.html

Solorzano, D. and Villalpando, O. (1998). The Chicano educational experience: A proposed framework for effective schools in Chicano students in an urban context, *Urban Education,* 36: 308–342.

Solum, L. (1987). On the indeterminacy crisis: Critiquing critical dogma, *The University of Chicago Law Review,* 54: 462.

Valdes, F., Culp, J. and Harris, A. P. (eds) (2002). *Crossroads, Directions, and a New Critical Race Theory.* Philadelphia: Temple University Press.

Valencia, R. R. (1997). *The Evolution of Deficit Thinking: Educational Thought and Practice.* Pennsylvania: Taylor & Francis Inc.

Wellman, D. (1977). *Portraits of White Racism.* Cambridge, England: Cambridge University Press.

Widiger, T. A. and Corbitt, E. (1996). Antisocial personality disorder. In T. A. Widiger, A. J. Frances, H. A. Pincus, M. B. First, R. R. Ross and W. W. Davis (eds). *(1996) DSM-IV Sourcebook* (Volume 2. pp. 703–716). Washington, D.C.: American Psychiatric Association.

Will, G. E. (1996). Playing the race card, *Portland Oregonian* (Nov. 29, at B8).

Yosso, T. J. (2005). Whose culture has capital? A critical race theory discussion of community cultural wealth. *Race, Ethnicity and Education,* 1(8): 69–91.

Cases Cited

Bell v. Wolfish, 441 U.S. 520 (1979)

Brown v. Board of Education of Topeka, Kansas, 384 U.S. 483; (1954)

McCleskey v. Kemp, 481 U.S. 279 (1987)

Miranda v. Arizona, 384 U.S. 436; 86 S. Ct. 1602; 16 L. Ed. 2d 694; (1966)

Powell v. Alabama, 53 S. Ct. 55, 287 U.S. 45 S. Ct. (1932)

Regents of the University of California v. Bakke, 438 U.S. 265; 407 (1978)

Tennessee v. Edward Garner et al., 471 U.S. 1; 105 S. Ct. 1694; (1985)

Post-Reading Questions

1   How is critical race theory different from strain theory? How does a critical race perspective further our understanding of the American criminal justice system?

2   Why does the late Nobel Laureate Toni Morrison suggest that the concept of race has become metaphorical?

3   What is meant by legal indeterminacy and interest convergence? In what ways can these be used in the criminal justice system?

4   According to the author, in what ways is the concept of legal indeterminacy demonstrated in the cases of *Tennessee v. Garner* and *McCleskey v. Kemp*?

5   What are some of the criticism of critical race theory? How are some of these criticisms refuted (or countered)?

PART III

DIVERSITY MATTERS AND JUSTICE SYSTEMS PROCESSING

"INJUSTICE ANYWHERE IS A THREAT TO JUSTICE EVERYWHERE."

– Martin Luther King Jr.

Racial Misuse of "Criminal Profiling" by Law Enforcement

Intentions and Implications

Patrick Ibe, Charles Ochie, and Evaristus Obiyan

Introduction

This [reading] investigates criminal profiling. Criminal profiling has always been an important law enforcement tool in solving crime. Profiling narrows the field of investigation by indicating the kind of person most likely to have committed a crime by focusing on certain behavioral and personality characteristics. It is a collection of leads, and has been described as an educated attempt to provide specific information about a certain type of suspect (Geberth, 1981), and as a biographic sketch of behavioral patterns, trend, and tendencies (Vorpagel, 1982). Behavioral forensic science has been used for years by law enforcement in crime solving by creating psychological profiles of criminals (Houck & Siegel, 2006). Particular psychological calling cards help and allow law enforcement to manage criminal events that may demand detail investigation. These behavioral analysts gather information from the victims and crime scenes to determine possible characteristics of the perpetrator(s). However, it must be emphasized that criminal profiling does not necessarily provide the exact identity of the offender and as a result, many law enforcement agencies around the world are still skeptical of the work of criminal profilers (Douglas, Ressler, Burgess, and Hartman, 1986).

This [reading] attempts to present an overview and history of criminal profiling used in the Criminal Justice System here in the United States, and would show that criminal profiling has been a legitimate investigation tool for law enforcement but is often misused in racially insensitive way by some law enforcement professionals. The [reading] examines progression of criminal profiling usage and should also show

how it turned into and has become a dreaded investigative tool for some segment of the U.S. society. The need to re-examine criminal profiling stems from (1) racial profiling which has and continues to be a public relations crisis for law enforcement and (2) profiling tends to be used by law enforcement agents more frequently on racial and ethnic minorities which may have unique psychological implications. Thus, it is imperative that attempts be made to reevaluate the current system that yields the best results necessary to restore the legitimacy of the "original intent of criminal profiling".

The issue is that law enforcement criminal profiling is otiose and often racist, and the society at large fails to credit the tool as a method or as the procedure or means of solving or clearing crime or preventing criminal tendencies sometimes with or without probable cause. The problem here is whether or not to keep it as a mechanism of solving crime problems or to eliminate it as racist and otiose. This [reading] examines validity/invalidity of criminal profiling, since it does not apply to society as a whole. Law enforcement should guide and monitor police discretions that lead to criminal profiling. Various theories have been advanced for changes in the criminal justice system particularly the police administration but none of these theories has advocated for upholding the use of criminal profiling officially nor quash it as a racist tool against minorities.

A number of theoretical and practical consequences flow from this [reading]. Looking at its phenomenological significance, one can identify several points regarding law enforcement criminal profiling as discussed supra. This [reading] will help to clarify the explanatory scope and potential of criminal profiling as applied by law enforcement or patrol officers without guideline by their superiors. This [reading] will be used as a tool for generic research initiative in law enforcement functions including patrol mechanism. Moreover, it will provide the possibility for comparative studies with other generic models as well as cross-cultural studies of this dimension of human and police culture. [...] [T]here would be a consensus in regard to criminal profiling in our criminal justice system on whether or not it would be guided and monitored as a tool for solving crime problems or to use it for racial discrimination against minorities.

Methodology

The method used in this [reading] is case study strategy commonly used to interpret and understand different phenomena. Here we are looking at the racial misuse of criminal profiling. In a case study, multiple methods and sources are employed in the collection and analysis of data. Such method includes in-depth interview, personal observations and secondary data collection. The second method used in this study is content analysis which is a type of qualitative method. Krippendorf (1980) defines context analysis as a technique for making inferences about the context, in which the data are found. Analysis of academic journal articles, books, and internet based documented source materials will also be used.

History and Review

What is today regarded as profiling was first used in the middle Ages by the Inquisition to analyze the beliefs of accused heretics. It was not until the 19th century that profiling was used in a truly systematic fashion in England by the police surgeon Dr. Thomas Bond who wrote a lengthy description of the unknown British serial killer "Jack the Ripper". Dr. Bond in his profiling notes detailed "Jack the Rippers" possible habits and psychosexual problems. This did not produce a positive result and the identity of the Ripper remains a mystery. In the U.S., the Californian psychiatrist J. Paul De River was the first to use profiling in assisting the police to catch a child killer in the 1937 case nicknamed the "babes of Inglewood Murders". Dr. James A. Brussel of New York profiled "the Mad Bomber" in the 1950s. His profiling helped in capturing and convicting George Metesky of the crimes. In late 1960s and 1970s Schlossberg developed profiles of many criminals including David Berkowitz-New York City's "Son of Sam". In the '80s in England the "Railway Rapist" (John Duffy) was apprehended through profiling. The "Red Ripper" (Andrei Chikitilo) the Soviet Union's most notorious multiple murder was apprehended through profiling.

The FBI formed its Behavioral Science Unit in 1974 to investigate serial rape and homicides cases. FBI agents Howard Teten and Pat Mullany created a system of profiling for the Bureau's Behavioral Science Unit in Quantico, Virginia. John Douglas and Robert K. Ressler the most famous FBI profilers refined profiling technique by breaking down killers into categories such as "organized" or "disorganized". They also developed methods that allowed profilers to more clearly determine if a crime scene had been staged to mislead investigators into surmising that the perpetrator was more disorganized than he actually was. Forensic science based profiling has gained a lot of popularity in recent years particularly in the media as can be seen from today's most top rated television shows such as Criminal Minds, CSI, and Law and Order, etc. Government agencies such as the FBI has used profiling for many years. According to Owen (2006), in 1985, the Behavioral Unit (BSU) was incorporated into the Federal Bureau of Investigation's (FBI's) national Center for Analysis of Violent Crime (NCAVC) which was set up at the FBI Academy in Quantico, Virginia.

After recognizing the effectiveness of profiling, the technique became a valuable tool in helping law enforcement fight against violent criminals (Owen, 2006). Of course, some crimes can be solved relatively easy because of conclusive forensic evidence such as blood and fingerprint matches of the offender. In this type of situation, a profiler would not be needed. On the other hand, when forensic evidence is not available, profilers will gather all possible information from the victim, crime scene, and other sources to develop a profile of the offender (Owens, 2006). Clearly, criminal profiling is an effective tool for law enforcement to solve crimes when specific evidence is not necessarily left during the criminal event (Owen, 2006). This helps investigators solve crime that would otherwise be a cold case and remains unsolved for years.

Innes (2005) points out that during the first half of the twentieth century, psychiatrist and psychologists dedicated their time to studies of criminal mind, but rarely applied them to forensic questions. However, the first important attempt to relate psychological analysis to determine future behavior of a person was made during World War II in 1943. According to Innes (2005) the U.S Office of Strategic Services requested the psychiatrist Walter Lange to develop a 'psych-dynamic personality profile' of Adolf Hitler. Most importantly, the OSS wanted to know his psychological makeup. In addition, Lange created a long detailed report about Hitler which also included a section predicting future behaviors. Lange predicted that Hitler would commit suicide to avoid capture by the Allied Troops. Lange's prediction was correct (Innes, 2005). Some scholars may declare this prophecy as mere coincidence. Nonetheless, using psychological assessment to explain future behaviors definitely gained notoriety among experts in the criminal justice system. At this point, forensic profiling was relatively new and not much evidence or literature was available. Recently, forensic psychiatrist Michael Stone developed a rating scale for 'who is most evil'. This rating scale may in the future contribute to criminal profiling of dangerous offenders who may deserve selective incapacitation.

According to Holmes and Holmes (1996) an offender profile is usually only called in when the police have exhausted all other leads, sometimes including psychics and astrologers. Profiling suggests the kind of person(s) that may have committed the crime by focusing on certain personality characteristics (Douglas et al., 1986). Remarkably, in a small number of cases, the criminal may be identified correctly and in most cases there is abundant bias in profiling against people of color and the poor. Criminal profiling is relevant in Criminal Justice because this is an investigative tool that assists investigators and police officers when trying to solve crime(s). Trying to solve certain crime or crimes would almost be impossible without creating some type of psychological profile considering the number of people in the U.S.

Alison, Bennell, Modros, and Ormerod (2002) clearly describe the theoretical approach of offender profiling as relying on trait perspective, which has two basic principles: 1) behavior is consistent across offenses and 2) stable relationship exist between criminal behaviors and background characteristics. Therefore, when describing behavior using trait approach, individuals will act very similarly throughout his or her life span. For example, if someone is aggressive or impulsive as a child or teenager, he or she will probably portray these same characteristics throughout life. Yet, traits are not directly observable; instead, they are inferred from conduct (Alison et al., 2002). As these authors explain, profiling uses latent behavior to infer personality characteristics from the original crime scene. Clues are not provided only at the crime scene, but also through the actual crime itself. Various crimes can typically give insight into the type of perpetrator who may have committed the crime. In most cases of rape, rapists do not necessarily seek sexual gratification as they do power and control of victim. Though some cases may appear relatively easy to answer, covert issues may be the motive behind a seemingly obvious offense.

Owen (2006) and Douglas et al., (1986) detailed adequately the various ways of preparing a criminal profile. As the authors describe, the FBI's Crime Scene Analysis (CSA) typically uses six logical steps which make up the profiling process: 1) *profiling inputs, 2) Decision process models, 3) Crime Assessment, 4) Criminal Profile, 5)* Investigation *and 6) Apprehension.*

PROFILING INPUTS: This involves collecting and assessing the evidence involving the case being profiled (i.e. photographs, results of autopsy, and many information needed to determine what happened before, during, or after the crime) This stage is particularly important, because this is the foundation of creating a profile.

DECISION PROCESS MODEL: This consists of arranging and classifying all the information from stage one into a logical pattern. This step will determine the possible number of victims or criminals involved.

CRIME ASSESSMENT: Here the profiler reconstructs the series of events which took place at the crime scene. This stage especially focuses on the behaviors of the victim and the criminal. This helps the profiler understand certain personality characteristic through behavior analysis in order to develop a criminal profile.

CRIMINAL PROFILE: The investigator begins to determine characteristics of the criminal such as background, psychological, and physical information. This stage will determine the age, race, gender and mental status of the perpetrator.

INVESTIGATIVE STAGE: This consists of using the actual profile in the investigation process. This will help investigators determine what information may need to be added or modified to the original profile.

APPRENHENSION STAGE: This may or may not take place depending on the success of the investigation in finding and arresting the criminal. However, even if the suspect is arrested, it is still important to cross reference the details or the profile with the detainee. As previously mentioned, criminal profiling does not always identify the specific perpetrator, rather it tries to understand and create the psychological profile of the criminal.

Furthermore, Owen (2006) also pointed out that investigative psychology was started in 1985 when David Canter, a Psychology instructor was asked to use his expertise in order to assist police with criminal investigation. Investigative Psychology is a technique that involves a series of steps, like the FBI's approach, but centers around five different phases of interpersonal interaction between the criminal and the victims as described by Owen. These five steps include: 1) Interpersonal coherence. This is based on the theory that criminals will interact with other people in their daily lives in similar ways as they interact with their victims. 2) Significant of time and place focuses on the time and location of the crime. This provides information about the criminal's possible routine or possible residence. The Criminal Characteristics step classifies the perpetrators responsible for a crime into the right criminal group. Upon classifying the perpetrator, investigators can gather more characteristic from these particular groups (i.e. rapists, murderers, or arsonist). The Criminal Career step consists of evaluating whether the perpetrator already has an existing record. If a criminal record is available, investigators can gather additional information about the suspect's previous criminal acts. Last, Forensic Awareness involves evidence at the crime scene which may indicate whether or not the perpetrator has any knowledge or awareness of the typical routines or techniques used when collecting evidence. For example, when a burglar breaks into a home, he or she more than likely has forensic awareness that fingerprints could be obtained if protective gloves are not worn during the crime (Owen, 200). It would mean that there is a positive correlation between number of crimes and forensic awareness-as the number of crimes increases so does the forensic awareness of the criminal. If the criminal appears to have a relatively high forensic awareness, he or she may have committed numerous crimes in the past with a higher degree of sophistication compared to inexperienced criminals. Therefore, investigators may be describing an individual with higher intelligence or more charisma than the average population.

Owen (2006) also added another category that is standard in profiling investigations and that is whether a criminal is organized or disorganized. Owen suggests that this category was an extremely valuable criterion for assessing the behavior of the perpetrator of the crime. As the term suggests an organized criminal carefully plans his criminal act decreasing the risk of being caught. An organized criminal tends to target specific victims according to age, gender, physical appearance, and lifestyle. Owen suggests that what makes this criminal so dangerous is the perpetrators ability to appear non-threatening to the victim (i.e. serial killer, Ted Bundy). This type of criminal typically does not represent the average criminal.

On the other hand, a disorganized criminal is completely different. He or she does not plan the crime; instead, he or she commits the criminal act suddenly or impulsively. The crime scene will appear chaotic or in total disarray. This individual could possibly leave more trace evidence than the organized type. FBI research indicates that disorganized criminals are often below average intelligence and are socially inadequate. These individuals will not have charm and social skills to lure their victims. When compared to organized types, a disorganized perpetrator may appear more like the average criminal. Owen goes further to create a summary of organized and disorganized crime scene offender characteristics. He concludes that all crime scenes are mixed to some degree, but establishing which category a crime scene or perpetrator falls under provides a starting point during the early stages of the investigation.

In his studies of psychological profiling of serial arson offenses Kocsis (2004) used questionnaire to determine characteristics of the offenders who may have committed a crime. The questionnaire successfully identified significant characteristics that assist in developing a more comprehensive profile. The major categories include *1) physical characteristics, 2) Cognitive process, 3) Offensive behavior, and social history and habits.* Physical characteristics determine these factors about the offender: gender, age, ethnic background, general build, hair color, hair style, and presence of facial hair. Cognitive process examines familiarity of location where the crime was committed, was the offender comfortable in these locations of the crimes, did the offender have knowledge of the victim prior to the offense, what was the primary motives of the crime, did the offense appear organized? Offenders behavior and possible residence of the perpetrator (i.e. did the offender live within a certain radius of the crime scene), did the offender take steps to conceal his or her identity when committing the crime, did the offender take any items from any of the crime scenes, was sexual activity related to the crime?, and if apprehended and questioned by the police, would the perpetrator possibly confess?. Last, social history and habits explore the offender's marital status, level of education, general employment history, military background, history of drug use, history of diagnosis of mental illness/disorder, how old is the offender's vehicle, condition and model of vehicle, and most importantly, does the offender have a criminal record for any previous crime(s).

Many characteristics are parallel to the category of organized or disorganized as mentioned previously. This can help investigators determine whether the perpetrator is precautious or impulsive. Both types are dangerous, but in different aspects. Kocsis (2004) suggests that all categories listed in the questionnaire are important. However, the last category exploring Social history and habits is more relevant to psychological profiling. These characteristics may identify the perpetrator's social skill and possible mental status. Many psychological assessments will include these facets of the individuals of interest. Alison et al. (2004) explained that traits and behaviors are typically stable over time. Therefore, this allows for future predictions of individuals.

According to Douglas et.al; (1986) a basic principle of profiling is that the cognitive process (i.e. ways and/or patterns of thinking) guide the person's behavior. Bennell et al (2002) suggest that when trying to complete a criminal profile, many traits will overlap with offenders that have committed the same or similar crimes. Yet, two profiles may not be exactly alike in all aspects. Through research and experience, criminal profilers have determined personality traits that appear consistent in certain offenses. Bennel et al. (2002) observed motivational typologies, which were outlined in a variety of rape cases which included the following types: power reassurance, power assertive, anger disciplinary, anger excitation, and profit. They state that power assertive and offender behavior suggest an underlying lack of self-confidence, as a sense of personal inadequacy. These characteristics are expressed through control, mastery, and humiliation of the victim. More importantly, the rapist is trying to demonstrate his sense of authority. Once more, these key personality traits relate to the perpetrator's social history and habits as described above. However, it needs to be reiterated that all perpetrators, such as rapists, are not all alike. Each criminal and case is different, but similar characteristics appear evident in more cases than not.

Additionally, there are two important variables to consider when discussing criminal profiling, the accuracy and validity of professionals. In a study, 77.2% of profiling reports provided by the FBI was indeed considered useful in providing an outside perspective on a case and in helping to focus on the investigation (Alison, West, and Goodwill, 2004). This particular study does lend profiling as a constructive tool for law enforcement. However, profiling may have some disadvantages such as biases.

According to Dabney, Dugan, Topalli, and Hollinger (2006) profiling is a focused and directed form of attribution formation. They describe attribution as helping us infer the intentions of others and how our behaviors may have affected them. Consequently, attributions are created through observations or social interaction and relevant cues that are important to immediate situation. Unfortunately, these attributions are integrated with our existing beliefs and cognitive schemas (Dabney et.al 2006). Therefore, attributions can have biases and results in incorrect profiling. For example, a robbery may have taken place, and two men were noticed at the scene, one a Caucasian and the other Hispanic male. Dabney et al. inferred that the Hispanic male will be questioned before the Caucasian and the reason is that some professionals are unable to resist the idea of cultural stereotyping when deciding which suspect to question first. This thus brings the issue of racial profiling and the misuse of profiling.

This [reading] started by discussing the usefulness of criminal profiling to law enforcement and how it is a vital law enforcement tool for solving crime. Unfortunately, criminal profiling has become racial profiling, thus has cast a serious shadow on the original intent and legitimate use of criminal profiling. How did this crime solving tool that was hailed as an important law enforcement tool turn into racially-biased tool and policy used against certain racial groups? To answer this question it is important to note that profiling can be proactive or reactive. Proactive profiling is "to make judgments about another, relative to possible criminal activity, based on a number of overt and subtle factors which may or may not include things such as a person's race, manner of dress, and grooming, behavioral characteristics, when and where the observation is made, the circumstances under which the observation is made, and relative to information the officer may already possess" (Fredrickson and Siljander, 2002:15). Reactive profiling is what has been glamorized in films and some T.V. shows when investigators use profiling to solve crimes that have already happened. Simply put proactive profiling involves an attempt to interdict and foil crime before it happens. It seems whenever proactive profiling is discussed in the context of police activity in areas where significant number of inhabitants are ethnic minorities, the charge of racial profiling is raised. Likewise, so-called "broken windows" policing (which pays attention to little things like vandalism, graffiti, broken windows, abandoned cars, and ill-kept property; on the assumption that such things broadcast a message that crime is welcome here) sometimes raises the charge of racial profiling because of the aggressive patrol and stopping of suspicious people involve. However, broken windows policing was very successful in cleaning New York City when consistently applied to crime problem there, at least according to most accounts (Carlson, 2002)

Racial profiling has been defined as the inclusion of <u>racial</u> or <u>ethnic</u> characteristics in determining whether a person is considered likely to commit a particular type of crime or an illegal act or to behave in a "predictable" manner. According to Amnesty International, racial profiling occurs when race is used by law enforcement or private security officials to any degree, as a basis for criminal suspicion in non-suspect specific investigations. Discrimination based on race, ethnicity, religion, nationality or on any other particular identity undermines the basic human rights and freedom to which every person is entitled. It further goes on to state that racial profiling is a serious human rights and problems affecting millions of people in the United States in even the most routine aspects of their daily lives. A year-long study conducted by the Domestic Human Rights Program of Amnesty International USA found that the unlawful use of race in police, immigration, and airport security procedures has expanded since the terrorist attack of September 11, 2001. The study further found that state laws provide insufficient and inconsistent protection against profiling. This practice continued despite promises by President George W. Bush shortly after taking office to end racial profiling, the number of Americans, ethnic, racial and religious groups whose members are at high risk of being subjected to this scourge has increased substantially.

The Domestic Amnesty International (USA) from July 2003 to August 2004 studied the current state of racial profiling by law enforcement agencies in the United States. The process began with the consultation of a wide range of community organizations and organizing of a series of public hearings across the United States throughout the Fall of 2003 (San Francisco/Oakland on September 9, Tulsa on September 30, New York, on October 2, Chicago on October 18 and 20, Dallas on November 15). At the hearings, victims, human rights advocates, experts and law enforcement officials testified about their experience with racial profiling.

The major findings of this study may be summarized as follows:

a. A staggering number of people in the United States are subjected to racial profiling. Approximately thirty—two million Americans, a number equivalent to the population of Canada reportedly have already been victims of racial profiling.

b. Approximately eighty—seven million Americans are at high risk of being subjected to future racial profiling during their lifetime

c. Racial profiling directly affects Native Americans, Arab Americans, Asian Americans, Hispanics Americans, African Americans, Persian Americans, American Muslims, many immigrants and visitors, and, under certain circumstances, white Americans.

d. Racial profiling happens to both men and women, affects all age groups, is used against people from all socio-economic backgrounds, and occurs in rural, suburban, and urban areas.

e. Racial profiling of citizens and visitors from Middle East, South Asia, and others, who appear to be from these areas or members of the Muslim and Sikh faiths, has substantially increased since September 11, 2011.

There is growing evidence that racial profiling and the misuse of criminal profiling is widespread. For example one of the earliest scholarly articles on this issue (Harris, 1997) states that:

> "The stopping of black drivers, just to see what officers can find, has become so common in some places that the practice has its own name: African Americans sometimes say they have been stopped for the offense of 'driving while black'------I have heard this phrase often from clients I represented in Washington, D.C., and its surrounding Maryland counties; among many of them, it was the standard way of describing the common experience of constant stops and harassment of blacks by police....... Profiling is not the work of a few 'bad apples' but a widespread, everyday phenomenon that will require systemic reform"

Quite a few studies support the claims of the existence of significant racial profiling in the jurisdictions in which data are available. In a New Jersey study while black and Hispanic motorists made up only 13.5 percent of the drivers on that state's highways, they represented 73.2 percent of those stopped and searched by the New Jersey State Patrol. In a similar study of traffic stops in Maryland from 1995 to 1997 revealed that, though black motorist made up only 17.5 percent of the drivers on certain roadways, they composed more than 72 percent of the motorists stopped and searched by the Maryland State Police. Yet another study in four large Ohio cities revealed that black motorists are two to three times as likely to be ticketed as white motorists (Harris, 1999). Yet another study, by the American Civil Liberties Union in Illinois, showed that, although Hispanics make up less than 8 percent of the state's population, they were 27 percent of those stopped and searched by a highway drug interdiction unit (Cole, 1999).

There are equally some arguments defending racial profiling especially given the different patterns of crime involvement by different ethnic groups. Kennedy (1999) argued that

> "Defenders .... Of racial profiling maintain that, in areas where young African American males commit a disproportionate number of street crimes, the cops are justified in scrutinizing that sector of the population more closely than others, just as they are justified in scrutinizing men more closely than women ... For {some} cops, racial profiling is a sensible, statistically based tool that enables law enforcement to focus their energies more efficiently; it lowers the cost of obtaining and processing information ... and {thus reduces} the overall cost of policing .... Racial profiling then ... is good police work ... empirically based, and above all, an effective tool in fighting crime".

Based on this assumption those who defend racial profiling generally do so on statistical grounds, citing some evidence that in certain jurisdictions, individuals associated with particular racial groups commit a disproportionate number of crime. In the Sourcebook of Criminal Justice, a federal data reveals that in 1996 nationwide, blacks, who made up approximately 12.8 percent of the nation's population, represent 43.2 percent of the persons arrested for Part I violent crimes, and 32.4 percent of persons arrested for Part I property crimes.

Psychologists exploring the personal impact of racial profiling concluded that racial profiling can inflict serious emotional anguish (Butts, 1999). The study by a researcher who conducted in-depth interviews regarding reactions to racial profiling and racialized law enforcement in different Washington D.C neighborhoods reveals that feelings of anger, powerlessness, and stigmatization are the norms for racial minorities subjected to criminal suspicion because of their race (Weitzer, 2000). In-fact, racial profiling imposes substantial burdens on persons who are innocent. Racial profiling has also been opposed as a violation of the Fourth Amendment's prohibition against unreasonable searches and seizures. Scholars have argued that a search or seizure based on an individual's race as a predictor of possible criminality violated the Fourth Amendment. (Maclin, 1990) In Whren v. United States the Supreme Court, however, has held that an officer's subjective motivation cannot be used to attack a search or seizure.

No other ethnic group has been affected negatively by racial profiling than African Americans. According to Ethnic Minority (2008) the most common example of police profiling is "DWB", otherwise known as "Driving While Black".

This refers to the practice of police targeting African Americans for traffic stops because they believe that African Americans are more likely to be engaged in criminal activities. Rarely do we hear about a criminal suspect as white because we think of the white criminal as "an individual deviant, a bad actor". We do not think of his actions as representative of an entire racial group (Volpp, 2002). African Americans have continued to be the repository for American fear of crime and to be treated as amalgamation of presumed group trait rather than as individuals. While racial profiling is illegal, a 1996 Supreme Court decision *Whren v. U.S.* Allow police to stop motorists and search their vehicles if they believe there is evidence of trafficking of illegal drugs or weapons. More traffic stops lead to more arrests, which further skews the racial profiling statistics against African Americans. Studies have shown that African Americans are far more likely to be stopped and searched. Are African Americans really committing more crimes or are they just caught more often because they are the target of police? This is a vicious cycle that even the strictest law enforcement advocates would admit is patently unfair. According to reports, racially profile arrests of drugs for African Americans have been one of the most troubling one.

Harris (1999) suggests that racial profiling is based on the premise that most drug offenses are committed by minorities, and this premise creates a profile that results in more traffic stops of minority drivers. He further states that the pervasiveness of racial profiling by the police in drug law enforcement is the result of an escalation in laws on drugs. Drug use and drug selling are not confined to racial and ethnic minorities; in fact, five times as many whites use drugs. The war on drugs, however, has targeted people of color and skin color and this has become a proxy for criminality. Consequences of racial profiling in law enforcement are evident in the demographics of the prison population. For example, Davis tell us that Blacks constitutes 13% of drug users in the United States, 37% of those arrested on drug charges, 55% of those convicted, and 74% of all drug offenders sentenced to prison. This leads Harris to conclude that the racial profiling premise that most drug offenses are committed by minorities is factually untrue, but that it has nonetheless become a self-fulfilling prophecy.

Because police are suspicious and search for drugs primarily among African Americans and Latinos, they find a disproportionate number of them with contrabands. Therefore, more minorities are arrested, prosecuted, convicted, and jailed, thus reinforcing the perception that drug trafficking is primarily a minority activity. This perception creates the profile that results in more stops of minority drivers. At the same time, white drivers receive far less police attention, many of the drug dealers and possessors among them go unchecked, and the perception that whites commit fewer drug offenses than minorities is perpetuated, and so the cycle continues says Harris. Harris further states that this vicious cycle carries with it profound personal and societal costs. It is both symptomatic and symbolic of larger problems at the intersection of race and the criminal justice system. It results in the persecution of innocent people based on their skin color. It has a corrosive effect on the legitimacy of the entire justice system. It deters people of color from cooperating with the police in criminal investigation, and in the court room, and it causes jurors of all races and ethnicities to doubt the testimony of police officers when they serve as witnesses, making criminal cases more difficult to resolve.

Employing a law and economics analysis in terrorism investigation Professor Lund (2003) argues that "governments are highly prone to excessive racial stereotyping and largely immune from forces that keep {practices like racial profiling} in check in the private sector". He further argued that the danger of government abuse arising from the *ex ante* use of race in terrorism investigation is too great when considered in light of the fact that "{m}any of the efficiency benefits of racial profiling----can be captured through the use other screening criteria, such as country of origin----age, sex, and travel patterns". Traditional profiling relies on the correlation between behavioral factors and the past experience of law enforcement in discovering criminal behavior associated with those factors, thus, it rests on the perceived accuracy of the profile as a predictor of criminality. When this is misused, that is when it is based on race it brings fear, anxiety, humiliation, anger resentment, and cynicism on the suspects. It also damages law enforcement and the criminal justice system as a whole. Other conservatives oppose racial profiling on "law and order" ground, that is, that it "makes law enforcement less effective" because "discriminatory police practices create unnecessary and unproductive hostility between police and the communities they serve" (Forman, 2001). When profiling is misused, it can inflict serious emotional anguish and stigmatization on the victim.

Yet despite overwhelming evidence, including the police department's own statistics on traffic stops, say Harris—officials in law enforcement continue to deny the reality of racial profiling on our nation's highways. Some deny that the phenomenon of racial profiling even exists, while others declare with indignation that their officers do not stop motorists on the basis of skin color. Still others argue without apology that making disproportionate numbers of traffic stops of African Americans and other minorities is not discriminatory, but rational law enforcement. But as one officer learned, such "honesty" can be a dangerous counterpoint to official denial of profiling. To demonstrate the resistance to acknowledge some reality in this issue, Harris cites a case where Carl Williams, New Jersey's Chief of Troopers, was dismissed in March 1999 by the Governor Todd Whitman soon after a news article appeared in which he defended profiling because, he said "mostly minorities" trafficked in marijuana and cocaine. Williams's remarks received wide media attention at the time when Whitman and other state public officials were already facing heightened media scrutiny over recent incidents of profiling and public anger over police mistreatment of black suspects. Governor Whitman and the Attorney General, Peter Veniero, recouped from Williams remarks somehow when they issued a statistical report on April 20, 1999, acknowledging that the problem of racial profiling is, as Veniero put it "real, not imagined". As events in New Jersey demonstrates, even when faced with lawsuits, statistical evidence from independent experts, public pressure and intensive news coverage, officials in law enforcement and government are not eager to acknowledge the problem of racial profiling. It is believed by many including the ACLU that addressing the problem will require a multi—faceted effort. Several law suits have been brought against states in racial profiling and police discriminatory practices by some civil rights advocates, but law suites are just the beginning as these cases are always difficult to win. Concerted efforts are needed by the public to fight this cancerous disease.

Evaluation of Offender Profiling

Generally, a number of misconceptions about profiling exist usually because of its fictional use. Profiling does not provide the specific identity of the offender which of course is not the purpose. The aim is to narrow the field of the investigation and suggest the type of person who commit-ted the crime (Douglas et al, 1986). There have been a lot of successes and failure in profiling. One of the most famous failures in the United States was the case of Albert DeSalvo (known as the "Boston Strangler", the profile put forward was that the offender was a male homosexual schoolteacher living alone. When he was arrested it was found that DeSalvo was a heterosexual construction worker living with his family. The case of the gateway sniper was another instance where profiling went completely wrong. John Allen Muhammad and John Lee Malvo terrorized the D.C. area from September 21, 2002 to October, 20th of the same year killing about ten people but all the profilers never taught that such crime will be committed by a black person. Most profilers taught it is a white male probably an ex-soldier.

Another notable failure was that of Rachel Nickel who was brutally murdered while walking on Wimbledon Common in South London. When the profile was put together and the suspect was arrested and confession was not forthcoming the case fell apart. Another classic failure was the case of Richard Jewell a security guard during the 1996 Olympics in Atlanta who discovered a bomb and began moving people to safety when the bomb exploded. The FBI had arrested him profiling him as a "lone bomber". But fortunately the case was solved after a series of abortion clinic bombing when Eric Rudolf was arrested and confessed to the Olympic bombing incident.

Equally, there have been successes recorded in this field. The murder by Carmine Calabro of a special education teacher on the roof of her Bronx apartment building turned out to be accurate. The profile appeared to be an important factor in reducing the number of suspects and eventually arresting the correct person. Profiling helped in apprehending Arthur Shawcross after a series of murders of prostitutes the profile suggested that the offender might return to the scene. Shawcross was observed masturbating in his car on a bridge near the scene, and was arrested and eventually confessed in custody. In some cases profiling can be shown to successfully identify some of the characteristics of the offender. A good example is the Green River case. Garry Ridgway who is regarded as the most prolific serial killer in U.S. history was apprehended through profiling. He admitted the murder of 48 women, mainly prostitutes over a 22 year period. In the end, Ridgway was apprehended as a result of DNA analysis, and a profile prepared by John Douglas was found to be reasonably accurate (Levi-Minzi and Shield, 2007).

Pinizzotto and Finkel (1990) argued that profiling is most effective in serial offenses because of the extensive research base, and least effective for fraud, burglary, robbery, theft and drug induced crimes. Agreeably, Kaufman (1998: 1223) made a number of recommendations in regard to profiling, including the following:

> "Police officers should be trained as to the appropriate use of, and limita- tions of criminal profiling. Undue reliance on profiling can misdirect an investigation. Profiling once a suspect is identified can be misleading and dangerous, as the investigators' summary of relevant facts may be colored by their suspicions. A profile may generate idea for further investigation and, to that extent, it can be an investigative tool. But it is no substitute for a full and complete investigation, untainted by preconceptions or stereotypical thinking."

Legislation at the federal and state levels and local voluntary efforts can advance the momentum to collect accurate data on the problem and rein in overzealous—and sometimes illegal-law enforcement practices.

The Fourth Amendment Impact

"The right of the people to be secure in their persons, houses, papers, and effects, against un- reasonable searches and seizures, shall not be violated, and no warrants shall issue, but upon probable cause, supported by oath or affirmation, and particularly describing the place to be searched, and persons or things to be seized" (U.S. Constitution: Fourth Amendment). Since the provision as enumerated in the fourth amendment, the United States Supreme court has issued several opinions broadening law enforcement discretionary authority. In fact, fourth amendment cases including but not limited to Carroll V. United States, Belton V. New York, Whren V. United States, Terry V. Ohio, Atwater V. The City of Lago Vista etc. have all broadened police powers and particularly and effectively given law enforcement personnel freedom to target minorities. Police are now able to set up vehicle stop and search without obtaining a judicial warrant. Racial profiling is indeed illegal in the United States, but the flexibility guarantees to them by the Supreme Court rulings make it easy for them to profile. Police stops and searches that are due to race and without any legal bases are improper and should be regarded as a fourth amendment violation.

The 2002 department of USDOJ national survey indicates that the police were more likely to carry out some type of search on African Americans who were found to be stopped 10.2% of the time, Hispanics are stopped 11.4% of the time and Caucasians 3.5% of the time. In the United States Supreme court cases mentioned earlier, the court clearly allows the police conduct of using simple traffic violation to justify a "Stop" though the actual intent was to conduct investigation into suspected or perceived criminal activities. A significant case is that of United States V. Arvizu in which the court announced that the 4th amendment does not prohibit investigatory stops as long as the "facts and circumstances" (Pelic, 2003) lead to reasonable suspicion that the occupant of the vehicle has indeed engaged in criminal event. The Arvizu case has strengthened police powers and reinforces the previous Supreme Court decisions that also increased law enforcement discretionary authority. In his analysis of the issue of racial profiling, Scott Belshaw (2007) argued that "the court in Atwater case permits the field officer a wide range of discretion when stopping and investigating citizens operating motor vehicles, standing in the street, or walking down the street ... this discretion is allowing the officer to make judgmental decisions which are fundamental to racial profiling issues". Devon Carbado (2010) postulated several hypothesis: That the fourth amendment jurisprudence is insensitive to and unconcerned with, the contemporary realities of race; that literature on race and the fourth amendment has not fully examined the ways in which current doctrine affects the everyday lives of people of color .... the suggestion that suspicion is racialized and that this racialization burdens people of color is not novel; and that the scholarship on race and the fourth amendment is under inclusive, focusing primarily on Blacks". Furthermore, Carbado argued that the "Supreme court has not explicitly articulated colorblindness as a guiding principle of the fourth amendment. As a result of this racial elision people of color continue to experience the fourth amendment more as a technology of surveillance than as a constitutional provision that renders them secure in their persons, homes, papers, and effects".

DJ Silton (2002) thought that in Whren v. United States, "the supreme court effectively declared the fourth amendment dead with respect to protecting citizens against racial profiling".

Furthermore, Silton argued that in the Whren's case, "the court held it reasonable for police offi-cers to pull cars over for nominal traffic violations with the specific intent to discover illicit drug use ... the result of this decision is that police officers have unfettered discretion to stop any car for any reason, since it is virtually impossible to drive without violating at least one traffic law". Several Supreme Court decisions seem to escalate incidents of racial profiling in their confused interpretation of the fourth amendment in Whren and which was reinforced in Ohio v. Ronette in which the court ruled that an officer need not tell a driver that they can refuse an officers' search request, Thornton v. United States in which the Court ruled that police can search a parked vehicle for drugs, guns, or other evidence of a crime while arresting the occupants, Wyoming v. Houghton where the court ruled that after arrest the police can search the closed purse of vehicle occupants even without probable cause, and in Maryland v. Wilson in which the court granted law enforcement agents the power to order vehicle occupants out regardless whether there is or no reason to believe that they were dangerous. All these cases have emboldened the police and have made it easy for them to engage in racial profiling. Fighting crime is surely a high priority. But it must be done without damaging other important values: the freedom to go about our business without unwarranted police interference and the right to be treated equally before the law without regard to race and ethnicity guaranteed by the Constitution. "Driving While Black" assails these basic American ideals, says Harris. And unless we address this problem, all of us—not just people of color—stand to lose.

Recommendations

Daigneault (2010) defined racial profiling as "that terrible vestige of segregation, intolerance, and hatred. It is his position that racial profiling "has to be fought on many levels, from terrorists profiling to drug dealer and other common criminal profiling". Daigneault suggested two ways to prevent racial profiling and we agree including education and cultural immersion. According to this author, we begin "from grade school and beyond ... . this is a way to help get rid of racial stereotypes that all African Americans and Latinos driving expensive cars are drug dealers, and not all people with Arabic or Persian accents are terrorists".

The proposed Traffic Stops Statistics act of 1997 was dead on arrival at the United States Congress. What we need is a strong federal law that gives individual States guidelines on the prevention and elimination of misuse of racial profiling. When the federal law is implemented it should mandate documentation of all traffic stops, searches and arrests. Furthermore, and as with the PCB recommendation for Washington DC Police, collect data on traffic stops, implement documentation of all stops, hire expert statisticians to help implement data collection, imple-ment officer education and training including intensive sensitivity training, and law enforcement agencies need to develop and adopt a racial profiling policy that all officers must abide by and in fact internalize.

In conclusion, this [reading] tried to demonstrate a number of issues. It not only has been able to show that criminal profiling has been and can be a legitimate law enforcement tool based on its history but also that its' original and legitimate law enforcement utility has been twisted. It has become almost like an illegitimate law enforcement concept because of how it is used by some law enforcement professionals. In the process, the [reading] narrated the history and how profiling was relevant in criminal justice because it is a useful investigative tool that assists investigators and police officer when trying to solve crime(s). As a relevant criminal investigative tool, it caught the attention of law enforcement agencies worldwide as well as the media. Profiling was described in this [reading] as the process of using available information about a crime and crime scene to compose a psychological portrait of the unknown perpetrator of a crime, usually a serial offender, through analysis of the scene left by the perpetrator. This [reading] also delved into the unfortunate misuse of criminal profiling and it became evident that it has turned into a racial and ethnic characteristic stereotyping used in determining whether a person is considered likely to commit a particle type of crime or illegal act or to behave in a "predictable" manner. The [reading] has demonstrated that criminal profiling has become a racial policy and tool used by some law enforcement as a basis for suspicion in non-specific investigation. It has evidently become a discriminatory concept based on race, ethnicity, religion, nationality, as well as other particular identity which without question undermines the basic human rights and freedom to which every person is entitled to. As suggested, concerted efforts should be made by all to root out racial profiling because it undermines the law enforcement efforts and it makes us all unsafe and it has proven to be a failure on the war on drugs. Finally racial profiling should be completely rooted out because it is illegal, inhuman, and should be used as originally intended as described in this [reading].

References

Alison, L., Bennel, C., Ormerod, D., & Macros, A., (2002). 'The Personality Paradox in Offender Profiling': *Psychology, Public policy, and Law*, 8(1), 115–135

Alison, L., Goodwill, A., & West, A., (2004) 'The Academic and Practitioner Pragmatists' views of Offender Profiling': *Psychology, Public Policy, and Law*, 10(1/2), 71–101

Atwater. G et al., v. The City of Lago Vista 532 US 318 (2002)

Belshaw, S., (2005) 'Racial Profiling and the Fourth Amendment' *E-Journal of Texas Criminal Justice.*

BJS, *Sourcebook of Criminal Justice Statistics*, published annually by U.S. Dep.t of Justice, Bureau of Justice Statistics, Using data gathered for FBI's Uniform Crime Report (UCR)

Butts, H., F., (1999) 'Psychoanalytic perspectives on Racial Profiling', 27 *J. AM. ACAD Psychiatry. L.* 633

Carbado., D.,W., (E) 'Racing the Fourth Amendment', 100 *Michigan Law Review* 946–1044, 064–974, 1043–1044 (March, 2002) (374 Footnotes)

Carlson, D., (2002). *When Culture Clash.* Uppers Saddle River, NJ: Prentice Hall

Cole, D., "The Color of Justice: Courts are Protecting, Rather than Helping to End, Racial to End, Racial Profiling by Police" *The Nation* 11 October, 1999

Dabney, D.A., Dugan, L., Topalli., & Hollinger R.C., (2006) the Impact of Implicit Stereotyping on Offender Profiling Unexpected Results from an Observation Study of Shoplifting. *Criminal Justice and Behavior*, 33(5), 646–674.

Daigneault, T., (2010 How to fight Racial Profiling: Helium, Politics, News and Issues. http://www.helium.com/items/506510 how-to-fight-racial-profiling.

Davis, H., (1999) 'Driving while Black: Racial Profiling on our Nation's Highways': *National Criminal Justice Reference Service*.

Davis, H., "Driving while Black" and other Traffic Offenses: The Supreme Court and Traffic Stops" *The Journal of Criminal Law and Criminology*, Vol. 87(2), 1997.

Douglas, J.E., Ressler, R.K., Burgess, A.W., & Hartman, C.R., (1986) Crime Profiling from Crime Scene Analysis: *Behavioral Science & Law*, 4(4), 401–421

Durose, M., et al., United States Department of Justice-Bureau of Justice Statistics Study: Contact Between Police and the Public: Findings of the 2002 National Survey. http://www.ojp.usdoj.gov/bjs/abstract/cpp02.htm

Forman, J., Arrested Development: The Conservative Case against Racial Profiling, *New Republic*, September 10, 2001 at 24.

Fredrickson, D, Siljander, R., (2002) *Racial Profiling: Eliminating the Confusion Between Racial Profiling and Criminal Profiling*. Springfield IL: Charles C. Thomas

Gerberth, V.J., (1981) Psychological Profiling: *Law and order*, pp 46–49.

Hicks, S.J., Sales, B.D., (2006) Criminal Profiling Developing an Effective Science and Practice. Washington, D.C: *American Psychology Association*.

Houck, M.M., Sales, J.A., (2006) *Fundamentals of Forensic Science* (pp. 7) San Diego, CA: Elsevier Limited

Innes, B., (2005*). Body in Question Exploring the Cutting Edge in Forensic Science*. New York: Barnes & Noble Publishing, Inc.

Kaufman, F., (1998) *Report of the Kaufman Commission on Proceedings Involving Guy Paul Morin*, Ontario: Ontario Attorney-General.

Kennedy, R., "Suspect Policy: Racial Profiling Isn't Racist. It Can Help Stop Crime. And It Should And It Should is abolished". *The New Republic:* September 13 & 20, 1999.

Kocsis, R., (2004) Psychological Profiling of Serial Arson Offenses an Assessment of Skills and And Accuracy, *Criminal Justice and Behavior*, 31(3), 341–361

Krippendorf, K., (1980) *Content Analysis: An Introduction to its Methodology*. Beverly Hills CA: Sage Publications

Levi-Minzi, M., Shields., M (2007) "Serial Sexual Murders and Prostitutes as Their Victims: Difficulty Profiling Perpetrators and Victim's Vulnerability as Illustrated by the Green River Case. *Brief Treatment and crisis Intervention*, 7:1, 77–89.

Lourie, R., *Hunting the Devil*, New York: Happer Collins (1993)

Maclin, T., the Decline of the Right of Locomotive: The Fourth Amendments on the Street, 75 *CORNELL L. Rev.* 1258, 1324 (1990)

Owens, D., (2006*). Criminal Minds the Science and Psychology of Profiling:* New York: Quintet Publishing Limited.

Pelic, J., (2003) United States v. Arvizu: Investigatory Stops and the Fourth Amendments, *Journal of Criminal Law and Criminology*, Vol. 93, 1094. Terry v. Ohio, 392 U.S. 1 (1968)

Pinizzotto, A., J., Finkel, N., J., (1990) Criminal Personality Profiling: An Outcome and Process Study. *Law and Human Behavior,* 14, 215–233

Schechter, H., *and the Serial Killer Files:* New York: Ballantine, (2003)

Silton, D., J., Profiling: A Covertly Racist Nation Rides Vicious Cycle, 20 *Law and Inequality: A Journal of Theory and Practice* 53–90, 67–81 (Winter 2002) (292 Footnotes).

Torres, A.N., Boccaccini. M.T., & Miller, H.A., (2006) Perception of the Validity and Utility of Criminal Profiling Among Forensic Psychologists and Psychiatrics. *Professional psychology: Research and Practice,* 37(1), 51–58.

Weitzer, R., Racialized Policing: Residents Perceptions in Three Neighborhoods, 43 *Law & Society Rev.* 129 (2000)

Volpp, L., 'The Citizen and Terrorist', 49 *U.C.A.L Rev.*1575, 1585 (2002)

Vorpagel, R.E., (1982) Painting Psychological profiles: Charlatanism, Charisma, or a new Science? Official Proceeding of the 88th Annual IACP Conference. The Police Chief. pp. 156–159.

Post-Reading Questions

1   According to the authors, what are some ways to prevent racial profiling? Which of these appear more practical?

2   Aside from federal law enforcement, should the federal government spearhead efforts to prevent racial profiling—or should it be left up to each individual state?

3   According to the authors, how did racial profiling evolve from a *legitimate* law enforcement tool to an illegitimate law enforcement tool?

4   Alison and colleagues (2002) describe the theoretical approach to offender profiling, relying on the trait perspective. What are its two basic principles of a trait perspective?

5   What can (or should) be done when law enforcement agencies fail (or refuse) to comply with racial profiling reporting requirements?

Reference

Alison, L., Bennel, C., Ormerod, D., & Macros, A. (2002). The personality paradox in offender profiling. *Psychology, Public policy, and Law,* 8(1), 115–135.

Abuses Resulting From Federal Immigration Enforcement Efforts

Lupe S. Salinas

Mexicans, the initial U.S. Latino group in 1848, actually lived in what is now the United States decades before the arrivals in 1620 of non-Hispanic Europeans at Plymouth Rock. Spaniards first founded St. Augustine, Florida, in 1565, and later, in 1610, founded the Santa Fe area in New Mexico (Weber 1973, 14). Notwithstanding, the white majority viewed Latinos as newcomers with no rights and abusively treated them as nonwhite people. This Anglo attitude arose from the nation's historical foundations, which envisioned a nation of free white men who would administer governmental affairs. The Founding Fathers provided that representation shall include the total of all free persons plus "three fifths of all other Persons,"[1] constitutionally recognizing slaves as property and as less than any white person.

Anglo American attitudes immediately caused conflict with the new Latino population. First, the adoption of Mexican persons as American citizens created tensions. Regardless of their citizen status, Anglos viewed Latinos scornfully as just "Mexicans," a blatant attitude that endured for over a century. Even if the Latino happened to be a soldier in uniform immediately after the end of World War II, he was still a "Mexican" to racist Anglo restaurant owners (Perales 1974, 156–57). During this one hundred–year period, millions of Mexicans and other Latinos entered the United States, some legally and many others surreptitiously. In the process of interactions, both the society at large and law enforcement encountered difficulties in distinguishing between immigrants on one hand and legal residents and citizens of Latino descent on the other. As a result, in this discussion of Latino injustices, the author also addresses the treatment of undocumented Latinos, since immigration enforcement inevitably snares U.S. citizens and resident aliens in the crossfire (Stevens 2011, 608, 618–35; Preston 2011; Perez and Lutz 2011).

For well over a century, America's immigration policy effectively promoted maintenance of a Caucasian-race majority. Congressional leaders and the Supreme Court followed this ideology, barring the admission of Chinese and promoting efforts to curtail Mexican immigration (Salinas and Torres 1976, 866–67). In 1924, Congress established the national-origins quota system, which limited immigration from Eastern Hemisphere countries to 150,000. Western Hemisphere immigration was not restricted.[2] In 1965, Congress made changes and limited Western Hemisphere visas to 120,000 per year.[3] For the first time in history, Congress placed Western Hemisphere countries under an immigration quota, an action that effectively increased undocumented entries. In 1976 Congress equalized the treatment towards the Eastern Hemisphere and the Western Hemisphere by limiting each hemisphere to 20,000 immigrants per country.[4] While on the surface this policy sounds equal, the law has adversely affected U.S. Latinos who have families in Mexico and other Latin American countries. These citizens now have to wait a disproportionately longer time—sometimes up to twelve years—to enjoy "family unity."

Peonage and Other Unfair Labor Conditions

The status of being immigrants, both legal and undocumented, as well as being poor and powerless American citizens, increases the chances of being a victim of peonage.[5] The Thirteenth Amendment to the United States Constitution provides that neither slavery nor involuntary servitude, except as a punishment for crime, shall exist within the United States.[6] The next Amendment, the Fourteenth, provides in relevant part that no State shall deprive any *person*[7] of life, liberty, or property, without due process of law, nor shall any State deny to any *person* within its jurisdiction the equal protection of the laws.[8]

Congress enacted an anti-peonage statute to enforce the Thirteenth Amendment. The law forbids one from holding or returning any person to a condition of peonage, or from arresting any person with the intent of placing him in, or returning him to, a condition of peonage. The statute provides for a maximum sentence of any term of years or life if the violation results in death, kidnapping or an attempt to kidnap, aggravated sexual abuse or the attempt to commit aggravated sexual abuse, or an attempt to kill.[9]

Historically, based on constitutional history, a discussion of slavery or peonage related to Africans. Today, however, peonage and slavery applies to persons of all races. In the *Slaughterhouse Cases*, a post-slavery case, the Supreme Court observed that the word "servitude" means more than just slavery, and it is intended to "forbid all shades and conditions of African slavery."[10] While the Court initially questioned whether persons other than African Americans could receive protection under the Thirteenth Amendment, the opinion dictated that the Amendment forbids any other kind of slavery, including "Mexican peonage or the Chinese coolie labor system."[11] The term "Mexican peon" appears in the writings of several sociologists and historians (Acuña 1972, 86–88, 137; Taylor 1934, 36, 325–29; Gonzales 1999, 122; Salinas 2005, 339–41). Concern over Mexican-descent worker abuses prompted LULAC to address Mexican peonage in its founding charter when Alonso S. Perales and other civil rights leaders founded the group in 1929 (Taylor 1934, 244).

In *United States v. Nelson*,[12] seafood company owner Benjamin Harrison Nelson hired a Houston man to supply him with undocumented workers. Nelson paid him $100 per alien. He would then deduct that amount at the rate of $10 a day, their daily wage. In other words, the first ten days they provided labor just to eliminate the debt. The aliens never knew up front that they had a built-in debt when they began their employment.

After working three days around the pungent odor of oysters and shrimp, two of the aliens went to collect their pay so they could leave. Nelson surprised them when he informed them that they owed him seven more days of labor to settle the debt. The two men, frustrated by the news, walked to the corner store to see if they could figure out a way to leave the bay-area town. They saw some Latino house painters and asked if they had room in the van to get back to Houston. The driver agreed, and as they headed down the road, a fellow worker advised Nelson that his indebted servants had escaped. Nelson and his son, armed with rifles, succeeded in racing down the road in their pickup trucks, forcing the painter's van to stop. Nelson and his son retrieved only the two aliens who still owed money for the transporting fee.

By pure chance, one of the painters knew one of the two men who were taken at gunpoint to the town. He notified that victim's family in Matamoros, Mexico, across from Brownsville, Texas. The family then informed a federal prosecutor, who drafted a search warrant for the seafood company premises. Based on the testimony of the victims and items found in the search, including a notebook with proof of the transporter payments, a federal grand jury indicted Nelson for peonage, kidnapping, and carrying away a person with the intent to hold that person as a slave. The grand jury also indicted Nelson for aiding and abetting the *coyote* (transporter) in the transportation of unauthorized aliens. After the jury found Nelson guilty, he appealed, and the Fifth Circuit Court of Appeals affirmed his convictions (Salinas 2005, 339–41).

Joint State and Federal Law Enforcement of Immigration Law

The collaboration between local and federal immigration officials in the apprehension and removal of undocumented immigrants is not new in American history. These cooperative efforts occurred during the notorious 1930s Operation Repatriation and again in the tactlessly named 1950s Operation Wetback. Two factors should affect whether future abuses occur as frequently. First, the U.S. Latinos sixty years ago did not have the numbers or the political muscle. Second, Supreme Court jurisprudence had not clarified what constitutes an "unreasonable" seizure, as recent federal court cases have accomplished.[13] While the larger, more vocal Latino community may not fully succeed in preventing the deprivations, Latinos are definitely better positioned politically.

The onset of the Great Depression's economic hardships caused politicians and small farmers to blame "the Mexican" for their misfortunes, and prompted federal and local law-enforcement deportations. President Herbert Hoover, for instance, blamed the economic woes on the presence of unauthorized workers (Acuña 1972, 190–91). By the late 1920s, Mexican-descent persons represented the largest number of undocumented workers (Acuña 1972, 141–42). The deportation enforcement unfortunately became contaminated with racist diatribes by Texas Congressman Box, who referred to Mexicans as a "degenerate" race (Gottheimer 2003, 157). He also expressed his goal of protecting American racial stock from further degradation through "mongrelization," his description of the "Mexican peon," the product of a Spanish peasant who had mixed with low-grade Indians (Box 1928).

Not surprisingly, these attacks contributed to the deportation fervor. In the process, agents nabbed adult American citizens (Balderrama and Rodriguez 1995, 98–107). Determining alien or citizen status by mere appearance is impossible. Naturally, the repatriation movement resulted in the inclusion of American-citizen children among repatriates, approximately 60 percent of all deportees (Balderrama and Rodriguez 1995, 183). In Los Angeles, the U.S. city with the largest and most concentrated Mexican population, officials discovered that "only a small percentage of the Mexicans were undocumented" (Rosales 2000, 80).

Notwithstanding the harsh anti-Mexican commentary and the drastic removal actions, American leaders in times of economic necessity usually relied on their Mexican *amigos* (friends). When World War II prompted U.S. involvement, Congress immediately initiated a temporary Bracero Program (from *brazos* or arms) to import Mexican workers to replace American men. This "temporary" statute lasted more than twenty years.[14]

After benefiting from Mexican labor for several years, President Eisenhower ungratefully approved Operation Wetback during the 1950s to deal with complaints of poor economic conditions and surplus labor. The Immigration Service operation involved the collaboration of federal, state, county, and municipal authorities in efforts to control the "invading force" of Mexican migrants (Samora 1971, 52; Copp 1971, xv). Once again, agents deported Mexican-descent permanent resident aliens and citizens by birth or naturalization along with undocumented persons (Rosales 2006, 335).

The Bracero Program contributed to an increase in unauthorized Mexican entry because it convinced other Mexican nationals that the United States had a high demand for labor. An excessive number applied. Obstacles to lawful admission prompted many to enter without permits. The extreme racial discrimination suffered by Mexicans in Texas led to Mexico's initial objection to providing that state with *braceros*. As a result, when employers demanded workers, this triggered an influx of undocumented aliens into Texas (Acuña 1972, 169–70; Samora 1971, 45). For instance, in 1950, some 500,000 undocumented Mexican aliens were apprehended, while only 120,000 Mexican contract laborers and 18,000 Mexican authorized immigrants entered the United States (Samora 1971, 197).

The Bracero Program's demise began with dissatisfaction among unions and laborers who asserted that imported labor displaced domestic labor (Galarza 1964, 16, 132, 145, 199–218). Upon the program's 1964 termination, Mexico warned American officials of future massive undocumented entries. After the program's end, the apprehensions of undocumented aliens increased from 86,597 in 1964 to 788,145 undocumented aliens in 1974, an increase of 810 percent (U.S. Immigration and Naturalization Service 1964, 7; U.S. Immigration and Naturalization Service 1974, iii, 9).

In 1978, Congress created the Select Commission on Immigration and Refugee Policy (SCIRP), a year after President Carter submitted a plan asking Congress to add 2,000 new Border Patrol agents. SCIRP met during the last year of the Carter administration and developed amnesty and employer sanction proposals (Salinas and Torres 1976, *passim*). In early 1981, the Hesburgh Commission (SCIRP) submitted its report to President Reagan, and SCIRP continued its work.[15] President Reagan eventually signed the Immigration Reform and Control Act of 1986 (IRCA) (Chishti, Meissner, and Bergeron 2011), a law primarily known for granting amnesty or legalization[16] to undocumented aliens, and for sanctioning employers who knowingly hire unauthorized workers.[17]

Fraud sadly occurred in the desire to receive residence. Another negative result included the lack of farsightedness of those involved in shaping the nation's future immigration needs. American employers had needs, and the immigration policy did not address them. IRCA beneficiaries petitioned for eligible family members, adding delay up to ten years or more and effectively increasing unauthorized immigration. What began as a petition for a few thousand extra border agents has multiplied to a request for over 20,000 by 2011 (Chishti, Meissner, and Bergeron 2011).

The continued surge in undocumented immigration fed the anti-alien politics during the 1994 congressional election. From this anger, adeptly exploited by Speaker Newt Gingrich, Congress in 1996 enacted two of the nation's harshest anti-immigrant statutes ever.[18] One statute not only expanded the definition of an aggravated felony to include misdemeanors, but also made the aggravated felony conviction retroactive for removal (deportation) purposes.[19] Since this time, the immigration battlefield has been malicious. National government policy changes resulted in more enforcement at the California border, and the presence of American vigilantes along portions of the Arizona border made the crossings more dangerous by respectively driving the migrants into the Arizona desert, and by having gun-toting civilians detain suspected aliens (Bender 2003, 135).

Under President George W. Bush, the government initiated Operation Return to Sender (Flaccus 2007, A4). Primarily billed as a concerted effort to nab criminal aliens, over 75 percent of those apprehended in the five-year period prior to 2009 were noncriminal persons employed in gainful endeavors (Bernstein 2009, A1). During this same Bush administration, Congress authorized billions of dollars for a fence to keep aliens from crossing our Southern border.[20]

Ironically, most Americans, including conservatives, praised President Reagan in 1987 for telling Soviet leader Gorbachev to tear down the Berlin Wall.

Classification and Typecasting of Undocumented Aliens as Criminals

Activists justify their anti-immigrant fervor by citing the moral depravity, economic drain, and rising crime rate that allegedly accompany undocumented aliens. Simultaneously, racist motives often surface. For example, Terry Johnson, a North Carolina sheriff, claimed that Mexicans have lower moral values than Americans, adding that Mexicans approve of having sex with 12-year-old girls. Another North Carolina sheriff raised concerns about the tolerance and ability of local police to enforce immigration law fairly. Sheriff Steve Bizzell complained that Mexicans rape, rob, and murder "American citizens." He admitted that, as the sheriff, he responded on behalf of people, apparently whites, who asked him what he was going to do about all "these Mexicans" (Weissman 2009).

Both sheriffs associated the Latino immigrant presence with an alleged growing crime rate. In rebuttal, a study of North Carolina court statistics documented that the incidence of criminal activity by foreign-born residents was actually lower than that of U.S. citizens. Furthermore, although the undocumented immigrant population has doubled since 1994, the violent crime rate in the United States has declined 34.2 percent and property crime has fallen 26.4 percent (Weissman 2009).

Federal Immigration Enforcement, Business Demands, and Resistance by States

Over the years, American businesses, particularly construction, service, and agricultural, have advocated for increased immigration. These business owners enjoy reliable workers and the low wages. Once an economic crisis occurs, however, opposition to undocumented workers escalates, even among those who once wanted their services. Recently, hot-tempered complaints about "illegals" prompted Arizona and copycat states to assume immigration duties reserved to the national government.

In 2010, Arizona enacted an "attrition through enforcement" statute.[21] In addition to the federal government's inaction, Governor Jan Brewer justified the state's law on the crime generated by migrants, including "beheadings" (Fox News 2010). Brewer added that agents found headless bodies in the desert, a claim the *Arizona Guardian* investigated and found to be "completely false" (Fox News 2010; Associated Press 2010). Even Senator McCain entered the fray by asserting that Arizona's forest fires had been caused by "illegals," a claim disputed by authorities (Katrandjian

2011). A *Washington Post* editorial condemned the governor's "mindlessness about headlessness" and other false claims about the crime rate increase and its alien link (Milbank 2010, A15). Shortly after these claims, the *Arizona Republic*, citing statistics from the FBI and Arizona police agencies, reported that the incidence of crime in Arizona border towns had been essentially unchanged for the ten years leading to 2010 (Wagner 2010).

In another move that upset these states-rights advocates, during the last days of President Obama's first term, the President enacted an executive order to exempt Dreamers[22] from immediate deportation (U.S. Department of Homeland Security 2012). In mid-2014, in response to an influx of Latino children at the Mexican border with Texas, Rep. Darrell Issa (R-CA) urged the end to the DACA program (Deferred Action for Childhood Arrivals) and the deportation of all 11 million undocumented aliens, Dreamers included. Despite the 2012 DACA order, ICE officers that year deported aliens at near record levels.[23]

In the process of carrying out such a massive enforcement effort, ICE and local police violated the civil liberties of many innocent people. ACLU and other civil rights lawyers fought legal battles on many fronts, decrying the numerous arrests, detentions, and deportations of innocent American residents and citizens erroneously suspected of being undocumented aliens. The litigators accused agents of racial profiling when they target Americans solely on the basis of their ethnicities, language, or even their accents (*New York Times* 2009). For instance, U.S. citizen Leonard Parrish moved from Brooklyn to Houston, Texas. He appeared at the county jail to obtain a bond upon discovering he had a misdemeanor warrant. The deputy concluded that Parrish was undocumented because of his foreign-sounding accent and placed an immigration hold on him, even though he presented documentation of legal status (Russell 2008).

Civil Rights Abuses Suffered by U.S. Latinos during Federal Immigration Enforcement

Several Latino organizations have been active for decades in the battle for justice for U.S. Latino equality. These groups, in chronological order, include LULAC, the League of United Latin American Citizens, founded in 1929; the American GI Forum, 1948; MALDEF, the Mexican American Legal Defense and Educational Fund, 1968; NCLR, the National Council of La Raza, also 1968; and the Puerto Rican Legal Defense and Educational Fund, 1972, known today as LatinoJustice PRLDEF.

Fortunately, other groups, like the American Civil Liberties Union (ACLU), and government agencies like the Department of Justice (DOJ) assist in the vindication of civil rights. Puerto Rican Americans, legislatively declared citizens even if born in Puerto Rico,[24] also suffer detentions by immigration agents who operate on suppositions rather than facts. In Chicago, Illinois, Eduardo Caraballo spent three days in jail after his theft arrest. Caraballo made bail promptly, but his immigration problems then began. He faced "deportation" on suspicion of unauthorized status (Perez and Lutz 2011).

Caraballo's investigators developed doubts by asking him specific questions about Puerto Rico that he could not answer to their satisfaction. Caraballo's mother had brought him to the U.S. mainland when he was eight months old, and he traveled only once to Puerto Rico. Chicago Congressman Luis Gutierrez complained that agents cannot "just judge people by their color or their features, by the way they look, they should actually investigate thoroughly, and they should do that before they put the hold on somebody" (Perez and Lutz 2011).

The case of Luis Alberto Delgado, an American by birth, involves a combination of racial profiling and abusive federal immigration practices, similar to those in the Caraballo case. Born in Houston and in possession of a Texas identification card, a social security card, and a birth certificate, Delgado was suspected by the deputy sheriff of using fake documents, since he spoke only Spanish (Carroll 2010). Based on this profiling, the deputy called for a Border Patrol agent to take over. At this point, an unreasonable seizure (prolonged detention without probable cause) had occurred.

Any law enforcement officer knows that when an undocumented parent is deported, the underage children also go with the parents to the country of origin. The Delgado case merely has another twist, i.e., a divorce where the mother chose to abandon Texas to live with family in Michoacan, in the interior of Mexico. Inexplicably, the federal immigration agent, supposedly trained to detect false documents, chose to disbelieve Delgado, and he failed to have someone with more expertise investigate the alleged falsification of documents.

After endless hours of doubting his birth claims, the agent managed to coerce a "voluntary" departure of the U.S. citizen. Delgado kept asking, without success, to be taken before a judge. Delgado finally relented and signed the agent's paperwork as a means of finding some other approach to his dilemma (Carroll 2010). Delgado remained in his "deported" status for nearly three months along the northern Mexican border, where he had no family, before immigration officials finally allowed his return (Lavender 2011). A question surfaces: If the agent really believed Delgado had false documents, why did he not pursue a felony charge of presenting forged documents, the alleged basis for his disbelief? This misrepresentation by any person is an extremely serious felony charge that amounts to an obstruction of justice.

In a case of recklessness or callous indifference, the U.S. government, in collaboration with the Los Angeles County Jail, deported U.S. citizen Pedro Guzman to Mexico. Guzman had been serving a 120-day jail sentence for a trespass committed under bizarre circumstances suggesting delusional behavior. Guzman signed a voluntary departure in May 2007 with immigration officials based in the jail. Guzman allegedly told a jailer that he was born in Mexico. Considering his mental condition, questions arose as to why officials neglected to investigate the detainee's jail records to confirm his citizenship and mental health situation. Three months later, Guzman called his sister from Mexico, telling her he did not know why he was in Mexico. He tried several times to return to his birth country, but federal agents at the bridge told him to stop playing games. The ACLU's legal director faulted the federal government and ICE for deporting Guzman, who returned in "a state of shock," trembling and stuttering (Hernandez 2007).

Deprivations of Liberty and Other Rights by Immigration Agents

An unfortunate misconception abounds that undocumented aliens in the United States do not merit protection under the Constitution. The Fourth Amendment refers to the right of the "people" to be free from "unreasonable searches and seizures."[25] Another relevant constitutional provision is the Fourteenth Amendment. This amendment mentions both "citizens" and "persons," an indication that the Founding Fathers distinguished between the two groups. In other words, persons subject to the jurisdiction of the United States include undocumented persons who receive constitutional protections.[26]

In *United States v. Otherson*,[27] Border Patrol agents admitted to beating aliens who had illegally entered the United States from Mexico. After they were found guilty, they appealed on the sole issue that the aliens are not protected by the criminal civil rights statute since, as undocumented persons, they were allegedly not "inhabitants of any State, Territory, or District."[28] The motive for the assault centered on an obscene gesture an alien had directed towards a Border Patrol aircraft. Otherson and his companions responded with violence. His partner slapped the alien several times and beat his hand with a nightstick. Otherson joined in, punching the alien in the stomach. Otherson then told a third agent about the incident, who then slapped and punched the alien.

On the following day, Otherson took two other aliens he had apprehended to an area where several aliens were being detained. An agent then slapped one man five or six times across the face. Otherson kicked another alien in the leg, hit him with his nightstick, and kicked his shoes into a canyon. The aliens were then taken to headquarters to be prepared for routine deportation. The proof indicated that Otherson's participation in the alien abuse involved a deliberate plan. The agent who apprehended the obscene-gesture alien overheard Otherson and other agents talk about "Who's the designated hitter?" or a similar question. Otherson explained to a trainee that they had to impose this punishment since "the criminal justice system doesn't do anything to these assholes."[29]

In this case of first impression, the Ninth Circuit decided if the term "inhabitant" excludes aliens who are in the United States without authority. After reviewing the legislative history, the appellate court concluded that the civil rights statute broadly protected "all persons within the jurisdiction of the United States,"[30] including those here without papers. As proof of the intent of the Senate, the court quoted the sponsor of the Civil Rights Act. He stated that the proposed 1870 legislation extended equal protection of the laws to "all persons who are in the United States"—i.e., to "all persons within the jurisdiction of the United States."[31] The court specifically noted that later amendments to the statute did not alter this meaning. As a result, the court concluded that the term "inhabitant," as used in section 242, includes all persons within the jurisdiction of the United States, including the aliens whom Otherson and his fellow agents admit beating and abusing.[32]

Another case involved a different type of inhumane treatment. Immigration agents arrested Serafin Carrera. The force used to seize him resulted inadvertently in Carrera's paralysis.[33] The U.S. Attorney filed a criminal civil rights charge against three agents for denying medical care to a person in their custody.[34] The prosecution did not allege that the force used by the agents in making the arrest constituted a specific intent to deprive him of his right to liberty and freedom from punishment. Instead, once the agents realized that Carrera was immobilized, the neglect to provide medical care constituted the constitutional deprivation. An officer squirted Carrera with pepper spray to determine if he was feigning an injury. When he did not react normally, the officers realized that Carrera was in serious need of medical care.[35]

Federal Immigration Agents and the Use of Deadly Force

Federal investigators began a review of U.S. Customs and Border Enforcement and Border Patrol policies on the use of deadly force after a wave of shootings by agents along the U.S.-Mexican border. One of the fatal shootings included a teenager who agents said was throwing rocks at them from across a fence in Mexico. Since 2010, at least eighteen people have been killed by Border Patrol agents. Eight of the deaths involved rock throwers (Associated Press 2012a).

In one of the rock-throwing allegations, a Border Patrol agent, Jesus Mesa Jr., shot and killed 15-year-old Sergio Hernández-Guereca near the El Paso–Juarez bridge. The family sued the United States and the agent. The Fifth Circuit Court of Appeals affirmed the dismissal against the government, but it allowed the action against the agent to proceed.[36] The family of the deceased alleged multiple avenues for liability, but the court allowed a trial only on the personal claim against the agent.[37] Judge Edward Prado concluded that a "noncitizen injured outside the United States as a result of arbitrary official conduct by a law enforcement officer located in the United States may invoke the protections provided by the Fifth Amendment,"[38] which include the right not to be subjected to the "conscience-shocking use of excessive force across our nation's borders."[39]

In another case, in 2008 prosecutors dismissed murder charges against a Border Patrol agent after two mistrials. Agent Nicholas Corbett arrested Francisco Javier Dominguez and three family members near the Arizona border. Corbett claims that when he ordered the Mexican nationals to surrender, Dominguez refused and threatened him with a rock. The witnesses contradict this story and claim the agent shot him without provocation. Corbett initially claimed that Dominguez was holding a rock while standing a few feet away (Holstege 2008). A forensic problem with Corbett's claim is that he was so close that his weapon upon discharge left powder burns on the victim's clothing. This means that the shooting occurred within a distance of one to two feet.

The evidence also indicates that the shot came from slightly behind and above the smaller man (Holstege 2008). Under those circumstances, the much larger agent was close enough to easily and physically control a man with a rock in his hand. This claim of being threatened by a rock, however, sufficed to create reasonable doubt among a jury of twelve citizens having to make a decision under circumstances where the volatile national immigration debate had inflamed emotions. For instance, during the trial, both anti- and pro-immigrant advocates conducted courthouse demonstrations (Holstege 2008). After a second mistrial, the victim's family filed a civil lawsuit, which alleged that Corbett had a reputation of anti-Latino hatred and violence. The government and Corbett, without admitting guilt, settled with Dominguez's family for $850,000 (Jackman 2011).

The Border Patrol considers the use of deadly force against rock throwers generally acceptable, noting that rocks can be deadly; but critics question comparing a bullet to a rock, particularly when the agent can retreat to a safer location. Sixteen members of Congress expressed concern as to whether the use of deadly force epitomizes a broader problem within the agency, and asked for an investigation. The Department of Homeland Security (DHS) inspector general began an investigation. In 2014, the commissioner of Customs and Border Protection (CBP) presented a report entitled *Use of Force Policy, Guidelines and Procedures Handbook*, which provides CBP law-enforcement agents with rules related to the use of force (U.S. Customs and Border Enforcement 2014, 38–42). The agency recognized that agents face hazardous conditions, but it found that "in several cases where agents shot at rock throwers, the force appeared to be excessive" (Preston 2014). The commissioner's most emphatic words zeroed in on the major purpose of the review: "The use of excessive force by CBP law enforcement personnel is strictly prohibited" (U.S. Customs and Border Enforcement 2014, i).

Another section of the handbook addresses the use of safe tactics in a confrontational situation. Primarily, the guidelines urge agents to "employ enforcement tactics and techniques that effectively bring an incident under control, while promoting the safety of the officer/agent and the public." Specifically, the procedures dictate that agents "should not place themselves in the path of a moving vehicle or use their body to block a vehicle's path," particularly when this action predictably necessitates the use of deadly force. Firing at the driver of a vehicle could disable that person, and the results of an out-of-control vehicle could result in the death of innocent passengers and bystanders or fellow officers (U.S. Customs and Border Enforcement 2014, 6).

Specifically, in response to the rock-throwing claims, agents "shall not discharge their firearms in response to thrown or launched projectiles unless the officer/agent has a reasonable belief, based on the totality of circumstances (to include the size and nature of the projectiles), that the subject of such force poses an imminent danger of serious physical injury or death to the officer/agent or to another person." To avoid the use of deadly force, agents are urged to seek cover or distance from the immediate area of danger and thus gain a tactical advantage (U.S. Customs and Border Enforcement 2014, 6).

Efforts to limit the rampant use of deadly force began with a 2013 independent law-enforcement review that recommended against the indiscriminate use of deadly force against rock throwers. The Border Patrol chief responded by stating that the agency will continue to allow its agents to shoot at rock throwers and vehicles (Childress 2013). This arrogant reaction perhaps lifts agent morale, but it creates a negative image of law enforcement and contributes to the deprivation of rights.

The policy as amended in 2013 (Childress 2013) and as it appears in the 2014 official handbook hopefully addresses the chief's concerns, or at least explains that not all lethal force will be banned in cases of rock throwers and vehicles. Agents of course are required to have a "reasonable" belief that they can suffer serious bodily injury or death by having a rock thrown at them. The agents also have to be astute enough not to jump in front of a vehicle whose driver is trying to escape. The potential loss of any life, including the agent's, does not justify such extreme behavior.

According to the DHS inspector general, rocks are the most common weapon used to assault agents. Another factor to consider is that the Border Patrol has grown quickly and is now the nation's largest police force. [...] The rapid growth has thus produced an agency with many officers with limited aptitudes and extremely dangerous attitudes about immigrants. Perhaps this combination has resulted in the numerous reports of excessive force, mostly along the border with Mexico. With almost twenty Border Patrol–attributed deaths since 2010, no one has been held accountable. One death, for example, included an agent shooting a 16-year-old boy eleven times for throwing rocks at him (Childress 2013).

The Brutal Death of Anastasio Hernández-Rojas

The death of Anastasio Hernández-Rojas[40] at the age of 42 is among the many fatalities involving immigrants and immigration agents since 2010. Hernández died in late May 2010, three days after being subjected to multiple baton strikes and electric shocks from a Taser repeatedly administered by an enforcement agent (Moran 2013). According to an investigator who talked to the agents, Hernández became "agitated and confrontational" after he was detained (Associated Press 2012a). San Diego police conducted Hernández's death investigation pursuant to an agreement the city has with Customs and Border Protection where deaths involving officers occur (Archibold 2010). The county medical examiner's autopsy report attributed his death to a heart attack, and included as contributing death factors an enlarged heart, the presence of methamphetamine, and a "prolonged struggle" that resulted in five broken ribs (Moran 2013).

Witnesses to Hernández's detention and assault by agents did not notice a confrontational person. Instead, they observed several federal agents surround Hernández as he lay handcuffed on the ground. Several witnesses recorded the action. The eerie sounds of Hernández crying out in pain for those two-and-a-half minutes affect even those aware of the worst crime stories. The word "torture" immediately surfaces. Hernández can be heard crying out in apparent pain for help. For 20 seconds, he cries out in a prolonged and horrible-sounding "Noooh" (Goodman 2012). Hernández then pleads with the men surrounding him in Spanish: "*Ayúdenme, por favor, señores, por favor"* (Help me, please, sirs, please). One can only imagine his hope that the crowd of *señores* (the male federal agents) will stop their colleagues who are beating and shocking him. These observing federal agents had a legal duty, but they did not intervene. They even stepped back so the stuns could be administered (Goodman 2012). One account claims that a supervisor arrived and allowed the assault to continue (Frey 2012).

At 44 seconds, another voice is heard yelling, *"Ya, déjenlo,"* which basically means, "Enough! Leave him alone." Then at 1 minute and 7 seconds, a voice states in English, "Hey! He's not resisting!" From 1:49 to 2:07, about 20 seconds, a voice exclaims: "Why you guys keep pushing on him? He's not even resisting!" (Goodman 2012). The Customs and Border Protection (CBP) federal agency insisted that Hernández's "combative" behavior necessitated the use of a baton and stun gun to "subdue the individual and maintain officer safety" (Costantini and Foley 2012). At the time of the application of this force, Hernández was handcuffed and unable to attack and harm the agents.

Additional footage later discovered by John Carlos Frey, an investigative reporter, raises questions about the propriety of the excessive force that agents directed at Hernández. The video, taken by Seattle resident Ashley Young as she crossed the bridge from Mexico to the United States, shows the crowd of agents standing around Hernández, who does not appear to be moving. Ms. Young asserts that Hernández was handcuffed. She did not witness Hernández lash out at the agents, but she heard an agent inexplicably yell for him to "quit resisting." The agents surely knew they were being watched by civilians, an apparent explanation as to why the agent yelled for him to cease moving. One must wonder whether a person who is subjected to a beating that resulted in broken ribs and to painful electrical shocks would not move involuntarily (Costantini and Foley 2012).

The agent with the Taser shot him five times with electric charges (Costantini and Foley 2012). As people gathered on the bridge and yelled to officers to stop the attack, Young says other agents approached and told them to keep moving. One officer demanded that two witnesses hand over their cell phones or delete the video they had taken, but she kept walking. She described the incident like witnessing a man being "murdered" (Caulfield 2012). Agents had reportedly hogtied Hernández prior to subjecting him to the Taser gun (Costantini 2012).

According to Eugene Iredale, an attorney representing Hernández's widow and five citizen children in a civil lawsuit,[41] the DOJ civil rights division began presenting evidence to a federal grand jury. Another family friend said two eyewitnesses to the incident were called to testify in July 2012. One possible witness is Humberto Navarrete, who made a cell-phone video that included audio of Hernández pleading for help, and passersby asking that he be left alone (Spagat 2012).

Prior to the videos, and while at the Border Patrol station, Hernández allegedly agreed to a voluntary deportation. The family's lawsuit disputes that, saying he did not agree to go and instead wanted a hearing before an immigration judge. In spite of this, a supervisor ordered Hernández to be deported at the bridge. As two agents removed his handcuffs and escorted him to a crossing point, Hernández bumped the agent. Another claimed that Hernández began to move around like a "tornado" while pushing and grabbing at the agents (Moran 2013).

As often occurs in the use of physical force against individuals being subjected to arrest, the stories vary. This occurred in the Rodney King beating case several years ago. The police claimed that King resisted. The federal jury eventually found some of the officers guilty. The video in the Hernández case should assist the prosecution. First, the video captures an agent sadistically applying electric shocks on a handcuffed man who is not in position to harm an agent. Second, the audio portion of the video captures the pleas for mercy of the victim as well as the invaluable present sense impressions and excited utterances of those persons whose voices are heard describing what they are observing. These comments represent potent prosecution evidence. Neither the identification nor the presence at trial of these individuals is required for the comments to be admissible since these types of out-of-court statements are generally deemed reliable and trustworthy.[42]

In the event of a civil-rights deprivation criminal prosecution, the government lawyers must contend with Hernández's enlarged heart and methamphetamine consumption. Methamphetamine causes increased heart rate and blood pressure and can cause irreversible damage to blood vessels in the brain, producing cerebral vascular accidents (strokes) (Missouri Department of Social Services 2005). Those eventually accused in a criminal trial and those who face civil litigation will likely claim that the methamphetamine caused his fatal heart attack.

The federal prosecution, if it ever occurs, will have to deal with these medical and social issues of Hernández's bad heart and his drug use, which may have been a small or a large amount of methamphetamine. Reports in the press have not been clear as to what amount he consumed or its effect. At the time the agents and Hernández had their encounter, however, the agents did not know Hernández consumed drugs or that he had an enlarged heart. In other words, the heart condition and drug use is irrelevant to the fact that officers acting under color of law summarily punished Hernández and, in the process, violated his civil rights. The appellate courts have universally held that the resulting death only has to be a proximate or foreseeable result of the wrongdoer's willful violation of the victim's rights.[43] Any factors that contribute to a quicker death obviously are relevant to a determination of an appropriate punishment.

The applications of the painful Taser stun gun, in addition to the baton strikes Hernández sustained, constitute a deprivation of a person's right not to be punished without due process of law. The relevant statue provides:

> Whoever, under color of any law, statute, ordinance, regulation, or custom, willfully subjects any person in any State, Territory, Commonwealth, Possession, or District to the deprivation of any rights, privileges, or immunities secured or protected by the Constitution or laws of the United States, or to different punishments, pains, or penalties, on account of such person being an alien, or by reason of his color, or race, than are prescribed for the

punishment of citizens, shall be fined under this title or imprisoned not more than one year, or both; and if bodily injury results from the acts committed in violation of this section or if such acts include the use, attempted use, or threatened use of a dangerous weapon, explosives, or fire, shall be fined under this title or imprisoned not more than ten years, or both; and if death results from the acts committed in violation of this section or if such acts include kidnapping or an attempt to kidnap, aggravated sexual abuse, or an attempt to commit aggravated sexual abuse, or an attempt to kill, shall be fined under this title, or imprisoned for any term of years or for life, or both, or may be sentenced to death.[44]

If death results, the punishment ranges from one year to a maximum period of life in prison. The likelihood of a death sentence in this type of case is minimal. In determining intent, jurors are often confused by the intent issue as it relates to the violation of one's rights and the resulting death. In other words, the federal prosecutor, in a criminal civil rights deprivation trial, does not have to prove that the person acting under color of law acted with the intent to kill. A prosecutor only has to prove that the agent acted with the intent to deprive the victim of his right not to be deprived of liberty without due process of law. Once that is shown, the penalty increases if the death resulted in any way from the deprivation.

As an appellate court stated in a civil rights case, "No matter how you slice it, 'if death results' does not mean 'if death was intended.'"[45] If a federal agent, in order to teach Hernández a lesson for resisting arrest, as the reports suggest, beats him and applies electric shocks multiple times while he is restrained, this conduct violates the deprivation of a right to due process that the Constitution guarantees to all "persons."[46] In a case where death results from a deprivation of rights, the punishment range is the only aspect of the statute that is affected.

Other legal concepts implicate a person's initial improper actions. Our law recognizes that the wrongdoer takes the victim as he finds him. In addition, our law recognizes what is called the acceleration theory, i.e., the idea that a wrongdoer can engage in an act that hastens or speeds up the inevitable result. If an agent's act accelerated Hernández's death, then he can be found criminally liable. Hernández's heart condition independently could cause medical problems. Even if Hernández was on the verge of death, American criminal law nonetheless permits a finding of culpability if his death is accelerated. Once again, these facts all go into the assessment of punishment and do not relate to the issue of guilt.

What role the electric shocks played in Hernández's death will perhaps remain a mystery, but medical studies indicate that risks increase when Tasers are applied to persons suffering from heart problems, or to anyone when the Taser is applied to the chest. For example, in August 2013, an 18-year-old healthy man ran from police after painting graffiti. The youth died from cardiac arrest within minutes after the officer applied a stun gun to his chest (Fagenson 2013).

Stun guns are used to physically incapacitate a person by discharging controlled electrical energy into the body with the intent to provide a safe means of subduing an uncooperative person. A team of Canadian medical doctors and other scientists conducted a study and determined that stun guns stimulate cardiac muscle in addition to skeletal muscle, thus potentially promoting lethal cardiac arrhythmias. While primarily utilized to impact motor function, intense pain is a collateral effect of the application of a stun gun. These experts observe that, depending on preexisting defects (e.g., a previous heart attack, drug intoxication), each person's heart may have a different susceptibility to life-threatening arrhythmia during stimulation (Nanthakumar and Massé 2008).

The Canadian experts utilized real stun guns operated by qualified law-enforcement personnel to test the effects on a pig's heart. They found that a stun-gun discharge can stimulate the heart. In another study, the experts attributed two animal deaths to ventricular fibrillation immediately after the electrical discharge. The experts further confirmed that even without catheters in the heart, stun gun discharges on the chest can stimulate the heart (Nanthakumar and Massé 2008).

Unlike prior studies, the evidence and the studies presented by Nanthakumar and Massé suggest that stun guns can stimulate the heart while discharges are being applied. They thus found it inappropriate to conclude that stun-gun discharges cannot lead to adverse cardiac consequences in all real-world settings. As a result, they recommend future studies involving people in order to resolve the conflicting theoretical and experimental findings and ultimately lead to the design of devices with electrical pulses that cannot stimulate the heart (Nanthakumar and Massé 2008).

Other deaths besides the 18-year-old man's mentioned earlier have occurred shortly after stun-gun discharges. After three stun-gun-related deaths in Houston, Texas, a review of Taser usage found that deputies appear to disregard national guidelines or product warnings in three key areas: stunning suspects in the chest, using Tasers against people who are not physically resisting, and stunning subjects multiple times. Even though the Taser manufacturer has warned law enforcement agencies to avoid stunning suspects in the upper chest over concerns of an adverse effect on the heart, officials with the sheriff's office in Houston say chest hits are safe (Pinkerton 2011, A1, A8).

Another problem with the use of Tasers is their indiscriminate use as an alternative to patient policing. Experts like the Police Executive Research Forum and the Justice Department note that a stun gun should only be used against those who actively resist or exhibit aggression. Another problematic finding in the use of Tasers is that 71 percent of those stunned were minorities (Pinkerton 2011, A8).

As to Hernández, considering what he endured in the custody of the federal agents, his death was foreseeable. Although he was only 42 years old, he experienced electric shocks from a stun gun and severe physical injuries, which included broken ribs associated with brutal force. His injuries were admittedly aggravated by his own debilitating health conditions. One thing is clear: Anastasio Hernández-Rojas would have continued to live if his rights had not been violated. Whether he would have lived one day, one month, or one more year and then suffered a fatal heart attack is irrelevant to the civil rights culpability. As the medical examiner stated, Hernández died from the totality of the experiences he suffered (Moran 2013).

Only time will tell if justice will be done. Probable cause that a civil rights deprivation occurred appears to be clear. A grand jury should return a true bill charging those responsible. This is not a finding of guilt, an issue that must be decided by the jury or the judge who hears the government's case. Many Latino activists fear that the "just another Latino" attitude will prevail, with nothing being done to vindicate the deprivation of the rights of Anastasio Hernández-Rojas. It has happened before in recent history. One can only hope that another Latino life is not given the same insulting treatment as that given to army veteran Jose Campos Torres or the renowned journalist Ruben Salazar [...].

In the end, the question arises as to whether the problem centers on the nation's immigration and Border Patrol police. In an op-ed in the *Los Angeles Times*, John Carlos Frey, a documentary filmmaker, deduced that insufficient training and little public oversight of the Border Patrol have led to problems, including violence against migrants (Frey 2012). Frey observed that in 2007, the Bush administration began efforts to strengthen border security. Eventually, this led to doubling the size of the Border Patrol, an agency of the Department of Homeland Security.

Since recruits were difficult to find, the agency lowered its standards and training regimens were relaxed. Individuals without a high school diploma could already join, and the agency also began to defer background checks. In less than two years, 8,000 new agents were hired. The Border Patrol, which had a force of 11,000 in 2007, by 2012 had more than 21,000 agents. Frey figured that nearly half of the Border Patrol force now includes rookies with two years of experience or less who are dangerously armed with batons, pepper spray, Tasers, rifles, and handguns (Frey 2012).

The Department of Homeland Security maintains secrecy about when and why police agents can fire a weapon. With insufficient training and little public oversight, it is not surprising that since May 2010 there have been at least eight documented cases of extreme use of force against unarmed and noncombative migrants resulting in death. Of eight recent killings by Border Patrol agents, not one agent has even been disciplined (Frey 2012). As long as this indifference to accountability continues, the message is that any person who throws a rock from across the border is subject to execution.

Notes

1 See U.S. Const. art. I, § 2 cl. 3.

2 Act of May 26, 1924, ch. 190, 43 Stat. 153.

3 Act of Oct. 3, 1965, Pub. L. No. 89–236, § 21(e), 79 Stat. 911.

4 Pub. L. No. 94–571 (Oct. 20, 1976) (effective January 1, 1977).

5 The author includes this related discussion on peonage in the immigration abuse section even though the unjust results arise from abuses by private persons.

6 U.S. Const. amend. XIII.

7 Emphasis added to show how the drafters of the Constitution distinguished "persons" and "citizens."

8 U.S. Const. amend. XIV.

9 18 U.S.C. § 1581 (2000).

10 Slaughter-House Cases, 83 U.S. (16 Wall.) 36, 69 (1873).

11 Ibid., 72.

12 The author prosecuted the peonage/slavery case, United States v. Nelson, No. 81–2105, in 1981.

13 U.S. Const. amend. IV; Melendres v. Arpaio, 989 F. Supp. 2d 822, 2013 U.S. Dist. LEXIS 73869, at 216 (D. Ariz. May 24, 2013); Melendres v. Arpaio, 695 F.3d 990, 1000 (9th Cir. 2012); Floyd v. City of New York, 959 F. Supp. 2d 540 (S.D.N.Y. 2013).

14 Agreement Between The United States of America and Mexico Respecting the Temporary Migration of Mexican Agricultural Workers, U.S.-Mex., Aug. 4, 1942, 56 Stat. 1759, amended by 57 Stat. 1152 (1943), (repealed 1964) (commonly known as the Bracero Program).

15 As special assistant to U.S. Attorney General Benjamin R. Civiletti, the author, along with other assistants of Cabinet members, senators, and members of Congress, collaborated to provide information to the SCIRP executive director in preparation of his final report.

16 8 U.S.C. § 1255a (2006).

17 8 U.S.C. § 1324a (2006).

18 The Antiterrorism and Effective Death Penalty Act (AEDPA), Pub. L. 104–142, § 401–443, 110 Stat. 1214, 1258–81 (1996), codified at 18 U.S.C. § 2339B (a) (7) (2006), combined with the Illegal Immigration Reform and Immigrant Responsibility Act (IIRIRA), Pub. L. 104–208, Div. C, 110 Stat. at 3009–546 through 3009–724 (1996), 8 U.S.C. § 1101 et seq. (2006), extensively amended the Immigration and Nationality Act of 1952 (INA), 66 Stat. 163 (1952), 8 U.S.C. § 1101 et seq. (2006).

19 8 U.S.C. § 1101(a)(43)(F) (2000) (definition of an aggravated felony).

20 Secure Fence Act of 2006, 120 Stat. 2638, Pub. L. 109–367, Oct. 26, 2006.

21 Ariz. Rev. Stat. Ann. tits. 11, 13, 23, 28, 41, as amended by Act of Apr. 30, 2010, ch. 211, 2010 Ariz. Sess. Laws 1070.

22 "Dreamers" is a label given to those children of undocumented parents who entered at school age and are still in the United States. The name derives from the acronym of the proposed bill, the Development, Relief, and Education for Alien Minors Act. The DREAM Act would provide these youngsters an avenue to remain in the country to study and/or serve in the military.

23 In FY 2012, ICE removed 409,849 individuals, with more than half of them persons with criminal convictions. Immigration & Customs Enforcement, Removal Statistics, http://www.ice.gov/removal-statistics.

24 Congress declared that persons born in Puerto Rico between 1899 and 1941, and residing in Puerto Rico or other United States territory, would be citizens of the United States, adding that all others born after January 13, 1941, would be citizens at birth. 8 U.S.C. § 1402 (2006).

25 U.S. Const. amend. IV.

26 Mathews v. Diaz, 426 U.S. 67, 77 (1976) (The Fifth Amendment Due Process Clause provides protection from discrimination against undocumented persons); Plyler v. Doe, 457 U.S. 202 (1982) (The Fourteenth Amendment Equal Protection Clause provides protection from discrimination against undocumented alien children).

27 637 F.2d 1276 (9th Cir. 1980).

28 18 U.S.C. § 242 (2006).

29 Otherson, 637 F.2d 1276, 1278 (9th Cir. 1980).

30 Ibid., 1281.

31 Ibid., 1282.

32 Ibid., 1283.

33 United States v. Reyna, No. 4: 02-CR-609 (S.D. Tex.) (Conviction obtained June 9, 2003). The court sentenced the three defendants, federal immigration agents, to imprisonment for periods ranging from 33 to 78 months. *United States v. Reyna* was affirmed in a related appeal by one of the three involved agents. United States v. Gonzales, 436 F.3d 560 (5th Cir.), cert. denied, 547 U.S. 1180 (2006).

34 The right to receive medical care for serious medical needs was established by the United States Supreme Court in *Estelle v. Gamble*, 429 U.S. 97 (1976) (deliberate indifference to serious medical needs of prisoners by custodians constitutes unnecessary and wanton infliction of pain).

35 Interview with Ruben Perez, assistant U.S. Attorney, Southern Dist. of Texas, in Houston, Texas (March 8, 2005). Perez, then chief of the Civil Rights Division, prosecuted the Carrera case against the three agents.

36 Hernandez v. United States, 757 F.3d 249, 2014 U.S. App. LEXIS 12307 (5th Cir. June 30, 2014).

37 Bivens v. Six Unknown Named Agents, 403 U.S. 388 (1971).

38 Hernandez v. United States, 757 F.3d 249, 2014 U.S. App. LEXIS 12307, at 55 (5th Cir. June 30, 2014).

39 Ibid., 57.

40 According to cultural tradition in Latin American nations, a Latino uses both the name of his father (Hernández) and his mother (Rojas). For brevity, Mr. Hernández-Rojas will be generally referred to as Hernández.

41 Estate of Hernández-Rojas v. United States, 2014 U.S. Dist. LEXIS 138495 (S.D. Cal. Sept. 29, 2014).

42 Fed. R. Evid., 803 (1) & 803 (2).

43 United States v. Hayes, 589 F.2d 811, 820 (5th Cir. 1979).

44 18 U.S.C. § 242 (Deprivation of rights under color of law).

45 United States v. Hayes, 589 F.2d 811, 821 (5th Cir. 1979).

46 U.S. Const. amends. V, XIV.

References

Acuña, Rodolfo. 1972. *Occupied America: The Chicano's Struggle toward Liberation*. San Francisco: Canfield Press.

Archibold, Randal C. 2010. "San Diego Police Investigate the Death of a Mexican Man Resisting Deportation." *New York Times*, June 2.

Associated Press 2010. "Tale of Arizona Desert's Decapitated Corpses Was Not True, Embattled Governor Admits." *Rawstory.com*, September 5. http://www.rawstory.com/rs/2010/09/05/tale-headless-corpses-arizona-desert-true-embattled-governor-admits/.

———. 2012a. "Homeland Security Probing Border Patrol's Use of Force Policies amid Claims of Brutality." *Washington Post*, October 18. http://soboco.org/washington-post-homeland-security-probing-border-patrols-use-of-force-policies-amid-claims-of-brutality/http.

Balderrama, Francisco E., and Raymond Rodriguez. 1995. *Decade of Betrayal: Mexican Repatriation in the 1930s*. Albuquerque: University of New Mexico Press.

Bender, Steven W. 2003. *Greasers and Gringos: Latinos, Law, and the American Imagination*. New York: New York University Press.

Bernstein, Nina. 2009. "Target of Immigrant Raids Shifted." *New York Times*, February 4.

Box, John. 1928. "Immigration Restriction." *Digital History*. http://www.digitalhistory.uh.edu/disp_textbook.cfm?smtID=3&psid=594.

Carroll, Susan. 2010. "Man Born at Ben Taub Returns after He's Wrongly Deported." *Houston Chronicle*, September 14.

Caulfield, Philip. 2012. "PBS Airs New Footage in Case of Illegal Immigrant Killed at Border (video)." *New York Daily News*, April 23.

Childress, Sarah. 2013. "Border Patrol to Keep Controversial Deadly Force Rules." *PBS*, November 5. http://www.pbs.org/wgbh/pages/frontline/criminal-justice/border-patrol-to-keep-controversial-deadly-force-rules/.

Chishti, Muzaffar, Doris Meissner, and Claire Bergeron. 2011. "At Its 25th Anniversary, IRCA's Legacy Lives On." *Migration Policy Institute*, November 16. http://www.migrationpolicy.org/article/its-25th-anniversary-ircas-legacy-lives.

Copp, Nelson G. 1971. *"Wetbacks" and Braceros: Mexican Migrant Laborers and American Immigration Policy*. San Francisco: R & E Research Associates.

Costantini, Cristina. 2012. "Anastasio Hernández Rojas Death Sparks Nationwide Call for Justice in Alleged Border Patrol Abuse." *Huffington Post*, May 4 (updated August 7, 2012).

Costantini, Cristina, and Elise Foley. 2012. "Anastasio Hernández-Rojas Death: Border Patrol Tasing Incident Complicated by New Footage (video)." *Huffington Post*, April 20.

Fagenson, Zachary. 2013. "Miami Teen Graffiti Artist Dies after Being Tasered by Police." *Reuters*, August 8. http://uk.reuters.com/article/2013/08/08/us-usa-florida-taser-idUKBRE9770XI20130808http.

Flaccus, Gillian. 2007. "L.A.-Area Immigration Sweep Nabs More Than 700." *Houston Chronicle*, January 24.

Fox News. 2010. "Governor Brewer: We Can't Continue to Be the Gateway for Illegal Immigration." June 17.

Frey, John Carlos. 2012. "What's Going on with the Border Patrol?" *Los Angeles Times*, April 20.

Galarza, Ernesto. 1964. *Merchants of Labor: The Mexican Bracero Story; An Account of the Managed Migration of Mexican Farm Workers in California, 1942–1960*. Charlotte, NC: McNally & Loftin.

Gonzales, Manuel G. 1999. *Mexicanos: A History of Mexicans in the United States*. Bloomington: Indiana University Press.

Goodman, Amy. 2012. "Death on the Border: Shocking Video Shows Mexican Immigrant Beaten and Tased by Border Patrol Agents." *Democracy Now*, April 24. http://www.democracynow.org/2012/4/24/death_on_the_border_shocking_video.

Gottheimer, Josh, ed. 2003. *Ripples of Hope: Great American Civil Rights Speeches*. New York: Basic Civitas Books.

Hernandez, Daniel. 2007. "Pedro Guzman's Return." *LA Weekly News*, August 7.

Holstege, Sean. 2008. "Mistrial Ends Murder Case against Ariz. Border Agent." *Arizona Republic*, November 5. http

Jackman, Janet Rose. 2011. "$850k Settlement for Family of Slain Illegal Immigrant." *Tucson Sentinel*, September 8. http

Katrandjian, Olivia. 2011. "John McCain's Illegal Immigrants Started Arizona Wildfires Disputed by Forest Service." *ABC News*, June 19.

Lavender, Mary B. 2011. "Hispanic Profiling Happened before Arizona's Stringent Immigration Law." *ABC News*, February 3.

Milbank, Dana. 2010. "Headless Bodies and Other Immigration Tall Tales in Arizona." *Washington Post*, July 11.

Moran, Greg. 2013. "Agents Give Their Account of Border Death." *U-T San Diego*, June 2.

Nanthakumar, Kumaraswamy, and Stephane Massé. 2008. "Cardiac Stimulation with High Voltage Discharge from Stun Guns." *Canadian Medical Association Journal* 178: 1451–57.

New York Times. 2009. "Wrong Paths to Immigration Reform." Editorial. October 12.

Perez, Alex, and B. J. Lutz. 2011. "American Citizen Faced Deportation." *NBC Chicago*, June 30.

Pinkerton, James. 2011. "Taser Warnings Go Unheeded among Harris County Deputies." *Houston Chronicle*, June 27.

Preston, Julia. 2011. "Immigration Crackdown Also Snares Americans." *New York Times*, December 13.

———. 2014. "Book Guiding Border Agents on Force Is Released." *New York Times*, May 30. http

Rosales, F. Arturo 2000. *Testimonio: A Documentary History of the Mexican American Struggle for Civil Rights*. Houston: Arte Público Press.

———. 2006. *Dictionary of Latino Civil Rights History*. Houston: Arte Público Press.

Russell, Rucks. 2008. "American Citizen Held in County Jail as Illegal Immigrant." *CBS Affiliate, Houston, TX*, October 17.

Salinas, Guadalupe, and Isaias D. Torres. 1976. "The Undocumented Mexican Alien: A Legal, Social and Economic Analysis." *Houston Law Review* 13: 863–916.

Salinas, Lupe S 2005. "Latinos and Criminal Justice in Texas: Has the New Millennium Brought Progress?" *Thurgood Marshall Law Review* 30: 289–346.

Samora, Julian. 1971. *Los Mojados: The Wetback Story*. Notre Dame, IN: University of Notre Dame Press.

Spagat, Elliot. 2012. "Grand Jury Probes Anastasio Hernández Border Death." *KPBS*, July 12.

Stevens, Jacqueline. 2011. "U.S. Government Unlawfully Detaining and Deporting U.S. Citizens as Aliens." *Virginia Journal of Social Policy & the Law* 18: 606–720.

Taylor, Paul S. 1934. *An American-Mexican Frontier: Nueces County, Texas*. Charlotte: University of North Carolina Press.

U.S. Customs and Border Enforcement. 2014. *Use of Force Policy, Guidelines and Procedures Handbook*. Washington, DC: U.S. Government Printing Office. http://www.cbp.gov/sites/default/files/documents/UseofForcePolicyHandbook.pdf.

U.S. Department of Homeland Security 2012. "Exercising Prosecutorial Discretion with Respect to Individuals Who Came to the United States as Children." June 15.

U.S. Immigration and Naturalization Service. 1964. *Annual Report of the Immigration and Naturalization Service*. Washington, DC: U.S. Government Printing Office.

———. 1974. *Annual Report of the Immigration and Naturalization Service.* Washington, DC: U.S. Government Printing Office.

Wagner, Dennis. 2010. "Violence Is Not Up on Arizona Border Despite Mexican Drug War." *Arizona Republic,* May 2.

Weber, David J., ed. 1973. *Foreigners in Their Native Land: Historical Roots of the Mexican Americans.* Albuquerque: University of New Mexico Press.

Weissman, Deborah M., Director of Clinical Programs, University of North Carolina at Chapel Hill School of Law. 2009. "State and Local Enforcement of Immigration Laws." Statement before the Committee on House Judiciary, Subcommittee on Constitution, Civil Rights, and Civil Liberties. *Congressional Quarterly,* April.

Post-Reading Questions

1   What are some difficulties in distinguishing between undocumented immigrants on the one hand and legal residents and citizens on the other hand?

2   What is the historical relationship between local and federal immigration officials in the removal of undocumented immigrants?

3   Why is the case of Louis Alberto Delgado unique to the debate surrounding illegal immigration?

4   Of the many cases of abuse and civil rights violations cited in this chapter, which one appears most egregious? In your estimate, what is an appropriate punishment for the officer? Be sure to qualify your position.

5   With respect to illegal immigration, what are some similarities between the Eisenhower and Trump Administrations? How do these differ from the Obama Administrations?

Blinding Prosecutors to Defendants' Race

A Policy Proposal to Reduce Unconscious Bias in the Criminal Justice System

Sunita Sah, Christopher T. Robertson, and Shima B. Baughman

P rosecutors may have more independent power and discretion than any other government offcials in the United States.[1] Prosecutors decide whether to initiate criminal proceedings, what charges to file or bring before a grand jury, how and when to prosecute individuals, and what penalties to seek. For a given criminal behavior, half a dozen charges might apply, ranging from minor misdemeanors to the most serious felonies. A prosecutor can decline to press charges altogether or stack charges by characterizing the same behavior as violating the law dozens of times (charging each phone call made as part of a drug transaction as a crime, for instance). Once charged, about 95% of criminal cases are resolved through plea bargaining, where prosecutors can defer prosecution, suspend a sentence, minimize factual allegations in ways that virtually guarantee a light sentence, or insist on the most severe penalties.[2] If a case does go to trial, a prosecutor's sentencing demand provides an influential reference point (an anchor) for a defense attorney's response in plea negotiations and the judge's final sentencing decision.[3]

Prosecutors typically do not need to articulate the bases for their discretionary decisions,[4,5] and these decisions receive only minimal scrutiny from the courts. Although the U.S. Constitution theoretically limits the discretion of prosecutors (to target a particular race prejudicially, for instance), such protections are exceedingly diffcult to invoke,[6] especially if a prosecutor's unconscious rather than intentional bias is in play.[7] This context prompts us to offer an important and novel proposal with the potential to help make the justice system blind to race.

Prosecutors, we believe, should be unaware of defendants' race whenever possible. Implementing such a significant change would be challenging, clearly. But evidence of persistent disparities regarding the proportion of racial minorities that are put in prison makes the need for change apparent. And growing evidence that prosecutors' unconscious biases contribute to that imbalance gives us a potentially powerful target for efforts to produce positive and vitally needed change.

Racial Bias in the Criminal Justice System

In 2010 in the United States, Blacks made up 38% of all prisoners, although they made up only 12% of the national population.[8] That same year, about one in 23 Black men was in prison, compared with one in 147 White men.[9] The causes of this racial disparity are many and complex. Socioeconomic factors (poverty and lower educational achievement, for example) play a role. So may inequitable police behavior that, for example, leads to Blacks being stopped and frisked more often than Whites are.[10,11]

Black defendants also tend to receive harsher sentences than White defendants do, even when both the severity of the crime and previous criminal history are taken into account.[12] For example, harsher punishment was applied to crimes related to crack cocaine versus powder cocaine in federal sentencing guidelines, which tended to punish Blacks more harshly because they were more likely to be arrested with crack cocaine than powder cocaine. To minimize this disparate impact on Blacks, Congress passed the Fair Sentencing Act in 2010, which reduced the unequal penalties and eliminated the five-year mandatory minimum sentence for simple crack cocaine possession. This new law addressed the racial bias perpetrated by the old regime that led to low-level crack dealers, who were often Black, receiving more severe sentences than wholesale suppliers of powdered cocaine.[13]

One important cause of the racial discrepancy among prisoners, however, is bias that affects discretionary decisions made by prosecutors.[14–17] A recent review of empirical studies examining prosecutorial decision making and race found that most of the studies suggested that the defendants' "race directly or indirectly influenced case outcomes, even when a host of other legal or extra-legal factors are taken into account."[17] Minorities, particularly Black males, "receive disproportionately harsher treatment at each stage of the prosecutorial decision-making process."[18] Indeed, prosecutors in predominantly Black communities have been shown to make racially biased decisions, such as overcharging Black youth,[19] which, in turn, perpetuates racial stereotypes.[20,21] Further, Black children in the United States are much more likely than White children to be sentenced as adults,[22] probably because Black juveniles are perceived to be older and less childlike than White juveniles.[23,24]

These data do not suggest that prosecutors are overtly racist, although some may be. Instead, research documents that bias can infect even people with the best of intentions, including physicians and other professionals.[25,26] Prosecutors are humans with bounded rationality, making decisions in a cultural milieu that shapes their perceptions and decisions on an unconscious level.[15,27,28] Generally, bias increases in ambiguous situations,[20,29-33] and [...] decisions on what and how many charges to file against a defendant are inherently ambiguous.

Behavioral science researchers have demonstrated that people unknowingly misremember case facts in racially biased ways.[34,35] For example, there is a greater tendency to remember aggressive actions (e.g., punches or kicks) if a suspect is Black.[34] In fact, it appears that the more stereotypically Black a defendant is perceived to be, the more likely that person is to be sentenced to death.[36] In one study, Stanford University students viewed photographs of Black men, rating each one on the degree to which the person's appearance was stereotypically Black. The students were told they could base their decisions on any of the features of the photographed subjects to make their decisions, including noses, lips, skin tone, and hair. Unbeknownst to the students, each man in the images had been convicted of murdering a White person. The men the students rated as appearing more stereotypically Black were more likely to have been sentenced to death in criminal proceedings.[36] Other research has demonstrated that lighter skin tones may lead to more lenient judgments and prison sentences.[20,37]

Although bias exists throughout the criminal justice system, bias in prosecutorial decisions has a potentially disproportionate impact, given that most criminal cases do not go to trial and prosecutors exercise such wide discretion in handling them. One might hope that selecting prosecutors of good faith and asking them to behave professionally could avert racial bias. In this vein, in 2014, the Department of Justice reaffrmed its policy that "in making decisions ... law enforcement officers may not use race."[38] Such a policy, although laudable, unfortunately cannot prevent unconscious bias.

Prosecutorial decisions are made in a more deliberative fashion than, for example, split-second decisions made by police to shoot or not shoot. However, even with deliberative decisions, the ability to self-regulate bias is diffcult: Moral reasoning is usually a post hoc construction, generated after a (usually intuitive) judgment has been reached,[39] often influenced by erroneous factors.[40] People exhibiting bias are typically unaware that they are doing so, and bias is often unintentional.[33,41,42] Educating people on unconscious bias often leads them to be convinced that other people are biased but that they themselves are not.[29] Accordingly, strategies to encourage people to become less biased are usually not suffcient.

One program that had some success in reducing racial disparities was the 2006 Prosecution and Racial Justice Program of the Vera Institute of Justice. Prosecutors collected and published data on defendant and victim race for each offense category and the prosecutorial action taken at each stage of criminal proceedings.[43] These data exposed that similarly situated defendants of different races were treated differently at each stage of discretion: initial case screening, charging, plea offers, and final disposition. For instance, in Wisconsin, the data showed that prosecutors were charging Black defendants at higher rates than White defendants for drug possession. With this information, the district attorney made an office policy to refer suspects to drug treatment rather than charging them in an attempt to reduce racial bias in charging. However, this approach requires a large investment from overburdened prosecutorial offices to collect and analyze their data to reveal trends in racial disparity. It also requires that individual prosecutors be motivated to consciously avoid bias or at least be motivated to appear unbiased.[44,45] This motivation is often led by societal norms or public pressure regarding racial attitudes and inequality, which varies by jurisdiction. There presently is no complete solution to eliminate racial bias in prosecutorial decisions.

Blinding: An Alternative Approach to Managing Bias

An alternative way to manage bias is to acknowledge its existence and create institutional procedures to prevent bias from influencing important decisions. The psychologist Robert Rosenthal, a leading methodologist, concluded that the best way to reduce the chances of bias unconsciously affecting decision processes is to keep the process "as blind as possible for as long as possible."[46]

Blinding (or *masking*) to improve decisionmaking has a long history in different domains. For example, having musicians audition behind a screen decreased gender bias and increased the acceptance rate of women into symphony orchestras.[47] In medical science, both subjects and researchers are, whenever feasible, kept unaware of who is in the treatment or control groups of clinical trials, in an effort to achieve unbiased results.[48] Meta-analyses have shown that such blinding reduces the number of false positives in science experiments.[49,50] Similarly, editors of scholarly journals routinely remove authors' names and institutions from submissions so they can assess articles on their scientific merits alone.[51] Likewise, to avoid possible favoritism, some professors mask students' identities on papers when grading.[52]

Blinding is already in use in other stages of the criminal justice process. For example, lineups are widely acknowledged to be best conducted by an officer who does not know which person is the suspect, so as not to pollute the eyewitness's perceptions.[53,54] This practice of blind administration of lineups was originally highly controversial. Iowa State University professor Gary Wells first proposed implementing blinding of police to suspect lineups in 1988,[55] although evidence of bias and erroneous identification had been accumulating for years before that. More than a decade later, in 1999, the U.S. Department of Justice published a set of best practices for conducting police lineups[56] that excluded blind procedures (although it acknowledged that having investigators who did not know which person in the lineup was the suspect was desirable) because blinding "may be impractical for some jurisdictions to implement" (p. 9).[56] Nevertheless, individual jurisdictions experimented with blind procedures.[57] By 2014, the National Research Council recommended unreservedly that all lineups should be conducted with the benefits of blinding.[58]

Blinding has also been recommended for forensic scientists and other expert witnesses, so that attorneys for either side in a case do not influence and undermine their scientific expertise.[32] More generally, the rules of evidence (which determine what is permissible in court) can be understood as an elaborate blinding procedure, designed to ensure that juries are not exposed to irrelevant or unreliable evidence, recognizing that for the purpose of assessing guilt, some factors are more prejudicial than probative.[59]

The Case for Blinded Prosecutors

The success of the long-standing practice of blinding in other contexts gives credence to our proposal that prosecutors should be blinded to the race of criminal defendants whenever possible. Prosecutors, like other professionals, cannot be biased by what they do not know. In addition to mitigating unconscious bias, the blinding of prosecutors also mitigates any conscious racism, which may infect some prosecutors.

Federal prosecutors already use a race-blinding procedure for death penalty decisions. The Department of Justice requires that attorneys on committees of capital cases (which determine death eligibility) review each defendant file only after information related to the race of the defendant has been removed.[60] Only paralegal assistants who collect statistics know the defendants' races. The question is how far this practice can and should be expanded. We believe there is potential for broader use of race blinding by other prosecutors. Prosecutors are a good target for race blinding given their substantial power and impact, particularly with two pivotal decisions: the filing of charges and the negotiation of plea bargains.

Charging Decisions

Prosecutorial practice varies in different jurisdictions. For petty offenses, a prosecutor may make key decisions in court while facing defendants, making blinding infeasible (unless that dynamic itself is reformed). In many jurisdictions, however, prosecutors do not see defendants in person when making initial charging decisions; these are based on information provided in police dossiers, in which race could be redacted. In fact, the trend is for such information to be conveyed to prosecutors electronically, making it easier to filter the race information, perhaps automatically by electronic tools or by intermediaries. In either case, race information could be retained for other uses such as identification or demographic tracking. As the Department of Justice capital-case review committees show, some assistants can have access to a full criminal file while decision-makers see only race-blind information.

Plea Bargaining

Although defendants retain the ultimate choice about whether to accept any deal, the prosecuting and defense attorneys actually negotiate that deal, and the prosecutor need not be exposed to the race of the defendant. In some jurisdictions, plea bargaining happens at arraignments with defendants in the same room. But this practice is neither uniform nor necessary. Thus, the two steps that are conclusive for the vast majority of cases—charging decisions and plea bargaining—can potentially be blinded to race.

Limitations, Challenges, and the Need for Pilot Testing

Although we argue for the value of race blinding procedures, we acknowledge that there will be difficulties and limitations in implementing such a policy. Race should have no legitimate role in the vast majority of charging decisions. However, in rare situations, such as prosecutions for hate crime, the race of an alleged perpetrator is relevant. In these cases, the necessary information can be provided to prosecutors.

For cases in which race is irrelevant, the blinding strategy will be effective at eliminating bias only to the extent that prosecutors are unable to infer race from other information available to them. Thus, it will be necessary to remove information that could reveal race, such as photos of a defendant; the defendant's name;[61] and, in racially segregated communities, the defendant's address. The practicalities of removing all race-related information could become complex. Further, race blinding may not be feasible if photos contain relevant information (such as defensive wounds on the defendant's skin) or eyewitness testimony describes a perpetrator's race.

To prevent prosecutors from inferring race from the defendants' names, court documents could instead identify defendants with assigned numbers (such as driver's license numbers). That said, removing names may have other unintended effects, such as reducing empathy, leading to harsher decisions toward anonymous defendants.[62] An alternative approach would be the use of random race-neutral pseudonyms to achieve anonymity without erasing all trace that a person is involved.

The severity of punishment is a question for the legislature. If race blinding succeeds, it levels the playing field for all by promoting equality, even if it decreases bias favorable to White defendants (often referred to as *White privilege*).[63–65] Both unjustified leniency for Whites and unjustified harsher punishments for Blacks were revealed in 2015 by the U.S. Department of Justice Civil Rights Division's investigation of the Ferguson (Missouri) Police Department. Of the many examples discussed in the report, one clearly highlighted the double standards: Whites were more likely to have citations, fines, and fees eliminated by city officials, whereas Blacks were punished for the same minor transgressions with expensive tickets and judgments punishing their perceived lack of personal responsibility (pp. 74–75).[66] That said, in other contexts, punishments may be harsher for Whites than for Blacks.[17] Blinding may create racial equity for both Black and White defendants.

Given that race blinding may not be feasible in some situations, may fail, or may have unintended consequences, the best path forward is to pilot-test this intervention and gauge its effectiveness. Pilot testing would allow researchers to uncover (and perhaps creatively address) challenges in the practical implementation of race blinding; evaluate on a smaller scale the precise impact, success, and value of race blinding; and expose any potential unintended consequences.[33,67–69] Sequential rollouts in different jurisdictions are also valuable, as they allow for continued monitoring and assessment in varying contexts.

In theory, prosecutors could be blinded to other information that may activate biases, including the race of the victim or the gender of the defendant or victim. These reforms should be considered on their own merits, including whether empirical evidence demonstrates that these variables are biasing prosecutorial decisions in a systematic fashion that is irrelevant to the proper application of the law. These considerations would also apply to whether blinding could be expanded to other decision-makers, including defense attorneys, judges, juries, and parole boards.

Impact and Cost Effectiveness

The need to eliminate race bias in prosecution is urgent. Racial biases can substantially distort decisions,[61,70] and prosecutorial bias alone leads to a substantial increase in the duration and severity of punishment for minorities. A study using 222,542 cases in New York County during 2010–2011 found that Black defendants were 10% more likely to be detained pretrial compared with White defendants charged with similar crimes, and they were 13% more likely to receive offers of prison sentences during plea bargaining.[71] Given that a prosecutor typically handles dozens of felonies and over a hundred misdemeanors per year,[72] the impact of racial bias is compounded. Approximately 27,000 state prosecutors deal with 2.9 million felony cases per year, and 6,075 federal prosecutors secure 82,000 convictions per year, not to mention the millions of prosecutorial decisions that are made on misdemeanor charges.[73,74] Two-thirds of those convicted of a felony go to prison, and the average sentence is about five years,[75] at a cost of $25,000 per prisoner per year.[76] Therefore, given that prosecutors are responsible for hundreds of person-years of incarceration annually and thus millions of dollars of public money, even a marginal reduction in bias may have a substantial effect.

These numbers have an impact that extends beyond the direct experiences of people sentenced to do time. As The Pew Charitable Trusts reported in 2010, the income of households and the educational success of children in those households decline when parents are put in jail.[77] The tangible and intangible costs to the prisoners, their families, and the broader society are tremendous.

Successfully blinding prosecutors to defendants' race may also improve the perceived legitimacy of prosecutorial decisions, which may enhance compliance with the law.[78] As important as anything else, it would advance some of the fundamental goals of our government: the equal treatment of all citizens and justice for all.

A New Standard: Blinding Prosecutors to Defendants' Race

If race blinding proves to be effective after pilot testing, we recommend that local and state prosecutors and the federal Department of Justice adopt race blinding as a uniform practice. We recommend that national and statewide associations of prosecutors (for example, the National District Attorneys Association), as well as broader organizations such as the American Bar Association (ABA), support implementation of the reforms. Furthermore, we recommend that this imperative be written into ethical codes and guidelines, such as the U.S. Attorneys' Handbook Chapter 9-27.000 (USAM) and Rule 3.8 of the ABA Model Rules of Professional Conduct (1983). Our reform also relies on the ethical behavior of attorneys, police, and other intermediaries who would not leak the race of the defendant to prosecutors. Adoption of this norm into the current ethical code could build on the current norms of confidentiality.

Race disparities pervade criminal justice decision-making in America. Among criminal-justice actors, the decisions of prosecutors are the least reviewable, are exercised with the most discretion, and are impactful. Blinding has been used as a tool to reduce gender and race discrimination in many fields, and its value is grounded in empirical evidence. We believe that blinding prosecutors to a defendant's race wherever feasible is a timely and important proposal.

We acknowledge that there will be practical implementation challenges and risks. Our primary aim with this proposal is to instigate a discussion on the merits and drawbacks of blinding prosecutors to race and to encourage pilot tests. The Department of Justice demonstrated the feasibility of race blinding for federal prosecutors[60] and state prosecutors could follow suit with similar procedures for their own death penalty cases. Expanding race blinding to other prosecutorial decisions may seem impractical; but, if the history of blind police lineups is any guide,[55] the jurisdictions most committed to racial equality and behaviorally informed policymaking will prove otherwise.

References

1. Bibas, S. (2009). Prosecutorial regulation versus prosecutorial accountability. *University of Pennsylvania Law Review, 157,* 959–1016.

2. Bibas, S. (2006). Transparency and participation in criminal procedure. *New York University Law Review, 86,* 911–912.

3. Englich, B. (2006). Blind or biased? Justitia's susceptibility to anchoring effects in the courtroom based on given numerical representations. *Law & Policy, 28,* 497–514.

4. Rabin, R. L. (1972). Agency criminal referrals in the federal system: An empirical study of prosecutorial discretion. *Stanford Law Review, 24,* 1036–1091.

5. Leonetti, C. (2012). When the emperor has no clothes III: Personnel policies and conflicts of interest in prosecutors' offices. *Cornell Journal of Law and Public Policy, 22,* 53–92.

6. Wayte v. United States, 470 U.S. 598 (1985).

7. McCleskey v. Kemp, 481 U.S. 279 (1987).

8. Guerino, P., Harrison, P. M., & Sabol, W. J. (2011). *Prisoners in 2010* (NCJ 236096). Retrieved from Bureau of Justice Statistics website: http://www.bjs.gov/content/pub/pdf/p10.pdf

9. Glaze, L. E. (2011). *Correctional populations in the United States, 2010* (NCJ 236319). Retrieved from Bureau of Justice Statistics website: http://bjs.ojp.usdoj.gov/content/pub/pdf/cpus10.pdf

10. Fagan, J., & Meares, T. L. (2008). Punishment, deterrence and social control: The paradox of punishment in minority communities. *Ohio State Journal of Criminal Law, 6,* 173–229.

11. Sommers, S. R., & Marotta, S. A. (2014). Racial disparities in legal outcomes on policing, charging decisions, and criminal trial proceedings. *Policy Insights from the Behavioral and Brain Sciences, 1,* 103–111.

12. Mitchell, O. (2005). A meta-analysis of race and sentencing research: Explaining the inconsistencies. *Journal of Quantatative Criminolgy, 21,* 439–466.

13. Fair Sentencing Act of 2010, Pub. L. No. 111-120, 21 U.S.C. § 1789, 124 Stat. 2372 (2010).

14. Tonry, M. (2011). *Punishing race: A continuing American dilemma.* New York, NY: Oxford University Press.

15. Burke, A. S. (2006). Improving prosecutorial decision making: Some lessons of cognitive science. *William & Mary Law Review, 47,* 1587–1633.

16. Smith, A. (2001). Can you be a good person and a good prosecutor? *Georgetown Journal of Legal Ethics, 14,* 355–400.

17. Kutateladze, B., Lynn, V., & Liang, E. (2012). *Do race and ethnicity matter in prosecution? A review of empirical studies.* Retrieved from Vera Institute of Justice website: http://www.vera.org/sites/default/files/resources/downloads/race-and-ethnicity-in-prosecution-first-edition.pdf

18. Johnson, J. L. (2014). *Mass incarceration on trial: A remarkable court decision and the future of prisons in America.* New York, NY: New Press.

19. Henning, K. N. (2013). Criminalizing normal adolescent behavior in communities of color: The role of prosecutors in juvenile justice reform. *Cornell Law Review, 98,* 383–462.

20. Levinson, J. D., & Young, D. (2010). Different shades of bias: Skin tone, implicit racial bias, and judgments of ambiguous evidence. *West Virginia Law Review, 112,* 307–350.

21. Correll, J., Park, B., Judd, C. M., & Wittenbrink, B. (2007). The influence of stereotypes on decisions to shoot. *European Journal of Social Psychology, 37,* 1102–1117.

22. Hartney, C., & Silva, F. (2007). *And justice for some: Differential treatment of youth of color in the justice system.* Retrieved from National Council on Crime and Delinquency website: http://www.nccdglobal.org/sites/default/files/publication_pdf/justice-for-some.pdf

23. Rattan, A., Levine, C. S., Dweck, C. S., Eberhardt, J. L., & Avenanti, A. (2012). Race and the fragility of the legal distinction between juveniles and adults. *PLOS ONE, 7*(5), Article e36680.

24. Goff, P. A., Jackson, M. C., Di Leone, B. A. L., Culotta, C. M., & DiTomasso, N. A. (2014). The essence of innocence: Consequences of dehumanizing Black children. *Journal of Personality and Social Psychology, 106,* 526–545.

25. Sah, S., & Fugh-Berman, A. (2013). Physicians under the influence: Social psychology and industry marketing strategies. *Journal of Law, Medicine and Ethics, 41,* 665–672.

26. Sah, S. (2013). Essays on conflicts of interest in medicine. *Business & Society, 52,* 666–678.

27. Johnson, S. L. (1988). Unconscious racism and the criminal law. *Cornell Law Review, 73,* 1016–1037.

28. Lawrence, C. R. (1987). The id, the ego, and equal protection: Reckoning with unconscious racism. *Stanford Law Review, 38,* 317–388.

29. Babcock, L., & Loewenstein, G. (1997). Explaining bargaining impasse: The role of self-serving biases. *The Journal of Economic Perspectives, 11,* 109–126.

30. Sah, S., & Larrick, R. (2015). *I am immune: A sense of invulnerability predicts increased acceptance of, and influence from, conflicts of interest* (Cornell University Working Papers).

31. Sah, S., & Loewenstein, G. (2010). Effect of reminders of personal sacrifice and suggested rationalizations on residents' self-reported willingness to accept gifts: A randomized trial. *Journal of the American Medical Association, 304,* 1204–1211.

32. Dror, I. E., & Cole, S. A. (2010). The vision in "blind" justice: Expert perception, judgment, and visual cognition in forensic pattern recognition. *Psychonomic Bulletin & Review, 17,* 161–167.

33. Sah, S. (2012). Conflicts of interest and your physician: Psychological processes that cause unexpected changes in behavior. *Journal of Law, Medicine & Ethics, 40,* 482–487.

34. Levinson, J. D. (2007). Forgotten racial equality: Implicit bias, decisionmaking, and misremembering. *Duke Law Journal, 57,* 345–424.

35. Oliver, M. B. (1999). Caucasian viewers' memory of Black and White criminal suspects in the news. *Journal of Communication, 49,* 46–60.

36. Eberhardt, J. L., Davies, P. G., Purdie-Vaughns, V. J., & Johnson, S. L. (2006). Looking deathworthy: Perceived stereotypicality of Black defendants predicts capital-sentencing outcomes. *Psychological Science, 17,* 383–386.

37. Viglione, J., Hannon, L., & DeFina, R. (2011). The impact of light skin on prison time for Black female offenders. *The Social Science Journal, 48,* 250–258.

38. U.S. Department of Justice. (2014). *Guidance for Federal law enforcement agencies regarding the use of race, ethnicity, gender, national origin, religion, sexual orientation, or gender identity.* Retrieved from http://www.justice.gov/sites/default/files/ag/pages/attachments/2014/12/08/use-of-race-policy.pdf

39. Haidt, J. (2001). The emotional dog and its rational tail: A social intuitionist approach to moral judgment. *Psychological Review, 108,* 814–834.

40. Gunia, B. C., Barnes, C. M., & Sah, S. (2014). The morality of larks and owls: Unethical behavior depends on chronotype as well as time of day. *Psychological Science, 25,* 2271–2274.

41. Pronin, E., Lin, D. Y., & Ross, L. (2002). The bias blind spot: Perceptions of bias in self versus others. *Personality and Social Psychology Bulletin, 28,* 369–391.

42. Pronin, E., Gilovich, T., & Ross, L. (2004). Objectivity in the eye of the beholder: Divergent perceptions of bias in self versus others. *Psychological Review, 111,* 781–799.

43. Davis, A. J. (2013). In search of racial justice: The role of the prosecutor. *New York University Journal of Legislation and Public Policy, 16,* 821–851.

44. Sah, S., & Loewenstein, G. (2014). Nothing to declare: Mandatory and voluntary disclosure leads advisors to avoid conflicts of interest. *Psychological Science, 25,* 575–584.

45. Plant, E. A. (2004). Responses to interracial interactions over time. *Personality and Social Psychology Bulletin, 30,* 1458–1471.

46. Rosenthal, R. (1978). How often are our numbers wrong? *American Psychologist, 33,* 1005–1008.

47. Goldin, C., & Rouse, C. (2000). Orchestrating impartiality: The impact of "blind" auditions on female musicians. *The American Economic Review, 90,* 715–741.

48. Schulz, K. F., & Grimes, D. A. (2002). Blinding in randomised trials: Hiding who got what. *The Lancet, 359,* 696–700.

49. Wood, L., Egger, M., Gluud, L. L., Schulz, K. F., Juni, P., Altman, D. G., ... Sterne, J. A. C. (2008). Empirical evidence of bias in treatment effect estimates in controlled trials with different interventions and outcomes: Meta-epidemiological study. *British Medical Journal, 336,* 601–605.

50. Psaty, B. M., & Prentice, R. L. (2010). Minimizing bias in randomized trials: The importance of blinding. *Journal of the American Medical Association, 304,* 793–794.

51. Snodgrass, R. (2006). Single- versus double-blind reviewing: An analysis of the literature. *ACM SIGMOD Record, 35*(3), 8–21.

52. Carrington, P. D. (1992). One law: The role of legal education in the opening of the legal profession since 1776. *Florida Law Review, 44,* 501–603.

53. Dysart, J. E., Lawson, V. Z., & Rainey, A. (2012). Blind lineup administration as a prophylactic against the postidentification feedback effect. *Law and Human Behavior, 36,* 312–319.

54. Garrett, B. L. (2014). Eyewitness identifications and police practices: A Virginia case study. *Virginia Journal of Criminal Law, 2,* 2013–2026.

55. Wells, G. L. (1988). *Eyewitness identification: A system handbook.* Toronto, Ontario, Canada: Carswell Legal.

56. U.S. Department of Justice, Technical Working Group for Eyewitness Evidence. (1999). *Eyewitness evidence: A guide for law enforcement* (NCJ 178240). Retrieved from https://www.ncjrs.gov/pdffiles1/nij/178240.pdf

57. Famer, J. J. J. (2001, April 18). Attorney general guidelines for preparing and conducting photo and live lineup identification procedures [Letter]. Retrieved from State of New Jersey website: http://www.state.nj.us/lps/dcj/agguide/photoid.pdf

58. National Research Council. (2014). *Identifying the culprit: Assessing eyewitness identification.* Washington, DC: National Academies Press.

59. *Federal Rules of Evidence: Rule 403. Excluding relevant evidence for prejudice, confusion, waste of time, or other reasons.* Retrieved from Legal Information Institute website: https://www.law.cornell.edu/rules/fre/rule_403

60. U.S. Department of Justice. (2001). *The federal death penalty system: Supplementary data, analysis and revised protocol for capital case review.* Retrieved from http://www.justice.gov/archive/dag/pubdoc/deathpenaltystudy.htm

61. Milkman, K. L., Akinola, M., & Chugh, D. (2012). Temporal distance and discrimination: An audit study in academia. *Psychological Science, 23,* 710–717.

62. Sah, S., & Loewenstein, G. (2012). More affected = more neglected: Amplification of bias in advice to the unidentified and many. *Social Psychological and Personality Science, 3,* 365–372.

63. Jensen, R. (2005). *The heart of Whiteness: Confronting race, racism and White privilege.* San Francisco, CA: City Lights Books.

64. Lowery, B. S., Knowles, E. D., & Unzueta, M. M. (2007). Framing inequity safely: Whites' motivated perceptions of racial privilege. *Personality and Social Psychology Bulletin, 33,* 1237–1250.

65. McIntosh, P. (1998). White privilege: Unpacking the invisible knapsack. In P. S. Rothenberg (Ed.), *Race, class, and gender in the United States: An integrated study* (4th ed., pp. 165–169). New York, NY: Worth.

66. United States Department of Justice, Civil Rights Division. (2015). *Investigation of the Ferguson Police Department.* Retrieved from http://www.justice.gov/sites/default/files/opa/press-releases/attachments/2015/03/04/ferguson_police_department_report.pdf

67. Loewenstein, G., Sah, S., & Cain, D. M. (2012). The unintended consequences of conflict of interest disclosure. *Journal of the American Medical Association, 307,* 669–670. doi:10.1001/jama.2012.154

68. Sah, S., & Loewenstein, G. (2015). Conflicted advice and second opinions: Benefits, but unintended consequences. *Organizational Behavior and Human Decision Processes, 130,* 89–107.

69. Sah, S., Loewenstein, G., & Cain, D. M. (2013). The burden of disclosure: Increased compliance with distrusted advice. *Journal of Personality and Social Psychology, 104,* 289–304.

70. Bertrand, M., & Mullainathan, S. (2004). Are Emily and Greg more employable than Lakisha and Jamal? A field experiment on labor market discrimination. *The American Economic Review, 94,* 991–1013.

71. Kutateladze, B. L., & Andiloro, N. R. (2014). *Prosecution and racial justice in New York County—Technical report* (Technical Report 247227). Retrieved from National Criminal Justice Reference Service website: https://www.ncjrs.gov/pdffiles1/nij/grants/247227.pdf

72. Gershowitz, A. M., & Killinger, L. (2011). The state (never) rests: How excessive prosecutor caseloads harm criminal defendants. *Northwestern University Law Review, 105,* 262–301.

73. Perry, S., & Banks, D. (2011). *Prosecutors in state courts—2007 statistical tables* (NCJ 234211). Retrieved from Bureau of Justice Statistics website: http://www.bjs.gov/content/pub/pdf/psc07st.pdf

74. U.S. Department of Justice. (2011). *United States attorneys' annual statistical report: Fiscal year 2010.* Retrieved from http://www.justice.gov/sites/default/files/usao/legacy/2011/09/01/10statrpt.pdf

75. Rosenmerkel, S., Durose, M., & Farole, D., Jr. (2009). *Felony sentences in state courts, 2006—Statistical tables* (NCJ 226846). Retrieved from Bureau of Justice Statistics website: http://www.bjs.gov/content/pub/pdf/fssc06st.pdf

76. Schmitt, J., Warner, K., & Gupta, S. (2010). *The high budgetary cost of incarceration.* Retrieved from Center for Economic and Policy Research website: http://www.cepr.net/publications/reports/the-high-budgetary-cost-of-incarceration

77. Western, B., & Pettit, B. (2010). *Collateral costs: Incarceration's effect on economic mobility.* Retrieved from Pew Charitable Trusts website: http://www.pewtrusts.org/~/media/legacy/uploadedfiles/pcs_assets/2010/collateralcosts1pdf.pdf

78. Tyler, T. R. (1990). *Why people obey the law: Procedural justice, legitimacy, and compliance.* New Haven, CT: Yale University Press.

Post-Reading Questions

1   What evidence is there to suggest that prosecutors can be racially biased in their decisions to charge and prosecute cases?

2   What is meant by "blinding prosecutors?" In what ways is this accomplished?

3   What are some limitations associated with efforts made toward blinding prosecutors?

4   What are some perceived benefits of blinding prosecutors to a defendant's race? Are there any hidden repercussions for defendants?

5   In what ways can prosecutors attempt to subvert or undermine the blinding process?

Racism, Fines, and Fees and the U.S. Carceral State

Elizabeth Jones

As is now well known, Philando Castile, a 32-year-old African American cafeteria worker, was shot dead by a Minnesota police officer during a routine traffic stop in July of 2016. The aftermath of the shooting was live-streamed on Facebook by his girlfriend, Diamond Reynolds, and the incident sparked nationwide protests. The not guilty verdict in officer Jeronimo Yanez's trial for second degree manslaughter once again caused protesters to hit the streets in June of 2017. Castile's mother decried after the acquittal that the system continued to fail black people. What is far less known about the case, however, is that the traffic stop leading to Castile's death was one in a series of many stops conducted by police for various violations. He had, it transpired, been stopped forty-six times, generating six thousand dollars' worth of fines. For Castile, these minor traffic violations could initiate months- and years-long cycles of court appearances, driving licence suspensions and fines.[1] In Ferguson, too, police officer Darren Wilson's shooting of unarmed Michael Brown in 2014 ultimately led to the uncovering of exactly the same pattern of systematically unconstitutional and racially disproportionate policing practices described in a Department of Justice (DOJ) commissioned investigation.[2] The report cited the experience of one black Ferguson resident involved in a minor illegal parking violation who was ultimately arrested twice, spent six days in jail, and paid $550 to the court. After two years of fee payments and court appearances for the citations, she still owed $541 towards her court-assessed fines and fees.[3] The DOJ discovered the biased police practices of the Ferguson police department were incentivised by a revenue-generating system funding the municipality and its court system. An email sent by the Ferguson City Finance Director to the Chief of Police read, 'unless ticket writing ramps up significantly before the end of the year, it will be hard to significantly raise collections next year'.

The assessment of fines for low-level offences, court costs, and fees for supervision, accompanied by their enforcement for non-payment, has become so prolific in America that, in March 2016, the DOJ issued a letter to various jurisdictions throughout the country which cautioned against assessing defendants with excessive monetary penalties for traffic citations, misdemeanours and low-level violations. It also advised local courts against using unconstitutional practices in enforcing fines and fees by punishing people, including incarcerating them, for their inability to pay. The DOJ letter highlighted the consequences of fines and fees, including escalating debt; repeated, unnecessary incarceration for non-payment; loss of jobs; and entrapment in a cycle of poverty.[4]

Exploring the prolific practice of local government imposition of fines and fees for low-level offences, accompanied by the state surveillance and punishment mechanisms for their collection, is important. It illustrates the embedded nature of colourblind racism[5] (i.e., that arising from the late 1960s post Civil-Rights era which describes racial inequality as resulting from supposedly nonracial dynamics) within the neoliberal political economy; and it also reveals the function of neoliberal ideals in *local* carceral state institutions that serve to produce inequalities along lines of race and class.[6] Unfortunately, there is a dearth of academic literature on the present use of fines and fees at the city and municipal level, so this study, therefore, relies primarily on local studies, the DOJ and news reports from the year 2000 onwards to demonstrate the scope of the problem.

There is no doubt that, nationwide, the use of ticketing and enforcement mechanisms has proliferated.[7] Writing an op-ed for the *Washington Post*, a Texas municipal court judge Doug Chakya said, 'I see 10 to 12 defendants each day who were arrested on fine-only charges: things like public intoxication, shoplifting, disorderly conduct and traffic offenses.'[8] Texas municipalities are not alone. In state after state, different legal schemes propagating and enforcing fines and fees have cropped up in various forms. Accompanying the spread of fines and fees, enforcement and collection efforts have also greatly intensified throughout local jurisdictions.

A Houston mayoral commission report found only 2,579 defendants were granted a community service option as a sentence in lieu of fines from the 30,000 defendants who were eligible. In Houston, between the beginning of 2012 and the end of 2015, approximately eight people were jailed per day for non-payment of fines and fees, and at least 1,000 of those individuals were listed as homeless.[9] Similarly, in New Orleans, in one month during 2010 alone, the American Civil Liberties Union (ACLU) identified thirty-two cases where defendants were given suspended sentences and told to pay a fine. However, if the fine were not paid within a specified time frame, the defendant would serve ten days in jail.[10] Two lawsuits were filed by the ACLU of Georgia against Dekalb County in both 2015 and 2016, one on behalf of a black teenager named Kevin Thompson, jailed in December of 2014 for five days because he could not afford to pay court-ordered fines, and another for improperly jailing poor people who couldn't afford to pay fees for misdemeanour probation supervision.[11]

A 2014 survey by National Public Radio, New York University's Brennan Center for Justice, and the National Center for State Courts showed that in Benton County, Washington, a quarter of people in jail for misdemeanours on a typical day were there for non-payment of fines and court fees.[12] The percentage of jail bookings in Tulsa involving inmates who had failed to pay court fines and fees more than tripled, from 8 to 29 per cent of 1,200 inmates between 2004 and 2013 according to reporting by the *Tulsa World*.[13] In July of 2016, a small municipality in St Louis County Missouri agreed to pay a $4.7 million settlement to almost 2,000 people jailed for non-payment of fines and fees.[14]

The neoliberal pursuit of 'lean government' and austerity measures has created a need to generate revenues through alternative means and the carceral state has increasingly begun to fulfil this role. Judges are unlikely to dismiss assessed fees because municipalities have become so dependent on the revenue. In 2009, Garrett and Wagner studied ninety-six North Carolina counties and found a decline in government revenue correlated with an increase in ticket-writing the following year.[15] Examples of the revenue generated by ticketing include the 12 per cent interest rate on unpaid fees assessed in Washington state and the 80 per cent increase in revenue generated in Ferguson over a two-year period.[16]

Discussing the Ferguson report at the Justice Department on 4 March, 2015, Attorney General Eric Holder said, 'once the system is primed for maximizing revenue—starting with fines and fees enforcement—the city relies on the police force to serve, essentially, as a collection agency for the municipal court rather than a law enforcement entity'.[17]

The disproportionate racial implications of fines and fees are also documented. A recent report from the campaigning coalition Back on the Road found that black drivers in California are more likely to have their licences suspended for failure to appear in court or failing to pay a ticket than whites. Black drivers in California were also found to be more likely to be arrested for driving with a suspended licence than whites for the same offence.[18] The impact of low-level carceral state contact in Ferguson was also most deeply felt by its black residents. As 67 per cent of the population, African Americans accounted for 85 per cent of vehicle stops, 90 per cent of citations, and 93 per cent of arrests by Ferguson police officers.[19] Based on findings that black residents were five times more likely than white residents to be arrested, the ACLU of Mississippi filed a lawsuit against the Madison County Sheriff's Department in May 2017 alleging it terrorised black residents with unconstitutional searches and seizures and excessive force.[20]

In *Blazing the Neoliberal Trail*, Timothy Weaver concluded that urban governments pursuing neoliberal policies ultimately reinforce racial and class inequalities in their cities.[21] The contemporary system of fines and fees utilised by local law enforcement and court officials is one such example of urban neoliberal policy; it elucidates the interaction between colourblind racism and the neoliberal political economic project within the context of the carceral state. How can we best situate and understand this disproportionate effect today of the low-level carceral state? How does the phenomenon challenge current academic notions regarding the impact of neoliberalism, the nature of the carceral state, mass incarceration and the criminalisation, punishment and containment of the poor, and the understanding of today's colourblind racism in place of yesterday's Jim Crow?

Carceral State Theorising and its Limitations on 'Race'

Recent burgeoning scholarship discusses the role of the carceral state in forming a group of politically, socially and economically disenfranchised citizenry, often concentrated in a handful of urban neighbourhoods.[22] There also exists a growing subset of academic literature connecting neoliberalism with state restructuring and the expansion of the punishment and surveillance mechanisms of the carceral state.[23] This literature positions neoliberal governance and policies as responsible for hyper-punitive policies and the uniquely American phenomenon of mass incarceration. Yet, very little of this scholarship on the expansion of the carceral state embeds colourblind racism within the neoliberal governance framework and explores the implications of it for local government institutions such as police departments, courts, surveillance mechanisms such as probation administration, and jail. Even more concerning is the way a focus on felony convictions and prison incarceration, i.e., mass incarceration, obscures the common, low-level forms of carceral state contact that produce and reinforce inequalities along race and class lines. Simply put, the size, scope and implications of the carceral state, particularly for urban communities of colour, are grossly underestimated. The conversation must move from mass incarceration in prison to one of mass criminalisation, to fully grasp that state's impact.

Marie Gottschalk in *Caught: the prison state and the lockdown of American politics* skilfully engages the interconnections between neoliberalism and the carceral state, but neglects to embed racial ideology within the neoliberalism paradigm itself.[24] Her contention that a focus on racial disparities disguises the function of the wider political economy and its role in an expanding carceral state treats neo-liberalism and racism as mutually exclusive. This reading of race, by Gottschalk and other scholars, as mutually exclusive from neoliberal policy and governance, misses the ways in which racism, in its current colourblind manifestation, is part and parcel of the neoliberal project. Race need not be a conversation that distracts from or is treated as distinct from other processes in the political economy leading to heightened incarceration, as it is instrumental to understanding both the historical and contemporary function and role of the American carceral state for managing black labour. An analysis of race within the context of neoliberalism is also instructive as to the ways race is a malleable social construction with contours that change and transform in response to shifts in the political economy.

The dominance and totalising nature of neoliberal urban governance that crowds out other alternatives and the transition to a bifurcated, postindustrial economy are relatively new phenomena arising in recent decades. However, the disproportionate racial consequences of the carceral state are foundational to American society. The legal machinery of the carceral state has always operated as a mediator between black labour and capitalist modes of production, particularly because race also functions as a hierarchical relationship 'rooted in the capitalist division of labour'.[25] Outgrowths of the economic role of race are both the social meaning attached to it, for example how space and phenomena are interpreted in racial terms, and the deployment of race as a salient political category driving policy decisions and the divvying out of resources by government institutions. The maintenance and control of black populations in connection to the economy remains as a social and political impetus to the American carceral state with its power to punish and surveil.

From Jim Crow to the Colourblind Racism of Neoliberalism

In the past fifty years, a shift from Jim Crowism (the official or legal policy or practice of segregating black people) to colourblind racism ('the ideological armor for a covert and institutionalized system in the post-Civil rights era'[26]) has manifested itself in the dominant neoliberal approach to governance and has justified an expansion of the carceral state while continuing to replicate racially disparate outcomes. Moving from Jim Crowism to colourblind racism occurred alongside the growth of neoliberal governance through free-market policies, privatisation, and a scaling back of social welfare programmes. (Which is not to say that neoliberalism is responsible for the shift towards colourblindness; rather, racial colourblindness became merged with neoliberal forms of governance to justify more punitive interventions in black urban communities.)

For Loïc Wacquant, who argued that the legal order of the Jim Crow South and its criminal justice appendages functioned to socially ostracise and extract the labour of newly freed black Americans,[27] in the current era, the carceral state operates to 'warehouse the precarious and deproletarianized fractions of the black working class'.[28] This assertion regarding state restructuring is only partially accurate in that it solely focuses on the phenomena of mass incarceration and prison populations instead of also including the broader apparatuses of the carceral state, such as the proliferation of assessing fines and fees for low-level offences. In the postindustrial economy, where unemployment among black urban populations is heightened and work is often temporary, low-wage, with minimal benefits, the carceral state also demobilises black populations through aggressive broken windows policing practices, continues to socially ostracise blacks by functioning as a poverty enhancer for those caught in its reach, and also extracts government revenue in an era of austerity through the imposition of fines and fees.

Historically, legal schemes and edicts criminalising a stratum of activities were most harshly imposed against blacks in the rural South, and were supported by an explicit logic maintaining racial separation.[29] In contemporary times, the ideological framework of neoliberalism, its colourblind market ideology and its rhetoric of individual responsibility serve to justify the *racially* disparate outcomes of the carceral state in *nonracial* terms. Not only does it rationalise away such disparities, the neoliberal project also deploys colourblind racism as an impetus for local carceral state policing and court practices. Writing on urban development projects, Christopher Mele argued that a racial colourblindness coincides 'with the political economic aims of neoliberalism' to legitimise 'policies and practices that reproduce and enhance sociospatial inequality'.[30] Further expounding on the connection between neoliberalism and colourblind racism, Eric Ishiwata wrote, 'colorblind racism has effectively recoded the incongruent effects of systemic racism in stringently individual and non-racial terms'.[31]

Looking at the now infamous local jurisdiction of Ferguson specifically, government officials predicated contact with the carceral state on a lack of personal accountability for appropriate behaviour.[32] The neoliberal rhetoric of individual responsibility was positioned to justify the municipality's fines and fees practices, and defendants were viewed as simply 'paying the fair share of government'. This rhetorical positioning of racially disproportionate carceral state outcomes as a function of individual responsibility in the market validates the expansive reach of criminal justice fines and fees in poor communities of colour. It is an example of Bonilla-Silva's explication of the ways in which racially disparate outcomes are explained away as market dynamics or shortcomings in culture.[33]

Managing Black Labour—Resonances From the Past

The modern phenomenon of fines and fees demonstrates how the carceral state plays a fundamental role in managing black labour, but the criminal justice system's disproportionate impact on black people has a striking historical precedent. Writing of the post-Emancipation era in the South, Du Bois claimed that the court system was being used to deprive newly freed blacks of their freedom.[34] Through a combination of an intricate network of lien laws, Black Codes, and the system of convict leasing, the courts constrained the economic freedom of blacks and also used criminal convictions to fill state coffers and benefit private interests.[35] In essence, the criminal justice system functioned to control black labour in the wake of Emancipation during the economic shift towards industrialisation in the South. During post-Emancipation, laws were passed criminalising low-level activities such as mischief and insulting gestures, as well as vagrancy and being unemployed. Heightened punishments accompanied these laws, criminalising a wide array of everyday life activities, and they were heartily enforced against blacks.[36] Throughout the South, statute books were written to reinforce planters' control over their labour force.[37]

This elaborate network of new crimes with their associated punishments operated in conjunction with a convict lease system in which prisoners were contracted out for labour. During the decade following Emancipation, the convict population grew ten times faster than the general population, prison populations became overwhelmingly black, and the length of sentences was extended.[38] Even as late as the second world war era, the criminalisation of petty activities, and the use of fines and fees as a mechanism for enforcement can be found:

With so many young men serving in the military and the demand for citrus products increasing with every month, growers were scrambling to find enough hands to work in the groves. Every able body was needed and in January 1945, Florida governor Millard Caldwell sent letters to all sheriffs in the state, urging them to 'use their good offices' to take vigilant action to enforce 'work or fight' laws that were designed to 'prevent loitering, loafing and absenteeism'. To further incentivize Florida law enforcement, Caldwell's statute allowed sheriffs to pocket all of the fines they collected up to a yearly maximum of $7,500.[39]

In essence, this brief exploration of fines and fees in the late-nineteenth century allows for a consideration of how the carceral state is integral in mediating the relationship between labour and capital in the political economy. The expansion of the carceral state during Emancipation and the more recent hyper-punitive turn, beginning in the 1970s, both with racially disparate effects, illustrate the interconnection between the carceral state and the political economy, particularly when economic shifts are taking place. We now live in a postindustrial era of dwindling job opportunities and precarious 'gig' and low-wage work. The similarities between carceral state practices in the two periods reveal how economic shifts transform the way the carceral state shapes and manages black labour.

Management for the Postindustrial Free Market

In contemporary times, the increasing imposition of criminal court fines and fees, and their disproportionate racial implications, are best understood as a roll-out of neoliberal urban governance unfolding in a postindustrial economy. Thus, the colourblind racism of neoliberalism moves beyond a simple rationalisation of disproportionate outcomes and serves as the foundation for racially unequal policies and practices. Neoliberalism has fundamentally changed the definition of what it means to be a citizen occupying urban space.[40] It views citizens as revenue generators, and participation in government is implicitly predicated on individual responsibility and participation in the free market. Further, neoliberal urban governance conceives of urban space as solely having value based on the profitability of its exchange in the market. All of these nuances of neoliberal ideology are tied to social constructions of race, and are 'rolled-out' via broken windows policing practices designed to maintain order in areas of concentrated poverty, and through harsher penalties and sentencing for even the pettiest of crimes.

The transition from Jim Crow practices of the carceral state, relegating black Americans to an exploited, captive labour population, to contemporary carceral state practices that both warehouse and extract revenues from urban populations is an example of what legal scholar Reva

Siegel identified as 'preservation through transformation'. While the status-enforcing regime may change over time, moving away from overt racial classifications to colourblindness, the fundamental relationships of power remain intact and continue to replicate unequal outcomes.[41] As the economy shifted from industrial to postindustrial and neoliberalism became the dominant form of ideology, conceptualisations of race also changed from Jim Crowism to colourblindness to justify increased carceral state intervention in urban centres. Heather Ann Thompson also captured this shift by comparing the criminalisation of rural African American spaces with the criminalisation of urban space in the post-second world war era that was responsible for the massive expansion of the American prison population.[42]

Within the context of the carceral state, the racially coded language of criminality, even in relationship to the most petty of offences, legitimises the unequal structural relationships embedded in the postindustrial political economy. Numerous scholars have noted the profound connectedness between race and crime and criminality in America that predates the era of neoliberalism.[43] But social constructions in the popular imagination conflating blackness with an inherent predilection towards criminality have merged with the neoliberal discourse of personal responsibility and individual accountability in a way that now justifies the systematically racially biased carceral state through 'law and order' politics. Politician advocates for the War on Drugs, including Nixon and Rockefeller, positioned drug trade participants as responsible both for their own condition and broader societal problems, including social and economic insecurity.[44]

Neoliberalism and Ordering Urban Space

A closer look at the ticketing and enforcement of misdemeanour offences, traffic violations, and the criminalisation of low-level activity reveals their relationship to a very specific element of neoliberal policy—its orientation towards urban space. The neoliberal requirement of greater order to increase the value of space in the market has shaped the function and form of urban crime control through a re-emergence of order maintenance policing practices, focused on petty, low-level activity. In the broken windows policing era, the conceptualisation of urban space as requiring order has led to policies imposing strong sanctions, including arrest, for even the smallest of perceived 'criminal' violations such as possessing an open container, loitering, and criminal trespass. These increasingly punitive law and order measures operate to criminalise even the most minor of behaviours.[45] 'Broken windows policing' ties into the neoliberal logic of urban space having worth solely based on its market value.[46] This conceptualisation of space is also inextricably linked to social constructions of race and the systematic operation of racism used to rationalise unequal economic relations.

Ideas about spaces of disorder and what type of areas require state intervention to maintain order via the deployment of the carceral state have always been coloured by race. The social meaning of space is integral to urban government policy, especially when 'inner cities' are equated with being black, poor, lacking in values and unstable families.[47] Even the winner of the 2016 presidential race articulated the idea of black people in urban centres as being at risk of violence and poverty and in need of law and order policies. The racially disproportionate deployment of 'stop and frisk' policing practices in communities of colour by departments in New York and Chicago are well documented.[48] The persistence of residential racial segregation and the ways in which poor communities and communities of colour are hyper-policed in the United States fuel the racially disproportionate effects of fines and fees, and also concentrate the poverty-enhancing effects of their assessment and collection.

According to Jamie Peck, author of *Neoliberal Constructions of Reason*, the roll-out phase of neoliberalism involves governmental actors seeking to intervene, ameliorate, and regulate the rising costs of public austerity and social abandonment. For him, neoliberalism's unfolding is realised through a combination of political action and institutional reinvention. The practice of using municipal court fines and fees to generate city revenues and the policing styles it incentivises are a keen example of the neoliberalisation of urban policy. And we see the institutional reinvention of urban police departments and court officials as 'collection agencies', to use the terminology of the former Attorney General Eric Holder.

While much of neoliberal ideology calls for a retreat from the state (so the market can reign), neoliberalism can simultaneously entrench the state's capacity to surveil and punish. The resulting state, characterised by a dismantling of its economic and social arms while simultaneously expanding its 'penal fist', is described by Wacquant as a centaur.[49] The imposition of fines and fees is a function of 'neo-liberal penality'; where government increasingly passes new criminal sanctions and heightens punishments as a logical state intervention to 'calibrate the calculations of rational actors'.

Conclusion

In the current climate, racially disproportionate carceral state practices, epitomised by fines and fees as reviewed in this [reading], are both produced and legitimised through the colourblind racism embedded in neoliberalism. There are clear material interests in pursuing racist carceral state practices for local police departments and court officials, similar to the fiscal incentives for governments and the planter class in the Jim Crow South. In the postindustrial era where austerity government has created a need for increased government revenue and there exist surpluses of labour, the carceral state is deployed to extract revenues from poor communities of colour through a system of fines and fees. Neoliberal conceptions of space as being valued solely for their exchange rate in the market help fuel broken windows policing practices, disproportionately carried out in poor communities of colour.

While this [reading] sketches a starting framework for understanding how neoliberalism and race are interconnected through an exploration of fines and fees, much more empirical research is needed on this subject, for many questions remain unanswered. For example, data is needed on the disparities in and among municipalities and their use of fines and fees. Also, do certain jurisdictions impose greater fines and fees on black defendants and, if so, what are the characteristics of those jurisdictions? What are the specific consequences for individuals and communities where the assessment of fines and fees of defendants is concentrated in a handful of neighbourhoods? Lastly, more reports such as that involving the Ferguson police department are needed to help bring to light the colourblind racist rhetoric of government officials and the use of the carceral state as a means of generating government revenue. These are just a few of the questions that need to be empirically studied to help further understanding of the ways fines and fees replicate anew inequalities along lines of race and class in different ways.

Acknowledgements

I would like to thank University of Louisville senior, Erica Wheeler for assistance in collecting research on fines and fees for this article.

References

1. E. Peralta and C. Corley, 'The driving life and death of Philando Castile', *NPR Morning Edition* [website], 15 July 2016, http://www.npr.org/sections/thetwo-way/2016/07/15/485835272/the-driving-life-and-death-of-philando-castile (accessed 25 January 2017).

2. See United States Department of Justice Civil Rights Division, 'Investigation of the Ferguson Police Department', 4 March 2015, https://www.justice.gov/sites/default/files/opa/press-releases/attach-ments/2015/03/04/ferguson_police_department_report.pdf (accessed 24 January 2017).

3. Remarks as prepared for delivery by Eric Holder, 'Attorney General holder delivers update on investigations in Ferguson, Missouri', *Justice News* [U.S. Department of Justice website], 4 March 2015, https://www.justice.gov/opa/speech/attorney-general-holder-delivers-update-investigations-ferguson-mis-souri (accessed 25 January 2017).

4. M. Apuzzo, 'Justice Dept. condemns profit-minded Court policies targeting the poor', *New York Times*, 15 March 2016, https://www.nytimes.com/2016/03/15/us/politics/justice-dept-condemns-profit-minded-court-policies-targeting-the-poor.html (accessed 25 January 2017).

5. It should be noted that the term colourblind in the UK, for instance, refers to a supposed un-noticing of colour by an individual. In the US it has a very different meaning, akin to 'indirect racism' by an institution or structure which purports to be using a non colour-related mechanism but effectively discriminates on race lines.

6. The term neoliberal is used here in reference to policies, governance and ideology centred on decreased social welfare spending, increased privatisation, and mechanisms emphasising and facilitating

free-market trade and capital investment. See N. Brenner and N. Theodore, 'Cities and geographies of "actually existing neoliberalism"', *Antipode*, no. 3 (2002), pp. 349–79; J. Peck and A. Tickell, 'Neoliberalizing space', *Antipode*, no. 3 (2002), pp. 380–404; D. Harvey, *A Brief History of Neoliberalism* (Oxford: Oxford University Press, 2005).

7. J. Shapiro, 'As Court fees rise, the poor are paying the price', *NPR News Investigations* [website], 19 May 2014, http://www.npr.org/2014/05/19/312158516/increasing-court-fees-punish-the-poor (accessed 25 January 2017).

8. E. Spillane, 'Why I refuse to send people to jail for failure to pay fines and fees', *The Washington Post*, 8 April 2016, https://www.washingtonpost.com/posteverything/wp/2016/04/08/why-i-refuse-to-send-people-to-jail-for-failure-to-pay-fines/?utm_term=.3585f89bcd79 (accessed 25 January 2017).

9. M. Barajas, 'Every year, Houston Municipal Courts send thousands of people to jail who won't (or can't) pay their fines', *Houston Press*, 6 May 2016, http://www.houstonpress.com/news/every-year-houston-municipal-courts-send-thousands-of-people-to-jail-who-won-t-or-can-t-pay-their-fines-8372240 (accessed 25 January 2017).

10. L. Maggi, 'New Orleans court costs, fines are unfair to the poor, 2 national reports find', *The Times-Picayune*, 4 October 2010, http://www.nola.com/crime/index.ssf/2010/10/court_costs_fines_in_new_orlea.html (accessed 25 January 2017).

11. M. Niesse, 'DeKalb traffic fines decline after court abolished', *The Atlanta Journal-Constitution*, 15 January 2016, http://www.myajc.com/news/news/local-govt-politics/dekalb-traffic-fines-decline-after-court-abolished/np5SL/ (accessed 25 January 2017); N. Choudhury, 'Poverty is not a crime, whether you live in Dekalb County or Ferguson or anywhere else', 19 March 2015, https://www.aclu.org/blog/poverty-not-crime-whether-you-live-dekalb-county-or-ferguson-or-anywhere-else (accessed 25 January 2017).

12. J. Shapiro, 'As Court fees rise'.

13. C. Smith and C. Aspinwall, 'Increasing number going to jail for not paying fines', *Tulsa World*, 3 November 2013, http://www.tulsaworld.com/news/local/increasing-number-going-to-jail-for-not-paying-fines/article_8b8d2229-c7ad-5e7f-aea2-baeb13390880.html (accessed 25 January 2017).

14. C. Robertson, 'Missouri city to pay $4.7 million to settle suit over jailing practices', *New York Times*, 15 July 2016, https://www.nytimes.com/2016/07/16/us/missouri-city-to-pay-4-7-million-to-settle-suit-over-jailing-practices.html (accessed 25 January 2017).

15. T. Garrett and G. Wagner, 'Red ink in the rearview mirror: local fiscal conditions and the issuance of traffic tickets', *The Journal of Law and Economics*, no. 1 (2009), pp. 71–90.

16. E. Spillane, 'Why I refuse'.

17. Remarks as prepared for delivery by Eric Holder.

18. T. Vega, 'The steep cost of driving while black in California', *CNN Money* [website], 11 April 2016, http://money.cnn.com/2016/04/11/news/economy/black-drivers-california-tickets/ (accessed 25 January 2017); 'Stopped, fined, arrested: racial bias in policing and traffic courts in California', *Back on the Road* [website], April 2016, http://eblc.org/backontheroad/reports.

19. Department of Justice, *Investigation of the Ferguson Police Department*, p. 4.

20. M. Rhodan, 'ACLU says Mississipi Sheriff's office repeatedly targeted African-Americans', *Time Magazine*, 8 May 2017, http://time.com/4771163/aclu-mississippi-ilegal-searches-black-residents/ (accessed 28 June 2017).

21. T. P. R. Weaver, *Blazing the Neoliberal Trail: urban political development in the United States and United Kingdom* (Philadelphia: University of Pennsylvania Press, 2016), p. 280. See also, C. Mele, 'Neoliberalism, Race and the redefining of urban redevelopment', *International Journal of Urban and Regional Research*, no. 2 (2013), pp. 598–617.

22. See M. Alexander, *The New Jim Crow: colorblindness in the era of mass incarceration* (New York: The New Press, 2012); A. Lerman and V. Weaver, *Arresting Citizenship: the democratic consequences of American crime control* (Chicago: The University of Chicago Press, 2014); R. Sampson and C. Loeffler, 'Punishment's place: the local concentration of mass incarceration', *Daedalus*, no. 3 (2010), pp. 20–31.

23. See L. Wacquant, 'Crafting the neoliberal state: workfare, prisonfare, and social insecurity', *Sociological Forum* no. 2 (2010), pp. 197–220; M. Gottschalk, *Caught: the prison state and the lock-down of American politics* (Princeton: Princeton University Press, 2015).

24. M. Gottschalk, *Caught*.

25. A. Reed, Jr, 'Marx, race, and neoliberalism', *New Labour Forum*, no. 1 (2013), pp. 49–57, p. 51.

26. E. Bonilla-Silva, *Racism without Racists: color-blind racism and the persistence of racial inequality in the United States* (Lanham: Rowan & Littlefield Publishers, 2010), p. 2.

27. L. Wacquant, 'From slavery to mass incarceration', *New Left Review*, no. 13 (2002), pp. 41–60, p. 53.

28. L. Wacquant, 'From slavery', p. 53.

29. L. Wacquant, 'From slavery'.

30. C. Mele, 'Neoliberalism, race, and the redefining of urban development'.

31. E. Ishiwata, '"We are seeing people we didn't know exist": Katrina and the neoliberal erasure of race', in Cedric Johnson, ed., *The Neoliberal Deluge: Hurricane Katrina, late capitalism, and the remaking of New Orleans* (Minneapolis: University of Minnesota Press, 2011), pp. 35–6.

32. Department of Justice, Investigation of the Ferguson Police Department.

33. E. Bonilla-Silva, *Racism without Racists*, pp. 74–8.

34. W. E. B. Du Bois, *Souls of Black Folk* (New York: Vintage Books, 1990), p. 124; W. E. B. Du Bois, *Black Reconstruction in America* (New York: The Free Press, 1998), pp. 167–80.

35. Du Bois, *Souls of Black Folk*; Du Bois, *Black Reconstruction*.

36. See M. Alexander, *The New Jim Crow* and Du Bois, *Souls of Black Folk*.

37. E. Foner, *A Short History of Reconstruction 1863–1877* (New York: Harper & Row Publishers, 1990), p. 250.

38. M. Alexander, *The New Jim Crow*, pp. 31–2. See also D. Blackmon, *Slavery by Another Name: the re-enslavement of black Americans from the Civil War to World War II* (New York: Anchor Books, 2008).

39. G. King, *Devil in the Grove: Thurgood Marshall, the Groveland Boys, and the dawn of a New America* (New York: Harper Collins Publishers, 2012), p. 79.

40. See M. Gottschalk, *Caught*.

41. R. Siegel, 'Why equal protection no longer protects: the evolving forms of status-enforcing state action', *Stanford Law Review*, no. 49 (1997), pp. 1111–48, p. 1113.

42. H. A. Thompson, 'Why mass incarceration matters: rethinking crisis, decline, and transformation in postwar American history', *The Journal of American History*, no. 97 (2007), pp. 703–34, p. 706.

43. See L. Wacquant, 'From slavery to mass incarceration'; M. Alexander, *The New Jim Crow*; K. Muhammad, *The Condemnation of Blackness: race, crime, and the making of modern urban America* (Cambridge: Harvard University Press, 2010); S. Body-Gendrot, *The Social Control of Cities? A comparative perspective* (Oxford: Blackwell, 2000).

44. M. Gottschalk, *Caught*.

45. See S. Herbert and E. Brown, 'Conceptions of space and crime in the punitive neoliberal city', *Antipode*, no. 4 (2006).

46. See M. Jay and P. Conklin, 'Detroit and the political origins of "broken windows" policing', *Race & Class* 59, no. 2 (2017).

47. M. Mahoney, 'Segregation, whiteness and transformation', *University of Pennsylvania Law Review*, no. 143 (1995), pp. 1659–84, p. 1674.

48. See American Civil Liberties Union of Illinois, 'Stop and frisk in Chicago', March 2015, http://www.aclu-il. org/wp-content/uploads/2015/03/ACLU_StopandFrisk_6.pdf (accessed 26 January 2017); New York Civil Liberties Union 'Stop and frisk data' [website], http://www.nyclu.org/content/stop-and-frisk-data (accessed 26 January 2017).

49. L. Wacquant, *Punishing the Poor: the neoliberal government of social insecurity* (Durham: Duke University Press, 2009), p. 4.

Post-Reading Questions

1   Why does the author describe the current system of fines and fees as embedded colorblind racism?

2   How do you feel about jailing offenders for non-payment of fines? In your opinion, does this alleviate or aggravate crime within communities? Be sure to qualify your position.

3   In what ways does the author critique the role of colorblind neoliberalism in the current growth of the carceral state? In what ways would you agree or disagree?

4   Beyond incarceration, what are some of the consequences of fines and fees for low-level offenses?

5   Explain your reaction to the following statement from former Attorney General Eric Holder:

Once the system is primed for maximizing revenue—starting with fines and fee enforcement—the city relies on the police force to serve, essentially as a collection agency for the municipal court rather than a law enforcement entity.

PART IV

DIVERSITY, PUNISHMENT,
AND CORRECTIONS

"NO CULTURE CAN LIVE, IF IT ATTEMPTS
TO BE EXCLUSIVE."

– *Mohandas K. Gandhi*

Legacies of Racialization of Incarceration

From Convict-Lease to the Prison Industrial Complex

A. E. Raza

The Civil War brought an end to the institutionalized enslavement of African Americans, yet through the 13th Amendment to the U.S. Constitution and various legal practices the current prison system has manifested itself into an institution of forced labor, which is increasingly being comprised of people of color. As such, this [reading] examines the material conditions that existed during the post-emancipation era in order to expose the racialized historical continuities of the prison system thereby demonstrating the way in which laws have in fact helped to create a racially unequal criminal justice system. By concentrating on the history of the post-emancipation South and its prison system as it relates to African Americans, this [reading] aims to illuminate how anti-black racism is central to the current era of incarceration. I do this by emphasizing the racial dimension of the prison system, focusing on the state of Georgia, which historically has subjugated African Americans via slavery, Black codes, and Jim Crow laws. Moreover, I argue that Georgia's post-emancipation criminal justice system contributes to its current state of incarceration, and should be understood as part of the legacies of the social and economic functions of slavery.

This [reading] is divided into three sections. The first section discusses the current state of the prison system, specifically the conditions in the state of Georgia. The second section traces the historical development of the racialized prison system by examining the 13th Amendment and the ambiguous definition of criminality. I then delineate the rise of the prison system in post-emancipation Georgia, paying particular attention to the convict-lease system and Black Codes specific to the state. In the third section I discuss the increasing imprisonment of women of color, and

A. E. Raza, "Legacies of the Racialization of Incarceration: From Convict-Lease to the Prison Industrial Complex," *Journal of the Institute of Justice and International Studies*, no. 11, pp. 159-169. Copyright © 2011 by University of Central Missouri. Reprinted with permission. Provided by ProQuest LLC. All rights reserved.

how that, too, is in fact a legacy of slavery, with its shared dimensions of sexual domination and oppression. I conclude with a discussion of the rise of the prison industrial complex.

Contemporary Georgia and its Prison System

The current figures associated with incarceration in the United States in general, and Georgia in particular, reveals that race plays a central role in imprisonment, which stems from a racialized system of enslavement that characterized both the antebellum and post-antebellum South. While slavery officially ended in the United States in 1865, the consequences of racialized enslavement are found today.[1] To begin, African Americans represent 12.8% of the U.S. population, yet make up 42% of the federal and state prison populations (Hoover Institute, 2006). In 2008 the total population of those held in custody at the federal, state, and local prisons and jails totaled approximately 2,311,2000 peoples (West, 2009). Among that total an estimated 913,800 were African Americans (West, 2009). These statistics reveal that on average African Americans are disproportionally imprisoned in the U.S., questioning the modern day assumption of a colorblind legal and criminal justice system.

The disproportionality discussed above is even more apparent when examining the state of Georgia's general population to the prison population. In 2008 the U.S. Census Bureau estimated the total population of Georgia at 9,685,7444 with whites accounting for 65% of the population followed by African Americans with 30% (US Census Bureau, 2008).[2] At the same time, the total prison population of Georgia was 54,016 with African Americans comprising over half of the inmate population with 33,114. When compounded with the other non-white inmates, 62% of the inmate population of Georgia consists of people of color (Georgia Department of Correction [GDC], 2008b).[3] Additionally, out of the 150,000 parolees in the state, African Americans account for 72,358. The most common offenses held by parolees are property offenses (51,378), and drug offenses (54,250) (GDC, 2008b, p. 17). It is significant that property offenses constitute the majority of probationary offenses, since, as will be discussed, the implementation of property laws was one of the most effective ways that the post-emancipation South was able to imprison the newly freed population.

The Georgia Department of Corrections' annual report for 2008 notes the budget history for the past six years showing an increase from $905,854,482 in 2004 to a projected annual budget of over one billion dollars for 2009 in order to keep correctional facilities operational (GDC, 2008b). There are over 100 facilities covered by the GDC including local jails and county prisons, employing 15,000 people. In 2008, the GDC entered into a contract with the private company, Bone Safety Signs, which would allow the company to operate a production plant within the state prison in Reidsville, Georgia. Under the contract Bone Safety Signs uses inmate labor, which is paid a wage that in turn goes to paying the cost of their imprisonment (GDC, 2008a).[4] At the same time the State also partnered with Western Union and ARAMARK. In addition to these contracts the GDC runs and operates a public corporation named Georgia Correctional Industries. This corporation began as a labor-based program established in 1960, which manufactures products such as office furniture, institutional furniture, road signs, janitorial chemicals, and print services to government agencies such as schools (Georgia Correctional Industries, n.d.). These private contracts and state-led manufacturing are very similar to the private contracts of the earlier prison management system embraced in the convict-lease system.

The consequences of imprisonment is complex and beyond the scope of this [reading], yet as can be seen from the data on Georgia it is apparent that the large inmate population coupled with the private contracts and convict labor is in line with the concept of the prison industrial complex. The prison industrial complex (PIC) can be understood as "a multifaceted system, maintained through cooperation between government and industry that designates prisons as a solution to social, political, and economic problems" (Herzing & Burch, 2003, para. 3).[5] Economically speaking, the PIC relies on the proliferation of prisons and supporting industries to create profits for corporations. Communication companies such as AT &T and Sprint provide telecommunications systems, while other corporations like American Express invest in prison constructions (Evans & Goldberg, 2009). Politically, the increase of prison populations and ex-felons creates a system that disenfranchises a large segment of the population. Felony disenfranchisement is, as Moore (2008) contends, a "holdover from exclusionary Jim Crow era laws like poll taxes and ballot box literacy tests [and] affects about 5.3 million former and current felons in the United States, according to voting rights groups" (para. 5). Likewise, Franklin (2000) argues that felony convictions and exclusionary citizenship laws explicitly function to prevent African Americans from the political process.

The reality of the PIC can be found today in Georgia where we observe the economic and political functions of prisons, such as corporate partnerships and the high rate of ex-convicts and parolees who are mainly people of color. The current state of imprisonment can be situated in the post-emancipation period which set the foundations for the PIC; economically situated within the convict-lease system, and socially in the anti-black racism of the time, both of which worked in unison to politically and economically disenfranchise African Americans.

Forced Labor after Emancipation

In 1865 Congress ratified the 13th Amendment to the U.S. Constitution, which states:

> Neither slavery nor involuntary servitude, except as a punishment for crime whereof the party shall have been duly convicted, shall exist within the United States, or any place subject to their jurisdiction.

What is central to this Amendment is the fact that while slavery and all other form of involuntary servitude were abolished it was found to be an appropriate method of punishment for criminals. Yet the definition of crime worthy of the punishment of slavery was never discussed within the Amendment, which allowed individual states to define crime in their own terms. In effect it allowed for the criminalization and re-enslavement of African Americans. As Angela Davis (2003) maintains, "in the immediate aftermath of slavery, the southern states hastened to develop a criminal justice system that could legally restrict the possibilities of freedom for newly released slaves" (p. 29). In many ways Black codes served to define criminality in terms of race, and shared many commonalities with the prior slave codes. This re-articulation of slave codes into Black codes "tended to racialize penalty and link[ed] it closely with previous regimes of slavery" (Davis, 2003, p. 31). This being said, the rise of the Black codes in Georgia supports the idea of recycling slave codes into legalized social control methods legitimized by the 13th Amendment's lack of a threshold definition for the qualifying criminality that could subject one to involuntary servitude.

Black Codes

Originally intended to outline and secure the legal rights of newly freed blacks, Black codes focused on property, contractual, judicial, and labor rights (Foner, 1983.). After the radical Republicans took control over Southern state governments beginning in 1867, Black codes were usurped and became a primary form to implement control over African Americans. Black code legislation was reformulated to include vagrancy laws, labor contract laws, travel restrictions, and employment laws (Hartman, 1997; Foner, 1983). This is supported by Wilson's (1965) study on post-emancipation Black Codes, which he argues, resulted from social beliefs such as blacks being regarded as 'lazy' and unwilling to work "without physical compulsion" and their "propensity for stealing" (p. 44 and 49).[6] In essence, these Black codes paternalistically sought to make newly freed slaves fit within the framework of the larger society by placing them into a subjugated position-one that was eerily similar to their position as slaves. Lichtenstein (1996), Mayers (1990, 1998), and Davis (2003) argue that while Black codes had economic implications, social control was an additional reason for their implementation. Mayers (1990) argues that black populations posed threats to both economic and political white hegemony, particularly black males due to their voting rights. While there are multiple reasons for the rise of Black codes, racism and white supremacy were major ideological factors that had real economic, political, and social results in the South.[7]

Historically, Georgia's laws were less overtly racist compared to other Southern states, such as South Carolina. This was concluded by scholars such as Bryant (1994) from the evidence that Georgia's legislature did not create Black codes formally, rather, they instituted laws that were more "subtle" in order to avoid northern criticism (p. 18). Additionally, Wilson (1965) found that Georgia's vagrancy law made no "apparent racial discrimination," yet blacks were primarily targeted as violating the vagrancy law.[8] In 1866 the Georgia Assembly passed trespassing laws, which imposed fines of imprisonment for those convicted of entering enclosed land. At the same time they also passed laws prohibiting "squatting or settling upon enclosed or unenclosed land of another whether public or private" (Hahn, 1982, p. 45). In that same year, Foner (1983) writes that Georgia "outlawed hunting on Sundays in counties with large black populations, and forbade taking [...] anything of "any value whatever" from private property, whether or not fenced" (p. 66). And so, while these laws were not formally written as Black codes they functioned to control the newly freed population.

In addition to the creation of laws targeting blacks, Georgia legislature increased penalties for convictions. Among the ways they did so, was by making crimes that were previously misdemeanors into felonies. For instance in 1875 Georgia made stealing hogs a felony; within two years of the implementation of this law the convict population more than tripled from 432 to 1,441 (Adamson 1983, p. 562). The legislature also increased penalties for felony convictions. Wilson (1965) found that "instead of the former maximum penalty of between fourteen and twenty years imprisonment, the new laws prescribed death for the offenses of burglary in the night, arson, when the building was occupied, horse and mule stealing, rape, and insurrection" (p. 105). The trend of racially implicit laws and the changes in penalties led to an increase in the penitentiary population, raising the question regarding the function of the prison system.

Convict-Lease System

W.E.B. Du Bois wrote in his 1901 essay, "Spawn of Slavery: The Convict-Lease System in the South," that prior to emancipation the criminal justice system was almost "exclusive to whites" (Du Bois, 2007, p. 117). Furthermore, Du Bois contends that the emancipation of African Americans caused a transformation of the southern criminal justice system which took on many of the same functions of slavery, including forced labor, as embodied in the convict-lease system. The convict-lease system was one of many prison management systems, although it is infamously associated with the post-Civil War South. This system was derived from earlier prison systems that began in the North, specifically the public accounts system and the contract system (Cable, 1969, p. 123). The former placed prisoners under the charge of the State and forced them to work in labor-intensive industries housed within the prison, while the latter system placed prisoners under official private contractors who were obliged by the state to follow specific guidelines. While these two systems were also used in the South prior to emancipation, the transition to the convict-lease system can be understood as both an economic and social consequence of Southern Reconstruction.

The convict-lease system resulted due to many reasons, one of which was for the prison system to achieve self-sustainability. Mayers (1998) argues that the economic depression and weakened infrastructure affecting the South after the Civil War allowed for this particular system to emerge. Georgia, for example, was in debt after the Civil War and by the end of the 1860s found itself with a $6.54 million debt (Mayers, 1998, p. 8). In addition, property values were falling, reconstruction failed to redistribute land causing intense poverty for freed blacks, and raising taxes for prisons was met with opposition. Consequently, the depressive situation in the South was exasperated by the lack of an industrial sector and limited flows of capital investment

(Norrell, 1991). Cable (1969) claims that the system sprang from the realization that the State had in its power a population that could be used in any manner it chose. The states in the South found that they could profit from their convict population, "allowing the possibility of waiving taxes while profiting the State's treasury" (Cable, 1969, p. 126). The industrialists and capitalists who went into lease agreements with the State paid a fee for the convicts as well as maintained the costs of "housing, feeding, clothing, and guarding all convicts" (Mayer, 1998, p. 9).

Economically, the convict-lease system provided an ample supply of cheap labor and the possibility to maximize profits. It also played an increasing role in preserving the Antebellum South's social and racial order. Adamson (1983) maintains that while convict-leasing provided "fiscal utility [...] in a real sense, the convict lease system was a functional replacement for slavery; it provided an economic source of cheap labor and a means to re-establish white supremacy in the South" (p. 556). This is apparent in the way in which the previous slave codes and public displays of punishment became embodied in laws that targeted newly freed blacks like the Black codes, Jim Crow laws, and the way in which prisoners were publicly displayed through the convict-leasing system and chain gangs.[9]

Georgia led the South in embracing the penitentiary management of the convict-lease system between 1868 and 1908 by promoting it as a panacea for economic and social problems (Mayers, 1998). Additionally, Mayers and Massey (1991) argue that its popularity was a result of it being seen as a way to "solve the dual problem of labor and capital scarcity" that Georgia found itself in after the Civil War (p. 269). Consequently, the convict-lease system in Georgia was justified as a solution to the States' problems, but it was not justified in its treatment of convicts, or the conditions under which they existed. In 1880, there were approximately 1,185 convicts consigned to three penitentiaries in three counties in eleven camps. According to Cable (1969) many of these camps did not maintain a hospital, physician, or chaplain, as required by law (p. 155). Du Bois (2007), in his study of Georgia prisons, noted that there was insufficient shelter for the convicts, and found one Georgia camp in 1895 extremely appalling, stating that "sixty-one men slept in one room, seventeen by nineteen feet, and seven feet high. Sanitary conditions were wretched, there was little to no medical attendance, and almost no care of the sick" (p. 119). While the leasing of convicts to private companies was the original idea behind the system, convict labor was chiefly extracted by the State in order to carry out public work projects, such as building roads. The Georgia Road Congress supported the use of felons to build roads and by 1895 expanded this harsh punishment to nonviolent felons and those with at least five-year sentences (Mayers & Massey, 1991). This is very much in line with today's GDC correctional industries where convicts, the majority of which are non-violent offenders, are employed by the State.

Incarceration and Gender

Of particular importance is the way gender was constructed in the convict-lease system. Much like slavery, the convict-lease system did not discriminate between genders. This was true in

Georgia where, in 1870, guards testified in Congress regarding the treatment of women convicts working on the railroads who, much like the men, were beaten by guards (Mayers & Massey, 1991).[10] Additionally, Du Bois (2007) found that:

> [...] [W]omen were mingled indiscriminately with men, both working and sleeping, and dressed often in men's clothes. A young girl at Camp Hardmont, Georgia, in 1895, was repeatedly outraged by several of her guards, and finally died in childbirth while in camp. (p. 119)

Furthermore Davis (2003) maintains that "black women endured the cruelties of the convict-lease system unmitigated by the feminization of punishment; neither their sentences nor the labor they were compelled to do were lessened by virtue of their gender" (p. 72). This can be contrasted to white women convicts who, at the same time, were sent to domestication training rather than forced labor (Davis, 2003).

In 2003 the female prison population in the U.S. reached over 100,000 for the first time, comprised of mainly women of color (Harrison & Beck, 2004). Although they do not face the same type conditions as exemplified in the convict-lease system, they continue to suffer from sexual abuse in the current prison system. For example, Human Rights Watch (HRW) reported that female prisoners live in constant fear of sexual abuse by guards, where "grievance or investigatory procedures, where they exist, are often ineffectual, and correctional employees continue to engage in abuse because they believe they will rarely be held accountable, administratively or criminally" (HRW, 1996, p. 13). The experiences of these women are even more disturbing when discussing the health care, prenatal care, and childcare denied or limited to them. For example, in the same HRW report it was found that "in some countries, women prisoners are shackled during childbirth," reporting this to be the case in the U.S. "where women who go into labor while imprisoned are chained with leg irons and belly chains during labor" (HRW, 1996, p. 13).

The state of women in prison share many similarities to the sub-human conditions of slavery and has faced criticism and evaluations from outside organization such as the UN, HRW, and the Friends World Committee for Consultations.[11] These conditions exemplify some of the shared logic between slavery and prisons, and have found similar criticism and opposition to end this form of punishment. The UN Commission on Human Right (UNCHR) found U.S. prisons, particularly California prisons, as unsafe reporting, "[i]t was also alleged that women in the units live in constant fear of rape" (UNCHR, 2001, para.99). Recently the Friends World Committee for Consultation released a 2008 report examining the treatment of women in prison and the UN Minimum Rules for the Treatment of Prisoners. This report corroborates the earlier findings of mistreatment and lack of resources in female prisons, but also concludes that race and ethnicity are unjustly linked to imprisonment. It found that internationally, indigenous women disproportionally represent the prison population, noting that in New South Wales, Australia, "Aboriginal women constitute 2% of the female population but 32% of the women's prison population" (Bastick & Townhead, 2008, p. 106). In the United States, women of color are also over-represented: "African American women are eight times more likely, and Latina women three times more likely, to be imprisoned than white women [...] two thirds of women in state and federal prisons are African American or Latina" (Bastick, & Townhead, 2008, p. 106).

From Convict-Lease to PIC

The transitions from previous systems of imprisonment to the convict-lease system coincided with the abolition of slavery and emancipation of slaves. In the South this system of imprisonment functioned not only to mitigate the economic depression it found itself in, but also to reestablish white supremacy through indirect means, primarily through harsh laws and penalties targeted against blacks. In many ways the 13th Amendment and the Black codes that followed Emancipation recreated involuntary servitude by justifying criminality to be punishable by slavery. This coupled with the post-Civil War depression in the South, and the new social dimension, allowed racism, laws, and the convict-lease system to emerge as a solution to the economic, social, and political threats posed by a free black population. Much like slavery the convict-lease system allowed for labor exploitation, mistreatment, and violence against blacks, with the similar sexual abuse of women. Moreover, the convict-lease system set up the foundation for government and private companies to extract labor and profits from inmates.

During this same period the U.S. was beginning to establish itself as a color-blind society, insisting that institutional racism was being eliminated. This idea of color-blindness before the law was cemented during the Civil Rights era of the 1960s yet was short-lived. As discussed by Lipstiz (1998) the economic restructuring taking place in the United States, characterized by deindustrialization and massive unemployment, negatively impacted working class and communities of color.[12] This was coupled with cutbacks in social services, creating a condition where people of color were unable to secure jobs or state aid. As a response to this paradox, the state, through racialized laws and policies, was able to imprison this surplus labor, thereby alleviating the economic consequences of structural adjustments, while at the same time securing a social hierarchy.[13] This is supported by Ruth Wilson-Gilmore's (2007) study where she found that the prison population in California grew 500% between 1982 and 2000, arguing that this growth can be attributed to the displacement of workers caused by the structural adjustment of the 1970s (p. 11). Similarly, Gilmore (2009) argues that most of those who found themselves imprisoned "were criminalized for crimes stemming from unemployment" (Gilmore, 2009, p. 1).

And so in this context of unemployment and social and economic instability we find the rise of the PIC. Recall that the PIC as an economic system involves both the State and private corporations working in collaboration to profit by imprisonment: The State secures employment for communities where prisons are held; private corporations profit from the construction and maintenance of prisons; and both profit from extracted prison labor. Integral to the success of this prison system are the prisoners themselves. The PIC is essentially an updated version of the convict-lease system, where not only are inmates used as labor, such as in Georgia, but they themselves are the raw materials facilitating the profitability and expansion of the PIC. Both the convict-lease and the PIC systems arose in the contexts of economic and social changes, emancipation and economic depression in the former and civil rights gains and economic restructuring in the latter. These similarities are important in developing an understanding, not only the current era of incarceration, but also the logic behind policies such as mandatory minimum sentencing.

As we enter the 21st century, the U.S. has the largest prison population in the world and is increasing due to the prison industrial complex, which much like the convict-lease system partners the State with corporations in order to profitably create a prison system that exploits inmates while expanding prison-led industries. While this paper attempted to expose the ways in which today's prison system can be understood as rooted in the racialized convict-lease system, it is imperative to note the similarities between the racist targeting of blacks in the South, Chinese in the West, and Mexicans in the Southwest during the late 19th century to today's prison population, which primarily consists of people of color. Furthermore, the legalized practice of racial profiling along the U.S.-Mexico border, and the War on Terrorism, can be seen as giving rise to new forms of "Black codes" targeting people of color.[14] This current situation shows the contradiction within the criminal justice system, which assumes the foundations of equality and colorblindness before the law, while in practice, functions differently. For this reason it is necessary to return to the historical moments that have led to this current situation. While this [reading] was limited in scope by focusing on the State of Georgia, it nonetheless provides evidence that the legacy of slavery in the post-emancipation criminal justice system can be found in today's prison system.

Notes

1 The legal definition of slavery in the United States is difficult to come by. In 1858 Thomas R. R. Cobb, examining U.S. slavery, defines it as "applied to all involuntary servitude, which is not inflicted as a punishment for crime" (p. 3–4). In his understanding of slavery Cobb references the civil code of Louisiana that defines a slave as "one who is in the power of a master, to whome he belongs" (Cobb, 1968, p. 4). Additionally, slavery is referenced in many court decisions and reports of the 1800's as involuntary servitude. For example see *Strader v. Graham (1850)*. Additionally, Kevin Bales (2004) presents all the current definitions of slavery from the Convention of Slavery in 1926, to the 2003 UN Convention on Transnational Organized Crime, all of which similarly conclude that forced labor is the main characteristic of slavery (p. 102). Hence, based on this authority this paper defines enslavement as involuntary servitude.

2 The figures from the 2010 U.S. Census reveals the total population of Georgia to be 9,687,653. Among that total 59.7% are reported to be White, and 30.5% African American (US Census Bureau, 2011).

3 This figure includes 65 reported Indians and 63 Asians.

4 The GDC reports that under this partnership inmates will be paid minimum wage. This minimum is far above other reports which have found that federal inmates were being paid anywhere between 5 cents and $1.65 an hour for work. See Egelko (2007, March 22).

5 Angela Davis (2003) notes that the term "prison industrial complex" was introduced by activist and scholars to challenge prevailing beliefs that an increased level of crime was the cause of rising prison population. Rather, Davis argues that prison construction, driven by ideologies of racism and profits, caused the increase (p. 84).

6 Wilson (1965) provides as evidence of these social beliefs, the view of one Georgian plantation overseer who in the fall of 1865 stated: "[M]onk and austen come back and stol two of the horses from the place" and "it seems that they want to Destroy everything you have" (Wilson, 1965, p. 50). This quote is originally from Sen. Exec. Docs., No. 2, 39th Congress, 1st session, p. 16.

7 According to Fredrickson (1981), white supremacy is defined as referring "to the attitudes, ideologies, and policies associated with the rise of blatant forms of white or European dominance over "non-white" populations" (xi).

8 Wilson (1965) notes that Georgia's vagrancy laws defined a vagrant person as someone able to work but choosing not to, or choosing to partake in illicit activities.

9 For example, note the similarities in imagery and symbolism of the chain gang to the coffle.

10 Mayers and Massey (1991) quote Zimmerman who wrote in 1947 that these guards "testified before a legislative committee in Georgia that women convicts who worked on the railroads were "whipped on their bare rumps in the presence of men" (p. 100).

11 The Friends World Committee for Consultation is part of the larger Quaker United Nations Office and is a non-governmental organization that seeks to "abolish war and promote peaceful resolution of conflicts, human rights, economic justice and good governance". ("Quaker United Nation Office", n.d.).

12 The United States in the late 1960s and early 1970s began an economic transition from a Keynesian model of economic growth to a neoliberal model. Under the new model heavy industries and manufacturing sectors were shipped abroad, while social programs and services were cut. Lipsitz (1998) argues that the consequences of deindustrialization were both socially and economically devastating for African Americans who had gained some upward mobility through industrialized labor.

13 During the Reagan administration the war on drugs was enacted in order to obfuscate the economic crisis resulting from the new economic order (Wilson-Gilmore, 1997). This 'war' was implemented as a response to the drug epidemic of the 1980s in urban black communities, and was presented to the public as a 'law and order' policy. Under the drug war, mandatory minimum sentencing was required, leading to the mass imprisonment of people of color. For example, at the federal level, the Anti-Drug Abuse Act of 1986 and 1988 required a five year minimum imprisonment for conviction of crack-cocaine possession (Mauer, 2001, p. 6). Furthermore, Mauer (2001) argues that the impact of drug-related sentencing led to the tripling of the national prison population between 1988 and 1996.

14 Nguyen (2005) historicizes the current Arizona border situations of vigilantes and border policies to the mid-1800s and the end of the Mexican American war, when lynching of Mexicans was practiced along the border (p. 94). She also writes of the post 9/11 conflations of immigrants and the US-Mexico border to terrorism (p. 103). While Rubio-Goldsmith, Romero, Rubio-Goldsmith, Escobedo, and Khoury (2009) relate the historic structural violence committed to Mexicans along the US Mexico border to the current practices of racial profiling.

References

Adamson, C. R. (1983). Punishment after slavery: southern state penal systems, 1865–1890. *Social Problems,* 30 (5), 555–569.

Bales, K. (2004). New *slavery: a reference book, Second Edition.* Santa Barbara, CA: ABD–CLIO Incorporated.

Bastick, M., and Townhead L. (2008). *Women in prison: a commentary on the UN standard minimum rules for treatment of prisoner.* Human Rights and Refugees Publications, Quaker United Nations Office. Retrieved from http://www.quno.org/geneva/pdf/humanrights/women-in-prison/WiP-CommentarySMRs200806-English.pdf

Bryant, J. M. (1994). We have no chance of justice before the courts. In J. C. Inscoe (Ed.), *Georgia in black and white.* Athens, GA: University of Georgia Press.

Cable, G. W. (1969). *The silent south.* Montclair, CA: Patterson Smith Publishing Corporation.

Coobes, T.R.R. (1968). *An Inquiry into the Law of Negro Slavery in the United States of America.* New York, NY: Negro Universities Press. Originally published in 1858.

Davis, A. (2003). *Are prisons obsolete?* New York, NY: Seven Stories Press.

Du Bois, W. E. B. (2007). The spawn of slavery: the convict-lease system in the South. In S. L. Gabbion (Ed), *W.E.B. Du Bois on crime and justice: laying the foundations of sociological criminology.* Burlington, VT: Ashgate.

Egelko, B. (2007, March 22). Lawyer slams prison wages: Tony Serra files suit on behalf of federal inmates for low rate of pay for labor by the incarcerated. *San Francisco Chronicles.* Retrieved from http://www.sfgate.com/chronicle/

Evans, L., and Goldberg, E. (2009). *The prison-industrial complex and the global economy.* Oakland, CA: PM Press.

Foner, E. (1983). *Nothing but freedom: emancipation and its legacy.* Baton Rouge, LA: Louisiana State University Press.

Franklin, H. B. (2000). *From Plantation to Penitentiary to Prison-Industrial Complex: Literature of the American Prison.* Black American Literature and Culture Division, Modern Language Association Convention, Washington, DC, December 30, 2000.

Fredrickson, G.M. (1981). *White supremacy: a comparative study in American and South African history.* New York, NY: Oxford University Press.

Mauer. M. (2001). The causes and consequences of prison growth in the United States. In D. Garland (Ed). *Mass imprisonment: social causes and consequences.* Thousand Oaks, CA: Sage.

Georgia Correctional Industries, Georgia Department of Corrections. (n.d). Website. Retrieved from www.gci-ga.com

Georgia Department of Corrections (Dec 18, 2008a). *New program allows prisoners to work for wages.* Press Release. Retrieved from http://www.dcor.state.ga.us/NewRoom/PressReleases/081218.html

Georgia Department of Corrections. (2008b). *Annual Report FY 08.* Retrieved from http://www.dcor.state.ga.us/Research/Annual/GDC_annual_report_FY2008.pdf

Gilmore, K. (2009). *Slavery and prisons: understanding the connections. Retrieved* from http://www.history-isaweapon.com/defcon1/gilmoreprisonslavery.html

Hahn, S. (1982). Hunting, fishing, and foraging: common rights and class relations in the postbellum South. *Radical History Review, 26,* 37–64.

Harrison, P., and Beck, A. (Nov, 2004). *Prisoners in 2003.* (Bureau of Justice Statistics Bulletin, NCJ 205335). U.S. Department of Justice. Retrieved from http://bjs.ojp.usdoj.gov/content/pub/pdf/p03.pdf

Hartman, S. (1997). *Scenes of subjection: terror, slavery, and self-making in nineteenth century America.* New York, NY: Oxford University Press.

Herzing, R., and Burch, M. (2003). *Critical resistance South: challenging the prison industrial complex.* Retrieved from http://november.org/stayinfo/breaking/CRSouth.html

Hoover Institute. (2006). *Facts on policy: prison demographics.* Retrieved from http://www.hoover.org/research/factsonpolicy/facts/16615876.html

Human Rights Watch, Women's Rights Project. (1996). *All Too Familiar: Sexual Abuse of Women in U.S. State Prisons.* New York, NY: Human Rights Watch. Retrieved from http://www.aclu.org/hrc/PrisonsStates.pdf

Lichtenstein, A. (1996). *Twice the work of free labor: The political economy of convict labor in the new South.* London, England: Verso.

Lipsitz, G. (1998). *The Possessive investment in whiteness: how white people profit from identity politics.* Philadelphia, PA: Temple University Press.

Mayers, M. (1990). Black Threat and Incarceration in Postbellum Georgia. *Social Forces,* 69 (2): 373–393.

Mayers, M. (1998). *Race, labor, and punishment in the new south.* Columbus, OH: Ohio State University Press.

Mayers, M., and Massey, J. (1991). Race, labor, and punishment in postbellum Georgia. *Social Problems,* 38 (2), 267–286.

Moore, S. (2008, September 13). States Restore voting rights for Ex-Convicts. *New York Times.* Retrieved from http://www.nytimes.com/2008/09/14/us/politics/14felony.html

Nguyen, T. (2005). *We are all suspects now: untold stories from immigrant communities after 911.* Boston, MA: Beacon Press.

Norrell, R. (1991). *James Bowron: The Autobiography of a new south industrialist.* Chapel Hill, NC: University of North Carolina Press.

Rubio-Goldsmith, P., Romero, M., Rubio-Goldsmith, R., Escobedo, M., Khoury, L. (2009). *Ethno-racial profiling and state violence in a Southwest barrio.* Aztlan: A Journal of Chicano Studies. 34(1), 93–123.

UN Commission on Human Rights. (2001, July). *Report of the mission to the U.S. on the issue of violence against women in the state and federal prisons, 1999.* Integration of the human rights of women and the gender perspective. UNESC,E/CN.4/1999/68/Add2. Retrieved from http://www.unhchr.ch/Huridocda/Huridoca.nsf/0/7560a6237c67bb118025674c004406e9?O pendocument

US Census Bureau. (2008). *Population Estimates, Table 3. Annual Estimates of the Resident Population by Sex, Race, and Hispanic Origin for Georgia: April 1, 2000 to July 1, 2008.* Retrieved from http://www.census.gov/popest/states/asrh/EST2008-03.html

U.S. Census Bureau. (2011). *State and County Quick Facts: Georgia* [Data file]. Retrieved from http://quickfacts.census.gov/qfd/states/13000.html

West, Heather. (June, 2010). *Prison Inmates at midyear 2009 Statistical Tables*. (Bureau of Justice Statistics Bulletin, NCJ 230113). U.S. Department of Justice. Retrieved from http://bjs.ojp.usdoj.gov/content/pub/pdf/pim09st.pdf

Wilson, T. B. (1965). *The black codes of the South*. Birmingham, AL: University of Alabama.

Wilson-Gilmore, R. (2007). *Golden gulag: prisons, surplus, crisis, and opposition in globalization California*. Los Angeles, CA: University of California Press.

Cases

Strader v. Graham, 51 U.S. 82; 13 L. Ed. 337 (1850)

Post-Reading Questions

1   In your estimate, which factors (both former and current) give rise to the prison industrial complex?

2   What factors account for the recent increase in incarceration among women of color?

3   From a historical perspective, what factors gave rise to the convict-lease system?

4   What—if any—are some similarities between the former convict-lease system and the current prison industrial complex? In what ways are they noticeably different?

5   Various scholars (including Angela Davis) have argued that the 13th Amendment has essentially allowed for the criminalization and re-enslavement of African Americans. In what ways do you agree or disagree? Be sure to qualify your position.

Five Theses on Mass Incarceration

Alessandro De Giorgi

According to the latest data published by the Bureau of Justice Statistics (BJS), in 2014 the prison population of the United States stood at 1,561,500 (BJS 2015a, 1). If prisoners held in local jails are added to the count, the population confined behind bars reaches 2,306,100 (for an incarceration rate of 725/100,000), to which one should add the more than 4,7 million individuals currently on parole or probation. In total, more than 7 million people are currently under some form of penal control—almost 3% of the US population, the equivalent of what would be the second-largest city in the United States after New York (BJS 2014a, 2015a, 2015b).

However, the sheer extension of the correctional population in the United States does not convey the race and class dimensions of the US penal state—the result of a four-decade-long carceral experiment devised from the outset as a political strategy to restructure racial and class domination in the aftermath of the radical social movements of the 1960s (cf. Alexander 2010; Tonry 2011; Wacquant 2009). As of 2014, 59% of the male prison population was either African American (37%) or Latino (22%). The largest overrepresentation of black prisoners is among males aged 18 to 19: With an incarceration rate of 1,072/100,000, young black men are 10 times more likely to be in a state or federal prison than whites (102/100,000). In 2014, 6% of black men aged 30 to 39 were in prison, compared to 2% of Latinos and 1% of whites of the same age (BJS 2015, 1). According to recent estimates, African American children born in 1990 of a high-school dropout black father had a 50.5% chance of having their male parent in prison by age 14, whereas for those born of a non-college-educated black father the probability was 30% (Wildeman 2009, 273). Black male high-school dropouts born between

1975 and 1979 had a 70% chance of spending some time in prison before reaching age 35 (Western and Wildeman 2009, 231).

In 2014, resuming a recent downward trend that had been momentarily reversed in 2013, the nation's prison population registered a modest 1% decline—15,400 fewer prisoners since the previous year. Approximately one third of this decline was due to a decrease in the federal prison population; once that number is subtracted from the count, the decline at the state level (where the vast majority of prisoners are held) goes down to a meager average of 200 fewer inmates for each US state in the period 2013–2014 (BJS 2015a, 2). Despite the ongoing national debate on the prison crisis and the recent wave of bipartisan initiatives to tackle the burgeoning costs of mass incarceration, in 2014 prison admissions actually rose in 18 states. Over the same period, California—whose 2011 Public Safety Realignment plan has been hailed by some as a blueprint for nationwide decarceration efforts—has witnessed a slight *increase* in the state prison population (+0.1%), largely due to the ongoing rise in the number of women behind bars (+1.3% in 2013–2014; ibid., 3). Indeed, since 2010 women have been the fastest-growing fraction of the US prison population, rising by an average of 3.4% annually, even as the number of incarcerated men was undergoing a modest decline (BJS 2014b, 6). These tendencies become even more evident if one observes the fluctuating population of local jails, which are increasingly transformed into modern-day poorhouses in charge of the low-cost warehousing of petty offenders now deemed unworthy of expensive stays in state prisons: In 2014 the total US jail population rose by 1.8% since the previous year, with the female jail population increasing by a notable 18% between 2000 and 2014 (BJS 2015b, 3).

Do these contradictory signals emerging from the penal field herald a turning point in the history of the American carceral state? Is it plausible, as Jonathan Simon (2014, 1) argues in his recent book, that "like a biblical flood, the age of mass incarceration is finally ebbing"? Can we expect that the same power elites who erected the penal state will also be willing (and able) to dismantle it? Should scholars, activists, and citizens opposed to the penal experiment of the last forty years support the current bipartisan initiatives to curb the prison population, or should the technocratic, "evidence-based" reform policies currently proposed be denounced as attempts to tinker at the margins of the carceral state, while leaving untouched the very foundations of this hypertrophic machinery of racial and social control (see Alexander 2014)?

Although providing any definitive answer to these questions may well be impossible—and is definitely beyond the scope of this [reading]—a reflection on their significance and implications in the present conjuncture seems as necessary as ever. In this direction the aim of this [reading], organized in the form of fire short theses on mass incarceration, is to assemble a critical map of some "discursive formations" (Foucault 1968/1991) that have emerged over the past few years around the US prison crisis, and to offer some alternative ideas for a "radical-reformist" agenda against mass incarceration.

Thesis 1
Against Technocratic Solutions: Re-Politicize Mass Incarceration

> Let me define the liberal wing of the Democratic Party. The liberal wing of the democratic party is now for 60 new death penalties ... The liberal wing of the Democratic Party has 70 enhanced penalties. The liberal wing of the Democratic Party is for 100,000 cops. The liberal wing of the Democratic Party is for 125,000 new state prison cells.
>
> —Joe Biden in 1994, as quoted in Coates (2015)

A cursory glance at the mainstream literature that has flourished around recent political initiatives to tackle the American correctional crisis reveals a common tendency to depoliticize and de-historicize the current penal crisis (see for example ALEC 2013, 2015; Chettiar and Wadlman 2015; The Hamilton Project 2014). In most public debates, particularly those wrapped in the now ubiquitous rhetoric of bipartisan collaboration, mass incarceration tends to be portrayed as a technical problem, a temporary aberration in an otherwise rational criminal justice system, the unintended consequence of past wars on crime and drugs whose legitimacy is left largely unquestioned, an accidental stumbling block in a long history of penal progress. For example, in his foreword to a recent publication boldly titled *Solutions: American Leaders Speak Out on Criminal Justice,* former president Bill Clinton—whose administration has been the single largest contributor to mass incarceration in the United States—writes:

> It has been two decades since there was sustained national attention to criminal justice. By 1994, violént crime had tripled in 30 years. Our communities were under assault. We acted to address a genuine national crisis. But much has changed since then. It's time to take a clear-eyed look at what worked, what didn't, and what produced unintended, long-lasting consequences. So many of these laws worked well, especially those that put more police on the streets. (Clinton 2015, v)

The carceral explosion prompted by US power elites during the past 40 years tends to be portrayed as a momentary deviation from the progressive achievements of the civil rights movement of the 1960s rather than as a planned backlash against them. Largely triggered by budgetary concerns over the rising costs of the carceral state, current reform initiatives aim to devise "smart on crime," "cost-effective," and of course "evidence-based" solutions to the mass incarceration crisis.

This framing of the crisis harbors several dangers. A first implication of these depoliticized and managerial approaches is the idea that the current penal crisis is not the outcome of a deliberate, decades-long project carried out by powerful politico-economic actors, but rather the consequence of a lack of data about the functioning of prisons and the largely predictable effects of penal policies. Once the crisis is framed in these falsely neutral terms, solutions to it can also be formulated in the reassuring language of technocratic efficiency and cost-benefits analysis, as exemplified, for instance, by the current emphasis on narrow reforms targeting recidivism, reentry, and justice reinvestment (the so called three-R approach). As Marie Gottschalk warns in her latest book:

> Encased in a shell of evidence-based research, the three-R approach is broadly seen as a way to wring politics out of penal reform. The aim is to devise penal reforms that attract overwhelming bipartisan consensus. But this goal comes at a high cost. It leaves largely unchallenged and unquestioned the political calculations and interests that built the carceral state in the first place. The narrow emphasis on evidence-based research related to recidivism fosters the impression that the birth of the carceral state was the result of bad or nonexistent research rather than bad politics or bad policy. (Gottschalk 2015, 17)

The result is that the moderate reform proposals forged within such elitist circles as the Right on Crime Coalition, ALEC, or the Coalition for Public Safety, while doomed to have a very limited impact on the number of incarcerated people in the United States (and virtually no effect on the living conditions they endure), "might actually entrench the carceral state even further over the long run" (ibid., 17) by restricting the spectrum of conceivable political responses to mass incarceration. Once again, the collective illusion fostered by a rhetoric centered on "common-sense reforms" or on generic calls to "re-stitch the fabric of our neighborhoods and communities" (Rodham Clinton 2015) is that the prison system can be fixed, social justice restored, economic inequalities reduced, and racial discrimination eliminated—all without challenging the legitimacy of the carceral state in the first place.

How should scholars and activists envision the project of re-politicizing the public discourse on mass incarceration? A crucial fact to keep in mind is that movements of resistance against mass incarceration (as against previous systems of racial and class domination) have historically developed outside—and to a great extent against—official reform circles. Such grassroots mobilizations have grown out of the lived experiences of individuals and communities entangled in the net of the carceral state. These movements don't speak the managerial language of fiscal austerity, cost containment, and evidence-based policies, but rather the social justice vocabulary of human dignity, justice, and equality for all (see for example Critical Resistance 2000; Gilmore 2007, 181–248; Richie 2012, 125–56). Of course, in most cases these radical movements are not perceived and treated as legitimate interlocutors in current public debates on the prison crisis—especially as the stage is increasingly monopolized by bizarre presidential campaigns and unholy alliances between right-wing lobbies and liberal think tanks (Democracy Now 2015).

In his recent *Mass Incarceration on Trial*, Jonathan Simon (2014) suggests that a necessary step to begin to address the structural roots of mass incarceration, as well as its devastating consequences for the human dignity of the populations most affected by it, would be an acknowledgment of fault by those powerful officials who have contributed the most to building the carceral state. In this vein, Simon proposes a model similar to the truth and reconciliation commissions instituted as part of transitional justice efforts in post-civil war or post-apartheid scenarios. According to this model, "those officials who led us into mass incarceration, those who planned and operated prisons they knew would deny prisoners basic human rights such as health care, should be asked to testify why they felt justified in doing so" (ibid., 169). I am inclined to see this proposal as a symbolically important, preliminary moment in a much broader process of public acknowledgment of the social injustice, institutional abuse, and state-sanctioned violence perpetrated by the penal system against poor and racialized populations in the United States. Such public conversations should lead to a full disclosure of the subterranean dealings between powerful interest groups—from gun lobbies to private prison profiteers, from corporate media to law enforcement unions—and the political elites that have built the machinery of mass incarceration. Crucially, the symbolic element of "truth and reconciliation" should be complemented by a concrete and sustained effort at redressing the social harms produced by the carceral state. This could happen through a federally subsidized program of *reparations:* not necessarily in the form of individual payments, but perhaps more realistically in the shape of massive public investments and social programs—along the lines of what Robert Sampson has recently called "affirmative actions for neighborhoods (Sampson 2015, 23–27)—to be instituted and run under the direct control of the communities most affected by the carceral state in all of its manifestations.

Thesis 2
The Struggle against Mass Incarceration Is a Struggle against Social Inequality

> Black men born in the US and fortunate enough to live past the age of eighteen are conditioned to accept the inevitability of prison.
> —George Jackson, *Soledad Brother* (1970, p. 9)

The mainstream penal reform discourse sketched above is fundamentally incompatible with any acknowledgment of the structural ties between the rise of the penal state and the dramatic increase in social inequalities in the United States over the past 40 years (see Piketty 2014,

150–56, 291–303, 347–50); such an acknowledgment would amount to a call for massive public spending in public services and social programs—the only way to begin to address the social harms produced by the carceral state across the most disadvantaged regions of the American social space. Instead, those arguments are fully compatible with—and indeed are often complemented by—policy reform initiatives that emphasize personal responsibility and the provision of "second chances" for deserving individuals, post-release programs aimed at shoring up labor market competition, and rehabilitation models purporting to address endemic social problems by making some individuals more employable. Perhaps the area in which this individualistic framing of exit strategies from the prison crisis emerges most clearly is the field of prisoner reentry, a banner increasingly waved in official reform discourses as the perfect metaphor of a successful path out of the carceral universe—a symbolically effective way to stage individual redemption as a remedy to structural problems (Gottschalk 2015).

Yet the evidence of a structural nexus between punishment and social inequality in capitalist societies has been there for quite some time. At least since the publication of Rusche and Kirchheimer's seminal *Punishment and Social Structure* (1939/1968), a large body of criminological literature has described the role played by penal and carceral control both in the governing of social marginality and in the reproduction of existing structures of inequality (see Beckett and Western 2001; Soss, Fording and Schram 2011; Wacquant 2009). Whereas earlier works in this materialist criminological tradition focused almost exclusively on the ancillary role played by the prison in the reproduction of class inequalities functional to the capitalist system, a more recent stream of critical literature has intersected this perspective with a critique of racial inequalities and other forms of social oppression (see Alexander 2010; Davis 2003; Gilmore 2007; Richie 2012). As it pertains to mass incarceration in the United States, this literature has emphasized in particular two complementary dynamics fostered by the growth of the penal state, both of which reveal the serious deficits of the current national conversation about the prison crisis.

A first line of analysis has focused on the power of the carceral state to artificially distort the official image (and public perception) of racial and class inequalities in the United States by rendering invisible a large fraction of the racialized poor. Like that of any other Western society, the US prison population is disproportionately selected among the unemployed/underemployed, modestly educated, and largely disenfranchised poor populations of color. The mass warehousing of these populations in penal institutions effectively disappears them from the public sphere as well as from official statistics on a variety of social issues, thus generating severe distortions in official indicators of social inequality. As Becky Pettit (2012, vi) writes in her book on the subject, "inmates and former inmates are categorically and systematically excluded from the data collection efforts that frame American social policy and social science research. Their exclusion clouds our understanding of the American economic, political, and social condition." The consequence of this state-sanctioned invisibility, which Pettit (ibid., 20–28) rightfully situates along a historical continuum of institutional neglect dating back to slavery and the "three-fifths" rule in the US constitution, is to artificially inflate official indicators of racial progress and equality in such disparate fields as educational attainments, employment levels, wage differentials, and even voter participation. In all these areas, the myth of black progress reveals, itself for what it is—a myth—whereas the broad invisibility of racialized poverty, in conjunction with the high visibility of some celebrated cases of individual success (e.g., Obama's presidency) allows for dominant narratives of racial progress to flourish (see Haney-López 2010).

At the same time as it obscures indicators of structural inequality in the United States, mass incarceration also actively contributes to it. It would be hard to overestimate the catastrophic social consequences produced by the rise of the penal state, particularly among African Americans and Latinos residing in disadvantaged urban areas.[1] In his work, Bruce Western has effectively illustrated how the mass incarceration of less-educated black and Latino men has not only "concealed declining employment and produced phantom reductions in wage inequality" (Western 2006, 108), but has also contributed to magnify and perpetuate the economic disadvantage of those caught in the net of the penal system, as well as of their families and communities. The ubiquitous presence of the prison in the lives of underprivileged young males of color inevitably casts the net of the penal state onto their families—destroying marriages, incapacitating fathers, traumatizing children, and impoverishing relatives who must cope with the high costs of having someone behind bars (ibid., 131–67; see also Comfort 2008). Furthermore, mass incarceration, particularly in conjunction with the the massive influx of the returning prisoners who are ejected on a daily basis by the American penal machine, also projects the crippling shadow of the penal state onto the larger inner-city neighborhoods from which most of the prison population is taken. High-incarceration communities suffer from exceptionally high levels of family instability, economic insecurity, civic disengagement, political disenfranchisement, segregated poverty, educational failure, and interpersonal violence—all social ills dramatically compounded, if not directly caused, by concentrated imprisonment (see Clear 2007).

The obstacles facing formerly incarcerated poor men and women of color as they struggle to reenter (or, more likely, enter for the first time) the labor force after prison have been broadly documented by the recent literature on the relationship between incarceration and labor markets (see for example Pager 2003; Raphael 2014; Thompson 2008, 108–21). Permanently marked by the stigma of a criminal record, disqualified from most middle-class jobs by their lack of marketable skills and formal education, and constantly targeted by pervasive forms of racial stigmatization, hyper-criminalized residents of the inner city find themselves confined into the most precarious sectors of the secondary labor market (Western 2006, 108–30). Most of them scramble to fill the growing ranks of the working poor, pushed by the parole system's injunction to "find a job, any job" into the arms of low-wage employers eager to hire the most vulnerable workers. The few who eventually do manage to find employment experience the untamed violence of "degraded work" (Doussard 2013) under neoliberal capitalism—one paycheck away from homelessness, abject poverty, and starvation.

It would be a mistake to consider these as unintended consequences of the American punitive turn, as social problems that could be addressed without dismantling the whole edifice of the penal state. The reproduction of a large army of disenfranchised poor people, rendered powerless to resist their exploitation in the labor market, and desperate enough that they will accept any condition of work as the only alternative to starvation or further incarceration, is not a collateral effect of the prison, but rather one of its main constitutive elements and historical *raisons d'être* (Melossi and Pavarini 1981; Rusche and Kirchheimer 1939/1968). This is why—absent a radical overhaul of the US welfare system with the goal of recognizing the human right to health, education, housing, and adequate living standards for all[2]—any plan to reduce the prison population, particularly through back-door solutions like letting some "nonviolent offenders" out, amounts to little more than replenishing the ranks of the (post)-industrial reserve army of labor (Marx 1867/1976, 781–802). If it is true that mass incarceration has reversed in part the victories of the civil rights revolution of the 1960s, perhaps the time has come for a new "social rights movement" to take up the unfinished struggle against social inequality and the carceral state that thrives on it.

Thesis 3
The Struggle against the Penal State Is a Struggle Against Privatization

> We are pursuing a number of initiatives intended to increase our occupancy and revenue … . The unique budgetary challenges governments are facing may cause them to further rely on us to help reduce their costs, and also cause those states that have not previously utilized the private sector to turn to the private sector to help reduce their overall costs of incarceration. We are actively pursuing these opportunities … . Increases in occupancy could result in lower operating costs per inmate, resulting in higher operating margins, cash flow, and net income.
> —Corrections Corporation of America, *2015 Annual Report*

The most frequent argument for penal reform circulating inside mainstream reformist circles—and definitely the one that has been able to attract most bipartisan consensus—is the unsustainable cost of the US carceral machine. Indeed, the increase in public spending on criminal justice over the past few decades has been astonishing. According to a 2014 policy memo published by the Hamilton Project (2014, 13), between 1980 and 2010 total correctional expenditures have more than quadrupled, jumping from $17 billion to $80 billion; at the same time per capita expenditures increased by 250%, going from an average of $77 per US resident in 1980 to $260 in 2010. A report published in 2012 by the Vera Institute of Justice (Henrichson and Delaney 2012, 9) reveals that the average per-inmate yearly cost of incarceration hovers around $31,200—more than three times the average annual tuition at a four-year public university. Not surprisingly, a significant factor in this dramatic increase is represented by the growing costs associated with the incarceration of elderly persons—a fast-growing fraction of the US prison population, due to the draconian lengthening of prison sentences since the early 1980s. For example, in a 2012 report the ACLU estimates that the number of state and federal prisoners age 55 and older grew from 8,853 in 1981 to 124,900 in 2012, with experts predicting that the number will reach 400,000 in 2030—an increase by 4,400% over a 50-year period (ACLU 2012, i). The same report estimates that the average yearly cost of detaining a person above the age of 50 is $68,270—more than twice the cost of incarcerating a younger person (ibid., vii).

Since at least the 1980s, the skyrocketing costs of the US prison system have worked as a magnet for private actors involved in the business of private detention and related "prison services," such as prisoner health care, phone services, transportation, food catering, and so on. Multinational corporations like Corrections Corporations of America (CCA, founded in 1983) and GEO Group (founded in 1984) have consistently lobbied federal and state legislators to gain access to the alluring business of incarceration-for-profit. Although not always successful in their efforts, these and other companies have managed to establish and control a profitable market in correctional services, particularly at the federal level and in states like Florida, Texas, New Mexico, Georgia, and California (Galik and Gilroy 2015, 4). As the cost of mass incarceration began to be felt by taxpayers in the form of massive reallocations of funds from welfare, health care, education, and other public services (see Beckett and Western 2001), the private prison business gained increasing traction with the promise of reducing costs while improving efficiency. Thus, between 2000 and 2013 the number of federal prisoners incarcerated in private facilities grew by 165%, with the share of federal prisoners privately detained rising from 10% to 19%; over the same time span, the number of state prisoners held in private prisons grew by 33.8% (Galik and Gilroy 2015, 1). In 2012, after several years of continuous expansion, CCA could count on 91,000 beds across 20 states and the District of Columbia, whereas GEO Group had 65,700 beds available in domestic correctional facilities. In total, the number of private prison beds in the United States is higher than the prison populations of Germany and France combined (Lee 2012).

It is worth keeping in mind, however, that despite this momentous growth, the overall fraction of US prisoners held in private facilities is still quite limited: As of 2013, more than 90% of the country's prison population (state and federal) was held in government-run facilities, and although an increasing share of prisoners do time in for-profit prisons, it is true, as Loïc Wacquant (2008, 31) suggests, that even "if commercial operators were made to vanish overnight ... the overall prevalence and social physiognomy of incarceration would remain untouched." In other words, the profit motive—and prison privatization more generally—cannot be considered as the main cause or even as a leading force behind the advent of mass incarceration in the United States; rather, as Marie Gottschalk argues, "mass incarceration helped transform the private prison

sector into a powerful and nimble political player that today poses a major obstacle to dismantling the carceral state" (Gottschalk 2015, 65). I would add that rather than representing purely
an obstacle to decarceration, prison corporations pose a subtler threat: In a political climate
dominated by concerns for cost containment and fiscal responsibility, they are able to devise
market-friendly strategies that could facilitate limited reductions in the prison population—such
as privately run probation services, halfway houses, electronic monitoring, post-release centers,
drug rehabilitation programs, and the like—while further widening the net and entrenching the
hold of the carceral state. If the push towards a more widespread privatization of prisons may
to some extent have been resisted—even by fiscally conservative politicians—on grounds of the
eminently public/sovereign nature of punishment in a modem nation-state, the opportunity to
devise market-friendly alternatives couched in the seemingly non-punitive language of prison
population reductions could definitely assist correctional corporations in overcoming such
resistance. In other words, the idea of privately delivered rehabilitation, treatment, and reentry
programs might be more easily welcomed as a viable alternative to the current prison crisis
precisely because those activities can be framed as "services" rather than as punishments.

The area of the US carceral state in which these dynamics have already emerged with particular virulence is the field of immigrant detention. Immigration control has long represented a
sort of laboratory in which, thanks to the less stringent constitutional safeguards limiting state
power as it applies to noncitizens, new strategies of penal control have been experimented on
illegalized "aliens," only to be later extended to criminalized citizens (cf. De Giorgi 2006, 111–38).
In 2013, close to 441,000 undocumented migrants had been detained by the US Immigration
and Custom Enforcement agency (Department of Homeland Security 2014, 1), and "nearly half
of immigrant detention beds were in private facilities, up from 10 percent a decade earlier"
(Gottschalk 2015, 68). The processing and detention of undocumented migrants currently rep-
resents one of the most promising areas of business expansion for private prison companies such
as CCA (ACLU 2014; Kirkham 2012). This development has been facilitated by the questionable
yet broadly accepted notion that immigration detention is not a punishment for a crime, but
simply a civil measure to ensure deportation; therefore, migrants warehoused in ICE-operated
(or privately subcontracted) detention facilities, or even in federal prisons or local jails while
awaiting deportation, are not considered prisoners, but "civil detainees" (García Hernandez 2014,
1348; Kanstroom 2000).[3] It is not difficult to glimpse some dangerous analogies between the
private subcontracting of the punitive (yet formally extra-penal) treatment of undocumented
migrants and the trend toward the privatization of supposedly non-punitive alternatives to
incarceration, such as probation, parole, drug treatment, reentry programs, and so on.[4]

A parallel development to prison privatization—and one likely to grow ever more significant,
if private corporations were to gain a more prominent role in the management of prisoners
and ex-prisoners—is the increasing tendency to shift part of the cost of detention unto the
prisoner him/herself, now construed as a "burden on the state's budget and a consumer of its
services" (Aviram 2015, 120). As public debates on mass incarceration are framed in terms of

cost containment and fiscal responsibility, US prisoners are expected to shoulder an increasing share of the cost of their own incarceration—from room and board to medical expenses—with the wholly predictable consequence that most of them will leave prison poorer than they were at the time of their arrest, and now further overwhelmed by debt (see Evans 2014). According to a year-long investigation conducted by NPR across the United States in 2013, in 43 states defendants can be billed for a public defender, in 41 states they can be charged for room and board; in 44 they can be charged for parole or probation costs; and in all states but two they can be charged a fee for wearing electronic monitoring devices—on top of legally imposed restitutions, child support payments, fines, and court fees (Shapiro 2014). If one considers that the prison population is disproportionately drawn from the poorest fractions of the US population, and that the small percentage of prisoners who are allowed to work in prison are paid symbolic wages such as $1 per day of work in Massachusetts, or $0.50 per hour in California (Evans 2014, 2), it is not difficult to see how the total debt owed by prisoners to the system has reached the astounding amount of $50 billion—equal to 62.5 percent of the total yearly correctional expenses of the United States (ibid., 4). Nor should it come as a surprise that, while criminal justice debt has become "a major revenue generator for states as well as for private debt collection agencies" (Ella Baker Center for Human Rights 2015, 15), criminalized people's inability to repay such debt has become a significant driver of imprisonment, particularly in local jails functioning as modern-day "debtor prisons" (Bannon, Nagrecha, and Diller 2010, 19–24). This is why the struggle against the penal state must be a struggle against the corporatization of state violence and the neoliberal ideology that sustains it.

Thesis 4
No End to the Penal State without a Radical Reform of Policing

> We want an immediate end to police brutality and murder of black people, other people of color, all oppressed people inside the United States.
> —Black Panther Party, Ten Point Program (1966)

In 1966, the year in which Huey P. Newton and Bobby Seale drafted the Ten Point Program from which the epigraph to this section is taken, police officers throughout the United States had killed a total of 298 people—193 of whom were recorded as "negro" in the statistics of the time (US Department of Health, Education, and Welfare 1968, 160). Fifty years later, the demands put forward in what would become the first political manifesto of the Black Panther Party still sound very actual, given the extraordinary levels of lethal violence characterizing the policing of "all oppressed people inside the United States" today. According to the statistics published annually by the FBI as part of the Uniform Crime Reporting Program (UCR), in 2014 the official number of "justifiable homicides"—the bureaucratic euphemism used to describe the killings of civilians by law enforcement—had reached 444 (FBI 2015). However, these numbers most likely underestimate the real extent of the phenomenon, given that law enforcement agencies around the country are not required to submit data on "justifiable homicides" as part of their participation to the UCR program—indeed, according to recent estimates, fewer than half of the 18,000 participating agencies actually contribute such information to the FBI (Molla 2014). In any case, today as in 1966, young African American males are dramatically overrepresented in these grim statistics. Based on data collected by the independent research group Mapping Police Violence, the actual number of homicides of civilians by police officers in 2014 was close to 1,100, and just during the first nine months of 2015 at least 240 black men and women had been killed by the police (Mapping Police Violence 2015).

Although the ordinary doses of state violence administered by the police to the most marginal fractions of the population go usually unnoticed, at times such instances of targeted violence are suddenly projected onto the public sphere and come to be perceived as extraordinary and intolerable by public opinion. This is what has happened in the United States in the wake of a streak of highly mass-mediated murders of unarmed young black men by police officers—from the execution of Oscar Grant at a BART station in Oakland on December 31, 2009 to the deadly chokehold against Eric Gamer in New York on July 17, 2014; from the shooting of 18-year-old Michael Brown in Ferguson on August 9, 2014 to the killing of 12-year old Tamir Rice in Cleveland on November 22, 2014; from the murder of Walter Scott in North Charleston on April 4, 2015 to the death of Freddy Gray while in police custody in Baltimore on April 19, 2015. Captured on videos that quickly circulated through social media and other news outlets, these and many other similar cases of police violence sparked protests across the United States, prompting the emergence of a broad mobilization against police brutality.[5] The demands formulated by the organizations active in the movement are very articulated, and an accurate cartography of such political platforms is beyond the scope of this [reading]. There are, however, some common threads uniting these grassroots efforts to stop police abuse, which include the demilitarization of the police; the end of racial profiling and "stop-and-frisk" practices; the introduction of restorative justice models; the development of best practices to curb the use of force; the creation of community alternatives to arrest and imprisonment; the decriminalization of "quality of life" offenses such as loitering, trespassing, public drunkenness, graffiti, and prostitution; and the requirement that all police officers wear body-mounted cameras capable of videotaping any encounter with civilians.[6] But what has been the institutional response to these mobilizations?

Although the regulation of police forces and of their activities takes place mainly at the state and local levels, the US federal government retains broad powers to initiate, promote, and shape police reforms that will unfold at other levels of government.[7] Indeed, in the aftermath of the militarized repression of demonstrations against police brutality in Oakland, Ferguson, and Baltimore, the Obama administration has undertaken a few—mostly symbolic—police reform initiatives, such as the investigation of some police departments by the Department of Justice's Civil Rights Division, and more recently the publication of Executive Order 13688, which limits the transfer of surplus military equipment from the Pentagon to domestic law enforcement and bans some military-style assault gear from local police departments (see Condon 2015; Law Enforcement Equipment Working Group 2015).

However, so far the most comprehensive institutional effort to assess current problems in policing and to envision possible solutions to the crisis has been the official report of the President's Task Force on 21st Century Policing, published in May 2015.[8] In order to better situate the Task Force's recommendations, it might be useful to return to one of the foundational texts on policing to have emerged from the radical criminological tradition in the United States—the classic *The Iron Fist and the Velvet Glove* (Center for Research on Criminal Justice 1975). In this publication, the authors distinguish between three main approaches to police reform as it relates specifically to the issue of police brutality. The first model is "corporate reform," which is inspired by the logic of "rationalization, professionalism, and managerial efficiency" (ibid., 186). Corporate police reformers emphasize the need to develop more sophisticated policing techniques, better technological equipment, special training programs, more effective crime prevention strategies, and so on. The second model is "liberal reform," the emphasis of which is more on "upholding democratic ideals of justice and equality than on the need for order and social control." In this vein, liberal reformers will propose such measures as "civilian review boards, improving the caliber of police administrators, demilitarization of the police and decriminalization of certain offenses" (ibid., 186). Finally, unlike the first two models—which have historically been proposed by more or less enlightened power elites—the third model originates out of popular struggles aiming at establishing a "service-oriented police under local, democratic control" (ibid., 189).

When observed through the critical lens of *The Iron Fist and the Velvet Glove*, the recommendations offered by the President's Task Force fall squarely under the "corporate reform" model. The whole report is imbued with neo-managerial ideology, from its blind faith in procedural justice as a panacea against hostile public perceptions of the police to its dull insistence on technical improvements—such as better training, better data reporting, better review of use of force incidents, and better technology (from Facebook to body-worn cameras and Tasers). It comes as no surprise that the report doesn't even mention the troubled history of race relations in the United States as a factor in the current crisis, or that neither the word "abuse" nor "brutality" ever appear in the report.

Yet militarized policing constitutes only the first cog in a much broader penal machine that has colonized increasing portions of our public spaces—from high schools to university campuses, from urban centers to suburban communities, from shopping malls to public transportation systems. This is why the struggle against police violence has to be a struggle not only to decolonize our cities from militarized policing, high-tech surveillance, and the many other exclusionary practices of the penal state, but most importantly to regain community control over the police.[9] In a radically democratized public space liberated from the deadly tentacles of the penal state, the police will no longer act as the discriminatory enforcer of an oppressive social order against the most marginal fractions of the population. Ideally, in such scenario the police as we know it would actually cease to exist, replaced—as Black Panther Party leader Huey P. Newton advocated in the first issue of this journal back in 1974—by a "Citizens' Peace Force that would provide a human environment for community experiment, growth, identity and responsibility, and, finally, an awareness of what role each must play as the human rights revolution drives toward its climax" (Newton 1974, 39).

Thesis 5
The Struggle for Decarceration Is a Struggle against Transcarceration

> "Alternatives" become not alternatives at all but new programs which supplement the existing system or else expand it by attracting new populations. I will refer to these two overlapping possibilities as "thinning the mesh" and "widening the net" respectively.
>
> —Stanley Cohen, "The Punitive City" (1979, p. 347)

In the edited volume that first popularized the concept among punishment and society scholars (Lowman, Menzies and Palys 1987), the term "transcarceration" was introduced to describe the tendency of contemporary systems of social and penal control to blur the boundaries between different institutions in charge of confining, treating, punishing, and disciplining deviant populations—from schools to prisons, from mental hospitals to community corrections. The term, coined by the editors of that volume as a critical response to the mainstream rhetoric of "deinstitutionalization" and "decarceration"—particularly as it related to the closing down of state mental hospitals in the 1960s and 1970s—effectively captures the structural ambivalence of deinstitutionalization in the United States. In the words of the authors, the term suggests that "what has been described recently as 'decarceration' is but a moment of the oscillation between inclusive and exclusive modes of social control; a transcarceral model of control is powered by an alternating rather than a direct current" (ibid., 2). Indeed, when the pendulum of social control swings towards deinstitutionalization or decarceration, particularly if this happens out of fiscal constraints rather than out of public concerns for human rights and social justice, social groups deemed deviant, dangerous, or problematic, far from being exempted from institutional control and surveillance, tend to be cycled between different social control settings (see also Cohen 1985, 87–114).

Transcarceration can happen as a corollary of the net-widening dynamics described by Stan Cohen—for example, when new community programs (e.g., drug rehabilitation, counseling services, community corrections, electronic monitoring, etc.) that are developed as supposedly less punitive alternatives to incarceration end up targeting behaviors that would not have been criminalized in the first place. In the current penal reform rhetoric we can see this tendency in action whenever solutions such as drug courts, mental health courts, prostitution courts, homeless courts, truancy courts, tobacco courts, fathering courts, teen courts, and family courts—just to name a few—are offered as alternatives to imprisonment, typically for so called "non-non-non" (non-serious, non-violent, non-sexual) offenders charged with "quality of life" crimes (see Berman and Feinblatt 2001; Neyfakh 2014).This trend is particularly harmful to any serious effort at dismantling the carceral state, because it further entrenches the latter's operations at the same time as it offers to the public the reassuring illusion that social services are indeed available to people who *earn* them through their law-abiding behavior. But if decarceration is to be pursued seriously, such services should be available in the community to everyone who *needs* them—rather than being selectively administered to stigmatized social groups in the coercive and disciplinary setting of a courtroom, under condition of behavioral modifications, and backed by the constant threat of imprisonment for those unwilling or unable to conform.

Transcarceration can also take place as the deliberate outcome of legislative measures that aim to shuffle certain segments of the confined populations from one institutional setting to another—usually out of fiscal concerns or court-mandated reforms. This is clearly the case of California, which since 2011 has embarked in an ambitious process of realignment of its correctional system in order to reduce chronic overcrowding in state prisons. California's legislature approved the Public Safety Realignment Act (AB 109 and AB 117) in the wake of the 2011 *Brown v. Plata* decision—in which the US Supreme Court ruled that prison conditions in the state's overcrowded penal institutions amounted to cruel and unusual punishment, and mandated that the state's prison population be reduced to 137.5 percent of stated capacity. This legislation redefines the division of labor between the state and local counties as it pertains to the penal management of criminalized populations, by diverting a large population of "non-non-non" offenders from state prisons to local jails and county-level "community corrections," such as probation and home detention (Lofstrom and Raphael 2013; Lofstrom, Raphael, and Grattet 2014; Martin and Grattet 2015). Since its inception, the realignment plan has resulted in a significant reduction in California's state prison population—from 160,700 in 2011 to approximately 131,000 in 2014—bringing the state into compliance with the court-mandated cap (Lofstrom and Raphael 2015, 2). Predictably, however, at the same time as the state prison population was declining, county jails witnessed a steady increase in their confined populations. According to recent estimates, over one-third of the overall reduction in the state's correctional population has been offset by the parallel increase in jail populations (ibid., 1)—a textbook example of transcarceration. Furthermore, the issue is not merely a numerical one. The increased resort to county jails to house people convicted to longer prison sentences raises important questions about the notoriously abysmal conditions of detention inside these facilities, which were not built for this purpose. As Gottschalk (2015, 270) argues, "designed and intended to house short-term, transient populations, jails do not have the medical facilities, programs, and security resources to meet the needs of inmates serving sentences counted in years, not months or weeks." A rather paradoxical outcome, for a plan that was originally devised to address the lack of medical care in state prisons.

Finally, transcarceration can take place as a side effect of deinstitutionalization plans that result in the state's neglect of vulnerable populations—for example, when large numbers of people are suddenly discarded from total institutions, without being provided the services and supports they need to conduct independent lives in the "free world." In this case, the unmet needs of these populations can trigger survival strategies that in turn result in further processes of criminalization and institutionalization. The closing down of mental hospitals in the 1960s-1970s—perhaps the most significant historical precedent of a planned effort to deinstitutionalize a large population of captive human beings—offers a clear case in point (see Harcourt 2011). As Stephen M. Rose (1979, 440) wrote many years ago:

> The rhetoric of deinstitutionalization seems to mask a brutal political and economic reality—the general abandonment of mentally disabled people who have been further debilitated, mentally and physically, by institutionalization. Evidence indicates that the new policy has brought with it a new set of mental health problems, including massive numbers of people needing rehospitalization; gross inadequacies in community resources for aftercare and rehabilitation; large-scale scandal, exploitation, and abuse in the new industry of operating community facilities; increased drug and alcohol dependency among released patients; and an apparent social and psychological decay among patients released into nursing homes, adult homes, or "welfare hotels."

The collateral effects of a deinstitutionalization process driven mostly by fiscal considerations—so much so that one of its most radical critics has characterized it as little more than "ideological camouflage, allowing economy to masquerade as benevolence and neglect as tolerance" (Scull 1977, 152; see also Warren 1981; Wolpert and Wolpert 1976)—are under everyone's eyes. Today hundreds of thousands of mentally ill persons, some of them formerly institutionalized, can be found barely surviving in homeless encampments, waiting in line at chronically overcrowded homeless shelters, pushing carts around dilapidated inner cities, or cycling in and out of jails and prisons, which have become the chief providers of mental health services in the United States today (see Dear and Wolch 1987; Lamb and Weinberger 2001; Raphael 2000).

It would be difficult not to see the similarities between the scenario just described and the situation currently faced by the thousands of former prisoners released every day from penal institutions across the United States only to return to the impoverished neighborhoods where they resided at the time of their arrest. In 2012 alone, 637,400 prisoners were discharged from

US prisons—an average of 1,714 per day (BJS 2013). Not unlike the patients discarded from state hospitals in the 1970s, former prisoners face disproportionately high rates of mental and physical illness, substance addiction, lack of social services, chronic poverty, and exploitative housing and employment conditions. Their chances of getting rearrested within few years from their release from prison are close to 70%, their risk of becoming homeless is disproportionately high, and their living conditions are often akin to bare survival. In the end, Andrew Scull's words once again effectively describe the condition characterizing the targets of transcarceration, whether through net-widening, institutional design, or state neglect; "What has changed is the packaging rather than the reality of their misery" (Scull 1987, 329).

Conclusion

The five theses presented in this [reading] are an attempt to illustrate the structural ambivalence of the mainstream penal reform discourse that has unfolded over the past few years in the wake of the US prison crisis. The main danger posed by the recent wave of technocratic reform proposals is that they will become the building blocks of a refurbished carceral state—one reformed enough to be more compatible with dominant fiscal and politico-economic imperatives, yet fundamentally unchallenged in its historical role as (re)producer of racial and class inequalities. However, not all penal reforms are the same, and although some reforms should be denounced from the outset as strategies to fine-tune the carceral machinery of social death, others might at least contribute to open some cracks in the edifice of mass incarceration.

This is not the venue to articulate what a radical penal reform agenda might look like—not least because developing such a platform can only be the task of a broad social movement against the penal state. However, even a cursory glance at the critical literature and activist mobilizations around mass incarceration could inspire a path toward some radical reforms—that is, reforms that promote decarceration rather than transcarceration, net widening, privatization, and the other dangers illustrated in this [reading]. Some of these reforms could take the shape of:

- a drastic reduction of the prison population, for example through the abolition of all mandatory minimums, truth in sentencing, and three strikes laws (see The Pew Center on the States 2012);
- the introduction of automatic geriatric releases for prisoners above the age of 65 (see Chiu 2010);
- the abolition of monetary bail (see Human Rights Watch 2010);
- the legalization and regulation of sex work (see Amnesty International 2015);
- the decriminalization of all drug use (see Greenwald 2009);
- the abolition of life-without-parole sentences (so-called death by incarceration) and their replacement with parole eligibility for lifers after 10 to 20 years (see Nellis and King 2009);

- the introduction of presumptive parole policies, whereby prisoners must be released at their first parole eligibility date unless serious disciplinary violations have occurred (see Drug Policy Alliance 2014);
- the abolition of court transfers from juvenile to adult courts (see Slobogin 2013).

Further reforms should target conditions of life for prisoners inside prisons and for ex prisoners upon release, to introduce those internationally accepted human rights standards that are foreign to the US carceral state. These reforms could start with:

- a repeal of the Prison Litigation Reform Act of 1996, specifically in its "exhaustion requirement," which prevents prisoners from challenging a condition of their confinement in federal court unless they have exhausted all administrative remedies available inside the correctional facility (see Human Rights Watch 2009);
- the complete abolition of solitary confinement (see Shames, Wilcox, and Subramanian 2015);
- the introduction of living wages for all prison labor and the recognition of the prisoners' right to form unions (see Kovensky 2014; Tibbs 2011);
- the reintroduction of conjugal visits for all prisoners and the introduction of contact visits in all county jails;
- the provision of free telephone and Internet services to all prisoners (see United Nations 2011);
- the abolition of felon disenfranchisement and the repeal of all welfare bans for former prisoners (see NAACP 2012);
- the introduction of a "residency principle" for incarceration and the establishment of a maximum distance (e.g., 100 miles) between a prisoner's place of custody and his/her last place of residence.

Although the reforms briefly sketched here (in a list that by no means is meant to be exhaustive) would probably advance the cause of decarceration more substantially than most of the proposals currently discussed in mainstream penal reform circles, we should never forget that "prison 'reform' is virtually contemporary with the prison itself: it constitutes, as it were, its programme," as Michel Foucault (1977, 234) famously wrote in one of the most-quoted paragraphs of his *Discipline and Punish*. The prison may ultimately be an unreformable institution, because every attempt at reform ends up being subsumed under the carceral logic, thus contributing to make it more compatible with changing cultural sensibilities and politico-economic arrangements and further entrenching the hold of the carceral state onto the fabric of society. Yet, denouncing all penal reforms as nothing more than obstacles on the road to the ultimate goal of a prison-free society is a luxury we cannot afford today—not in light of the tremendous suffering mass incarceration exacts on the most vulnerable fractions of the US population.

Notes

1 In a recent article on the impact of mass incarceration on poverty rates in the United States between 1980 and 2004, Robert DeFina and Lance Hannon (2013, 581) argue that "had mass incarceration not occurred, poverty would have decreased by more than 20%, or about 2.8 percentage points. At the national scale, this translates into several million fewer people in poverty had mass incarceration not occurred."

2 As required, for example, by the 1976 International Covenant on Economic, Social and Cultural Rights, signed but never ratified by the United States.

3 A point of view repeatedly confirmed by courts across the United States, despite wide evidence that the treatment to which migrants are subjected in private detention facilities is in many cases worse than the already inhumane conditions endured by detainees in regular prisons, due to insufficient food, recurring staff abuse, chronic lack of medical care, and frequent resort to isolation (see ACLU 2014, 26–51).

4 For a journalistic account of the business opportunities that prison corporations expect will emerge in the wake of current penal reforms, see Segal (2015).

5 Among the vast archipelago of organizations active on these issues, the one that has gained most visibility is perhaps the #BlackLivesMatter movement *(http://www.blacklivesmatter.org)*, created in response to the murder of unarmed 17-year-old Trayvon Martin by neighborhood watch volunteer George Zimmerman in Sanford, Florida, on February 26, 2012.

6 See, for example, the guiding principles published on the #BlackLivesMatter website *(http://black-livesmalter.com/guiding-principles/)*, or the demands published on the website of Ferguson Action *(http://fergusonaction.com/demands/)*.

7 Past presidential administrations have resorted to such powers over the last decades, mostly favoring a "tough on crime" and militaristic stance that has contributed to the current legitimation crisis in policing. One of the most significant of such federal initiatives has been the infamous civil asset forfeiture program introduced by the US Congress in the early 1980s (and then expanded several times) as a tool in the so-called war on drugs, which allows budget-stricken police departments to keep up to 80% of the proceeds of seizures of any asset—monetary or otherwise—allegedly connected to criminal activities, particularly drug-related crimes. In January of 2015, US Attorney General Eric Holder has introduced a modest reform to the program, establishing new limits to the ability of the federal government to partake in seizures effected by state or local police departments (Office of the Attorney General 2015).

8 The 116-page-long report features several recommendations and "action items" articulated into five "pillars" of reform: (1) Building Trust & Legitimacy; (2) Policy & Oversight; (3) Technology & Social Media; (4) Community Policing & Crime Reduction; and (5) Officer Wellness & Safety. In this section I will not provide a detailed or comprehensive analysis of the document, but only a broad critique of its general approach to the issue of police violence and police reform.

9 One of the most politically advanced efforts to establish a model of community control of the police was developed in Berkeley in 1971, in the form of a grassroots initiative to introduce a Community

Control of the Police Amendment to the city's Charter. The amendment would have replaced the hierarchical, monocratic, and militaristic structure of the Berkeley Police Department with a system of democratically elected, all-civilian "police councils" with full powers to direct, prioritize, and control police activities in Berkeley (Red Family 1971). Supported by a large coalition of political groups and grassroots community organizations, the initiative gathered 15,000 signatures but was defeated at the polls in 1971.

References

ACLU

2012   *At America's Expense: The Mass Incarceration of the Elderly.* New York: American Civil Liberties Union. At *https://www.aclu.org/files/assets/elderlyprisonreport_20120613_1.pdf.*

2014   *Warehoused and Forgotten: Immigrants Trapped in Our Shadow Private Prison System.* New York: American Civil Liberties Union. At *https://www.aclu.org/warehoused-and-forgotten-immigrants-trapped-our-shadow-private-prison-system.*

ALEC

2013   *Criminalizing America: How Big Government Makes a Criminal of Every American.* Arlington, VA: American Legislative Exchange Council. At *http://www.alec.org/publications/criminalizing-america/.*

2015   *Recidivism Reduction: Community-Based Supervision Alternatives to Incarceration.* Arlington, VA: American Legislative Exchange Council. At *http://www.alec.org/publications/recidivism-reduction/.*

Alexander, Michelle

2010   *The New Jim Crow: Mass Incarceration in the Age of Colorblindness.* New York: The New Press.

2014   "A System of Racial and Social Control." *PBS Frontline,* April 29. At *http://www.pbs.org/wgbh/pages/frontline/criminal-justice/locked-up-in-america/michelle-alexander-a-system-of-racial-and-social-control/.*

Amnesty International

2015   "Global Movement Votes to Adopt Policy to Protect Human Rights of Sex Workers," August 11. At *https://www.amnesty.org/en/latest/news/2015/08/global-movement-votes-to-adopt-policy-to-protect-human-rights-of-sex-workers/.*

Bannon, Alicia, Mitali Nagrecha, and Rebekah Diller

2010   *Criminal Justice Debt: A Barrier to Reentry.* New York: Brennan Center for Justice. At https://www.brennancenter.org/publication/criminal-justice-debt-barrier-reentry.

Beckett, Katherine and Bruce Western

2001 "Governing Social Marginality: Welfare, Incarceration, and the Transformation of State Policy." *Punishment & Society* 3(1): 43–59.

Berman, Greg and John Feinblatt

2001 "Problem-Solving Courts: A Brief Primer." *Law & Policy* 23(2): 125–40.

Bureau of Justice Statistics

2013 *Prisoners in 2012: Trends in Admissions and Releases, 1991–2012.* Washington, DC: Department of Justice.

2014a *Probation and Parole in the United States, 2013.* Washington, DC: Department of Justice.

2014b *Correctional Populations in the United States, 2013.* Washington, DC: Department of Justice.

2015a *Prisoners in 2014.* Washington, DC: Department of Justice.

2015b *Jail Inmates at Midyear 2014.* Washington, DC: Department of Justice.

Center for Research on Criminal Justice

1975 *The Iron Fist and the Velvet Glove: An Analysis of the U.S. Police.* San Francisco, CA: Crime and Social Justice Associates.

Chettiar, Inimai and Michael Waldman (eds.)

2015 *Solutions: American Leaders Speak Out on Criminal Justice.* New York: Brennan Center for Justice. At *https://www.brennancenter.org/publication/solutionsamerican-leaders-speak-out-criminal-justice*.

Chiu, Tina

2010 *It's About Time: Aging Prisoners, Increasing Costs, and Geriatric Release.* New York: Vera Institute of Justice.

Clear, Todd

2007 *Imprisoning Communities: How Mass Incarceration Makes Disadvantaged Neighborhoods Worse.* Oxford, UK: Oxford University Press.

Clinton, William J.

2015 "Foreword." In *Solutions: American Leaders Speak Out on Criminal Justice,* edited by Inimai Chettiar and Michael Waldman, v–vi. New York: Brennan Center for Justice. At *https://www.brennancenter.org/publication/solutions-american-leaders-speak-out-criminal-justice*.

Coates, Ta-Nehisi

2015 "The Black Family in the Age of Mass Incarceration." *The Atlantic,* October. At *http://www.theatlantic.com/magazine/archive/2015/10/the-black-family-in-the-age-of-mass-incarceration/403246/.*

Cohen, Stanley

1979 "The Punitive City: Notes on the Dispersal of Social Control." *Contemporary Crises* 3: 339–63.

1985 *Visions of Social Control: Crime. Punishment and Classification.* Cambridge, UK: Polity Press.

Comfort, Megan

2008   *Doing Time Together: Love and Family in the Shadow of the Prison.* Chicago: The University of Chicago Press.

Condon, Stephanie

2015   "A Year after Ferguson, Washington Still Working on Police Reforms." *CBS News,* August 11.

Corrections Corporation of America

2015   *Annual Report.* At *http://www.sec.gov/Archives/edgar/data/1070985/000119312515061839/d853180d10k.htm.*

Critical Resistance

2000   *Critical Resistance to the Prison-Industrial Complex. Social Justice* 27(3), Special Issue.

Davis, Angela Y.

2003   *Are Prisons Obsolete?* New York: Seven Stories Press.

De Giorgi, Alessandro

2006   *Re-Thinking the Political Economy of Punishment: Perspectives on Post-Fordism and Penal Politics.* Aldershot, UK: Ashgate.

Dear, Michael J. and Jennifer R. Wolch

1987   *Landscapes of Despair: From Deinstitutionalization to Homelessness.* Princeton, NJ: Princeton University Press.

DeFina, Robert and Lance Hannon

2013   "The Impact of Mass Incarceration on Poverty." *Crime & Delinquency* 59(4): 562–86.

Democracy Now

2015   "Strange Bedfellows: Why Are the Koch Brothers & Van Jones Teaming Up to End Mass Incarceration?" July 15. At *http://www.democracynow.org/2015/7/15/strange_bedfeltows_why_are_the_koch.*

Department of Homeland Security

2014   *Immigration Enforcement Actions: 2013.* At *http://www.dhs.gov/sites/default/files/publications/ois_enforcement_ar_2013.pdf.*

Doussard, Marc

2013   *Degraded Work: The Struggle at the Bottom of the Labor Market.* Minneapolis: University of Minnesota Press.

Drug Policy Alliance

2014   *New Solutions Campaign: Presumptive Parole Act.* Trenton, NJ: Drug Policy Alliance. At *http://www.jdrugpolicy.org/sites/default/files/New_Solutions_Parole_Reform_Presumptive_Parole_Act.pdf.*

Ella Baker Center for Human Rights

2015   *Who Pays? The True Cost of Incarceration on Families*. Oakland, CA: Ella Baker Center for Human Rights. At *http://ellabakercenter.org/who-pays-the-true-cost-of-incarceralion-on-families*.

Evans, Douglas N.

2014   *The Debt Penalty: Exposing the Financial Barriers to Offender Reintegration*. New York: John Jay College of Criminal Justice. At *http://justicefellowship.org/sites/default/files/The%2014Debt%20Penalty_John%20Jay_August%202014.pdf*.

Federal Bureau of Investigation

2015   *Crime in the United States, 2014*. At *https://www.fbi.gov/about-us/cjis/ucr/crime-in-the-u.s./2014/crime-in-the-u.s.-2014/cius-home*.

Foucault, Michel

1968/1991   "Politics and the Study of Discourse." In *The Foucault Effect: Studies in Governmentality*, edited by Graham Burchell, Colin Gordon, and Peter Miller, 53–72. Chicago: The University of Chicago Press.

1977   *Discipline and Punish: The Birth of the Prison*. London: Penguin Books.

Galik, Lauren and Leonard Gilroy

2015   *Annual Privatization Report 2015: Criminal Justice and Corrections*. Los Angeles: The Reason Foundation. At *http://reason.org/news/show/apr-2015-criminal-justice*.

García Hernández, César Cuauhtémoc

2014   "Immigration Detention as Punishment." *UCLA Law Review* 61: 1346–414.

Gilmore, Ruth

2007   *Golden Gulag: Prisons, Surplus, Crisis, and Opposition in Globalizing California*. Berkeley: University of California Press.

Gottschalk, Marie

2015   *Caught: The Prison State and the Lockdown of American Politics*. Princeton, NJ: Princeton University Press.

Greenewald, Glenn

2009   *Drug Decriminalization in Portugal: Lessons for Creating Fair and Successful Drug Policies*. Washington, DC: Cato Institute.

Hamilton Project

2014   *Ten Economic Facts about Crime and Incarceration in the United States*. Washington, DC: The Brookings Institution. At *http://www.brookings.edu/research/reports/2014/05/10-crime-facts*.

Haney-López, Ian F.

2010   "Post-Racial Racism: Racial Stratification and Mass Incarceration in the Age of Obama." *California Law Review* 98(3): 1023–74.

Harcourt, Bernard E.

2011   "Reducing Mass Incarceration: Lessons from the Deinstitutionalization of Mental Hospitals in the 1960s." University of Chicago Public Law & Legal Theory Working Paper No. 335.

Henrichson, Christian and Ruth Delaney

2012   *The Price of Prisons: What Incarceration Costs Taxpayers.* New York: Vera Institute of Justice.

Human Rights Watch

2009   *No Equal Justice: The Prison Litigation Reform Act in the United States.* New York: Human Rights Watch.

2010   *The Price of Freedom: Bail and Pretrial Detention of Low Income Non-Felony Defendants in New York City.* New York: Human Rights Watch.

Jackson, George

1970   *Soledad Brother: The Prison Letters of George Jackson.* New York: Coward-McCann.

Kanstroom, Daniel

2000   "Deportation, Social Control, and Punishment: Some Thoughts about Why Hard Laws Make Bad Cases." *Harvard Law Review* 113(8): 1890–935.

Kirkham, Chris

2012   "Private Prisons Profit from Immigration Crackdown, Federal and Local Law Enforcement Partnerships." *Huffington Post,* June 7. At *http://www.huffingtonpost. com/2012/06/07/private-prisons-immigration-federal-law-enforcement_n_1569219 .html.*

Kovensky, Josh

2014   "It's Time to Pay Prisoners the Minimum Wage." *New Republic.* August 15. At *http://www .newrepublic.com/article/119083/prison-labor-equal-rights-wages-incarcerated- help-economy.*

Lamb, Richard H. and Linda E. Weinberger

2001   "Persons with Severe Mental Illness in Jails and Prisons: A Review." *New Directions for Mental Health Services* 90: 29–49.

Law Enforcement Equipment Working Group

2015   *Recommendations Pursuant to Executive Order 13688 Federal Support for Local Law Enforcement Equipment Acquisition.* Washington, DC: Bureau of Justice Assistance. At *https://www.bja.gov/publications/LEEWG_Report_Final.pdf.*

Lee, Suevon

2012   "By the Numbers: The U.S.'s Growing For-Profit Detention Industry." *ProPublica,* June 20. At *http://www.propublica.org/article/by-the-numbers-the-u.s.s-growing-for-profit- detention-industry.*

Lofstrom, Magnus and Steven Raphael

2013   *Public Safety Realignment and Crime Rates in California.* San Francisco: Public Policy Institute of California.

2015   *Realignment, Incarceration and Crime Trends in California.* San Francisco: Public Policy Institute of California.

Lofstrom, Magnus, Steven Raphael, and Ryken Grattet

2014   *Is Public Safety Realignment Reducing Recidivism in California?* San Francisco: Public Policy Institute of California.

Lowman, John, Robert J. Menzies, and T.S. Palys (eds.)

1987   *Transcarceration: Essays in the Sociology of Social Control.* Aldershot, UK: Gower.

Mapping Police Violence

2015   "National Trends." At *http://mappingpoliceviolence.org/nationaltrends/*.

Martin, Brandon and Ryken Grattet

2015   *Alternatives to Incarceration in California*. San Francisco: Public Policy Institute of California.

Marx, Karl

1867/1976   *Capital: Volume I*. London: Penguin Books.

Melossi, Dario and Massimo Pavarini

1981   *The Prison and the Factory: Origins of the Penitentiary System*. London: Macmillan Press.

Molla, Rani

2014   "Why the Data on Justifiable Homicide Just Won't Do." *The Wall Street Journal*, September 2. At *http://blogs.wsj.com/numbers/why-the-data-on-justifiable -homicide-just-wont-do-1725/*.

NAACP

2012   *Silenced: Citizens Without a Vote*. Baltimore, MD: National Association for the Advancement of Colored People.

Nellis, Ashley and Ryan S. King

2009   *No Exit: The Expanding Use of Life Sentences in America*. Washington, DC: The Sentencing Project.

Newton, Huey P.

1974   "A Citizens' Peace Force." *Crime & Social Justice: A Journal of Radical Criminology* 1 (Spring-Summer): 36–39.

Neyfakh, Leon

2014   "The Custom Justice of 'Problem-Solving Courts'." *Boston Globe*, March 23. *At https:// www.bostonglobe.com/ideas/2014/03/22/the-custom-justice-problem-solving-courts/ PQJLC758Sgw7qQhiefT6MM/story.html*.

Office of the Attorney General

2015   *Prohibition on Certain Federal Adoptions of Seizures by State and Local Law Enforcement Agencies*. Washington, DC: US Department of Justice. At *http://www.justice.gov/opa/ pr/attorney-general-prohibits-federal-agency-adoptions-assets-seized-state-and- local-law*.

Pager, Devah

2003   *Marked: Race, Crime, and Finding Work in an Era of Mass Incarceration*. Chicago: The University of Chicago Press.

Pettit, Becky

2012   *Invisible Men: Mass Incarceration and the Myth of Black Progress*. New York: Russell Sage Foundation.

The Pew Center on the States

2012   *Time Served: The High Cost, Low Return of Longer Prison Terms*. Washington, DC: The Pew Charitable Trusts.

Piketty, Thomas

2014   *Capital in the Twenty-First Century.* Cambridge, MA: Belknap Press.

President's Task Force on 21st Century Policing

2015   *Final Report of the President's Task Force on 21st Century Policing.* Washington, DC: Office of Community Oriented Policing Services. At *http://www.cops.usdoj.gov/pdf/ taskforce/taskforce_finalreport.pdf*

Raphael, Steven

2000   "The Deinstitutionalization of the Mentally Ill and the Growth in the U.S. Prison Populations: 1971 to 1996." Working Paper, University of California, Berkeley.

2014   *The New Scarlet Letter? Negotiating the U.S. Labor Market with a Criminal Record.* Kamazoo, MI: W.E. Upjohn Institute for Employment Research.

The Red Family

1971   *To Stop a Police State: The Case for Community Control of Policing.* Berkeley, CA.

Richie, Beth E.

2012   *Arrested Justice: Black Women, Violence, and America's Prison Nation.* New York: New York University Press.

Rodham Clinton, Hillary

2015   "Keynote Speech at the David N. Dinkins Leadership & Public Policy Forum," Columbia University, New York, April 29. At *https://www.hillaryclinton.com/feed/ its-time-end-era-mass-incarceration/*.

Rose, Stephen M.

1979   "Deciphering Deinstitutionalization: Complexities in Policy and Program Analysis." *The Milbank Memorial Fund Quarterly. Health and Society* 57(4): 429–60.

Rusche, Georg and Otto Kirchheimer

1939/1968   *Punishment and Social Structure.* New York: Columbia University Press.

Sampson, Robert

2015   "Individual and Community Economic Mobility in the Great Recession Era: The Spatial Foundations of Persistent Inequality." At *https://www.stlouisfed.org/~/media/ Files/PDFs/Community%Developinent/Econ%20Mobility/Sessions/SampsonPaper508. pdf.*

Scull Andrew T.

1977   *Decarceration. Community Treatment and the Deviant: A Radical View.* Englewood Cliffs, NJ: Prentice-Hall.

1987   "Decarceration Reconsidered." In *Transcarceration: Essays in the Sociology of Social Control,* edited by John Lowman, Robert J. Menzies, and T.S. Palys, 316–37. Cambridge, UK: Gower.

Segal, David

2015   "Prison Vendors See Continued Signs of a Captive Market." *The New York Times,* August 29.

Shames, Alison, Jessa Wilcox and Ram Subramanian

2015   *Solitary Confinement: Common Misconceptions and Emerging Safe Alternatives.* New York: Vera Institute of Justice.

Shapiro, Joseph

2014   "As Court Fees Rise, The Poor Are Paying the Price." *NPR News,* May 19. At *http:// www.npr.org/2014/05/19/312158516/increasing-court-fees-punish-the-poor.*

Simon, Jonathan

2014   *Mass Incarceration on Trial: A Remarkable Court Decision and the Future of Prisons in America.* New York: The New Press.

Slobogin, Christopher

2013   "Treating Juveniles Like Juveniles: Getting Rid of Transfer and Expanded Adult Court Jurisdiction." Vanderbilt University Law School, Public Law & Legal Theory Working Paper No. 13–37.

Soss, Joe, Richard C. Fording, and Sanford F. Schram

2011   *Disciplining the Poor: Neoliberal Paternalism and the Persistent Power of Race.* Chicago: The University of Chicago Press.

Thompson, Anthony C.

2008   *Releasing Prisoners, Redeeming Communities: Reentry, Race, and Politics.* New York: New York University Press.

Tibbs, Donald F.

2011   *From Black Power to Prison Power: The Making of Jones v. North Carolina Prisoners' Labor Union.* New York: Palgrave.

Tonry, Michael

2011   *Punishing Race: A Continuing American Dilemma.* Oxford, UK: Oxford University Press.

United Nations

2011   *Report of the Special Rapporteur on the Promotion and Protection of the Right to Freedom of Opinion and Expression.* New York: United Nations. At *http://www2.ohchr. org/english/bodies/hrcouncil/docs/17session/A.HRC.17.27_en.pdf.*

US Department of Health, Education, & Welfare

1968   *Vital Statistics of the United States, 1966: Volume II—Mortality.* Washington, DC: US Government Printing Office.

Wacquant, Loïc

2008   "The Place of the Prison in the New Government of Poverty." In *After the War on Crime: Race, Democracy and a New Reconstruction,* edited by Mary Louise Frampton, Ian Haney-López. and Jonathan Simon, 23–36. New York: New York University Press.

2009   *Punishing the Poor: The Neoliberal Government of Social Insecurity.* Durham, NC: Duke University Press.

Warren Carol A.B.

1981   "New Forms of Social Control: The Myth of Deinstitutionalization." *The American Behavioral Scientist* 24(6): 724–40.

Western, Bruce

2006   *Punishment and Inequality in America.* New York: Russell Sage Foundation.

Western, Bruce and Christopher Wildeman

2009   "The Black Family and Mass Incarceration." *The Annals of the American Academy of Political and Social Science* 621: 212–42.

Wildeman, Christopher

2009   "Parental Imprisonment, the Prison Boom, and the Concentration of Childhood Disadvantage." *Demography* 46(2): 265–80.

Wolpert, Julian and Eileen R. Wolpert

1976   "The Relocation of Released Mental Hospital Patients into Residential Communities." *Policy Sciences* 7: 31–51.

Post-Reading Questions

1. In what ways does the present prison industrial complex perpetuate racial and class inequalities?

2. What are some ways to drastically reduce the current prison population? What are some forces of resistance to your ideas?

3. In terms of prison reduction, what are some of the pros and cons of presumptive parole policies whereby prisoners must be released by their first parole eligibility date?

4. What are the pros and cons of the proposed abolition of court transfers from juvenile to adult court? What are some forces of resistance?

5. How do you view the proposed "affirmative action for neighborhoods" most affected by mass incarceration? What are some forces of resistance?

Women Behind Bars

An Illuminating Portrait

Cathy McDaniels-Wilson and Judson L. Jeffries

The United States has the highest documented incarceration rate in the world (Pager, 2007). As of year-end 2007 the rate was 743 people incarcerated per 100,000 people; compared to 600 people incarcerated per 100,000 in Russia, 100 people incarcerated per 100,000 in Europe and 80 people incarcerated per 100,000 in Japan (Walmsley, 2009; Human Development Report, 2007/2008). Ninety three percent of prisoners in the U.S. were males, hence the reason why when many Americans think of prisoners they tend to think of males, albeit, in many cases, Black[1] males. Since 1980 the Black male population has grown exponentially, mainly as a result of mandatory sentencing that came about during the "war on drugs" (Alexander, 2010; Parenti, 2000). In fact, over the past twenty years, the Black male prison population has rivaled the Black male college student population (Alexander, 2010; Boothe, 2010; Robinson, 2008; Parenti, 2000). This may explain why the bulk of the literature about prisons has focused on African American males.

What many do not realize is that while the number of Black male inmates has spiraled out of control so has the number of female inmates. Unfortunately, little attention has been paid to female incarceration. A cursory look at the numbers shows that the incarceration of females[2] is increasing at a staggering rate. According to the Bureau of Justice Statistics, there were more than 2,297,400 inmates in federal, state, and local prisons and jails in 2010 (Minton, 2011). Of that number 201, 200 were women. The number of women imprisoned since the mid-1980s has grown steadily. In fact between 1980 and 2006 the number of women entering prison in the U.S. rose 400%, double the rate of men over that same period (Kerness, 2006). A report by the Bureau of Justice Statistics (2010) also showed that by midyear of 2009, female incarceration rates varied sharply by race. In 2009, the likelihood of being in prison or jail for Black females (with an incarceration rate of 333 per 100,000) was twice that of Hispanic females (142 per 100,000) and over 3.6 times that of White females (91 per 100,000) (Minton, 2011). Of women in prison 92,100 were White, 64,800 were Black and 32,300 were Latina.

Mass incarceration, as a major social phenomenon has garnered significant attention among academics, thus it is not surprising that the number of books and journal articles on the subject is in no short supply. However, the majority of these works focus on the disproportionate incarceration rates of African American males (Alexander, 2010; Thompson, 2010; Robinson, 2008; Pager, 2007). By contrast the surge in the number of women prisoners in the U.S., however, has been given short shrift. By focusing on the histories of sexual abuse that females bring with them to their prison terms in the state of Ohio this [reading] seeks to help fill that void.

A review of the literature will show, that no one has systematically studied the lives of women inmates to the degree that this work does. In doing so, we explore the degree to which females inmates were sexually abused prior to entering prison. Over the years, some have claimed that women inmates often have an extensive history of sexual abuse. Using Ohio as our case study we set out to test this hypothesis. This work delved into the lives of more than 1,500 women in all of the correctional facilities in the state of Ohio where women are admitted. This [reading] also presents the reader with a sense of women's sexual abuse history across race. Because very little diversity exists within the female prison population in Ohio this study focuses primarily on Black and White women prisoners.

Female Inmates in Ohio: A Brief Portrait

The numbers of female prisoners in Ohio may not be as sobering as those nationally, but the numbers are still cause for concern. According to the Ohio Department of Rehabilitation and Corrections (2010), in the state of Ohio, in 2001, of the 45,259 total inmates, 2,788 were female; consisting of 6.16% of the total prison population. Nearly ten years later, in 2010, there were a total of 50,880 people incarcerated, 3,911 of which were females, comprising 7.7% of the total population. As far as the racial demographic goes, of the current 3,911 female offenders, 31.4% identified themselves as Black/African American, 67.0% European American, 0.1% Hispanic, 0.05% Native American, 0.31% Asian, and 0.08% identified as Other. In terms of age, 36% of the women incarcerated were between the ages of 15–29, 31.2% were 30–39, and 22.9% were 40–49; 8.2% were 50–59 and 1.48% were age 60 years and older. The highest represented age group in prison; was the 25–29 age cohorts while the average age of a female inmate was thirty-five (Ohio Department of Rehabilitation and Corrections, 2010).

The proliferation of the female prison population suggests a striking trend in female criminal activity. The most serious offenses as reported by the Ohio Research Office of Policy and Offender Reentry summary reveal that even among those, there is a significant amount of variability ranging from forgery to aggravated murder. On the whole, the sample evaluated by the Research Office of Policy and Offender Reentry had committed more crimes against actual persons (such as aggravated robbery, felonious assault, and involuntary manslaughter), followed by drug offenses, as well as offenses against justice/public administration, and property offenses.

Going Behind the Walls of Ohio's Prisons

In the early to mid-1990s, the first author had an opportunity to teach at the Franklin pre-release center for women in Columbus, Ohio. Unlike some other institutions, the Franklin pre-release center offered an array of professional development endeavors, including the opportunity to earn a college degree in the social sciences. The first author taught two psychology courses over a period of several years. The first author's foray into the prison system in 1993, involved teaching an introductory course in Psychology. Although the experience was gratifying, the first author found "The Psychology of Women" course, which was taught in 1996, to be most enlightening. In this course the biological, sociological, and cultural influences of the psychology of women were examined. Topics included gender socialization, sex roles; the impact of gender on personality and achievement and mental health. While teaching this particular course the first author was struck by the stories that women voluntarily shared regarding the events that they believed led to their incarceration. There seemed to be an underlying theme of victimization across the board. This observation does not negate, however, the horrific and in some cases heinous crimes, that were committed by some of her students. Intrigued by this unanticipated discovery, she decided to explore the issue further.

Based on the author's clinical experiences with non-incarcerated women and men who have reported histories of abuse, it was believed that the pathway perspective on offending would be especially helpful in studying women inmates and the prevalence of sexual abuse.[3] According to Belknap (2007) the pathway perspective views traumatic and other troubling antecedent events as significant risk factors in girls' subsequent deviance and offending behaviors. Indeed, there is a body of research that appears to rely heavily on this approach (Belknap, Winter, & Cady, 2003; Chesney-Lind & Rodriquez, 1983; Belknap & Holsinger, 1996; James & Meyerding, 1977; Silbert & Pines 1981). Grounded in this literature, we set out to systematically explore the extent and complexities of sexual abuse in the lives of women inmates in Ohio.

Significance of Research

This research is significant for several reasons. First, this research provides an in-depth look into the often complicated and intricate lives of a prison population that has often been overlooked by scholars and others. Second, this research enables the reader to see the degree to which the sexual abuse histories of Black and White women prisoners are similar or different. Third, this work shows how widespread the histories of sexual abuse are among women inmates prior to being imprisoned. Fourth, this research spotlights an issue that is increasingly becoming a major societal problem, but not given the attention it deserves, especially by those who are well-positioned to address it. Fifth, some women inmates have deep psychological scarring and/or suffer from pervasive mental health disorders that stem from incidents of sexual abuse. Tragically, instead of receiving treatment or being hospitalized, they are oftentimes imprisoned and forgotten.

Literature Review

There is a small, but growing body of literature that examines the history of sexual abuse in the lives of incarcerated women. A portion of the literature only minimally assessed the sexual abuse experiences of the participants, oftentimes only asking a single question, such as "Have you ever been abused?", does not make for a rich data set (Belknap, Holsinger & Dunn, 1997). Moreover, a fair amount of the work studies sexual abuse of female inmates while in prison (The Sexual Abuse of Female Inmates, 2003). It is well-documented that women are sometimes violated once in prison, but unfortunately, many female inmates are the victims of sexual abuse long before entering prison. Some have even argued that the horrific experience of being sexually abused, oftentimes, leads to a life of criminal activity that eventually results in imprisonment.

The majority of the work on female inmates, however, is in the area of female criminality as distinct from male criminality. A fair amount of it is theory-based, with little to no supporting empirical evidence (Chesny-Lind, 1986). Moreover, it is important to be mindful that previous attempts to analyze data gleaned from women's histories' of abuse have relied heavily on male-generated paradigms as an overlay to the challenges women face, which has, to a large degree, resulted in a superficial analysis and/or misinterpretation of the facts (see Belknap, 2007; Chesney-Lind & Rodriguez, 1983; Smart, 1976). There has been, however, over the past decade, an increase in both the amount and quality of work in the area of female criminality.

This recent body of work has helped us better understand the role of violence in the lives of incarcerated women. More specifically, we now know that criminal offending and subsequent incarceration is one of the aftereffects of female sexual abuse history (Belknap & Holsinger, 2006; Gaarder & Belknap, 2002; Browne et al., 1999; Girshick, 1999). One of the most frequently cited socio-cultural explanations of violence against women and girls is rooted in feminist theory, which suggests that violence against women generally, emanates from potent socializing messages from the media, music, peer groups, the families, the legal system and other American institutions; all of which leads to widespread acceptance and normalization of gender-based violence. This holds special significance for African American women (Wyatt, 1992; 1990). Scholars who have studied the prevalence and types of abuse across race have produced a body of work that, to a large degree is both contradictory and inconclusive. Some of the weaknesses of those studies include an underdeveloped theoretical thrust, flaws in methodological approach, sample bias, and the like (Comack, 1996; Richie, 1996; Priest, 1992). Given these shortcomings, it is not surprisingly, that few differences between Black and White women have been found.

A brief review of the research on childhood sexual abuse and its impact across race and ethnicity is crucial to our understanding of women's survival, health, and resiliency. It has been well-documented that a history of childhood sexual abuse is an important factor in the onset of delinquent behavior (Belknap, Holslinger & Dunn, 1997). Ramos, Carlson, and McNutt (2004) examined lifetime abuse, and the resultant effects on the mental health of Black women. One of their more interesting findings indicated that Black women who experienced childhood abuse were more likely to report adult partner abuse than those who were victimized as adults, but not as children. Overall, though, the authors found more similarities than differences when it came to types of childhood abuse and adult abuse between Black and White women. Similarly, in a more recent study, Amonde et. al (2006) found no significant racial differences in the nature, severity, or aftereffects of childhood sexual abuse between these two groups. What they did find, however, was that in terms of age of onset, White women were more likely to experience abuse before the age of seven than Black women (Amonde et. al, 2006). In their sample White women were two and a half times more likely to experience abuse before age seven than were Black women. African American women, however, were more likely to report abuse that occurred during adolescence. Black women also reported a higher incidence of perpetrators living within the household, suggesting that there may be differences in family structure between Black and White women.

Method

In 1996, research participants were solicited from three separate penal institutions in the state of Ohio. They were: the Ohio Reformatory for Women (ORW) in Marysville, Ohio, housing minimum-, medium-, and maximum-security prisoners, opened in 1916, is the oldest prison for adult women in Ohio and the reception site for all incoming offenders; the Franklin Pre-Release Center (FPRC) in Columbus, Ohio, opened in 1988, houses minimum- and medium-security women prisoners who serve the majority of their sentences at FPRC; and the Northeast Pre-Release Center (NPRC), also opened in 1988, is a minimum-security women's prison in Cleveland, Ohio. At the time, these three correctional facilities were the only prisons in Ohio that housed women. Of the three facilities, only the Ohio Reformatory for Women is located in a rural area. The prison was once a functioning farm, complete with dairy cattle, hogs, and grain, which the inmates ran. The FPRC and the NPRC are located in the largest (Columbus) and second largest (Cleveland) cities in the state of Ohio. Although ORW no longer operates as a farm, it is still commonly known as "the farm."

A *call for participation* was sent to the inmates in all three correctional facilities; hence every inmate was given the opportunity to participate in the study. Eight hundred and eighty five women out of a total of 2,903 inmates (which produced a response rate of 44.1%) participated in the 1996 study. All participants had to be at least 18 years old. Each participant was asked to complete the two surveys. Also ten inmates [from each site] were randomly selected for a face-to-face interview with the examiner.

A comprehensive set of questions was developed in order to assess several factors. Some of the questions inquired about the age of onset, the relationship of victim to offender, and whether the acts of violence were intrusive or nonintrusive. The first measure used for the women's sexual abuse history is a modified version of the Koss and Oros (1982) Sexual Experiences Survey. The original version consisted of 13 closed-ended (yes or no) questions that gave inmates an opportunity to identify behaviors that were not only unusual, but unsettling, and males the opportunity to identify behaviors that could be characterized as aggressive and violating. The SES that was designed for this study consisted of 15 items ranging from "someone misinterpreting the level of sexual intimacy you desire," to more intrusive, violent, sexually aggressive or assaultive behaviors. In the modified SES, participants who reported experiencing a violation were asked (a) the number of times they experienced an encounter and (b) the gender of the abuser(s). Even with these modifications, it was determined that an additional survey was needed, as it was important to document the Victim-Offender Relationship (VOR) as well as the victim's age at the time the violation or abuse occurred.

A decision was made to develop the Sexual Abuse Checklist Survey (SACS) to document a more detailed account of the types of sexual violations and abuses that occurred. The SACS specifically identified the following potential VORs: father, stepfather, grandfather, mother, stepmother, grandmother, uncle, aunt, brother, sister, male cousin, female cousin, male neighbor, female neighbor, male lover or boyfriend, female lover or girlfriend, male date, female date, husband, male counselor, female counselor, male minister or clergy, female minister or clergy, male teacher, female teacher, male stranger, and female stranger. For VORs not indicated on the list, blank spaces were provided so that respondents could describe the relationship, type of abuse and their age(s) at the time of the violation. Adjacent to each potential abuser, the following potential abuses were listed, and the respondents were asked to circle as many as were applicable: nudity, disrobing, genital exposure, being observed (i.e., showering, dressing, toileting), kissing, fondling, masturbation, finger penetration of vagina, finger penetration of anus, oral sex on the victim, oral sex on the abuser, penile penetration of vagina, and penile penetration of anus. A comment section was included at the bottom of this survey for additional thoughts or reflections. Both the modified SES and the SACS were pilot-tested at a nearby counseling center on the campus of a major research university, in several introductory to psychology classes, as well as several local halfway houses. What follows is a rather detailed account of the levels and types of sexual violations and sexual abuses experienced by these women.

Results

Nearly all of the women in this study admitted being sexually abused at some point in their lives. Even more disturbing is that the overwhelming majority (70%) of the participants identified multiple acts of abuse, and at least one would meet the legal definition of rape in most states, which is non-consensual sexual intercourse that is committed by physical force, threat of injury, or other duress. Additionally, under a variation known as "statutory rape," some states make it unlawful for an adult to engage in sexual intercourse with a person who has not reached the age of consent (usually 18 years of age). Of the reported incidents of multiple abuses, more than half reported childhood sexual abuse. The most frequent perpetrators were male strangers, lover/boyfriends, uncles, husbands, and brothers.

Additional descriptions of the sample include the following: 45% of the participants were White women and 53% were Black women. Of these, only 28% graduated from high school, while 15% reported having taken some college courses. An examination of family structure revealed that the overwhelming majority (85%) of the inmates were parents with an average of 2.4 children per participant. The majority had been employed before incarceration, was single, and had a positive history of polysubstance use. The frequency with which Black women inmates reported a history of polysubstance abuse (a combination of both drugs and alcohol abuse and dependence) was noticeably higher (56.1%) than that of White women (43.5%) in the sample study.

Information regarding their prior arrests and convictions for each offender was obtained from two sources at the time of this investigation: the Bureau of Criminal Investigations, a nationwide reporting agency, and the National Criminal Information Center, a reporting agency via the Federal Bureau of Investigations. More than half (56.3%) of the inmates had a prior history of juvenile arrests while 43.7% had a prior adult arrest history. The most serious offenses committed by this sample were categorized into three groups: crimes against people, drug offenses, and property offenses. A significant number of offenders were indicted for crimes against people (43.8%), about one-fourth for drug offenses (22.6%), and one-fourth for property offenses (19.8%).

An area that was of particular interest to the authors was the differences and variations in sexual violations across race. In this study, "sexual violations" are defined as sexual experiences that are rarely prosecuted. Many individuals do not view them as sexual abuse, but some scholars have identified them as exploitative and troubling (e.g., Basile, 1999; Kelly, 1988; Russell, 1984). Examples include acquiescing to sex in response to verbal threats to end the relationship and/or succumbing to various types of verbal coercion or pressure. We defined "sexual abuses," on the other hand, as sexual experiences that are usually considered both criminal and culturally unacceptable, such as rape and molestation. However, the traditional definition of "rape" can vary across jurisdictions, over time, and across studies (McDaniels Wilson & Belknap, 2008).

On the Sexual Experience Survey, White females reported significantly higher rates of sexual violations than did Black women. For example, when asked if someone ever misinterpreted one's level of sexual interest, 63% of White women responded affirmatively compared to 48% of Black women who answered yes. To the question "Have you ever kissed, pet, fondled under verbal pressure" 54% of White women said yes, compared to 40% of Black women who reported in the affirmative. In response to the question "Did you ever experience penetration as a result of verbal pressure," 54% of White women and 38% of Black women indicated that they had. Additional responses to questions that addressed issues of abuse revealed a similar pattern. When asked, "Has someone used their position of authority to force penetration?" 24% of White women said yes while 15% of Black women responded affirmatively. Finally when asked, "Has anyone used alcohol and or drugs to penetrate?" 44% of White women and 34% of Black women indicated yes. An additional question on this measure was designed to assess how the victim conceptualized her abusive experiences. Clinicians often encounter women who experience a sexual violation or an abusive act, but fail to conceptualize or define their experience as a violation or abusive act. To better assess this phenomenon, the participants were asked to respond to the following question "Have you ever been raped or gang raped?" Of the White women, 15% reported that they had been gang raped, while on 7.9% of the Black women affirmed the same experience. Still, it is possible that some women were unwilling to admit to someone whom they did not know that they had either been raped or gang raped. It is also possible that some women were in denial and/or wholly unwilling to acknowledge being the victims of such a heinous crime.

Findings from the Sexual Abuse checklist, which identified the relationship between the victim and the perpetrator also revealed noticeable differences for White and Black women. For many years, researchers have attempted to examine whether there are identifiable factors within family systems that may place some children at greater risk of experiencing sexual violations or abuse within their own families. One school of thought that attempts to explain why some children may be at greater risk than others focuses on the concept of the extended family. For example, the African American family is often extended and multigenerational, which creates a communal and collective family structure (Wilson et al., 1995). Belgrave and Allison (2010) state that included within this family network are immediate family members, extended members, (i.e., aunts, uncles, cousins, etc.) friends, neighbors, fictive kin (individuals who are not biologically related but are considered family. They are often referred to as cousin, uncle, aunt and the like) and church members. This extended family situation sometimes places children in the presence and/or care of individuals who may be less repulsed by the idea of sexually abusing a child than would someone who may be related to the child. This is not to say that children are not abused by those who are biologically related to them, because they are. The point is, the stronger the biological link between the potential abuser and the abused; the less likely [seemingly] he or she would be to commit such a horrific act. For example, a father may be more hesitant to sexually abuse his own daughter than he would his niece. Similarly, a brother may be more hesitant to sexually abuse his own sister than he would a cousin. The same argument can be made regarding biological vis-à-vis non-biological family members. Simply put, biological relatives may be less likely to sexually abuse children with whom they share the same blood line than they would children who are considered family, but are not related, biologically. Again this is not to say that such things do not occur, only that the stronger the link the more repulsed the potential abuser might be, making it more difficult for the potential abuser to engage in such behavior, not only because of the penalties associated with the crime, but the resultant heavy burden that one would carry on his/her conscience.

When differences among victim-offender relations by race are examined, one sees striking disparities between Black and White women. White women reported higher incidents of abuse by each of the following five perpetrators: male cousins, husbands, male dates, male lovers, and male strangers (see Table 14.1).

Table 14.1   Perpetrators of Abuse for Inmates Reporting Abuse.

PERPETRATORS OF ABUSE	VS. WHITE WOMEN	VS. BLACK WOMEN
Male cousins	15%	6.4%
Husbands	24.9%	5.9%
Male dates	21%	11.4%
Male lovers	21%	11.9%
Male strangers	32.3%	22.3%

Additional information on this measure also shows that White women experienced a significantly higher level of both non-intrusive (disrobing, genital exposure, verbal inappropriateness) and intrusive (oral, anal vaginal intercourse, or oral sexual) acts by their perpetrators than did Black women. Sexually abusive behavior, victim-offender relations, and age of onset were also analyzed. The data were also analyzed from two different developmental spectra, by defining children as up through age 12 and adolescents starting at age 13. Examining the types of experiences both groups of females reported between the ages of 0–12 by race, we see that White females report experiencing more abuse by family members and acquaintances at this age than do Black females and that Black females report experiencing more abuse by a stranger between the ages of 13–17 than do White females. Below are excerpts extrapolated from face-to-face interviews with three of the inmates:

> "I just would like to say, once one person does it to you, it's almost normal to allow others to do it. I learned how to zone out."

> "I was raped at least 3 times by the time I was 20."

"I have been abused from birth, throughout my life. Never having no one to talk to, or haven't reported this before. Still it's very painful in many ways. Not being able to ever talk about this even in prison, they only want to punish me, but no one ever asks why I become an addict, or why I did the things I did."

These findings were both revealing and unsettling. The levels of abuse reported by both Black and White women speak to the magnitude of abuse that many women experience even at an early age, at the hands of people who, historically, are expected to assume the role of protector and nurturer. So disturbed were we by what we uncovered, a decision was made to revisit this issue; to assess whether the abuse that female inmates experience had changed over time. In 2010, we questioned, whether or not Black women, White women, Latinas, Asian American, or Native American women experienced more or less sexual abuse and/or sexual violations than occurred fifteen years earlier. Moreover, we set out to ascertain what role those charged with the responsibility of protecting and nurturing these women might have played in that abuse.

The Follow-up: December 2010

A follow-up assessment of sexual abuse and violations was conducted in December 2010. Out of a total of 4,920 inmates from the four Ohio prisons that housed women, 760 incarcerated women participated in the study. Again, a *call for participation* was sent out to all four facilities, thus giving each inmate the opportunity to participate. The correctional facilities were: The Ohio Reformatory for Women which housed 2,865 women, the Franklin Pre-Release Center, which comprised of 470 women and the North Pre-release center, which admitted 522 women. A fourth prison, the Trumbull Correctional Institute, which opened in 1992 and houses 1,073 inmates was added in 2010, as it was believed that doing so would result in an even richer data set. Moreover, at the time of the first study, Trumbull, a small rural/suburban town of 2,200 residents, located in Leavittsburg, Ohio, was an all-male correctional facility. That changed, in 2005, when women started being admitted.

None of the women in the 2010 study were in the 1996 cohort, yet the 2010 follow-up produced few surprises; therefore presenting the data here would not be the best use of space and/or time. Sadly, much of what we encountered in terms of misery and circumstance mirrored the 1996 cohort. The racial demographics were similar as were the crimes committed against and by the female inmates. What was confirmed for us is that many women commit crimes not necessarily for the sake of committing crime itself, or for the thrill of eluding the law, but as a response to the social and psychological reality of their lives. More frightening than anything, however, is the fact that, many women inmates continue to suffer from multiple bouts of abuse by multiple perpetrators, which leads to feelings of hopelessness, low self-worth, drug abuse and criminal activity. If there was an appreciable difference, between the two cohorts, it was the gripping discursive comments offered by the 2010 cohort. The comments were gleaned from answers given to a number of open-ended questions that were asked. The open-ended questions encouraged a full, meaningful answer that allowed the subject to use her own knowledge and/or feelings to think about a person and/or event that affected her.

One important aspect of this research is the opportunity for participants to tell their own story, unfiltered. These discursive narratives allows subjects to paint a more vivid portrait of their sexual abuse experiences than do the open-ended/close ended questions that appear on a standardized questionnaire/survey. Moreover, these personal narratives afford participants an opportunity to delve into their oftentimes complex and nuanced life story, which for some, is cathartic. Many of the inmates had heretofore never taken the time to jot down their feelings. Once this was done, some inmates found it easier to analyze certain events that they perhaps had refused to deal with, deliberately blocked out or were unwilling to acknowledge. Finally, these discursive comments, add to the study a rich human dimension that cannot be captured by quantitative data alone.

Below are several compelling and emotional excerpts from interviews conducted with both Black and White females from the 2010 sample. These personal vignettes provide the reader with a sense of the depth and scope of the abuse, experienced by some of the study's participants.

"It happened from about the age of 7 or eight, to about the age of 15, and I didn't tell anyone until I was 18 years old."

"I don't trust anyone. I don't. 'Cause it was a family member that did it, and a family friend that did it, and because of that, I have a really hard time letting people in, I don't—I'm not an emotional person, I don't like being touched at all. I like my personal space a lot. I like my privacy a lot."

"The first time I had mentioned it was to my mother, and I love my mother, but it was kind of brushed under the rug. No-nonsense-type stuff. "Go home and we'll get a 12-pack and everything will be all right"—type situation. I was raped when I was 14, I reported it. I had the support of my family when I reported it. After I reported it; during the court procedures, everybody turned their back on me and I had no support, so I stepped down and they dropped it from rape to "conduct with a minor" and he got 18 months. So after that, I didn't talk anymore."

"I had two different sexual abuses. One was when I was very young. It was my brother. I didn't tell anybody about that until my twenties. I told my psychologist, and up until that point, for years and years and years, I felt very guilty. So when I shared it with my psychologist, he told me that playing around with your family members is fairly common. He reduced my guilt tremendously. And I don't know why it took me so long to tell him, either, because it weighed on me for many, many, many years. Now, when I was abused by a neighbor's grandfather, my parents told me they didn't believe me and not to talk about

it. Obviously that didn't sit well. And the last time I was abused was from an acquaintance, male, and I believe he raped me, and I called the police at the hospital and gave them a report, and that felt good."

Fifteen years has passed since the initial investigation into the sexual abuse histories of incarcerated women, yet as one can see from the disturbing narratives above, similar themes surfaced among the 2010 cohort. Given the horror of sexual abuse, it is not altogether surprising that many women might seek solace or attempt to escape reality by engaging in some thrill seeking criminal activity; that if caught, would result in imprisonment.

Discussion

Until recently, the study of female incarceration was virtually ignored, principally because there was a perception that prison was for men (Kerness, 2006). By 2004, U.S. legislators and others recognized that women were entering prison at a higher rate than men (Austin, 2006). The findings of this study suggest the notion that many female inmates have experienced some type of sexual abuse prior to entering prison is not without merit. Moreover, the perpetrators of this abuse range from male friends and lovers to uncles, husbands and brothers. For some, the thought of a female/women being raped by her brother may seem particularly repulsive, yet it occurs more often than one might imagine.

This research also demonstrates that there are clear differences between the lived experiences of Black and White women. For example, 56.1% of Black women inmates reported a history of polysubstance abuse compared to 43.5% of White female inmates. One possible explanation is that unlike White women, Black women suffer from what some refer to as a triple disadvantage. In other words, Black women are not only the victims of racial discrimination, but sexism and classism as well. Consequently, the stress brought on by this level of oppression may be sometimes overwhelming, leading Black women to turn to a combination of legal and illegal substances in order to help them cope with the daily grind. Another possible explanation is that drugs are perhaps both more plentiful and accessible in inner city Columbus where there is a higher density of people of color than in the outlying areas where the population is predominantly White. In urban areas there are often more liquor stores [per capita and per square mile] and/or stores where alcohol can be purchased than there are in non urban areas (Roberts, 2003). In their article *Health Risk and Inequitable distribution of liquor stores in African American neighborhoods* LaVeist and Wallace (2000) found that liquor stores are disproportionately located in predominantly Black neighborhoods, even after controlling for socioeconomic status. Moreover, researchers have long argued that the large number of liquor stores in Black communities, influence the heavy use of alcohol among African Americans (Clucas & Clark, 1992). In many African American communities, for example, liquor stores often outnumber

Black churches (Roberts, 2003; William & Gorski, 1997). The cities of Columbus and Cleveland are no exception.

For years, scholars have debated whether or not there were differences between the abuse experiences, the prevalence, and the disclosure patterns between Black and White women. Some believe that there are no major differences in the prevalence of sexual abuse. Gail Wyatt (1990) conducted a ten-year comparison of prevalence rates between Black and White women who were the victims of sexual abuse and found that 29% of Black women and 39% of White women reported childhood sexual abuse. Further analysis compared the responses of White women to Black women, which revealed that overall, White women reported higher rates or sexual violations than Black women (Wyatt, 1990).

The feminist literature lays out a trajectory or pathway that leads women toward criminal involvement. Belknap (2010) explains that the feminist pathway perspective starting in the late 1970s identifies the impact that traumatic life experiences have on both delinquent girls and incarcerated women. The feminist pathways perspective emphasizes how deeply social life is patterned on the basis of gender, and thus, how variables such as trauma can take on different meanings not only for females, but males as well. Moreover, the pathways approach seeks to understand and explain how the broader intersections of gender, race, and economic inequities impact an individual's life experiences, opportunities and choices. This perspective helps us understand problem behaviors displayed by adolescents and adults who have been abused. The findings from our studies support the work of Chesney-Lind (1986), Daly (1992) & Ritchie (1996). Each have suggested that the examination and inclusion of gender and gender related elements as they relate to criminal activity is central to any theory that attempts to explain why sexually abused women tend to lead lives that result in incarceration.

Based on the experiences of the majority of women currently or previously incarcerated in the state of Ohio, many met the diagnostic criteria for post-traumatic stress disorder, depression, and anxiety in particular.[4] Given the emotional trauma that sexual abuse induces one can only imagine the mental state of many female inmates. According to the State of Ohio Office of Criminal Justice Services (2006), female prisoners and jail inmates had higher rates of mental health problems than did male inmates. White inmates were more likely than African Americans or Latinas to have mental health problems, and those inmates who were 24 years of age or younger tended to have the highest rates of substance abuse problems. Based on the experiences and symptoms reported in this study, many of the participants would meet the diagnosis of "severe mentally ill."[5] To compound matters, those with severe mental illnesses are especially vulnerable in spaces such as prisons where the possibility of being segregated from others is highly likely. Research suggests that prolonged periods of isolation, via lock down or seclusion, where there is decreased contact from others, or even a lack of natural lighting, can increase the symptomatology of those with severe mental illness (National Commission on Correctional Health Care, 2002).

It deserves mentioning that the number of first-time inmates with mental illnesses is increasing, so much so, that there is a growing concern among some about the number of such inmates flooding the criminal justice system and whether or not their emotional or mental health needs are being met (National Commission on Correctional Health Care, 2002). A recent three-year study conducted by the National Commission on Correctional Health Care and other expert groups delivered a final report to Congress in 2002 that read:

> Prisons and jails offer a unique opportunity to establish better disease control in the community by providing improved health care to inmates before they are released. The report established conclusively that thousands of inmates are being released into the community every year with undiagnosed and/or untreated mental illness. Over all these reports show that a more cost-effective and therapeutic outcome (both for mentally ill individuals and the greater community) could be achieved through adequately providing treatment to these individuals while they are incarcerated. (p. 3)

Over the years, prison officials have become increasingly aware of the extent of mental illness within the penal system; however, in the case of women with extensive abuse histories, specific knowledge about these experiences has often been lacking. The criminal justice system has been designed and managed, based on policies, procedures, and practices consistent for the management of male offenders. The heartfelt comments from one of the study's participants is a testament to the need for change within the criminal justice system and how it is presently ill-equipped to deal with women and the many issues with which they face. Said this inmate,

> "I sincerely hope you are able to effect change. Given my own history, I find it extremely difficult to gain any sense of empowerment with male correctional officers yanking open the door to my cell at any time. I feel it's harmful to be subjected to the constant supervision of male officers—many of whom are younger and not particularly educated. Their screaming, shouting, and firm fisted approach to maintaining security often causes me to have post traumatic episodes or flashbacks".

Conclusion

It is no surprise that programs for female offenders are often either lacking in substance or absent altogether. Indeed, it is well documented that the needs of female offenders have historically been both underserved and in some cases, trivialized (Austin, 2006). Movement toward creating gender-based programs would entail giving proper consideration to the gendered nature of offending. Given the preponderance of abuse in the lives of women inmates, it is imperative that a system be created to address women's needs in a way that would take into consideration the various pathway dimensions that often lead to their incarceration, their behavior while incarcerated, and needs that are specific to women while incarcerated.

Certain considerations need also be taken into account where women of color are concerned. The issue of rape and sexual assault experiences for many women of color is complex and unique. Black women have historically been stereotyped as wild, uncontrollable, and even crim-inal (Davis, 1985). In her paper, "Constituting American: Black Women, Sexual Assault, and the Law," Irving (2007) examined a number of rapes cases in the Philadelphia area from 1995–2000 and found that sexual assault cases involving Black women were often dismissed despite strong supporting evidence to the contrary. Based on this Irving maintained that the justice system dis-criminates based on race and class, thus leaving many women of color, especially Black women without proper legal protection against sexual abuse (Irving, 2007). Wyatt goes even further, arguing that the inattention to sexually abused Black women can be traced back to the history of sexual exploitation of slaves more than 250 years ago (Wyatt, 1992). Women held as slaves were regularly forced to comply with the sexual advances of their masters. If they resisted, they were beaten, sometimes brutally. There was, of course, little recourse for women held as slaves. Consequently, an enormous number of female slaves became concubines for their masters. It is not a far-fetched idea, that for Black women, America's long history of slavery may have a lingering effect on their attitudes about rape and their right to be protected. As Wyatt asserts, due to this context, African American women's help-seeking behaviors are likely to be atypical. In her 1992 study addressing the "Sociocultural Context of Rape," Wyatt suggested that nearly 65% of her sample of African American women failed to disclose their experience with sexual abuse until well in adulthood (Wyatt, 1992). Thus, understanding the nature of disclosure patterns is an important treatment consideration. Outcome measures are also important when assessing the variation in life experiences, adaptive styles, and modes of recovery among all women, especially Black women.

The number of women inmates in Ohio who were sexually violated before entering prison is staggering. Moreover, the data show that the problem transcends race and age. Research such as this should sound an alarm among those who are well positioned to address the issue. Too often, sexual abuse is not taken as seriously as other crimes especially when it occurs within the home or a marriage. Consequently, there is a lack of urgency or interest in identifying the kinds of resources needed to combat the problem and the ramifications of sexual abuse. Indeed, understanding the potential far-reaching consequences of this horrific crime would go a long way in helping prison officials and others meet the unique and complex needs of a steadily increasing prison population.

Notes

1 The words Black and African American are used interchangeably throughout this paper according to sound and context.
2 The words female and women are used interchangeably throughout this paper according to sound and context.
3 The author to whom this sentence refers is Cathy McDaniels-Wilson.
4 In addition to being a professor the first author is also a licensed psychologist with a private practice. Given her unique position in the area of mental health she is well equipped to make this diagnosis.
5 Ibid.

References

Alexander, M. (2010). *The New Jim Crow: Mass Incarceration in the Age of Colorblindness.* New York: New Press.

Amonde, M., Griffin, M.L. & Fraser, I.R. (2006). The Childhood Sexual Abuse among Black and White women from two-parent families. *Child Maltreatment*, 11, 237–246.

Austin, J. (2006). *Assessment of Ohio Prison Admission Trends For Female Prisoners and Their impact on the prison population.* Washington, D.C.: The JFA Institute.

Basile, K. C. (1999). Rape by acquiescence. *Violence Against Women*, 5, 1036–1058.

Belgrave, F. Z., & Allison, K. (2005). *African American Psychology: from Africa to America*, (2nd Ed.) California: Sage Publications.

Belknap, J. (2010). "'Offending Women': A Double Entendre." *Journal of Criminal Law & Criminology*, 100, 1060–1098.

Belknap, J. (2007). *The Invisible Woman: Gender, Crime, and Justice, 3rd Edition.* Belmont, CA. Wadsworth Publishing Company.

Belknap, J. K, & Holsinger, K. (2006). The Gendered Nature of Risk Factors for Delinquency. *Feminist Criminology*, 1, 48–71.

Belknap, J., E. Winter, & B. Cady. (2003). "Professionals' Assessments of the Needs of Delinquent Girls: The Results of a Focus Group Study," In B. E. Bloom (Ed.), *Gendered Justice*. (pp. 209–240). Durham, NC: Carolina Academic Press.

Belknap, J., K. Holsinger, & M. Dunn. (1997). Understanding Incarcerated Girls: The results of a Focus Group Study. *Prison Journal*, 77, 381–404.

Boothe, D. (2010). *Why are So Many Black Men in Prison?* Memphis: Full Surface Publishing.

Browne, A, B., Miller, & E. Maguin. (1999). Prevalence and severity of lifetime physical and sexual victimization among incarcerated women. *International Journal of Law and Psychiatry*, 22, 301–322.

Chesney-Lind, M. (1986). Women and Crime: The Female Offender. *Journal of women in culture and society*, 12, 78–96.

Chesney-Lind, M. & Rodriguez, N. (1983). Women under Lock and Key. *Prison Journal*, 63, 47–65.

Clucas, A., & Clark, V. (1992). Module II 7: Drug and Alcohol Problems in Special Populations. In M.A. Naegle (Ed.), *Substance Abuse Education in Nursing*, Vol. 2, (pp. 531–547). New York: National League for Nursing.

Comack, E. (1996). *Women in Trouble: Connecting Women's Law Violations to their Histories of Abuse*. Halifax, N.S.: Fernwood Publishing.

Daly, K. (1992). Women's Pathways to Felony Court: Feminist Theories of Lawbreaking and Problems of Representation. *Review of Law and Women's Studies*, 2, 11–52.

Davis, A. (1985). *Violence Against Women and the ongoing challenge to racism*. Latham, NY: Kitchen Table Press.

Gaarder, E., & J. Belknap. (2002). Tenuous Borders: Girls Transferred to Adult Court. *Criminology*, 40, 481–517.

Girshick, L. B. (1999). *No Safe Haven: Stories of Women in Prison*. Boston: Northeastern University Press.

Human Development Report 2007/2008 (HDR 2007/2008). For prison population per 100,000 people see Table 27 on page 322 of the full report.

Irving, T. (2007). Constituting American: Black Women, Sexual Assault, and the Law. *Culture Health and Sexuality*, 9, 536.

James, J., & J. Meyerding. (1977). Early Sexual Experiences and Prostitution. *American Journal of Psychiatry*, 134, 1381–1385.

Kelly, L. (1988). *Surviving sexual violence*. Minneapolis: University of Minnesota Press.

Kerness, B. (2006). *Speaking Truth to Power: Women in Prison*. Speech given on January 14, 2006, before the United Nations Committee on the Elimination of Discrimination Against Women.

Koss, M.P., & Oros, C.J. (1982) Sexual Experiences Survey: a research instrument investigating sexual Aggression and victimization. *Journal of consulting and clinical Psychology*, 50, 455–457.

LaVeist, T. A., & Wallace, J.M. (2000). Health Risk and Inequitable distribution of liquor stores in African American neighborhoods. *Social Science & Medicine*, 51, 613–617.

McDaniels-Wilson, C., & J. Belknap. (2008) The Extensive Sexual Violation and Sexual Abuse Histories of Incarcerated Women. *Violence Against Women*, 14, 1090–1127.

Minton, T. D. (2011). Jail Inmates at Midyear 2010-Statistical Tables. Bureau of Justice Statistics, April 14. http://bjs.ojp.usdoj.gov/index.cfm

National Commission on Correctional Health Care (2002) www.ncchc.org/resource/guidelines

Ohio Department of Rehabilitation and Corrections: Research Office of Policy and Offender Reentry. (2010) www.drc.state.oh.us/web/Reports.oorc.htm

Pager, D. (2007). *Marked: Race, Crime, and Finding Work in an era of Mass Incarceration*. Chicago: University of Chicago Press.

Parenti, C. (2000). *Lockdown America: Police and Prisons in the Age of Crises*. London and New York: Verso.

Priest, R. (1992). Child Sexual abuse histories among African American college students: A Preliminary Study. *American Journal of Orthopsychiatry*, 62, 475–476.

Ramos, B.M., Carlson, B.E. & McNutt, L.A. (2004). Lifetime abuse, mental health, and African American Women. *Journal of Family Violence*, 19, 153–164.

Richie, B. E. (1996). *Compelled to Crime: The Gender Entrapment of Battered Black Women*. New York: Routledge.

Roberts, O. (2003). *Streets of Glory: Church and Community in a Black Urban Neighborhood.* Chicago: University of Chicago Press.

Robinson, D.A. (2008). *Blacks: From the Plantation to the Prison.* Georgia: Going Against the Grain Publications.

Russell, D. E. H. (1984). *Sexual Exploitation.* Beverly Hills, CA: Sage.

Silbert, M. H., & Pines, A. M. (1981). Sexual Abuse as an Antecedent to Prostitution. *Child Abuse and Neglect,* 5, 407–411

Smart, C. (1976). *Women, Crime and Criminology: A Feminist Critique.* London: Routledge and Kegan Paul.

Thompson, H. A. (2010). Why Mass Incarceration Matters: Rethinking Crises, Decline, and Transformation in Postwar American History. *Journal of American History*, 117, 703–734.

U.S. Department of Justice, Bureau of Justice Statistics. (2010) Sourcebook of Criminal Justice Statistics.

Walmsley, R. (2009). *World Prison Population List. 8th edition.* International Centre for Prison Studies School of Law, King College London.

William, R., & Gorski, T.T. (1997). *Relapse Prevention Counseling for African Americans: A Culturally Specific Model.* Independence, MO: Herald House/Independence Press.

Wilson, M.N., Green-Bates, C., McCoy, L., Simmons, F., Askew, T., & Curry-El, J, (1995). African American family life: The dynamics of interactions, relationships, and roles, In M. Wilson (Ed), *African American family life: Its structural and ecological aspects* (pp. 5–21). San Francisco: Josey-Bass.

Wyatt, G.E. (1990). The Aftermath of child sexual abuse of African American and White American women: The victim's Experience. *Journal of Family Violence*, 5, 61–81.

Wyatt, G.E. (1992). The sociocultural context of African American and White American Women's rape. *Journal of Social Issues*, 48, 77–91.

Post-Reading Questions

1   Many of the assertions in this chapter result from firsthand experiences within the institution. What are some advantages and disadvantages of teaching at an institution before writing about one's experiences?

2   When conducting field studies, what can be done to guard against onlooker bias?

3   What are some of the problems researchers encounter when attempting to document the sexual abuse of female prisoners?

4   What are some advantages and disadvantages of having sexual abuse victims speak and elaborate on their victimization experiences?

5   What are some of the differences found in this study that distinguish Black and White victims of sexual assault? How are these differences explained in feminist literature?

Transgender Inmates

The Dilemma

Hal Brotheim

It's the midnight shift in a county jail receiving center when a local police officer and a female arrestee walk in—or so you think.

After medical screening, the arrestee is assigned to female booking personnel. At the same time, someone from medical staff enters the center and a female deputy calls for a sergeant. This female arrestee is actually a male in the transgender process. A big discussion begins. Who determines the arrestee's gender? Sworn staff and medical staff point at each other.

This scenario is not as farfetched as it sounds. The number of transgender inmates is rising, albeit slowly, but our jails and prisons are not adapting to this rise. So how do facilities handle these inmates?

Some agencies ask arrestees which gender they identify with. Others have medical personnel do an examination and render an opinion. However, some just place the arrestee in administrative segregation.

To prevent conflict, a policy that provides specific direction for both security and medical staff to determine gender must be in place before a transgender arrestee arrives in booking.

Key Terms

Definitions of terms describing those who are transgender can vary widely. Even within the transgender community there is some disagreement about appropriate terminology. Different terms are used to refer to a person's sexual orientation, which is a separate issue from his or her gender identity, which, in turn, may or may not match the evident physical anatomy.

The term *transgender* refers to a person who is born with the traits and physical characteristics of one sex (i.e., male or female), but self-identifies as another gender (i.e., feminine or masculine). A transgender person can be pre-operative, post-operative, or non-operative.

Intersex people develop before birth with a genetic disorder of sex representation/ differentiation. They are born with indeterminate genital structures that are not entirely male or female and may show a combination of both male and female features. These genital structures may also be underdeveloped. Indicators may be present both externally and/or internally. However, the external indicators may not be physically obvious. Some individuals outwardly appear male or female but internally have a mixed sexual anatomy. No intersex person has a complete set of both male and female organs. Intersex persons may identify themselves as either male or female, and their sexual orientation may be straight, bisexual, gay, or lesbian relative to their gender identity.

Gender identity refers to a person's internally felt sense of his or her own gender (sex), without regard to physical traits present at birth. Gender identity can match—or not match—a person's physical characteristics.

There is broad variation in the definition of "gender identity," and the meaning changes as societal norms, mores, and values evolve. Definitions also can be specific to individual cultures. Generally, gender identity is what a person feels him- or herself to be internally—either male or female. In most people, the gender identity and physical characteristics are aligned (male body with male identity, female body with female identity). However, this is not always the case.

In the medical and mental health fields, there is growing acknowledgment of a condition called "gender identity disorder." According to the *Diagnostic and Statistical Manual of Mental Disorders* (American Psychiatric Association, 2000), gender identity disorder is the presence of persistent and strong cross-gender identification. Such persons do not merely want to be a member of the other gender, but they may also experience discomfort with their own physical characteristics as well as suffer clinically significant distress or impairment in social, occupational, or other important areas of functioning. Persons with gender identity disorder often report feeling out of place in their bodies. As adults, many of these persons express a strong desire to live as members of the opposite sex. Increasingly, gender identity disorder is emerging during childhood.

Gender expression of gender identity manifests through dress, demeanor, and language. Quite apart from one's birth sex as male or female, an individual may identify as a particular gender and express that gender in various ways. For example, males express masculinity in different ways, and females express femininity in different ways. Likewise, transgender individuals express femininity and masculinity in different ways—and ways that may not be consistent with their sex at birth.

Sexual Quandary Triad is a sexual identity with three components. One side of the "sexual triad" is physical characteristics such as specific genitalia, breasts, and facial and body hair. The second is gender identity, and the third is sexual orientation.

For the majority of human beings, *physical characteristics* are either male or female. Intersex persons are an exception, even when the differences may not always be apparent from a simple external examination. Transgender persons who are transitioning to a new physical sexual identity can also present ambiguous physical characteristics. The most common procedure in a jail for determining an offender's "sex" is a visual examination by an officer or medical staff. The outcome of this examination is the pronouncement of either "male" or "female," with management, supervision, and housing practices pertinent to that sex. When physical sex is not easy to determine, problems can arise.

Conflict

The issue starts the moment a transgender person is arrested and enters the custody environment. In the criminal justice system, humiliation, abuse, and confusion occur at the very outset for transgender persons. Traditionally, the criminal justice system classifies arrestees as male or female and houses them accordingly. However, there is no widely published protocol regarding where a transgender individual must be housed or even how gender is determined (Turnbull, 2006).

Responding to incidents of violence and discrimination against transgender arrestees, the Los Angeles Police Department and San Francisco County Sheriff opened segregated housing for biologically male and female suspects who identify themselves as members of the opposite sex (Quinones, 2012).

Surveys conducted by the Bureau of Justice Statistics in 2009 indicate that transgender arrestees experienced sexual victimization at a rate 13 times higher than a random sampling of other offenders in the same facility. Such evidence indicates that transgender offenders are at increased risk for sexual victimization while in custody. Agencies that ignore this may be placing themselves at risk for litigation. Changes in Federal and State legislation, court decisions, settlement agreements, and Prison Rape Elimination Act (PREA) standards are also important factors in the management of these vulnerable offenders in the correctional setting.

Gender Determination

Once a person is taken into custody—even before that person is brought to the custodial environment—a protocol of determination needs to be followed.

Transgender people who have not had genital surgery are usually classified according to their birth sex for purposes of corrections housing regardless of how long they may have lived as members of the "other gender" and regardless of how much other medical treatment they may have undergone (*Farmer v. Brennan,* 511 U.S. 825, 829 [1994]; *Farmer v. Haas,* 990 F.2d 319, 320 [7th Cir. 1993]). This situation places male-to-female transsexual women at great risk of sexual violence. Transsexual people who have had genital surgery are generally classified and housed according to their reassigned sex. One mechanism to protect transsexual women who are at risk of violence due to being housed in male prisons is to separate them from other prisoners via "administrative segregation."

If an individual does not self-identify as transgender, the following guidelines are suggested:

- When the intention of a person's gender presentation is clear to a reasonable person (based on attire and other objective clues), use that as a basis for gender determination.
- When a person's sex is unclear or staff members are uncertain of a person's gender identity, it is appropriate to ask how the individual wishes to be addressed ("Sir," "Ma'am") and the name that the individual wishes to be called. This name should be documented as an "AKA" (also known as) if it differs from the individual's legal name.
- If a transgender person is unwilling to provide information that enables staff to know what name or gender is preferable, staff could make a determination about the person's gender based on gender expression (clothing, language, demeanor, etc.) and any other evidence available, including a sanctioned visual examination by appropriate personnel.
- Are there any objective criteria present that indicate which gender an arrestee identifies with despite what he or she is displaying, such as the obvious presence (male) or absence (female) of an Adam's Apple (laryngeal prominence), deep voice, facial hair, or large breasts?
- If sufficient clues indicate a transgender inmate, then a visual exam may be necessary. It is highly recommended that any visual exam be conducted by trained medical staff. The transgender person should be examined in a very professional manner that is unlikely to shock the average citizen. A prior agreement or protocol should be put in place with facility medical staff for these exams.

QUESTIONS FOR JAILS TO ASK

Medical Care Concerns

- What different medical and mental health services must we provide transgender offenders?
- Is there a question or inquiry during the intake medical triage regarding inmate gender identification?
- Is there a need for a greater level of service and support for the sexual reassignment process than the jail now provides?
- What is the potential psychological impact of impeding the sexual reassignment process while a person is in jail?
- Does this impact rise to the level of a "serious medical need"?
- Who is qualified to determine "serious medical need"—a general practitioner, or a specialist in sexual reassignment surgery?

Recordkeeping Concerns

- Do we book transgendered or mid-change persons into our records management information system as male or female?
- Is the official sex of an offender going to be based on the offender's perception of his or her sex rather than current physical characteristics?
- Do we begin by asking offenders to state their gender identity?
- Will gender identity have as big an impact on offender management as an inmate's sex?
- What is the basis for determining the designation of sex in the records management system? Does this information

come from the detainee? The arresting officer? The booking officer? Medical staff?

- Do we change sex information in our data systems on future bookings once the surgical procedures are completed?

Security Concerns

- Do we conduct searches differently with transgender inmates based on their gender identity?

- Do we ask inmates who they want to be searched by, male or female staff?

- Do we match the sex of the officer conducting the search to the gender identity of the offender?

- Is it intrusive if the search of a transgender offender is conducted by a member of the opposite sex?

- Is there a perception of being violated similar to that which could be experienced by a person with female anatomy and female gender identity if searched by a male officer?

- Is there an issue of intrusiveness when a male with a female gender identity is searched only by a male officer?

- If an inmate with female gender identity is more comfortable being searched by a female officer, do we comply?

- On a strip search, should there be a policy that searches of transgender inmates are conducted by a "mixed" team of one male and one female officer?

- How should we approach searches of intersex inmates?

- The results of the exam should be officially documented, stating the reason for and circumstances of the exam, the person who performed the examination, who was present, where it was conducted, and the outcome of the exam.
- In addition to such documentation, any information obtained about an individual's transgender status should be provided to appropriate departmental staff for the purpose of ensuring safe and appropriate treatment.
- Most importantly, any exam of an arrestee's naked body by medical or security staff should be done only on an arrestee who is assigned housing, and *not* on arrestees who may be released on their own recognizance, cite, or post bail.

Responsibilities of the Jail

The government's obligation upon incarcerating a citizen, derived from the 8th and 14th Amendments of the U.S. Constitution, is to provide reasonable protection for that person. Jails have a duty to take reasonable measures to guarantee inmates' safety from assault, suicide, fires and other facility dangers, and preventable illness. We are charged with preventing assault and the excessive use of force as well as suicide and self-harm. We must respond to serious medical and mental health needs; and we must avoid unconstitutional conditions of confinement. The fundamental question is, "How do we uphold our obligations when managing transgender offenders?"

Once a person is taken into custody ... a protocol of determination needs to be followed.

Most jails have adopted the position that any sexual behavior in the facility is a violation. Sex between any persons in a correctional setting is forbidden, period. Whether that behavior is homosexual, heterosexual, or bisexual is of no consequence. Our focus is on the potential for victimization, regardless of sexual orientation. Most jails have clearly defined policies on the housing, supervision, and management of heterosexual, gay, and lesbian offenders, but what about transgender and intersex offenders? We all acknowledge the legal requirement that strip searches are conducted by a member of the same sex (except in exigent circumstances), and we accept the legal implications of violating this caveat.

The following guidelines should be implemented to ensure that contacts with transgender individuals are professional, respectful, and courteous and will not lead to complaints and lawsuits:

- Do not use language that a reasonable person would consider demeaning to another person, in particular language that refers to a person's gender identity, gender expression, or sexual orientation.
- Show respect for transgender persons' identity and gender expression, which includes addressing them by their preferred name and using gender pronouns appropriate to an individual's gender self-identity and expression. When a person self-identifies as transgender, respect the expressed gender and do not question it.

Housing

Housing heterosexual inmates is straightforward, all other classification factors being equal. For gay and lesbian inmates, many jails do not have a blanket policy of segregation. A decision to segregate gay or lesbian inmates is usually based on an articulated risk or is derived from current or previous institutional behavior where the need for segregation has been identified or a request for protective custody has been made.

Transgender people typically are placed directly into protective custody with little opportunity to waive out. Some transgender persons are in the process of changing their physical characteristics via sexual reassignment when they reach our jails. The process involves counseling, lifestyle changes, hormone replacement therapy, and ultimately surgical procedures either to implant or remove breasts and reconstruct the genitalia. During the process of sexual reassignment, many live as members of the sex they plan to be. This raises questions for jail managers in several spheres of operations.

Medical Care Concerns

Some case law recognizes that a person who is undergoing the sex reassignment process has a "serious medical need" for the continuation of

Housing Concerns

- Do we house inmates differently based on transgender status and gender identity?
- Do we disregard physical characteristics in making housing decisions?
- Do we place a trans-woman in a female housing unit even though she still possesses male genitalia?
- Do we house a person with female physical characteristics but a male gender identity with males?

hormone treatments (*Wolfe v. Horn,* 130 F.Supp.2d 648 [E.D.Pa. 2001]; *Kosilek v. Maloney,* 221 F.Supp2d 156 [D. Mass. 2002]). For example, one decision holds that transsexualism [transgenderism] has been characterized as a "serious medical need." But little has been said thus far concerning the continuation of surgical procedures. Advocates of the transgender community would argue for continuation based on the negative psychological and physical impact of stopping the process. For jails holding inmates for periods of a year or less, this may be considered to have minimal impact. However, some jails house inmates for five years or more; what are their responsibilities then?

Conclusion

Transgender persons have the same rights and deserve the same protections as any other arrestees. By asking the right questions and treating a transgender person with respect, jails can avoid conflict during the booking process and decrease the risk of lawsuits.

References

American Psychiatric Association. (2000). *Diagnostic and statistical manual of mental disorders* (4th ed., text rev.). Washington, DC: Author.

Quinones, S. (2012, April 15). LAPD plans separate jail for transgender suspects. *The Los Angeles Times.* Retrieved from http://articles.latimes.com/2012/apr/15/local/la-me-transgender-lockup-20120415

Turnbull, L. (2006, December 21). County adopts guidelines on transgender inmates. *The Seattle Times.*

Author's Note

During the research for this [reading], several California jails were contacted. The topic raised some very spirited conversations and provided much food for thought among jail managers and administrators who are in the process of reviewing their own policies.

Post-Reading Questions

1 What distinctions—if any—are there between the terms "transgender" and "gender identity"?

2 Within a correctional institution, who should have the responsibility to determine the arrestee's gender? Would you allow transgendered arrestees to assist in this determination? Be sure to qualify your position.

3 Should we house inmates differently based on transgender status and gender identity? Be sure to qualify your position.

4 What are some of the difficulties associated with managing transgender inmates?

5 How would you go about developing a protocol for housing transgendered inmates?

Correctional Treatment

Developing a Successful Program

Wesley Wagner

U nless a paroled person commits a terrible crime or a news article reports the possible early release of a number of convicted felons because of overcrowding, correctional treatment is not discussed beyond the world of corrections or criminal justice. For the majority of people, corrections is an "out of sight, out of mind" or "as long as it is not in my back yard" topic. This should not be the case. Because the vast majority of people whom we send to correctional facilities ultimately return to their communities, it should be everyone's concern. The correctional treatment that offenders receive during their incarceration determines how productive they will be as members of society or whether they become part of the high recidivism rate. This [reading] discusses correctional treatment programs that are being used in correctional facilities and whether they help inmates become better individuals.

Barriers to Implementation

Change is a constant in everyone's life. This is especially true in correctional treatment programs—after all, their goal is to change an offender's life habits. However, this change can also affect the work assignments of correctional staff and the manner in which they perform their duties. To understand this process, correctional staff must look at their own lives, recall how hard it is to initiate change, and be willing to be part of that change (Latessa, 2004). This is the first step toward successful change for both inmates and staff.

Before a correctional treatment program is implemented, it must be approved by the facility's administration. Not only does the evidence-based practice on which it is based need to be explained, but the administration has to know how the program will work and how the outcome is better for society (Latessa, 2004). Even though policymakers maintain a tough stance on crime, public opinion still strongly supports effective offender rehabilitation programs. However, the public also wants a tough stance on crime; therefore, rehabilitation programs must not appear to have a soft approach to crime (Latessa, 2004).

One of the most common difficulties encountered when initiating change is the lack of information communicated to line staff. To encourage a positive response, the presentation of a new treatment program must show staff how the program will improve the safety and security of the institution and the role they will play in the success of the program (Latessa, 2004).

Leadership is another key component in the implementation of a successful correctional treatment program. Because they are the ones who manage programs on a daily basis, frontline supervisors must be directly involved in the program—from the developmental stage through implementation (Latessa, 2004). When supervisors have an important role in a treatment program, they can demonstrate to staff how the program should be managed.

Risk Factors

Risk factors are the most important consideration for a correctional agency when looking at ways to develop successful treatment programs. Different risk factors have different effects and each is treated differently. Risk factors that most classification tools consider are:

- **Static.** These are factors in an offender's past that cannot be changed. They can predict the likelihood that an individual will recidivate. Some examples of these factors are age, previous convictions (both type and frequency), and age at first incarceration (Gendreau, Little, & Goggin, 1996).

- **Dynamic.** These are the factors that can change and that are regarded as suitable areas for improvement in correctional treatment. These criminological needs include antisocial cognitions, values, and behaviors (Gendreau et al., 1996).

When deciding on acceptable risk, both static and dynamic factors should be considered. Static factors determine whether an offender is a good candidate for treatment. Dynamic factors direct the treatment itself by changing offenders' criminological needs and reducing the likelihood of their future criminal behavior.

Four additional risk factors specifically help to predict criminal activity:

- **Antisocial behavior history.** If an offender has a history of antisocial behavior, correctional staff should consider the number of times the offender was involved in antisocial behavior (Andrews & Bonta, 2010). Examples of antisocial behavior are arrests, convictions, probation violations, and behavior while institutionalized.

- **Antisocial personality pattern.** If an offender has an antisocial personality pattern, the offender's behavior may be impulsive and pleasure seeking, and he or she has no regard for the feelings and well-being of others (Andrews & Bonta, 2010).

- **Antisocial cognition.** This thought process rationalizes the criminal activity in the mind of an offender. For example, offenders might think that victims deserve what they got and that the criminal justice system is corrupt and already stacked against them.

- **Antisocial associates.** These are other individuals who support an offender's criminal behavior (Andrews & Bonta, 2010).

Effective Intervention

Effective intervention is achieved through well-designed, established programs that involve four principles: risk, need, treatment, and fidelity. Programs that use these principles have seen a reduction in recidivism at a significant level (Latessa & Lowenkamp, 2006). Research shows that a well-planned program can reduce recidivism more than punishment alone (Latessa & Lowenkamp, 2006).

Risk

Under this principle, those classified as most at risk for recidivism are targeted for treatment. High-risk offenders are more likely to be antisocial. When they do socialize, it is with individuals who also exhibit criminal behavior. On the other hand, a low-risk offender has a good social background and friends who avoid getting into trouble with the law (Latessa & Lowenkamp, 2006). Because low-risk offenders are less at risk for committing another crime, facilities would do well to budget their money for offenders with a high risk of recidivism. Additionally, because of the antisocial and criminal behavior of high-risk offenders, low-risk offenders should be separated from high-risk offenders (Latessa & Lowenkamp, 2006).

Need

The need principle looks at an offender's actual need for correctional treatment. It targets the factors that can lead an individual to crime, such as antisocial peer association, drug or alcohol abuse, antisocial traits, and values and beliefs that are criminal in nature (Latessa & Lowenkamp,

2006). The program then addresses an offender's needs through physical fitness, self-esteem, and other factors that are not part of the offender's criminal pattern (Latessa & Lowenkamp, 2006).

Treatment

The treatment principle considers how to achieve the best results from treatment. This is specifically done with programs that are behavior-oriented (Latessa & Lowenkamp, 2006). Such programs are successful because they concentrate on present circumstances and the risk factors that control an offender's behavior. Instead of trying to correct past transgressions (although therapeutic, this does not mitigate an individual's criminal nature), the program works toward changing the current risks associated with crime (Latessa & Lowenkamp, 2006). The second part of this principle provides treatment that is action-oriented, not simply discussion. Treatment programs that involve kinesthetic learning—where offenders actually practice and learn problem-solving skills—have been shown to effectively reduce recidivism (Latessa & Lowenkamp, 2006).

Fidelity

The fidelity principle is a catch-all principle. Program integrity and quality contribute to the effectiveness of a program. An offender's motivation to participate in a program also ensures a better chance of success. Employee training is part of this principle to ensure continuity and belief in the program. To reinforce the program's message when the treatment has concluded, a proper after-care system for offenders should be established. All of these factors allow the program to achieve maximum effectiveness if the program has been delivered in its entirety. According to recent studies, if the program is not delivered in its entirety, this increases rather than decreases the recidivism rate (Latessa & Lowenkamp, 2006).

Cognitive-Behavioral Therapy

A number of studies identify treatments that work best for reducing recidivism. At the top of the list is cognitive-behavioral therapy (CBT). Two major meta-analyses by different researchers have proven that CBT contributes to a drop of between 20 and 30 percent in recidivism rates compared to control groups (Landenberger & Lipsey, 2005).

Although CBT programming varies and each program may provide different types of treatment, CBT develops the decision-making process of offenders. They learn how to think before acting and how to evaluate the consequences of their actions. CBT teaches offenders a more

MONEYBALL AND CORRECTIONS

In his book, *Moneyball*, Michael Lewis looks at the evidence-based practices used by Billy Beane to produce a winning season for the Oakland A's, even as he dealt with budget concerns. Cullen, Myer, and Latessa (2009) point out eight lessons that corrections professionals can learn from evidence-based baseball and the *Moneyball* program.

- As with the Oakland A's, the correctional world is under a budget constraint crisis. Because of this, it is important to use programs that have a proven success rate because high-risk offenders who go without treatment have a high likelihood of committing more crimes.

- Before *Moneyball*, baseball, like corrections, was based on custom rather than scientific evidence. Because of a lack of scientific knowledge on building correctional treatment programs, a lot of correctional programs have failed.

- In corrections, appearances are sometimes more important than the actual effectiveness of a program. Many programs have been implemented because of how they look and not for their actual success with offenders.

- The wrong theory leads to stupid decisions. An example of this in corrections is the belief that offenders' low self-esteem causes their criminal activity. Programs that try to boost self-esteem have proved to be a waste of time. Corrections needs programs based on empirical evidence that demonstrate crime deterrence.

- Actuarial data lead to better choices and decisions than personal experience or gut feelings. When making a

socially acceptable understanding of the law. Through activities and exercises, CBT restructures the distortions and errors that characterize criminal thought processes. Interpersonal conflict and peer pressure are resolved through interpersonal problem solving.

The offender's social skills are guided toward more socially acceptable behaviors. Offenders learn how to consider the effects of their actions on other people. In addition, they learn how to identify the triggers that spark their anger and ways to control that anger. The offenders learn to better understand right and wrong and develop moral reasoning with training. By using behavior contracts, behavior modification can be achieved and appropriate behavior can be reinforced. Offenders gain the ability to recognize and cope with situations that could return them to criminal behavior and they learn how to halt these situations through relapse prevention. Individual attention such as one-on-one counseling is also used to reinforce group treatment (Landenberger & Lipsey, 2005).

The most influential aspects of CBT programs were studied in this order: individual attention, anger control, and cognitive restructuring (Landenberger & Lipsey, 2005). The information provided in these programs is not the only important factor. The total amount of time spent in a program is also a major factor. The number of treatment sessions per week, the actual hours in treatment per week, total hours of treatment, and total duration of treatment in weeks were analyzed. The studies concluded that total hours had the most positive overall effect on the efficacy of the programs, and the duration of the programs in weeks had the smallest effect (Landenberger & Lipsey, 2005).

Successful Parameters

The parameters of a successful CBT program come from a meta-analysis of 97 correctional programs and 13,676 offenders. The first parameter is to target the right kind of offenders to receive the maximum effect from the correctional program. This is done by using one of the classification tools that assesses the risk-level of the offender in terms of recidivism (Lowenkamp, Latessa, & Holsinger, 2006). High-risk offenders have shown the best results in treatment programs compared to low-risk offenders.

The length of a program is another important parameter. High-risk offenders need to be in treatment longer than low-risk offenders. Very few programs consider the offenders' risk level when deciding the duration of a program (Lowenkamp et al., 2006). High-risk offenders are classified as high risk because of the factors that increase their criminal lifestyle. Any program designed for this group should target more than one of these risk factors.

Because so much emphasis is placed on duration of treatment, one of the biggest challenges is sentencing guidelines in the courts. Will the high-risk offender have enough time for a program to be effective? This is why sentence length and the type of services offered should be considered when assessing an offender's risk level (Lowenkamp et al., 2006). Of course, the most important parameter of a successful criminal justice program is the number of options available to the sentencing judge. A good classification instrument can be used to determine an offender's risk factor. However, unless the judge has many options from which to choose, the classification process is a waste of time.

Thinking for a Change

One CBT program that has been effective is Thinking for a Change (TFAC), developed by Bush, Glick, and Taymans in 1997 (Lowenkamp, Hubbard, Makarios, & Latessa, 2009). TFAC integrates two types of CBT treatments: cognitive skills and cognitive restructuring. It teaches pro-social skills and attitudes through problem solving (Lowenkamp et al., 2009). The program consists of 22 lessons that range from basic, such as active listening and learning to ask appropriate questions and other important social skills, to more complex restructuring techniques such as recognizing the types of thinking that lead to criminal behavior, and understanding how actions affect others (Lowenkamp et al., 2009). In this way, the TFAC program demonstrates the importance of interpersonal communication skills and helps offenders develop such skills. The offender also learns how to overcome thought patterns that lead to criminal behavior.

Evidence-based Practices

There are many barriers to the implementation of evidence-based practices. First, everyone must recognize that change is difficult. Offenders who are receiving treatment will have difficulty changing; however, correctional personnel need to understand that even for them, change is hard (Latessa,

decision about an offender, all the data must be reviewed to avoid mistakes. Making a decision without considering the evidence is irresponsible and a travesty of justice.

- Those who oppose the treatment model in corrections use destructive techniques to defeat the use of evidence-based approaches. People who are against correctional treatment will hold its successes to impossible standards of proof.

- A major cost is associated with correctional facilities ignoring programs whose success has been scientifically proven.

- The final lesson of *Moneyball* for the world of corrections is that evidence-based practices are going to be hard to ignore.

More and more programs are reporting success with evidence-based corrections; it will be hard for anyone involved in the development of these programs not to take note.

Source: Cullen, F. T., Myer, A. J., & Latessa, E. J. (2009). Eight lessons learned from *Moneyball* The high cost of ignoring evidence-based corrections. *Victim and Offenders Journal of Evidence-Based Policies & Practices*, 4.197–213.

2004). A second barrier is convincing stakeholders to invest completely in the program. Although the general public is receptive to effective programs, policymakers are not always as confident. Because they are the front line in providing treatment, correctional and treatment staff should actively promote the program. To gain stakeholder confidence, staff may need to provide an explanation of the program with evidence showing that the program is effective. All leadership levels of the program—top to bottom—must be involved and interact on a day-to-day basis. A communication breakdown at any level causes a program to be ineffective (Latessa, 2004).

Successes and Failures

Over the years, a number of programs have helped reduce recidivism. Although they have different names, the umbrella of CBT covers them all. Each program is linked by some basic understandings and guidelines. The Canadian theory of rehabilitation uses the same principles:

- A social psychological perspective is used to focus on the causes of recidivism (Cullen & Gendreau, 2000).
- The programs target the known predictors of recidivism, especially dynamic risk factors that can be changed.
- CBT is used.
- Offenders are matched to a program that complements them the most (Cullen, Myer, & Latessa, 2009).
- The program ensures that only high-risk offenders are targeted because this is the most successful area.
- Staff must ensure that therapeutic integrity is engrained in the intervention program (Cullen et al., 2009).

Conclusion

With the economic downturn, local, State, and Federal agencies are challenged to find ways to decrease the incarcerated population. The common "get-tough" attitude on crime has not proven to reduce recidivism. Although both offenders and staff may resist change, different studies and parameters being introduced in correctional facilities across the Nation indicate that change is necessary. By classifying offenders with specific risk factors and applying the principles of effective intervention, correctional programming such as CBT and TFAC has produced successful results. Not only offenders benefit from this therapy, but also correctional facilities, correctional staff, and communities.

References

Andrews, D., & Bonta, J. (2010). *The psychology of criminal conduct* (5th ed.). New Providence, NJ: Mathew Bender & Company.

Andrews, D., Zinger, I., Hoge, R., Bonta, J., Gendreau, P., & Cullen, F. (1990). Does correctional treatment work? A clinically relevant and psychologically informed meta-analysis. *Criminology, 28*(3), 369–404.

Cullen, F. T. & Gendreau, P. (2000). Assessing correctional rehabilitation: Policy, practice, and prospects. In Horny, J., Martin, J., Peterson, R., & Rosenbaum, D. (Eds.). *Policies, processes, and decisions of the criminal justice system* (Vol. 3). Washington, DC: U.S. Department of Justice.

Cullen, F. T., Myer, A. J., & Latessa, E. J. (2009). Eight lessons learned from *Moneyball*: The high cost of ignoring evidence-based corrections. *Victim and Offenders Journal of Evidence-Based Policies & Practices, 4.* 197–213.

Gendreau, P., Little, R., & Goggin, C. (1996). A meta-analysis of the predictors of adult offender recidivism: What works! *Criminology, 34*(4), 48–69.

Landenberger, N. A., & Lipsey, M. W. (2005). The positive effects of cognitive behavioral programs for offenders: A meta analysis of factors associated with effective treatment. *Journal of Experimental Criminology.* Retrieved from http://restorativejustice.pbworks.com/f/Landenberger_Lipsey.pdf

Latessa, E. J. (2004). The challenge of change: Correctional programs and evidenced-based practices. *Criminology & Public Policy, 3*(4), 547–560.

Latessa, E. J., Cullen, F. T., & Gendreau, P. (2002). Beyond correctional quackery: Professional responsibility for evidence-based practice. *Federal Probation, 66*(2), 43–49.

Latessa, E. J., & Lowenkamp, C. (2006). What works in reducing recidivism. *St. Thomas Law Journal, 3*(3), 521–535.

Lowenkamp, C. T., Latessa, E. J., & Holsinger, A. (2006). The risk principle in action: What we have learned from 13,676 offenders and 97 correctional programs. *Crime & Delinquency* 51(1), 77–93.

Lowenkamp, C. T., Hubbard, D., Makarios, M. D., & Latessa, E. J. (2009). A quasi-experimental evaluation of thinking for a change: A "real world" application. *Criminal Justice & Behavior* 36(2), 137–146.

Lowenkamp, C. T., Latessa, E., & P. Smith (2006). Does correctional program quality really matter? The impact of adhering to the principles of effective intervention. *Criminology & Public Policy,* 5(3), 575–594.

Post-Reading Questions

1   What is meant by the author's assertion that corrections exist in an "out of sight, out of mind" atmosphere. What are some recent incidents that appear to counter this assertion?

2   Based on past research, what are some common difficulties encountered when initiating change within correctional institutions?

3   Risk factors are an important consideration in the development of successful prison programs. How does your author distinguish between static and dynamic risk factors?

4   Most prison programs are developed with the inmate in mind and appear to ignore the needs of correctional staff. What are some needs and limitations associated with correctional staff that should also be addressed?

5   What can be done to create job opportunities for newly released offenders to ensure their successful re-entry and lower the chances for recidivism?

PART V

THE PROMISE OF CULTURAL DIVERSITY

"A LOT OF DIFFERENT FLOWERS MAKE
A BOUQUET"

– *Muslim Origin*

Dismantling the School-to-Prison Pipeline

A Survey from the Field

Matt Cregor and Damon Hewitt

Our nation's school discipline rates have reached all-time highs. As suspension, expulsion and school-based arrest rates grow, racial disparities in discipline continue to widen. Despite a wealth of research on the harms of these exclusionary discipline practices and their ties to school push-out, media outlets are filled with stories of ever younger students being suspended, expelled or arrested for matters that, prior to "zero tolerance" disciplinary policies, were once handled by a call home. As the "School-to-Prison Pipeline" reaches a crisis stage, both new and familiar voices are emerging to reform school discipline. Here we review recent research on school discipline and highlight promising efforts to eliminate racial disciplinary disparities and dismantle the School-to-Prison Pipeline.

A Current Look at the School-to-Prison Pipeline

According to the most recent data from the U.S. Department of Education's Office for Civil Rights (OCR), over 3 million students are suspended at least once each year and over 100,000 are expelled. U.S. public school discipline rates have never been higher—roughly double today what they were in the 1970s. In *Test, Punish, and Pushout,* Advancement Project (www.advancementproject.org) provides some alarming glimpses into school discipline trends at the local level:

- In Chicago, the number of out-of-school suspensions quadrupled to 93,312 between 2001 and 2007.

- In Texas, more than 128,000 students were pushed out of school and into alternative schools in 2007.
- In Pennsylvania, the number of school-based arrests almost tripled between 1999 and 2006, to 12,918.

Racial disparities in discipline continue to widen.

With these absurd numbers also come appalling stories. Last year, national media covered the arrest of a 12-year-old in New York for doodling on her desk with an erasable marker and the long-term suspension of a six-year-old in Delaware for bringing his Boy Scout knife for show-and-tell.

High disciplinary rates persist despite a significant body of research on the harms of exclusionary discipline. The American Academy of Pediatrics found that suspension and expulsion jeopardize children's health and safety and may exacerbate academic failure. The Centers for Disease Control & Prevention found that out-of-school youth are more likely to be retained a grade, drop out of school, become teen parents, and engage in delinquent behavior. Indeed, a 2003 study by Robert Balfanz found that school suspension is a top predictor for those students incarcerated by ninth grade. Beyond impacting those excluded, the American Psychological Association (APA) found that zero tolerance policies fail to make schools safer and that schools with high suspension rates score worse on standardized tests. In a recent publication in *Educational Researcher,* Anne Gregory, Russ Skiba and Pedro Noguera explore the connection between racial disparities in discipline and educational achievement.

Race continues to play a central role in school discipline. In *Race is Not Neutral,* a forthcoming publication, Russ Skiba reviewed the disciplinary data of over 400 elementary and middle schools from across the country and found that African-American and Latino students received harsher punishments for similar misbehavior than their white peers. In related research, Skiba found that students of color were disproportionately disciplined for "subjective" offenses (e.g., "disrespect"), while their white peers were disproportionately disciplined for "objective" offenses (e.g., smoking). According to OCR, African-American students are nearly 3 times as likely to be suspended and 3.5 times as likely to be expelled as their white peers. Latino students are 1.5 times as likely to be suspended and twice as likely to be expelled as their white peers.

Disparities in discipline encompass all of our nation's historically disenfranchised youth. The APA found that students with disabilities are disciplined at a rate roughly twice that of their non-disabled peers. In November 2010, the *New York Times* reported that gay and lesbian students receive harsher punishment than their straight peers in school disciplinary matters. Recent research suggests that disciplinary rates and disparities may be most pronounced in the middle school grades. [...]

School administrators' approaches to discipline play a significant role in disciplinary activity. In *Opportunities Suspended,* Advancement Project and the UCLA Civil Rights Project found that building principals used exclusionary discipline in direct proportion to their stated support for zero tolerance disciplinary practices. (The University of Virginia's Youth Violence Project—http:// youth violence.ed school.virginia.edu—has done excellent related research, examining how schools with similar demographics can have such divergent discipline rates.)

Federal and state laws and policies also play a significant role in shaping the disciplinary practices at the school level. While the Gun-Free Schools Act of 1994 may have inspired the proliferation of zero tolerance policies, a number of more recent laws and grant opportunities continue to incentivize exclusionary approaches to discipline. The U.S. Department of Justice's Community Oriented Policing Services ("COPS") grants provide funds for school districts to hire or staff law enforcement at their schools. While such grants are intended to further school safety, school arrests are skyrocketing as schools have come to rely on law enforcement to handle routine disciplinary matters. Such over-reliance on school police recently led the Florida legislature to amend its zero tolerance statute to limit the types of infractions for which a student could be arrested.

Aspects of the No Child Left Behind Act (NCLB) contribute to the Pipeline as well, and U.S. suspension and expulsion rates have spiked since the law's enactment. While NCLB correctly "shined the light" on educational disparities along racial, language, disability and socioeconomic lines, the law's accountability structure, with its narrow focus on standardized test scores, has given schools the perverse incentive to push out those students who exhibit challenging behavior or who do not meet testing standards. In December 2010, a group of organizations released a position paper recommending policy changes for the reauthorization of the Elementary and Secondary Education Act (ESEA) as a means to begin dismantling the Pipeline through federal law. To review and endorse the paper, please visit Fair Test's website at www.fairtest.org and email stop schoolstojails@advancementproject.org by January 31, 2011.

Turning the Tide: Steps toward Dismantling the School-to-Prison Pipeline

Although national trends show disciplinary rates on the rise, an increasingly diverse group of stakeholders has begun to turn the tide on exclusionary discipline at the state and local levels. Teachers unions in Los Angeles and Ohio have advocated for better classroom management practices. Juvenile courts are working with school districts to reduce school-based arrests. Parent, student, civil rights and human rights organizations have secured meaningful changes at the local, state and federal levels. For example:

A wealth of research shows the harms of exclusionary discipline.

- In Denver, Padres y Jóvenes Unidos, a parent and student organizing group, led a multi-year campaign that resulted in significant changes to Denver Public Schools' discipline code and practices. Denver's new code is premised on the principles of restorative justice—techniques for de-escalating and resolving conflicts and strengthening bonds between students, their peers and their teachers. The code restricts the types of offenses for which students can be suspended, expelled and arrested. Padres y Jóvenes Unidos also partnered with Denver Public Schools to obtain a grant for professional development in restorative justice. As a result, the district's arrest rate is down significantly and its suspension rate is down 44%. See *Education on Lockdown*, a joint publication by Padres y Jóvenes Unidos and Advancement Project, for more information (www.advancementproject.org). See the International Institute for Restorative Practices website for additional information and case studies on restorative practices: www.iirp.org.

- To address spiraling school arrest rates in Clayton County, Georgia, the local juvenile court assembled representatives from the county's school district, law enforcement agencies and mental health agencies to develop a "school offense protocol." The protocol limits the types of arrestable infractions and provides alternatives to court referral for school officers. Both school safety and student achievement have improved since implementation: Incidents of weapons possession are down 70% while the district's graduation rate is up 20%.

- In Los Angeles, CADRE, a parent organizing group, secured passage of Los Angeles Unified School District's *Discipline Foundation Policy*. The policy is built on human rights principles and calls for the district-wide implementation of Positive Behavior Supports (PBS)—an evidence-based approach to improving school discipline shown to reduce disciplinary incidents, support gains in academic achievement, and improve staff morale and perceptions of school safety (www.pbis.org). PBS implementation has led to significant reductions in exclusionary discipline in some L.A. schools. However, failure to implement and enforce the policy district-wide leaves many schools that could benefit most from the policy no different than they were before its adoption. CADRE members and allies have investigated the district's implementation efforts and recently released a shadow report on what the school district must do to fulfill its promises under its PBS policy (www.cadre-la.org).

At press time, a broad coalition of advocates and community groups secured unanimous passage of the Student Safety Act in the New York City Council. The Act requires reporting of school-based arrests, summonses and other forms of exclusionary discipline. (www.nyclu.org)

While districts like those described above are implementing school-wide strategies for reducing exclusionary discipline, more must be done to eliminate the racial disciplinary disparities. PBS, for instance, has been found to reduce suspensions for students of all races at similar rates, but PBS implementation alone does not close racial disciplinary gaps. Schools in the Midwest are combining best practices like PBS with focused efforts to address racial bias. After being cited for racially disproportionate placements in special education, Eau Claire Public Schools in Wisconsin melded its PBS efforts with "beyond diversity" trainings and trainings in culturally responsive pedagogy. The district's disciplinary rates and racial disparities are down significantly. Alton Middle School in Illinois combined similar practices along with restorative justice training to reduce its out-of-school suspension rate, and its discipline and achievement disparities are narrowing (see the December 2009 Newsletter of the Illinois PBIS Network, the country's largest network of PBS schools: www.pbisillinois.org). Indiana University's Equity Project is piloting similar efforts toward Culturally Responsive PBIS in Indiana schools. (http://www.indiana.edu/−equity/index.php)

To reduce racial disparities in discipline, OCR has stepped up collection of disciplinary data and its enforcement of Title VI. (See the PRRAC Researcher Report in [...] *P&R* for more on OCR's renewed Title VI enforcement efforts. Visit www.wakehelp.org for information on a recent Title VI complaint that involves disciplinary disparities in Wake County, NC.) Beyond Title VI, a number of promising legal strategies are developing to challenge the School-to-Prison Pipeline in state and federal courts. For example, the Southern Poverty Law Center has employed class administrative complaints under the Individuals with Disabilities Education Act (IDEA) to win district-wide implementation of PBS and other practices. For a survey of current legal strategies to address the Pipeline, see *The School-to-Prison Pipeline: Structuring Legal Reform,* a book released in late 2010 by Catherine Kim, Dan Losen & Damon Hewitt (New York University Press).

Despite a shifting Congressional landscape, a number of efforts are under way on Capitol Hill to effect school discipline reform through federal law. The Congressional Black Caucus has stated that reforming zero tolerance and reducing racial disciplinary disparities are among its consensus priorities for ESEA reauthorization. Rep. Carolyn McCarthy (D-NY) has introduced legislation (H.R. 5628) to ban corporal punishment for all schools receiving federal funds, and to provide grant funds for PBS implementation. The ACLU and Human Rights Watch released an excellent report on corporal punishment in schools: *Impairing Education*—www.aclu.org. Senator Michael Bennet (D-CO) has introduced a bipartisan bill (S. 3733) that calls for additional use of PBS in state education plans. A number of community organizations, educators and civil rights groups have come together under the umbrella of the Dignity in Schools Campaign and the Alliance for Educational Justice to prioritize discipline reform in the ESEA context.

Federal and state laws and policies play a significant role.

Much work remains to address exclusionary discipline policies and related disparities, but more than a decade's work by community organizers, researchers, educators and advocates is beginning to show great progress in dismantling the School-to-Prison Pipeline.

Resources

Catherine Kim, Daniel Losen & Damon Hewitt. 2010. *The School-to-Prison Pipeline: Structuring Legal Reform.* New York: New York University Press.

Robert Balfanz et al. 2003. "High Poverty Secondary Schools and the Juvenile Justice System," in Johanna Wald & Daniel Losen, eds., *Deconstructing The School to Prison Pipeline*. San Francisco: Jossey-Bass, 77–78.

The Alliance for Educational Justice: www.allianceforeducationaljustice.org

The Dignity in Schools Campaign: www.dignityinschools.com

NAACP Legal Defense and Educational Fund, Inc: www.naacpldf.org

www.schooltoprison.org (a password-protected legal forum on pipeline issues)

Advancement Project/Stop the Schoolhouse-to-Jailhouse Track: www.stopschoolstojails.org

Poverty & Race (July/Aug. 2005) has a series of articles on the school-to-prison pipeline. Back issue available at www.prrac.org

American Bar Association. 2009. *Resolution 118A: The Right to a High-Quality Educational Program; Resolution 118B: The Right to Remain in School; 118C: The Right to Resume Education.* www.abanet.org

Post-Reading Questions

1   What factors account for racial disparities in school discipline?

2   What is the theorized connection between school discipline and eventual incarceration? What are some differences between those who are disciplined—even expelled—yet remain law abiding?

3   How do the principles of restorative justice help remedy exclusionary disciplinary practices?

4   In what ways might cultural diversity training and culturally responsive pedagogy impact racial disparities in disciplinary practices?

5   As a school administrator, what would you do to address racial disparities in school disciplinary practices?

Breaking the Cycle

Implicit Bias, Racial Anxiety, and Stereotype Threat

Rachel D. Godsil

Our country is in the midst of a racial cataclysm. Deaths of black men and boys at the hands of police, combined with grand juries' failure to indict, have spurred grief, rage and protest across the country. The reactions to the events are not uniform, however. A deep polarization along racial lines has emerged that contributes to the feeling among many people of color that black lives don't matter.

Neither these tragedies nor the racial disconnect that followed occur in isolation. People of color experience obstacles rooted in racial or ethnic difference with alarming frequency. And yet most Americans espouse values of racial fairness. How can we make sense of these seeming contradictions? And how can we work to change the conditions that set the stage for daily challenges and tragic endings that are linked to race?

In November 2014, the Perception Institute, along with the Haas Institute for a Fair and Inclusive Society, and the Center for Police Equity, issued the first in a series of reports entitled, *The Science of Equality: Addressing Implicit Bias, Racial Anxiety, and Stereotype Threat in Education and Health Care,* co-authored by Rachel Godsil, Linda Tropp, Phillip Atiba Goff and john powell. The goal of this series of reports is to synthesize and make accessible the advances in neuroscience, social psychology and other "mind sciences" that have provided insight into otherwise confounding contradictions between our country's stated commitment to fairness and the behaviors that lead both to tragic outcomes and day-to-day indignities linked to race.

Our report includes a lengthy discussion of social psychological research focusing on "implicit bias"—the automatic association of stereotypes or attitudes with particular social groups. We place particular emphasis on new research on reducing bias or, as Patricia Devine and colleagues describe, "Breaking the Prejudice Habit" (Devine 2014) and research identifying best practices to prevent implicit bias from affecting decision-making and behavior.

Understanding implicit bias can help explain why a black criminal defendant charged with the same crime as a white defendant may receive a more draconian sentence, or why a resume from someone named Emily will receive more callbacks than an otherwise identical resume from someone named Lakeisha. This work confirms that people of color whose experiences of the world make abundantly clear that "race matters" are not simply oversensitive, while also explaining how whites who consider themselves non-racist may be sincere, even if their behavior sometimes suggests otherwise.

This is not meant to suggest that racialized outcomes are only a result of individual actions; cumulative racial advantages for whites as a group have been embedded into society's structures and institutions. However, as john powell and I argued in these pages in 2011 ("Implicit Bias Insights as Preconditions to Structural Change," *P&R,* Sept./Oct. 2011), there are two key reasons why structural racism cannot be successfully challenged without an understanding of how race operates psychologically. First, public policy choices are often affected by implicit bias or other racialized phenomena that operate implicitly. As a result, the changes in policy necessary to address institutional structures are dependent upon successfully addressing implicit biases that can affect political choices. Second, institutional operations invariably involve human behavior and interaction: Any policies to address racial inequities in schools, workplaces, police departments, courthouses, government offices and the like will only be successful if the people implementing the policy changes comply with them (Crosby & Monin, 2007).

Although implicit phenomena have the potential to impede successful institutional change, implicit racial bias is not the only psychological phenomenon that blocks society from achieving racial equality. We risk being myopic if we focus only on people's cognitive processing, and we also risk unintended consequences if we focus our interventions only on addressing implicit bias. Our experiences, motivations and emotions are also integral to how we navigate racial interactions. These can translate into racial anxiety and stereotype threat which, independent of bias, can create obstacles for institutions and individuals seeking to adhere to antiracist practices. Indeed, research suggests that some forms of anti-bias education may have detrimental effects, if they increase *bias awareness* without also providing skills for managing anxiety.

Racial anxiety refers to discomfort about the experience and potential consequences of interracial interactions. It is important to distinguish this definition of racial anxiety from what social scientists refer to as "racial threat," which includes the anger, frustration, uncertainty, feelings of deprivation and other emotions associated with concern over loss of resources or dominance. People of color may experience racial anxiety that they will be the target of discrimination and hostile treatment. White people tend to experience anxiety that they will be assumed to be racist and will be met with distrust or hostility. Whites experiencing racial anxiety can seem awkward and maintain less eye contact with people of color, and ultimately these interactions tend to be shorter than those without anxiety. If two people are both anxious that an interaction will be negative, it often is. So racial anxiety can result in a negative feedback loop in which both parties' fears seem to be confirmed by the behavior of the other.

Skills are needed for managing racial anxiety.

Stereotype threat refers to the pressure people feel when they fear that their performance may confirm a negative stereotype about their group (Steele, 2010). This pressure is experienced as a distraction that interferes with intellectual functioning. Although stereotype threat can affect anyone, it has been most discussed in the context of academic achievement among students of color, and among girls in science, technology, engineering and math (STEM) fields. Less commonly explored is the idea that whites can suffer stereotype threat when concerned that they may be perceived as racist. In the former context, the threat prevents students from performing as well as they ought, and so they themselves suffer the consequences of this phenomenon. Stereotype threat among whites, by contrast, often causes behavior that harms others—usually the very people they are worried about. Concern about being perceived as racist explains, for example, why some white teachers, professors and supervisors give less critical feedback to black students and employees than to white ones (Harber et al., 2012) and why white peer advisors may fail to warn a black student but will warn a white or Asian student that a certain course load is unmanageable (Crosby & Monin, 2007).

In other words, cognitive depletion or interference caused by stereotype threat can affect how one's own *capacity*, such as the ability to achieve academically, will be judged; this causes first-party harm to the individual whose performance suffers. However, as is explored in more detail below, stereotype threat about how one's *character* will be judged (i.e., being labeled a racist) can cause third-party harms when suffered by an individual in a position of power.

Implicit bias, racial anxiety and stereotype threat have effects in virtually every important area of our lives. In the first report, we illustrate the interrelated implications of the three phenomena in the domains of education and healthcare. Education and healthcare are of critical importance for obvious reasons, and an abundance of research has highlighted the role race plays in unequal outcomes in both domains.

The report also emphasizes the interventions that are emerging in the research that institutions can begin to use to prevent continuing racialized obstacles. Ideally, this work will happen at the structural and institutional level—but many of us don't want to wait, and the social science research shows that we are not wholly without agency or tools. The interventions described below can, even in absence of wide-scale institutional change, help individual teachers or medical providers begin at least to ameliorate implicit bias, racial anxiety and stereotype threat.

"Debiasing" and Preventing Effects of Implicit Bias

While the research on debiasing is fairly new, recent studies by Patricia Devine and colleagues have found success in reducing implicit racial bias, increasing concern about discrimination and awareness of personal bias by combining multiple interventions to "break the prejudice habit." The strategies quoted below (thoughtfully utilizing findings from research by Nilanjana Dasgupta and others) included:

- *Stereotype replacement:* Recognizing that a response is based on stereotypes, labeling the response as stereotypical and reflecting on why the response occurred creates a process to consider how the biased response could be avoided in the future and replaces it with an unbiased response.
- *Counter-stereotypic imaging:* Imagining counter-stereotypic others in detail makes positive exemplars salient and accessible when challenging a stereotype's validity.
- *Individuation*: Obtaining specific information about group members prevents stereotypic inferences.
- *Perspective-taking:* Imagining oneself to be a member of a stereotyped group increases psychological closeness to the stereotyped group, which ameliorates automatic group-based evaluations.
- *Increasing opportunities for contact:* Increased contact between groups can ameliorate implicit bias through a wide variety of mechanisms, including altering their images of the group or by directly improving evaluations of the group.

The data showing reduced bias from Devine and colleagues "provide the first evidence that a controlled, randomized intervention can produce enduring reductions in implicit bias" (Devine et al. 2012). The findings have been replicated by Devine and colleagues, and further studies will be in print in 2015.

Whites can also suffer stereotype threat.

Preventing Implicit Bias from Affecting Behavior

To the extent that debiasing is an uphill challenge in light of the tenacity of negative stereotypes and attitudes about race, institutions can also establish practices to prevent these biases from seeping into decision-making. Jerry Kang and a group of researchers (Kang et al. 2012) developed the following list of interventions that have been found to be constructive:

Doubt Objectivity: Presuming oneself to be objective actually tends to increase the role of implicit bias; teaching people about non-conscious thought processes will lead people to be skeptical of their own objectivity and better able to guard against biased evaluations.

Increase Motivation to be Fair: Internal motivations to be fair rather than fear of external judgments tend to decrease biased actions.

Improve Conditions of Decision-making: Implicit biases are a function of automaticity (Daniel Kahneman's "thinking fast"—Kahneman, 2013). Thinking slow by engaging in mindful, deliberate processing and not in the throes of emotions prevents our implicit biases from kicking in and determining our behaviors.

Count: Implicitly biased behavior is best detected by using data to determine whether patterns of behavior are leading to racially disparate outcomes. Once one is aware that decisions or behavior are having disparate outcomes, it is then possible to consider whether the outcomes are linked to bias.

Interventions to Reduce Racial Anxiety

The mechanisms to reduce racial anxiety are related to the reduction of implicit bias—but are not identical. In our view, combining interventions that target both implicit bias and racial anxiety will be vastly more successful than either in isolation.

Direct Inter-group Contact: Direct interaction between members of different racial and ethnic groups can alleviate inter-group anxiety, reduce bias, and promote more positive inter-group attitudes and expectations for future contact.

Indirect Forms of Inter-group Contact: When people observe positive interactions between members of their own group and another group (vicarious contact) or become aware that members of their group have friends in another group (extended contact), they report lower bias and anxiety, and more positive inter-group attitudes.

Stereotype Threat Interventions

Most of these interventions were developed in the context of the threat experienced by people of color and women linked to stereotypes of academic capacity and performance, but may also be translatable to whites (Erman & Walton, in press) who fear confirming the stereotype that they are racist.

Social Belonging Intervention: Providing students with survey results showing that upper-year students of all races felt out of place when they began but that the feeling abated over time has the effect of protecting students of color from assuming that they do not belong on campus due to their race and helped them develop resilience in the face of adversity.

Wise Criticism: Giving feedback that communicates both high expectations and a confidence that an individual can meet those expectations minimizes uncertainty about whether criticism is a result of racial bias or favor (attributional ambiguity). If the feedback is merely critical, it may be the product of bias; if feedback is merely positive, it may be the product of racial condescension.

Behavioral Scripts: Setting set forth clear norms of behavior and terms of discussion can reduce racial anxiety and prevent stereotype threat from being triggered.

Growth Mindset: Teaching people that abilities, including the ability to be racially sensitive, are learnable/incremental rather than fixed has been useful in the stereotype threat context because it can prevent any particular performance from serving as "stereotype confirming evidence."

Value-Affirmation: Encouraging students to recall their values and reasons for engaging in a task helps students maintain or increase their resilience in the face of threat.

Remove Triggers of Stereotype Threat on Standardized Tests: Removing questions about race or gender before a test, and moving them to after a test, has been shown to decrease threat and increase test scores for members of stereotyped groups.

Interventions in Context

The fundamental premise of this [reading] is that institutions seeking to alter racially disparate outcomes must be aware of the array of psychological phenomena that may be contributing to those outcomes. We seek to contribute to that work by summarizing important research on implicit bias that employs strategies of debiasing and preventing bias from affecting behavior. We also seek to encourage institutions to look beyond *implicit bias* alone, and recognize that *racial anxiety* and *stereotype threat* are also often obstacles to racially equal outcomes. We recommend that institutions work with social scientists to evaluate and determine where in the institution's operations race may be coming into play.

The empirically documented effects of implicit bias and race as an emotional trigger allow us to talk about race without accusing people of "being racist," when they genuinely believe they are egalitarian. The social science described in this report helps people understand why inter-racial dynamics can be so complicated and challenging for people despite their best intentions. The interventions suggested by the research can be of value to institutions and individuals seeking to align their behavior with their ideals. Yet for lasting change to occur, the broader culture and ultimately our opportunity structures also need to change for our society to meet its aspirations of fairness and equal opportunity regardless of race and ethnicity.

Works Cited

Crosby, J. R. & Monin, B. (2007). Failure to warn: How student race affects warnings of potential academic difficulty. *Journal of Experimental Social Psychology, 43,* 663–670.

Dasgupta, Nilanjana, 2013. "Implicit Attitudes and Beliefs Adapt to Situations: A Decade of Research on the Malleability of Implicit Prejudice, Stereotypes, and the Self-Concept," in P.G. Devine & E.A. Plant (eds.), *Advances in Experimental Social Psychology* (Vol. 47, pp. 233–79).

Devine, P. G., Forscher, P. S., Austin, A. J., & Cox, W. T. L. (2012). Long-term reduction in implicit race bias: A prejudice habit-breaking intervention. *Journal of Experimental Social Psychology, 48,* 1267–1278.

Devine, Patricia, et al. *Breaking the Prejudice Habit* (Guilford Publications, 2014).

Erman, S. & Walton, G. M. (in press) (2014). Stereotype threat and anti-discrimination law: Affirmative steps to promote meritocracy and racial equality. *Southern California Law Review.*

Harber, K. D., Gorman, J. L., Gengaro, F. P., Butisingh, S., William, T., & Ouellette, R. (2012). Students' race and teachers' social support affect the positive feedback bias in public schools. *Journal of Educational Psychology, 104*(4), 1149–1161.

Kahneman, Daniel, *Thinking Fast and Slow* (Farrar, Straus and Giroux, 2013)

Kang, J., Bennett, M., Carbado, D., Casey, P., Dasgupta, N., Faigman, D., Godsil, R. D., Greenwald, A. G., Levinson, J. D., & Mnookin, J. (2012). Implicit bias in the courtroom. *UCLA Law Review, 59*(5), 1124–1186.

Steele, C. M. (2010). *Whistling Vivaldi: And other clues to how stereotypes affect us.* New York, NY: Norton.

Post-Reading Questions

1   If you suspected a coworker (or someone close to you) was not aware of his or her racist attitudes, how would you go about bringing it to his or her attention?

2   How would you define an implicit bias? What are some examples that are consistent with your definition?

3   How might the concept of "doubt objectivity" help prevent implicit biases from seeping into one's decision making?

4   According to the author, what are some ways of de-biasing and preventing the effects of implicit bias? Of these, which appears most practical?

5   Should criminal justice agencies employ implicit bias testing (i.e., the Implicit Association Test) during the hiring process? What are some pros and cons of doing so?

Why Racial Integration Remains an Imperative

Elizabeth Anderson

In 1988, I needed to move from Ann Arbor to the Detroit area to spare my partner, a sleep-deprived resident at Henry Ford Hospital, a significant commute to work. As I searched for housing, I observed stark patterns of racial segregation, openly enforced by landlords who assured me, a white woman then in her late twenties, that I had no reason to worry about renting there since "we're holding the line against blacks at 10 Mile Road." One of them showed me a home with a pile of cockroaches in the kitchen. Landlords in the metro area were confident that whites would rather live with cockroaches as housemates than with blacks as neighbors.

We decided to rent a house in South Rosedale Park, a stable working-class Detroit neighborhood that was about 80% black. It was a model of cordial race relations. Matters were different in my place of employment, the University of Michigan in Ann Arbor. At the time, a rash of racially hostile incidents targeting black, Latino, Native American and Asian students was raising alarms. Although overtly racist incidents got the most publicity, they did not constitute either the dominant or, in aggregate effect, the most damaging mode of undesirable racial interactions on campus. More pervasive, insidious and cumulatively damaging were subtler patterns of racial discomfort, alienation, and ignorant and cloddish interaction, such as classroom dynamics in which white students focused on problems and grievances peculiar to them, ignored what black students were saying, or expressed insulting assumptions about them. I wondered whether there was a connection between the extreme residential racial segregation in Michigan and the toxic patterns of interracial interaction I observed at the university, where many students were functioning in a multiracial setting for the first time.

Elizabeth Anderson, "Why Racial Integration Remains an Imperative," *Poverty & Race*, vol. 20, no. 4, pp. 1-2, 17-19. Copyright © 2011 by Poverty & Race Research Action Council. Reprinted with permission. Provided by ProQuest LLC. All rights reserved.

My investigations led me to write my book, *The Imperative of Integration,* which focuses primarily (but not exclusively) on black-white segregation. Since the end of concerted efforts to enforce *Brown v. Board of Education* in the 1980s, activists, politicians, pundits, scholars and the American public have advocated non-integrative paths to racial justice. Racial justice, we are told, can be achieved through multiculturalist celebrations of racial diversity; or equal economic investments in *de facto* segregated schools and neighborhoods; or a focus on poverty rather than race; or more rigorous enforcement of anti-discrimination law; or color-blindness; or welfare reform; or a determined effort within minority communities to change dysfunctional social norms associated with the "culture of poverty." As this list demonstrates, avoidance of integration is found across the whole American political spectrum. *The Imperative of Integration* argues that all of these purported remedies for racial injustice rest on the illusion that racial justice can be achieved without racial integration.

Readers of *Poverty & Race* are familiar with the deep and pervasive racial segregation in the U.S., especially of blacks from whites, which was caused and is currently maintained by public policies such as zoning, massive housing discrimination and white flight, and which generates profound economic inequalities. Segregation isolates blacks from access to job opportunities, re-tail outlets, and commercial and professional services. It deprives them of access to public goods, including decent public schools and adequate law enforcement, while subjecting them to higher tax burdens, concentrated poverty, urban blight, pollution and crime. This depresses housing values and impedes blacks' ability to accumulate financial and human capital. If the effects of segregation were confined to such material outcomes, we could imagine that some combination of non-integrative left-liberal remedies—color-blind anti-poverty programs, economic invest-ment in disadvantaged neighborhoods, vigorous enforcement of anti-discrimination law, and multiculturalist remedies to remaining discrimination—could overcome racial inequality.

Non-Integrationist Remedies Are Insufficient

Such non-integrationist remedies are insufficient because they fail to address the full range of effects of segregation on group inequality. *The Imperative of Integration* documents three additional effects that can only be undone through integration: social/cultural capital inequality, racial stigmatization, and anti-democratic effects. These effects recognize that segregation isn't only geographic, and so can't be undone simply by redistributing material goods across space. More fundamentally, segregation consists of the whole range of social practices that groups with privileged access to important goods use to close ranks to maintain their privileges. This includes role segregation, where different groups interact, but on terms of domination and subordination.

Everyone knows that who you know is as important as what you know in getting access to opportunities. This idea captures the social capital effects of racial segregation. In segre-gated societies, news about and referrals to educational and job opportunities preferentially circulate within the groups that already predominate in a given institution, keeping disadvantaged groups off or at the back of the queue. Cultural capital also matters: Even when the gatekeepers to important opportunities do not intentionally practice racial discrimination, they often select applicants by their "fit" with the informal, unspoken and untaught norms of speech, bodily comportment, dress, personal style and cultural interests that already prevail in an institution. Mutually isolated communities tend to drift apart culturally, and thereby undermine disadvantaged groups' accumulation of the cultural capital needed for advancement. Integration is needed to remedy these inequalities.

Avoidance of integration is found across the whole American political spectrum.

Segregation also stigmatizes the disadvantaged. When social groups diverge in material and social advantages, people form corresponding group stereotypes and tell stories to explain these differences. These stories add insult to injury, because people tend to attribute a group's disadvantages to supposedly intrinsic deficits in its abilities, character or culture rather than to its external circumstances. Spatial segregation reinforces these demeaning stories. Ethnocentrism, or favoritism towards those with whom one associates, induces self-segregated groups to draw invidious comparisons between themselves and the groups from which they are isolated. They create worldviews that are impervious to counterevidence held by members of out-groups with whom they have little contact. They tend to view extreme and deviant behaviors of out-group members, such as violent crimes, as representative of the out-group. Role segregation also creates stereotypes that reinforce outgroup disadvantage. People's stereotypes of who is suited to privileged positions incorporate the social identities of those who already occupy them. Occupation of dominant positions also tends to make people prone to stereotype their subordinates, because dominant players can afford to be ignorant of the ways their subordinates deviate from stereotype.

Popular understandings of racial stigma and how it works lead people to drastically underestimate its extent and harmful effects. We imagine racially stigmatizing ideas as consciously located in the minds of extreme racists. Think of the KKK member who claims that blacks are biologically inferior and threatening to whites, proclaims his hatred of them, and discriminates against them out of sheer prejudice. Most Americans despise such extremists, disavow explicitly racist ideas, and sincerely think of themselves as not racist. Most say that racial discrimination is wrong. It is tempting to conclude that negative images of blacks are no longer a potent force in American life.

Tempting, but wrong. While the old racist images of black biological inferiority may have faded, they have been replaced by new ones. Now many whites tend to see blacks as choosing badly, as undermining themselves with culturally dysfunctional norms of single parenthood, welfare dependency, criminality, and poor attachment to school and work. Since, on this view, blacks are perfectly capable of solving their own problems if they would only try, neither whites nor the government owe them anything.

These ideas don't have to be believed, or even conscious, for them to influence behavior. Mere familiarity with derogatory stereotypes, even without belief, can cause unwitting discrimination. No wonder that even people who consciously reject antiblack stereotypes have been found to discriminate against blacks. This is because stereotypes typically operate automatically, behind our backs. In addition, we need to multiply our models of *how* racially stigmatizing ideas cause discrimination. Pure prejudicial discrimination, as in the KKK case, offers just one model. Economists stress statistical discrimination, in which decision-makers use race as a proxy for undesirable traits such as laziness or criminal tendencies. But often stereotypes work by altering *perceptions*. For some white observers, that rambunctious black youth shooting hoops in the park looks aggressive and hostile, although if he were white, he would be perceived as harmlessly horsing around. Other times they work by making well-meaning people anxious. Nervous about appearing racist, whites may avoid blacks, or act stiffly and formally toward them. The very desire to avoid discrimination can cause it.

Racial stigmatization also harms blacks through paths other than discrimination. This is why *The Imperative of Integration* argues that the standard discrimination account of racial inequality needs to be replaced by a broader account, based on the joint effects of segregation and stigmatization. Negative effects of stigmatization not mediated by discrimination include "stereotype threat"—anxiety caused by the fear that one's behavior will confirm negative stereotypes about oneself—which depresses blacks' performance on standardized tests. In addition, stigmatizing images of blacks are not just in people's heads; they are in our culture and public discourse. TV news and police dramas disproportionately depict criminals as black and exaggerate the extent of black-on-white crimes. Such taken-for-granted stigmatizing public images of blacks amount to a massive assault on the reputation of blacks, a harm in itself. They also generate public support for policies that have a disproportionately negative impact on blacks. White support for the death penalty jumps when whites are told that more blacks than whites are executed. White hostility to welfare is tied to the public image of the welfare recipient as a single black mother, even though most recipients are white.

Such impacts of racial stigmatization on democratic policy formation reinforce the anti-democratic effects of spatial and role segregation. Democracy isn't only about the universal franchise. It requires a trained elite, institutional structure, and culture that is systematically responsive to the interests and voices of people from all walks of life. This requires that people from all walks of life have effective access to channels of communication to elites, and that they be able to hold them accountable for their decisions. Segregation blocks both communication and accountability. There is nothing like face-to-face confrontation to force people to listen and respond to one's complaints. Out of sight, out of mind: Segregated elites are clubby, insular, ignorant, unaccountable and irresponsible. The history of the Civil Rights Movement demonstrates how mass disruptive protests were needed to teach segregated elites, and whites at large, fundamental lessons about democracy and justice that they were incapable of learning on their own.

Segregation also stigmatizes the disadvantaged.

Racial Segregation: A Fundamental Cause of Racial Injustice

So racial segregation is a fundamental cause of racial injustice in three ways: It blocks blacks' access to economic opportunities, it causes racial stigmatization and discrimination, and it undermines democracy. It stands to reason that racial integration would help dismantle these injustices. We can think of integration as taking place by stages. We start with formal desegregation: ending laws and policies that turned blacks into an untouchable caste by forcing them into separate and inferior public spaces. This is an essential step toward destigmatization. While stigma still exists, blacks' public standing is better now that they can no longer be forced to the back of the bus. Next comes spatial integration, in which racial groups actually share common public spaces and facilities. This enables blacks to get access to many of the public goods—notably, safe, unblighted, relatively unpolluted neighborhoods with decent schools and public services— that most whites enjoy. Studies of integration experiments involving low-income families, from Gautreaux to Moving to Opportunity, show that spatial integration yields important material and psychic benefits to formerly segregated blacks, notably better housing, lower stress and greater freedom for children to play outdoors.

The next step is formal social integration: cooperation on terms of equality in institutions such as schools, workplaces, juries and the military. This is where some of the biggest payoffs of integration occur. Extensive interracial cooperation on equal terms expands blacks' social and cultural capital, leading to better education and job opportunities. Sustained formal social integration under moderately favorable conditions, including institutional support and cooperative interaction, also reduces prejudice, stigma and discrimination, often to the point of promoting informal social integration—interracial friendship and intimate relations.

Formal social integration also improves the responsiveness of democratic institutions to all social groups. Racially integrated police forces are less violent toward blacks and more responsive to community concerns than racially homogeneous ones. Integrated teaching staffs are less punitive toward black students and less likely to consign them to lower educational tracks. Integrated juries deliberate longer, take into account more evidence, make fewer factual mistakes, and are more alert to racial discrimination in the criminal justice process than all-white juries. Part of the greater intelligence of integrated juries is due to the diverse information provided by blacks, who are more likely to raise critical questions, such as the reliability of whites' eyewitness identification of blacks. Deliberation in an integrated setting also makes whites deliberate more intelligently and responsibly: They are less likely to rush to a guilty judgment, and more likely to raise and take seriously concerns about discrimination in the criminal justice process, than in all-white juries. The need to justify oneself face-to-face before diverse others motivates people to be responsive to the interests of a wider diversity of people. In public opinion polling, too, whites express more racially conciliatory positions when they think they are talking to a black pollster.

The Imperative of Integration argues that the evidence on the positive effects of racial integration, combined with theory and evidence that these effects cannot be achieved in other ways, provide a powerful case for re-instituting racial integration as a policy goal. Integration needs to be pursued on multiple fronts, including housing vouchers to promote low-income black mobility into integrated middle-class neighborhoods, abolition of class-segregative zoning regulations, adoption of integrative programs by school districts, extension and aggressive enforcement of differential impact standards of illegal discrimination to state action, and deliberate selection for racially integrated juries. I also argue that voting districts should be integrated in such a way that politicians cannot be elected without running on platforms with multiracial appeal. This will correct a serious downside of majority-minority districting, which is that remaining districts tend to favor race-baiting politicians running on a politics of white racial resentment. In many parts of the U.S., race relations have relaxed enough to enable blacks, even when a minority in their district, to elect their preferred candidate in coalition with a critical mass of racially tolerant whites, Latinos, Asian Americans and Native Americans.

Stereotypes typically operate automatically, behind our backs.

The Imperative of Integration also argues for alternative models of affirmative action. Right now, discussion of affirmative action is dominated by two models: diversity and compensation. The diversity model stresses the supposed connections between racial diversity and diversity of cultures and ideas. It doesn't do much to support affirmative action in industries such as construction and manufacturing, where the culture and ideas of most employees make little difference. Nor does it explain why selective schools should preferentially admit African Americans and Latinos, as opposed to foreign students. The compensatory model portrays affirmative action as making up for past discrimination. This encourages people to believe that racial inequalities are due to long-past deeds, overlooking the powerful continuing causes of racial injustice rooted in current segregation and stigmatization. It also supports public impatience with affirmative action. No wonder the Supreme Court, even while upholding affirmative action in *Grutter v. Bollinger,* expressed the view that affirmative action will no longer be needed in 25 years.

Once we understand that current racial inequality is rooted in current racial stigmatization and segregation, affirmative action can be understood differently. *De facto* segregation creates referral networks that exclude blacks from information and recommendations to job openings in firms that employ few blacks. Role segregation within firms creates stereotypes of qualified workers that mirror the identities of those who already occupy those roles. Non-stereotypical workers are therefore *perceived* to be unqualified for such roles even when they could fill them successfully, and so are excluded even when managers believe they are hiring on merit. Affirmative action within firms serves to block these and other racially exclusionary practices. This is *discrimination-blocking* affirmative action. *Integrative* affirmative action explicitly adopts racial integration as an institutional goal, in the name of promoting democratic responsiveness to the full diversity of people whom the institution is supposed to serve, overcoming racial inequalities in social and cultural capital, and breaking down racial anxieties, prejudices and stereotypes through integrated, cooperative work teams.

Any argument for restoring racial integration to a central place in the public policy agenda must address three objections. Conservatives oppose integrative policies on grounds of color-blindness. In *The Imperative of Integration,* I argue that the color-blind principle is conceptually confused, because it conflates different meanings of race and different kinds of racial discrimination. It is one thing to discriminate out of pure prejudice against a group with a different appearance or ancestry, or to treat race as a proxy for intelligence or other merits; quite another to take race-conscious steps to counteract racial discrimination and undo the continuing causes of racial-based injustice. Affirmative action, properly administered, does not compromise but rather promotes meritocratic selection. Some on the left oppose integrative policies because they fear the destruction of autonomous black institutions and cultural practices in the name of assimilation and object to the psychic costs of integration on blacks. I argue that integration is distinct from assimilation, since its aim is not to erect white practices as the norm, but rather to *abolish* white exclusionary practices and replace them with practices inclusive of all. And, while integration is stressful, as people learn to cooperate across racial lines the psychic costs of integration decline. Finally, readers of *Poverty & Race* will be familiar with the argument that integration is an unrealistic fantasy. We know, however, that the experience of integration is self-reinforcing: people of all races who grew up in more integrated settings tend to choose more integrated settings later in life. So we should not foreclose all hope. After all, only a few years ago the idea of a black president was regarded by many Americans to be an unrealizable dream.

Further Readings

Estlund, Cynthia. *Working Together: How Workplace Bonds Strengthen a Diverse Democracy.* New York: Oxford UP, 2005.

Frankenberg, Erica & Gary Orfield, eds. *Lessons in Integration: Realizing the Promise of Racial Diversity in American Schools.* Charlottesville: Univ. of Virginia Press, 2007.

Gaertner, Samuel & John Dovidio. *Reducing Intergroup Bias: The Common Ingroup Identity Model.* Philadelphia: Psychology Press, 2000.

Kinder, Donald & Tali Mendelberg. "Cracks in American Apartheid: The Political Impact of Prejudice Among Desegregated Whites." *Journal of Politics* 57:2 (1995): 402–24.

Pettigrew, Thomas & Linda Tropp. "A Meta-Analytic Test of Intergroup Contact Theory." *Journal of Personality and Social Psychology* 90:5 (2006): 751–83.

Sanders, Lynn. "Democratic Politics and Survey Research." *Philosophy of the Social Sciences* 29.2 (1999): 248–80.

Sklansky, David Alan. "Not Your Father's Police Department: Making Sense of the New Demographics of Law Enforcement." *Journal of Criminal Law and Criminology* 96:3 (2006): 1209–43.

Sommers, Samuel. "On Racial Diversity and Group Decision Making: Identifying Multiple Effects of Racial Composition on Jury Deliberations." *Journal of Personality and Social Psychology* 90:4 (2006): 597–612.

Tilly, Charles. *Durable Inequality.* Berkeley and Los Angeles: Univ. of California Press, 1999.

Wells, Amy & Robert Crain. "Perpetuation Theory and the Long-Term Effects of School Desegregation." *Review of Educational Research* 64:4 (1994): 531–55.

Post-Reading Questions

1   In what ways do current housing and employment practices promote racial integration? In what ways do these practices undermine racial integration?

2   In what ways is the avoidance of integration evident across the political spectrum? Of these, which appears more racially divisive?

3   Which of the following forms of "capital" is *least* attainable as a result of racial segregation: social capital, cultural capital, financial capital, or political capital? Which form do you value more (and why)?

4   In what ways does racial segregation further stigmatize those who are disadvantaged?

5   Why do you think the author maintains "racial segregation is a fundamental cause of racial injustice"? To what extent would you agree or disagree? Be sure to qualify your position.

CONCLUSION
A Promising Future for Cultural Diversity (If Only)

Perhaps the promise of multiculturalism and cultural diversity in our justice systems is best reflected in the makeup of college campuses around the nation as classrooms have become increasingly more culturally, racially and ethnically diverse, for it is here that we value the perspective of people from all different backgrounds in hopes that they will be prepared for a global society.[1] Our recognition and appreciation for the increased cultural diversity on college campuses parallel the need to recognize the importance of cultural diversity within the criminal justice system.

Throughout this book, we have explored a variety of issues reflected in a justice system often characterized as "broken," suffering from the oppression of racial stereotypes, discrimination, and miscarriages of justice. As a result, one can only imagine how things might have been had our justice systems reflected more diversity in the makeup of its workforce and operations (U.S. Equal Opportunity Commission, 2016). However, much like charity—which begins at home—an appreciation for cultural diversity must also begin in our homes. Otherwise, it appears superficial to advocate diversity in our systems of justice when within our own communities and work spaces cultural diversity is noticeably absent. Having once read a passage that said, "diversity includes all of us," I wondered whether this passage fulfills its promise when applied to our justice systems. Therefore, I invite readers to consider whether an increase in cultural diversity translates into less racial stereotyping, discrimination, and miscarriages of justice. Moreover, would more diversity lead to increased levels of respect, fairness, and functionality for our justice systems? To test these "considerations" and to draw your own conclusions, I am inviting you to engage me in a friendly game of "*what if.*"

As you may recall, the readings in Part I highlighted our obsession and dysfunctional preoccupation with skin color and how the harboring of implicit biases, alongside racial/ethnic stereotypes, blinds us to the reality that we are all basically the same. Yet, the prevalence of societal racism and discrimination continues to obscure, devalue, and degrade people of color, rendering them not only invisible but (somehow) more deserving of punishment and condemnation. The evidence suggested that some victims are more worthy of saving than others while others are falsely arrested

291

and wrongfully convicted—in a rush to judgment—based on racialized stereotypes. One can only ask, *What if* we all were not so "caught up" in skin color, accents, language, and dialects where we saw others as simply human beings? As strange as it may seem, *people of color* also tend to discriminate against family, friends, and others who look like them. And yet, these same people are quick to raise the "hue and cry" when felt discriminated against by others who do not look like them. While the invidious effects of colorism are not our axe to grind, it does present an array of problems and dilemmas that are difficult to reconcile.

What if we took a stroll down memory lane highlighting the repeated tragedies and miscarriages of justice that resulted, in part, from a lack of cultural diversity within our justice system? These are reflected in the form of ethnic and racial stereotypes and their nexus to racial profiling, a longstanding and deeply troubling national problem despite claims that the United States has entered a "post-racial era" (American Civil Liberties Union, n.d.). *What if* all police were mandated to undertake cultural sensitivity training? *What if* all police departments were more culturally diverse and representative of the community they served? Would we see the same degree of police corruption in the form of coerced false confessions, false arrests, falsification of evidence, perjury, police brutality, unwarranted surveillance, and illegal searches, among other behaviors? These practices alienate communities from law enforcement, hinder community policing efforts, and cause law enforcement to lose credibility and trust among the people they are sworn to protect and serve. When we embrace cultural diversity throughout our justice systems—which promotes human understanding—we can alleviate many of these miscarriages of justice, including police corruption.

Part II entertained theories and ideas of a subculture, the proverbial breeding grounds for "street crime" presumably committed by persons of color, to the benign neglect of White-collar, corporate, and environmental crime, where Whites as the main culprits. These readings served to advance our understanding of the relations between cultural diversity, racism, and crime. One of the readings asked, "*What if* we reexamined the notion of a subculture and acknowledged that many behaviors are more reflective of adaptive lifestyles and are not necessarily 'sub' (or below) the standards of some youthful behaviors?" Instead, *what if* we focused on the legal system and criminal law as seen through the lens of critical race theory? Doing so, forces us to examine the demographics of legislative bodies that create laws in the first place. For example, most state legislatures are racially homogenous and lack racial/ethnic diversity as nearly 82% of all state legislatures are White/Caucasian (National Conference of State Legislature, 2016). In the most extreme case, North Dakota's state legislature is comprised of 99% Caucasians. In contrast, Puerto Rico's legislature is comprised of 100% Latinx. In concert with race, it is equally important to note that age, gender, religious affiliation, and sexual orientation also weigh heavily in the creation of laws that benefit some more so than others.

The tenor of readings in Part III displayed serious concerns about the continued use and abuse of racial profiling, exclusionary immigration policies, the distrust of state and federal prosecutors, and the financial burdens imposed on poor persons—many of whom are a minority—through monetary sanctions. As shown through social media, the use of racial profiling in connection with police brutality and use of deadly force against unarmed citizens is eerily reminiscent of an antebellum south and our country's *original sin* (i.e., slavery). Indeed, we have witnessed similar fatalities on the southwest border in our highly politicized war against illegal immigration. Beyond arrest, the unethical practices of some prosecutors, coupled with their own abuses of power, invite scrutiny of the profession's demographic makeup as well.[2] In each of these areas, it is fair to ask, "*What if* most criminal justice agencies were more culturally and racially diverse? Moreover, would it matter if more women and persons of different sexual orientations, language, and religious persuasions were key decisions makers?

As anticipated throughout these readings, the cumulative weight of a system lacking in cultural diversity reveals itself in the latter stages, especially in the area of corrections. The articles in Part IV serve as reminders of the origins of a justice system where cultural diversity was once virtually nonexistent. Whether it is the theoretical underpinnings of the convict-lease system or discursive analyses of the prison industrial complex, we have witnessed the racialization of these institutions in their design, execution, and steady march toward the goal of enslavement through mass incarceration. In the process, we explored the widespread frequency of sexual assault and other abuses confronting male, female, and transgendered inmates. If you are wondering what cultural diversity resembles in these settings, consider the following questions: *What if* more correctional officers had family members "caught up" in the system or came from oppressed backgrounds characterized by occasional "run-ins" with the law? Would it affect their regard and treatment of those in their custodial care? Does the correctional treatment that offenders receive during their incarceration determine how productive they will be as members of society? Would the integrity and professional work ethic of the staff matter? *What if* correctional personnel thought most inmates were "lost causes" and that whether they are rehabilitated is not their concern? Rather, they are more concerned with maintaining custody and control of the institution. I have had correctional officers tell me this during a prison tour! *What if* these concerns varied by the degree of cultural diversity among staff within an institution? While opposing voices might dismiss these questions as merely an invitation to speculate on a hypothetical, these reflect reality and deserve serious consideration.

The concluding articles in Part V highlighted the promise of efforts to eliminate racial disparities in school discipline in hopes of dismantling the school-to-prison pipeline. However, while the guiding light of these efforts should reflect the leadership of our school systems, it begs the question of whether educators have a vested interest in seeing all children succeed. A serious consideration of this question welcomes a retrospective look at the landmark school desegregation case of *Brown v. Board of Education of Topeka Kansas* in 1954. As most readers know, this ruling overturned the "separate but equal" doctrine and set into motion the legal precedent that would be used to overturn laws enforcing segregation in other public facilities. Today, more than 60 years after this historic decision, the debate continues over how to combat racial inequalities in our nation's school system, largely based on residential patterns and differences in resources between schools in wealthier and economically disadvantaged districts across the country (Cornia, 2004). Despite widespread and lingering opposition to school desegregation, the ruling helped to galvanize the civil rights movements and combat racial inequalities far beyond the classroom. Without question, it also made public spaces more diverse. This leads us to ask, "*What if* racial inequality was less disparate? Would issues of structural inequality, academic failure, high school dropout rates, and disproportionate discipline continue to plague our educational system, creating gateways into the juvenile and adult criminal justice systems?"

While we have grown accustomed to the phrase "race matters,"[3] we must also realize that *cultural diversity also matters* in the administration of justice. It matters because it impacts the way justice is administered in terms of what criminal justice practitioners look like—from the police to prosecutors, to judges, to correctional personnel and beyond. Each chapter in this book takes readers on a soul-searching journey, inviting them to wonder *what if* our system were more culturally diverse? Would we continually witness the constant barrage of racially charged incidents that exhaust our resources, hope, and patience? As a reader, you were asked to weigh in and draw your own conclusions. As for me, I see a very promising future for cultural diversity, for not only does it include all of us, it enriches our criminal justice system and the lives of everyone involved. Moreover, cultural diversity is a special form of social and cultural capital. It terrelates with financial and political capital and provides opportunities for us to live up to our human potential. In conclusion, *what if* the next time you are in class, at a cookout, a birthday party, a wedding, or social gathering, that it included more people who did not look like you? What if ... only?

Notes

1 According to U.S. Census data, as of 2018 there were 18.4 million students attending college, where women comprise 54.9% of undergraduate students and 59.8% of graduate students. In terms of race and ethnicity, White students represented 54%, followed by Latinx at 18%, Blacks at 14%, Asian and Pacific Islanders at 7%, and American Indian/Alaska Native at .8% (with 5% not reporting their identity). See U.S. Census Bureau (2018).

2 According to the American Bar Association's National Lawyer Population Survey, 88% of the nations "active" prosecutors are White. See American Bar Association (2019).

3 Author, scholar, and social activist Cornel West is at the forefront of thinking about race. In *Race Matters* he addresses a range of issues far beyond the context of criminal justice-related matters. For more information, see West (1994).

References

American Bar Association. (2019, August 5). *Legal profession statistics*. Retrieved from https://www.americanbar.org/about_the_aba/profession_statistics/

American Civil Liberties Union. (n.d.). *Racial profiling*. Retrieved from https://www.aclu.org/issues/racial-justice/race-and-criminal-justice/racial-profiling

Cornia, G. A. (Ed.). (2004). Inequality, growth, and poverty in an era of liberalization and globalization (No. 4). Oxford University Press on Demand.

National Conference of State Legislature. (2016). *Legislators' race and ethnicity 2015*. Retrieved from http://www.ncsl.org/Portals/1/Documents/About_State_Legislatures/Raceethnicity_Rev2.pdf

U.S. Census Bureau. (2018, December 11). *More than 76 million students enrolled in U.S. schools*. Retrieved from https://www.census.gov/newsroom/press-releases/2018/school-enrollment.html

U.S. Equal Opportunity Commission. (2016, October). *Advancing diversity in law enforcement*. Retrieved from https://www.eeoc.gov/eeoc/interagency/police-diversity-report.cfm

West, C. (1994). *Race matters*. Boston, MA: Beacon.

INDEX

CPSIA information can be obtained
at www.ICGtesting.com
Printed in the USA
FSHW020526120520
70140FS